Advance Praise for *The Political Speechwriter's Companion*

"What Strunk and White's *Elements of Styl*̲ _____ ____ ̲ ̲obert Lehrman's *The Political Speechwriter's Comp*̲ ̲ ̲poken one. *The Political Speechwriter's Companion* is a gift fr̲ ̲ one of the country's most gifted speechwriters."

—The Honorable William Cohen, U.S. Senator (R-Maine, 1979–1997)
U.S. Secretary of Defense (1997–2001)

"The right words at the right time change a losing campaign into a winning one. Bob's book will help any aspiring candidate or writer to choose wisely. Speechwriting is an art and a skill. Bob's new book will help readers develop their skills into an art."

—The Honorable James R. Sasser, U.S. Senator (D-Tenn., 1977–1995)
Ambassador to China (1996–1999)

"A superb book! Lehrman has combined his knowledge about how to write an effective speech with solid principles of public speaking. With a wealth of examples to illustrate his points, Lehrman provides the speechwriter and the speaker with a good foundation for crafting an eloquent speech. The interviews with high-profile speechwriters are fascinating. A must-read for speechwriters and speakers at any stage in their communication career."

—Andrew D. Wolvin, University of Maryland
Author of *The Public Speaker/The Public Listener*

"Stunning, thoughtful, and original. Whether you hold office or work for someone who does, you should read—and learn from—this book by one of America's best speechwriters."

—Samuel Berger, Chair, Stonebridge International
National Security Adviser for President Bill Clinton (1996–2001)

"Smart and innovative! Bob Lehrman teaches us how to build an idea into a speech that engages and soars. As a former speechwriter myself, I learned new insights and angles from every page, and there's nothing else like it out there. It belongs in every political classroom, office, and campaign."

—Leonard Steinhorn, American University
Author of *The Greater Generation: In Defense of the Baby Boom Legacy*

"This book raises the craft of speech writing to a public art form. Lehrman's experience as a White House speechwriter and a teacher of young writers makes him a lively and instructive guide to one of the oldest forms of mass communication to Republicans and Democrats alike."

—Noam Neusner, Principal, 30 Point Strategies
Speechwriter for President George W. Bush (2001–2003)

"With *The Political Speechwriter's Companion*, Bob Lehrman attaches method to the madness and rhythm to the rigor of speechwriting—while reminding us why this profession can be endlessly stimulating and just plain fun. Bob's book is indispensable."

—Michael Long, director, White House Writers Group
Speechwriter for U.S. Senator Fred Thompson (R-Tenn., 1996–1998)

"A bad speech can bore an audience to tears; a great speech can change the world. Veteran speechwriter Bob Lehrman offers wise counsel to writers and speakers alike on how to avoid the former and aspire to the latter in *The Political Speechwriter's Companion*. It's an indispensable guide that proves as engaging as it is useful."

—Mark K. Updegrove, Presidential Historian
Author of *Baptism by Fire* and *Second Acts*

"Chock full of examples, information, and advice, Lehrman's book illuminates and enthralls; it critiques and informs. Lehrman not only teaches, he inspires and lifts our faith in the power of the written word intended to be spoken. If speechwriting is your craft, read this book; if speech giving is part of your vocation, read this book; it never disappoints."

—Robert L. Mallett, Deputy Secretary, U. S. Department of Commerce (1997–2001)
Senior Vice President, Pfizer Inc and President, Pfizer Foundation (2001–2009)

"An eloquent, clear guide to political speechwriting. Bob Lehrman's book is an invaluable tool for both writers and speakers."

—William Ferris, Chairman, National Endowment
for the Humanities (1995–2001)
Joel R. Williamson Eminent Professor of History,
University of North Carolina, Chapel Hill

"Bob Lehrman has packed a career's worth of oratorical knowledge into this indispensable guidebook. Whether you are a teacher, student, speechwriter, or politician, it will show you how to turn the often frigid waters of the blank page into waterfalls of inspiration, wisdom, and wit."

—Terry Edmonds, Chief Speechwriter for
President Bill Clinton (1998–2001)

"There's a reason that Robert Lehrman is the first phone call I make when I have an important speech to give. He's poured the thoughtfulness, passion, and expertise he brings to every speech into this invaluable resource. Like Bob's speeches, his book is filled with clear and compelling information, illustrative anecdotes, and even a joke or two along the way. I've learned a lot from Bob in years of working with him, but I learned even more from *The Political Speechwriter's Companion*. From fundamentals for beginners to tips even seasoned pros can use, I highly recommend this wonderful resource to anyone looking to develop or hone their communications skills."

—Nan Aron, President, Alliance for Justice

"Bob Lehrman knows how to make words pop and sizzle. By sharing some of his secrets, he has created an engaging step-by-step guide to political speechwriting that goes beyond the predictable and gets at essential truths about how we communicate with each other. Along the way, he gives political junkies a treat, tugging us, through telling anecdotes, into the backstage spaces—the motorcade limos and White House offices—where he made his name as a Washington wordsmith."

—Manuel Roig-Franzia, Reporter, *Washington Post*

"If communication matters in your life, then Bob Lehrman's new book should be part of your resource library. The elements of good speech writing are all here—structure, clarity, delivery, persuasion, humor, and leaving your audience with a memorable close. Bob wrote speeches for me when I was the Majority Whip in the U.S. House of Representatives. He made me a far better speaker. My audiences were happier and so was I."

—David Bonior, U.S. Representative (D-Mich., 1976–2003)

"Bob Lehrman has taken his background as both a high-level political speechwriter and an academic lecturer to produce a unique how-to compendium that is a fascinating learning tool for experienced as well as apprentice wordsmiths of all interests. Lehrman highlights hundreds of techniques that make a speech informative or entertaining, and sometimes both. By sharing his decades of lessons, Lehrman has produced a book that will educate and entertain new generations of speech-writers across the political spectrum. His explanations of how speeches can influence viewpoints and votes enlighten a little understood aspect of public life."

—Richard Cohen, *The Almanac of American Politics*

"Bob's book is a hugely valuable guide for anyone who wants to give speeches, write speeches, or lead others—whether in politics or in business. If you want to know how to inspire, how to persuade, how to unite Americans for a great cause, read his chapter on 'Language People Remember.' I keep Bob's book on my shelf, next to *Bartlett's*."

—Alex Castellanos, Partner, National Media Inc.
CNN commentator, advisor to Mitt Romney's 2008 presidential campaign

"No one is better qualified than Bob Lehrman to guide political speechwriters, both neophytes and veterans—and in this volume he does so with insight and grace. *The Political Speechwriter's Companion* will reward casual readers and serious professionals."

—Clark S. Judge
Managing Director, White House Writers Group, Inc.
Special Assistant and Speechwriter for President Reagan (1986–1989)

"This book is a peek behind the curtain of Bob Lehrman's magic. For those of us who want Bob to write every speech—and after all, that's why I wanted him to join Al Gore's staff—it is a priceless guide to his unique skills. Bob writes with passion, clarity, humor, and power. In this book, he shares his gift, and years of experience, insight, and critical thinking. If you must communicate ideas, policy, and passion—in any and every walk of life—this book will make you better at it. There is no one with Bob's talents and no other book like this one. I still want Bob to write every speech, but now I can send him a draft and ask him to work from that. This book is staying where I can reach it fast."

—Marla Romash
Communications Director for Vice President Al Gore (1992–1995)

"Here is a cookbook that comes with all of the delicious ingredients for good speeches. The basics from soup to nuts are all here, as well as the sweeteners that make for great public presentations."

—Juan Williams,
Emmy Award–winning NPR commentator
Author, *Eyes on the Prize* and *Thurgood Marshall: American Revolutionary*

The Political Speechwriter's Companion

A Guide for Writers and Speakers

ROBERT LEHRMAN

American University

CQ PRESS

A Division of SAGE
Washington, D.C.

CQ Press
2300 N Street, NW, Suite 800
Washington, DC 20037

Phone: 202-729-1900; toll-free, 1-866-4CQ-PRESS (1-866-427-7737)

Web: www.cqpress.com

Photo Credits
Earl Dotter: 87
Michael Thaul Lehrman: 282, 362

Cover design: Silverander Communications
Composition: C&M Digitals (P) Ltd.

♾ The paper used in this publication exceeds the requirements of the American National Standard for Information Sciences—Permanence of Paper for Printed Library Materials, ANSI Z39.48-1992.

Printed and bound in the United States of America

13   2 3 4 5

Library of Congress Cataloging-in-Publication Data

Lehrman, Robert A.
   The political speechwriter's companion : a guide for writers and speakers /
   Robert A. Lehrman.
      p. cm.
   ISBN 978-1-60426-549-1 (pbk. : alk. paper) 1. Speechwriting.
2. Political oratory. 3. Public speaking. 4. English language—Rhetoric. I. Title.

PN4142.L44 2009
808.5′1—dc22

                                                                                    2009033614

To Richard Yates (1926–1992),
for showing me what language should do—
and what I might

Contents

Part III: How to Do It

Preface

Speechwriting is a "particularly low form of rhetoric," historian and sometime speechwriter Arthur M. Schlesinger Jr. once said. It doesn't have to be.

As someone who writes both speeches and novels, I am struck by how often I see similarities between the two forms—and no, not because politicians have been known to make things up. At its best a political speech doesn't just convey information or argue a point. It can be a dramatic monologue built around ideas, able to move, excite, entertain, and inspire, sometimes through narrative. Nothing low about that. In the 2008 presidential election Americans saw that, and not just from Barack Obama; speechwriters created skillful, moving, and thoughtful speeches for Hillary Clinton, John Edwards, Mike Huckabee, and Sarah Palin, among others.

Their speeches weren't typical, though, and the reasons are no mystery. Political speeches are usually written at breakneck speed, sometimes by committee, and often by people whose main interest is policy, not language. And few books exist to help them learn how to do it.

The Political Speechwriter's Companion aims to fill that gap. This is a book for students interested in learning the language of politics and those already *using* it: the sixty thousand elected officials in America and the hundreds of thousands more who work for them. It is for the more than two hundred thousand people who run for elective office every two years: state reps and senators, governors, members of Congress, mayors, and city council members. It is a book for anyone in government making a speech about policy and for the heads of nonprofits trying to influence them. It is a book for an eighty-year-old senator who's decided he wants to be more compelling—and for a nineteen-year-old student running for alderman from the ward containing his college. It is a book not just for those writing speeches full time but for anyone who has to write one—including politicians, who do occasionally write their own or just want to see what they can demand from their staff. And it is a book for political consultants who think hard about what the message should be and might want to see what's possible when it comes to expressing it.

It is mostly, but not entirely, about technique—so for those of you who would be tempted to slam the book shut, let me be the first to admit that technique has its limits.

This is hardly an original thought. Bernard Grebanier, who wrote an excellent playwriting book about fifty years ago, acknowledged it too. "It was not Aeschylus and Sophocles who read Aristotle but he who read them," he wrote. I'm not Aristotle, Grebanier said. But, he added, his own teaching experience taught him that looking at the techniques of great playwrights could help budding playwrights of his day.

I've tried to do the same thing here. Systematic teaching seems to help most people, whether they're learning tennis, piano, or screenwriting. Why not speechwriting? In fact, this book tries to teach speechwriting the way coaches teach tennis: they may give you a little background, but usually they take you out on the court right away to systematically teach strokes. You will see this approach through most of the book's sections.

WHAT'S INSIDE

- **PART I: Background.** First you learn about political life, some theories of persuasion, and what you need to know about audiences. Then you focus on structure, especially a kind that turns out to be incredibly useful for the varied needs of political speech.

- **PART II: Elements**. The rhetorical equivalent of strokes in tennis, language, anecdote, wit, and support—the LAWS of speechwriting—are really the core of this book. You examine the way language can be both clear and memorable; how story and humor can enliven, move, and inspire; and what kinds of evidence best persuade political audiences.

- **PART III: Applications.** Learning the strokes doesn't make you a tennis player. It's not enough to have a great forehand doing crosscourt drills. You have to know how to apply it—to attack, defend, or run the other guy into the corner to set up a winner. In Part III you learn how to *apply* what you've learned, from the first line of a speech to the last.

- **DELIVERY.** Many readers will not only write speeches, they will also give them. For those who only write, you need to understand what a speaker goes through to see why many of the suggestions in this book make sense. And for those of you who speak, this special section covers the basics of effective delivery and some practical ways to become good at it—if you're willing to endure the constant and sometimes humiliating practice that it takes.

- **APPENDIX.** Again, tennis players face different opponents; they dictate different strategies. The most common speeches in political life involve different strategies as well. And so you will find a section outlining the different ways to approach the most common types: stump, floor, keynote, commencement, eulogy, and roast.

Analogies are always imperfect. You'll also find two chapters (in part IV) about the morally fraught and grueling world of politics for which sports analogies would be a stretch: one on ethical conflicts and another on ways speechwriter and speaker can work well together. But I can't end without one more comparison with sports, a lifelong passion that unfortunately far outstripped my abilities on the field.

THE IMPORTANCE OF EXAMPLES

In virtually no sport is it enough just to play—or even practice. You have to watch others. A coach can tell you what to incorporate into your game, but examples show you. And so this book is laced with examples of what others have done. You can't steal their language, but you can imitate their approaches.

Which is what all writers do. Someone who wants to be a novelist—as I did, for example—grows up reading thousands of stories and novels, all models for the unconscious imitation we use when we write. But speechwriters usually learn on the job. Except for the Gettysburg Address, the "I Have a Dream" speech, and a few other staples of high school lit courses, most speechwriters start paying attention to speeches only when they have to write one.

In my experience, even the best work speechwriters have done in the past is new to just about everyone. I want speechwriters to see what's worked. In my speechwriting course at American University, I see—semester after semester—that this makes a difference. You should read through and think about each example in the chapters that follow.

Many of them come from the 2008 presidential campaign, and for good reasons. First, memories fade fast. More readers will pay attention to a 2008 John McCain speech they remember than a 1988 Michael Dukakis speech they don't. Second, in 2008 oratory became a campaign issue. This was largely—not entirely—because of Barack Obama's skillful drafts and his undeniable power as a speaker. It's worth examining the speeches that created such a stir.

But the techniques this book covers were not invented in 2008. I use examples taken from the last half-century of American politics, and some from farther back. Language and tone may change over the decades, but Obama's strategies, structure, and techniques go back to Churchill, Lincoln—and Aristotle.

Because we learn not just from success but also from failures, some chapters use examples of speeches that did not work.

And since the odds are that someone who writes a good opening is more likely to have closed well, and because by following one speech through we can examine how things planted in an opening recur later, you will see some speeches come back again and again: Ronald Reagan's wonderful Farewell Address, for example, or Arnold Schwarzenegger's 2004 Republican National Convention keynote.

You will see examples from speeches nobody remembers, but not many by people nobody remembers. For obvious reasons, the most imaginative speechwriters in American politics work not at the statehouse but the White House; to best illustrate the points in each chapter means using a lot of their work.

The reader I have in mind, though, is not a U.S. president. It's me—or at least the me I was running for city council in Iowa City, Iowa, back in 1969, and putting together my first stump speech. Looking back I can see that the things

I needed—desperately—for those League of Women Voters debates were not much different from those that made Ronald Reagan effective from the Oval Office. Every technique in this book can be applied at every level. Not only presidents live the political life.

USEFUL FEATURES

I'm especially happy with the features of this book and grateful to CQ Press for encouraging—and in some cases insisting—on them. There are five. Each aims to clarify the points this book makes.

• **Annotated Speeches.** In each chapter we examine a variety of techniques in isolation, but in real life, speeches use them in combination. To show how that works, I have annotated excerpts so you can see for yourself without destroying your ability to read on. In chapter 7, for example, you'll see Mike Huckabee's entire 2008 Republican National Convention speech, while in chapter 15, you'll read through an annotated version of Al Gore's entire 1995 speech to the Women's Legal Defense Fund.

• **Behind the Scenes.** I'm sorry to tell you that I don't have a monopoly on wisdom. Seven people allowed me to interview them and get the benefit of theirs. That means you get to see how five of the most distinguished and best speechwriters in the country go about their work, what one of the best political speech consultants tells her clients about delivery, and what one of the leading consultants on political management urges when it comes to managing speechwriting in a political office. Later, I'll acknowledge them by name; right now, I encourage you to read and think about what they say.

• **The Speechwriter's Checklist.** Most chapters are full of suggestions, but you don't have to take notes. At the end of these chapters you will find a checklist of the things you need to remember most as you are thinking, creating, and drafting speeches.

• **As Delivered**. If this book had been published ten years ago we would have had to include a long section of speeches to study. Luckily, the Internet and YouTube have made that unnecessary. You can read, listen, and watch online most of the speeches mentioned or excerpted in the chapters that follow. Each "As Delivered" box includes a URL that points to the text's companion Web site, where you can find a series of links to speeches and experience them in a way no amount of description could provide.

• **Web Site (college.cqpress.com/politicalspeech).** Here you'll find the speeches that are most important for this book. Some are available now on YouTube, but that may not always be the case. That's the point of the Web site: any example we use will be available for years. In addition, the site contains articles, examples, and exercises this book couldn't include without weighing as much as a phone book.

So far, we've examined what kinds of things you'll find in the book. But what about how to approach them? You could read this book straight through, but not every reader has the same needs. Some of you may want to turn right to the chapter on delivery; others may be more interested in structure or the research on what makes arguments persuasive. That's fine with me, and the book is easy to navigate so that you can dip in and out of the text to quickly find the advice you need.

For those new to delivering or writing speeches, the book is written so each section prepares you for the next. But there's a reason the word *companion* is in the title. Like a lifetime friend, you may want to spend time with this book, drop it for a while—then pick it up again. That's fine too.

Whether you read from beginning to end or skip around, please don't forget the way this preface opened: technique is important but not everything. As you read about antithesis, analogy, or Monroe's Motivated Sequence, remember this: a gift for language and a passion for issues will contribute more to a speech than technique alone ever can.

ACKNOWLEDGMENTS

Readers of this book will see that I recommend the absolute minimum number of acknowledgments you can get away with. But that's in speeches. This book is different: I owe too many people too much.

First among those I owe is my friend, colleague, and coteacher, Eric Schnure. Since we met in Al Gore's office in 1993, we have written, taught, and lectured together. Eric has influenced this book at every stage, and I'm grateful for his involvement.

Second, I'm grateful to the people at CQ Press, beginning with someone no longer there: Aron Keesbury, who saw a way to take both me and CQ Press in a new direction and persuaded the company to buy my proposal. CQ Press then had the wisdom to assign me to editor Jane Harrigan, whose insight and keen sense of what each chapter might need made me swear at myself with each of her e-mails—then get back to work.

Working under the insightful and always encouraging Charisse Kiino, Chief Acquisitions Editor, was a pleasure. Christina Mueller, editorial assistant at CQ Press, was also a delight to work with, combining firmness about deadlines with sensitivity to language. And I've been helped by the skillful work of Talia Greenberg, copy editor; Taryn McKinnon, intern; Allyson Rudolph, production editor; and Judy Myers, designer.

For their helpful professional and scholarly reviews, I'd like to thank Pete McRoberts, Kristine Bruss, Steven Keller, Margot Friedman, John R. Luecke, Gerald Sussman, Todd Frobish, Megan Rooney, Alexandra Veitch, and Tom Hollihan, among others. But here, wishing there was no need, I must mention one other. Journalist, congressional candidate, and marine Bill Cahir provided especially useful and insightful suggestions. Bill then reenlisted in the Marine Corps, and as this book went to press was killed in Afghanistan. I didn't know

Bill well; I wish I had. I am grateful for his advice, and immensely saddened by his death.

It is awkward to return from acknowledging a death to acknowledgments about a book. With apologies, I must. In addition to the readers who took part in CQ Press's review process, a number of speechwriters and friends put in long hours critiquing the manuscript. I'm grateful to Russ Block, Margot Freedman, Stephen Goldstein, Dave Helfert, Jonathan Penner, and Bob Stewart. I'm also grateful for the meticulous work my research assistant, Margaret Bolton—herself a talented writer—put in during the final stages.

And thanks to seven people who agreed to let me interview them so readers could get insights I lacked. In addition to Eric Schnure, three are Democrats: David Kusnet, Lissa Muscatine, and Rick Shapiro. I've benefited from talking to them for a long time. And since Washington is a very partisan town, I'm also grateful to three thoughtful people profiled in the book who don't share my political views but trusted me when I told them that when it came to political speech I would be rigorously nonpartisan: David Frum, Landon Parvin, and Carol Whitney.

Nobody learns to write speeches in a vacuum. I learned a lot from the brilliant strategist and media person—and now friend—the communications director for Vice President Gore, Marla Romash. I've also learned from the writings of others, especially the textbooks of Stephen Lucas and Andy Wolvin. In fact, readers should frequently visit www.americanrhetoric.com, the Web site created by the indefatigable Lucas, author of *The Art of Public Speaking*. I'm grateful for his groundbreaking work and encourage you not only to read his book but also to watch the speeches delivered.

I'm especially grateful to Lenny Steinhorn, a former speechwriter and now my boss at American University, and author of two prescient books. Lenny not only suggested I teach at AU but taught me through all the conversations we've had about teaching, writing, and politics. Thanks, Lenny, for being so encouraging when both the course and this book were only ideas in my head.

I've been involved with politics for much of my adult life. This book is informed by every campaign and every political office I ever joined. I thank Art and Mary Jo Small, who long ago yanked me back from Students for a Democratic Society to work for Sen. Eugene McCarthy; my cousin, Sandy Berger; and the many people who taught me politics when I worked in Illinois for Gov. Dan Walker, in the Senate for Lloyd Bentsen, in the House for Majority Whip David Bonior, and—of course—in the White House for Vice President Gore.

Do students understand that teachers learn from them? I won't name any—because I'd be leaving out others who are equally deserving. But there hasn't been a class where I haven't learned from my students how to be both a better teacher and better speechwriter.

Sometimes a client becomes a friend. That's true of former Commerce Department deputy secretary and Pfizer Foundation president Robert

Mallett, whose friendship and warmth I value and whose great skill as a speaker influenced this book. It's also true of Alliance for Justice founder and president Nan Aron, who's taught me a lot about what's possible to achieve in Washington and how speeches help.

And I am grateful for the opportunity to work for Al Gore, whose visionary approach to issues becomes clearer every year, as well as for David Bonior, the introspective, sensitive, and principled former House majority leader.

I started out writing fiction. I learned much from classmates like Jonathan Penner and Mark Dintenfass, and from teachers like Kurt Vonnegut and, especially, the great Richard Yates—author of *Revolutionary Road*—to whom this book is dedicated. His ideas influence everything I write.

I've had two friends who kept urging me to work on this book: Robert Molofsky and Ashi Tandon—thank you. And Sean Rowe, who worked so hard at his own writing that I had to work hard to keep up: thank you.

I wish my parents were alive to hold this book in their hands—especially my mother, who nurtured my love for language from the moment I was born. Their influence persists in the comments of my perceptive brother, David, and in their grandchildren—my two brilliant, talented, and lovable sons, Eric and Michael.

And finally, thank you, thank you, Susan Thaul, friend and lover still, for listening to every idea I had, reading every draft, scribbling over it, and managing to make me feel I'd done something that someday might be good.

The Political
Speechwriter's Companion

Introduction

Why Speechwriting Matters

They spoke seven days apart: first the skinny black senator from Illinois, winner over Democratic rivals who hadn't even heard of him five years earlier; then the white-haired senator from Arizona who had been in the public eye for almost four decades. And what Barack Obama proposed at an outdoor stadium in Denver and John McCain at a convention hall in St. Paul differed in tone, delivery, and ideas both about what was wrong with the country and how to fix it.

But in other ways, their acceptance speeches to the 2008 Democratic and Republican national conventions were quite similar. Both speakers used the theme of change. Both addressed not just the people in front of them but all Americans, speaking to them directly, often about the same problems.

> These are tough times for many of you. You're worried about keeping your job or finding a new one. . . .
>
> McCain

> Tonight, more Americans are out of work and more are working harder for less. More of you have lost your homes.
>
> Obama

The two speakers used the same basic structure—a modified version of Monroe's Motivated Sequence, the popular five-step problem-solution format designed to make listeners act. Both used direct juxtaposition, immediately contrasting their (good) ideas with their opponent's (bad) ones.

> My tax cuts will create jobs. His will eliminate them.
>
> McCain

> Unlike John McCain, I will stop giving tax breaks to corporations that ship jobs overseas.
>
> Obama

Both used a technique politicians sometimes call *litany.* In formal rhetoric it's described another way: lists of examples using the same grammatical structure and often the same opening words for each sentence. Obama used litany at least sixteen times and McCain, twelve.

> We believe everyone has something to contribute. . . . We believe in
> low taxes. . . . We believe in a strong defense.
>
> McCain

> We measure progress by how many people can find a job that pays
> the mortgage. . . . We measure progress in the twenty-three million
> new jobs that were created when Bill Clinton was president. . . . We
> measure the strength of our economy . . . by whether somebody with
> a good idea can take a risk. . . .
>
> Obama

Both used rhetorical techniques like *antithesis,* a contrast based on parallel structure that audiences find easy to remember.

> All you ask is that government stand by your side and not in your
> way.
>
> McCain

> Our government should work for us, not against us.
>
> Obama

Before closing, both used stories to inspire: McCain about his experience as a prisoner of war in Vietnam, honoring his imprisoned comrades who had "fought for me"; Obama about Martin Luther King's "I Have a Dream" speech, echoing King's pledge "We cannot turn back." And both drew lessons from their stories in a traditional way.

> I'm going to fight for my cause every day as your president!
>
> McCain

> America, we cannot turn back!
>
> Obama

Finally, both launched a "call to action" litany from those lessons.

> Fight for what's right! Fight for our children's future!
>
> McCain

> We cannot turn back. We cannot walk alone. We must pledge. . . .
>
> Obama

In short, McCain and Obama demonstrated that even when politicians find little common ground on issues, they share beliefs in one area: rhetoric.

Speechwriters produce much of that rhetoric. I'm one. It is, in some ways, a strange career, not least because until recently it was almost a rule of political life for politicians to pretend that they write the words they speak. In 1988, I wrote a Democratic National Convention tribute to Jimmy Carter for Ed Muskie, the former Maine governor, senator, and Carter's secretary of state.

Muskie walked to the podium carrying the speech I had given him. But before starting, he turned to Texas governor Ann Richards, who had introduced him.

"Madame Chairperson," he said, "as you know, I like to do things my own way. So I will complete this assignment reading from my own handwritten notes."

Handwritten notes? I had written almost every word! At that point I had been a speechwriter long enough to know that reading other people's words can make politicians uncomfortable. But why would Muskie go out of his way to conceal what I had done, unless he thought there was something shady about it?

Some people do argue that speechwriting is by definition unethical, partly because of the secrecy, and partly because skillful speechwriters can distort audiences' judgment about candidates by making them appear more articulate than they are in real life. But politicians aren't the only public figures who ask others to write their own material. So do talk show hosts or Supreme Court justices whose clerks write actual decisions. Nobody protests.

The fact is, people want their politicians to speak a lot. And if they had to write those speeches, they would be doing nothing else. Over roughly the last hundred years, that has made political speechwriters not just essential for politics but also to the public conversation about policy. Out of their printers emerge arguments that support or oppose war, universal health care, the right to choose an abortion, or a $700 billion economic "stimulus." When I worked in the White House for Vice President Al Gore, I wrote his speeches commemorating the fiftieth anniversary of D day and the twenty-fifth anniversary of the moon landing, his remarks at Nelson Mandela's inauguration, and his eulogy for firefighters had who died in action. On my fiftieth birthday, while my wife and kids waited, I spent all day in the office writing a speech on the value of fatherhood—and thought it was well worth putting off my party, because I believed the role I'd been given was a privilege. With all its occasional moral ambiguity, imperfect solutions, and endless need for compromise, I still feel that way.

The secrecy is another matter. The last few years have seen some of the secrecy surrounding speechwriting erode, at least at the presidential level. It's about time. Few would argue that Barack Obama lost votes because reporters wrote stories about his gifted chief speechwriter, Jon Favreau. Concealing the identity of speechwriters only lends ammunition to those who see politics as corrupt.

As it occasionally is. Americans often use the word as an insult, probably because they believe politics is so pervasive. Even politicians do, running in campaigns against "career politicians" and offering to rise "above politics."

They shouldn't be so hard on themselves. In my experience, politicians are complex, often surprisingly introspective, passionate about issues, and nuanced in their beliefs. They chafe at the limits that political life imposes on their intellectual and personal lives. There's no evidence that they are any more corrupt than the rest of us.

And while they've chosen a heady occupation, many pay a price: a bifurcated routine in which their families live hundreds of miles away while they rent tiny apartments in state capitals or Washington, D.C.; in which weekends are chances to rush back to the district and race from pancake breakfasts to ribbon cuttings to fund-raisers as part of the perpetual campaign of political life. A small battalion of aides schedules their days, transports them to and fro, writes their letters, signs their names, insists on meetings, and bombards them with stacks of memos to a degree that frustrates people who might like to go to their daughter's lacrosse game or read a novel now and then.

In the White House, I used to be amazed by the briefing book that aides handed Gore each night, dividing the next day into fifteen-minute segments from the moment he stepped into his limo (*"7:30 A.M.: CIA briefing"*) to the moment, often near midnight, when he returned to the mansion. Once I asked him how he found the time to explore any of the issues he dealt with.

"You spend the intellectual capital you come here with," Gore replied, allowing me to hear just a hint of exasperation.

How to change political life is beyond the scope of this book. How to make speeches better reflect that intellectual capital is not. But to learn what to put *in* those speeches you should first figure out what politicians need *from* them. Let's begin by looking at those needs, why they differ from those of other speakers, and what they imply about the sometimes terrifying act of writing a speech that satisfies them.

LAYING THE FOUNDATION

"Say, who the hell's been writing this stuff?
It comes perilously close to the truth."

Bernard Schoenbaum. Published in *The New Yorker*, December 7, 1992.

chapter 1

The Political Speech

Denver. November 1994. Our motorcade heads downtown past snowbanks while police cars with flashers on hold back traffic. Al Gore, then a mere vice president of the United States, is on his way to speak to the Council of Jewish Federations. The speech is one of four on his schedule, all calculated to get the Clinton administration out of trouble. Republicans won control of Congress in the disastrous elections two weeks earlier, prompting speculation that Bill Clinton would abandon principle and move to the right.

The other day in Jakarta, Indonesia, someone had asked Clinton about Republican House Speaker Newt Gingrich's proposal for a constitutional amendment allowing prayer in schools. The president said he would "not rule anything out."[1] The *Washington Post* reported this response on its front page, outraging Jewish groups, and we've hastily scheduled this speech to reassure them. Much of Gore's speech will do that, but right now I'm worried about the opening I wrote.

A heel injury has forced Gore to limp toward the podium before speeches, supporting himself with a flamboyantly orange cane. Since the accident he likes to start speeches with a string of heel jokes. I had wanted to find him a Jewish one, but nothing seemed appropriate until my intern, Julie Fanburg, came down from the library with a brilliant discovery.

That week's Torah portion was about Jacob, who was born grasping the heel of his twin brother, Esau. Jacob—*Ya-a-kov,* in Hebrew—actually means "heel"! Perfect!

Or was it too arcane? These are mostly secular Jews, after all. Inside the auditorium, Gore asks me if the crowd will get it. Apparently, he's worried, too. I take a chance. They should, I say. I'm Jewish. Presumably I know. Gore gives me the wordless stare that means I'd better be right.

At the podium, though, he starts out saying, tentatively, almost apologetically, "This may be a stretch." Uh-oh.

But now he's locked into the joke. "I'm told there's a special biblical significance to my appearance this morning, given my heel injury," he says, over-explaining because he's unsure. "The Torah—."

The audience explodes with laughter. I'm startled. So is Gore. But he isn't too taken aback to improvise. "I hadn't *realized,*" he says, pretending absolute incredulity, "so many of you *read* the—. . ."

More laughter. "Jacob was born grasping—I say this for those *few* who have not read—. . ."

Now everybody's roaring. Staffers are high-fiving me. *You wrote that? Great!* Finally, I'm relaxed.

Can one, somewhat serendipitous remark really matter so much? Weren't the policy points in his speech more important? Of course they were; but speeches are about policy *and* personality for politicians. Are they smart? Funny? Compassionate? Do they care? Voters care about these questions, so politicians must. A joke can mean a lot.

That day in 1994 was unusual even for a vice president. We did the four speeches as a day trip: *Air Force Two* took us from Washington to Denver, where in addition to the Council, Gore talked to a Native American convention; then on to Orlando for a meeting of state Democratic Party chairs; and finally to New York for another Democratic group before heading back to Andrews Air Force Base. But while not many people other than those in the White House—or running for it—go racing around the country to speak, living large chunks of their lives at thirty-seven thousand feet, Gore's speaking needs that day differed only in degree from those of, say, a candidate for the school board.

What are those needs, and how do they make political speeches different from speeches by the rest of us?

POLITICIANS NEED TO SPEAK MORE

Only in politics would four speeches constitute a moderate load. Even first-term members of Congress sometimes speak more: at a prayer breakfast, at the caucus, on the floor, on the steps of the Capitol for off-the-cuff remarks to visiting school groups—and, after adjournment, maybe at a meeting of shop stewards or in a nearby restaurant for a fund-raiser.

Working for Texaco in the 1980s, I wrote for CEOs who thought speaking once a week was a lot. Later, back in politics, I wrote about 150 speeches a year for my bosses. And those were just the prepared texts; politicians often speak with only a few talking points, or nothing at all. In his book *The Rhetorical Presidency,* Jeffrey K. Tulis calculates that from George Washington through William McKinley, American presidents only spoke about ten times a year—and almost never about policy. Today, especially during campaigns, even a state senator might talk ten times a day.

Such a schedule creates special needs. First, politicians must have material they can recycle. Everybody knows that's true during a campaign, but these are the days of perpetual campaigns, and major politicians cannot possibly generate enough speech drafts to cover every appearance. They wouldn't want to even if they could. Who wants a formal text for a group of thirty eighth graders, or a half-drunk crowd pushing around the microphone at a fund-raiser? The solution: remarks you give so often you can use them without notes.

Some politicians resist that option on the grounds that recycled speeches are unoriginal—and uninteresting. "Yeah, absolutely," Michelle Obama replied when asked in 2008 if she got bored giving the same speech over and over again.[2] Still, most politicians eventually see that the sheer amount of day-in, day-out speaking makes recycling necessary.

That heavy, never-ending speech load leads to a second necessity: politicians must rely on material prepared by others. Clearly, people using hundreds of speeches a year can't write them all. That's true even for skillful writers, like Barack Obama or Virginia's senator-novelist Jim Webb. That day in Denver and Orlando, how could Gore have mastered the nuances of Middle East issues, biblical names, church and state questions, Native American concerns, and the volatile disputes of Democratic Party politics? He had to rely on two speeches I wrote, and on talking points from staffers who had the time to think about them.

Some politicians detest using speechwriters—as, apparently, did Ed Muskie. In modern politics, they don't have a choice; they would have to spend all their time writing and none legislating.

POLITICIANS NEED TO PERSUADE

During ten years of corporate writing, I didn't once produce a speech in which the speaker sounded angry, raised a voice, or pounded a lectern. All these things happen regularly in politics; they help make it fun. Emotions don't always reach the level they did in 1849, when a speech by a Massachusetts abolitionist congressman, Charles Sumner, so incensed a Southern colleague that he attacked Sumner at his desk, beating him unconscious with his gutta-percha cane. But when politicians sound furious, it's usually not an act.

After all, you argue at home about what's for dinner, or whether the kids can play video games before finishing their homework; why shouldn't politicians get mad when they disagree about ways to cure cancer, allow poor kids to go to college, or declare war? When Republicans see Democrats arguing for a minimum wage increase that in their view costs thousands of jobs, or when Democrats see Republicans voting for a missile defense system they believe makes life more dangerous, it's silly for them to react as though they were chatting over drinks.

The contentiousness of political life means politicians need little of something that takes up a lot of space in public speaking textbooks: *informative speech,* the speech that should, as one text puts it, "convey knowledge or understanding."[3] There's room for informative speech in politics; just ask a campaign organizer who's explaining the results of a poll to workers. But the bread and butter for political speechwriters involves *persuasion,* the "process of creating, reinforcing, or changing people's actions."[4] Politicians are not in the business of conveying information; they are advocates.

On the stump they persuade people to vote for them. On the floor they persuade people to support or oppose a bill. So when Gore moved on through his speech to the Council, he made the case for separation of church and state;

when he went across town to the Native American convention, he argued that Native Americans should be considered a sovereign nation; that night, talking to Democrats, he tried to convince them that the administration had learned its lesson from the dreadful results of the 1994 elections.

Persuasive speeches—all three. Moreover, they were essentially only one kind of persuasive speech. In chapter 2 we will examine the three most common kinds of questions that involve persuasion: questions of fact (*Did Saddam Hussein have weapons of mass destruction?*), value (*Is that good or bad?*), and policy (*Should we invade his country to get rid of them?*). But in politics, politicians deal with the first two questions mostly to help persuade about the third.

Voters don't want politicians to opine about values, they want them to solve problems. The solutions may be political (*Change the president!*) or based on issues (*Stop greenhouse gases!*). Either way, they're urging—advocating—action, or *policy.*

Politicians work to persuade about policy even when you might think they have no reason to persuade. Floor speeches rarely change a single vote, but reporters—and thus their readers—would look askance at a party that abandoned the effort to make a case for its position. So politicians take floor speeches seriously. And while politicians fill the bulk of their speaking schedule with friendly audiences, even friends need to hear evidence reinforcing their beliefs: numbers that remind them of where the other side has screwed up, or anecdotes that remind them of why they are Democrats or Republicans. That's what helps persuade them to walk a precinct, write a check, or vote for the speaker.

But for politicians it is not enough to be persuasive. They need something equally important.

POLITICIANS NEED TO BE LIKED

Doesn't everybody? Not the way politicians do. Really, most of their appearances are group job interviews before crowds who will decide, at least by voting, whether they get the job. With the advent of video, cable, and an Internet that lets people see damning mistakes posted before politicians stop talking, speeches can win or lose a lot of votes. And while political races principally turn on issues, *personality* influences voters, too. Voters usually want their politicians likable: humble, appreciative, energetic, moral, exciting, witty, and—within limits—compassionate.

Being liked doesn't necessarily mean saying only what the audience wants to hear. It does, however, mean soft-pedaling those views the audience resents and highlighting those it likes.

POLITICIANS NEED TO STAY UPBEAT

In 1979 Jimmy Carter used an energy speech to deliver a sermon. In the words of Patrick Anderson, who had been his campaign speechwriter, he "embraced [pollster] Pat Caddell's mumbo jumbo about a national crisis of the spirit."[5]

The result: what historians call Carter's "malaise" speech, using a word that never appeared in Carter's speech but in Caddell's memo. Speaking from the Oval Office, Carter warned Americans that their "erosion of confidence in the future" was "threatening to destroy the social and the political fabric of America." He not only blamed voters for their problems but promised no solution. "No one ever took his speeches seriously again," wrote Anderson.[6]

Really, the speech wasn't so bleak; but the controversy it inspired shows how unusual *any* measure of pessimism is in politics. People do not want to hear that they are at fault, or that there may be no solutions. They want to know they *can* win the election, though the polls say no; that government *can* and *will* help; that a bill *will* pass.

In a sense, they want speeches to resemble a well-made Hollywood feature, raising serious issues, like corruption, but providing a happy ending by the closing credits. "We chose hope over fear," Barack Obama was careful to say in his inaugural address. There are ways to be optimistic without sounding mindless. But the relentless need to promise success imposes sharp limits on the complexity of political debate.

Politics also imposes limits on another kind of complexity, for reasons we examine next.

POLITICIANS NEED TO BE UNDERSTOOD

In 2008 Wesleyan professor Elvin T. Lim analyzed every single American presidential inaugural speech, using one gauge of complex language: the Flesch-Kincaid reading level assessment.[7] Lim was distressed to find that in the nineteenth

---

BOX 1.1   The Flesch-Kincaid Readability Test

The Flesch-Kincaid Readability Test is a simple but effective formula that can tell you how many Americans are likely to understand what you've written.

For those of you using Microsoft Word, it's the little box that pops up after Spelling and Grammar Check. It looks like the image shown here. Note the elements besides grade level; sentence length and percentage of passive voice can really help speechwriters.

My rule of thumb for speech: I worry about sentences longer than thirteen words, speeches with more than 3 percent passive sentences, and scoring at a grade level over eight.

Readability Statistics	☒
Counts	
Words	8022
Characters	39486
Paragraphs	256
Sentences	185
Averages	
Sentences per Paragraph	1.2
Words per Sentence	39.4
Characters per Word	4.7
Readability	
Passive Sentences	29%
Flesch Reading Ease	43.4
Flesch-Kincaid Grade Level	13.9
	OK

century, those speeches were written for college graduates and averaged sixty-word sentences; that is three times longer than they are today.

Actually, the change makes perfect sense. Thomas Jefferson wrote his inaugural for a tiny educated elite, not backwoods farmers in Virginia or slaves forbidden to learn reading. Since the Twentieth Amendment gave women the right to vote, politicians have needed to speak to everyone. That means reaching a population averaging a seventh-grade reading level. In fact, speeches written at a seventh-grade level may be too complicated for a lot of Americans; unlike readers, listeners can't go back if they're confused.

Luckily, writers have been reasonably effective with short sentences and simple words—the one who thought up "I come to bury Caesar, not to praise him," for example. Because power in speech depends so much on concrete detail and repetition, simplicity precludes neither profundity nor power. We see this in one of 1988 presidential candidate Jesse Jackson's best moments from his "Keep Hope Alive" speech:

> Most poor people are not on welfare. They work hard every day. . . . They catch the early bus. They work every day. They raise other people's children. They work every day. They clean the streets. They work every day. They drive vans and cabs. They work every day. They change the beds you slept in at these hotels last night and can't get a union contract. They work every day.

What makes this passage so effective after more than two decades? The reasons include Jackson's use of repetition and his ability to pick examples that create a shock of recognition in the audience (both elements we will examine later in the book). But look at how easy it is for average Americans to understand, with its short sentences, concrete examples, and words everyone knows. Jackson uses fifty-six one-syllable words out of seventy-one, and of the fifteen words that have two syllables, the word *every* accounts for six. That it is simple doesn't mean it is simple-minded. The Flesch-Kincaid test measures Jackson's excerpt at a little below fourth-grade level, but it made people with doctorates weep.

In order to write so voters understand, speechwriters should feel comfortable using sentence fragments or beginning expressions with "But"; and if they program their computers to put wavy lines underneath anything grammatically incorrect, they should think twice about clicking on Accept Change.

They should also keep their speeches short. Often, politicians get invitation letters asking them to speak for forty-five minutes. The smart ones say yes to the invitation and no to the format. Audience surveys show that after twenty minutes, the attention of an audience is virtually zero. It even is for me, and I have a professional interest in what's being said. I look at the dessert tray and wonder if I can snarf another cookie without being conspicuous.

Of course, the live audience is not the politician's only concern. Unlike most speakers, politicians have at least two: the people sitting in front of them and the secondary audiences reading news stories or watching snips on TV or YouTube. Speeches can have influence after they end, which leads to a final point.

POLITICIANS NEED PUBLICITY

In the early 1990s, when I worked for House Majority Whip David Bonior, the House Democratic leadership used to hold press conferences up in the Capitol's Radio-Television Correspondents' Gallery. I would stand in the back with Bonior's press secretary while reporters filed in, shirts out, ties pulled down, looking skeptically at the pinstriped politicians on the riser.

Usually, reporters didn't take notes. They had the press releases and, in those pre-laptop days, tape recorders. But every once in a while there was a quotable line, and twenty hands would click pens and jot it down. We used to take great pride in predicting which lines would make the pens jump: in other words, which were sound bites—not *bytes* as in computer language, but *bites* as in bite-sized.

To some, sound bites represent everything that is wrong with politics. While it's true that only about eight seconds of the average speech now make news—not much time to capture the complexity of an issue—sound bites are not meaningless. Take these, for example:

Give me liberty or give me death.

It's morning in America.

Yes we can.

All three implied significant messages, easily understood by those who heard them. And, because they were quotable, they reached audiences many times larger than the live one.

To recap, your material should be:

- persuasive—about problems and solutions;
- likable;
- upbeat;
- understandable by average folks;
- quotable; and
- able to be used again and again.

Wouldn't it be nice if there were a format that could include all the special needs of those in political life? Actually, there is. That is, there exists one structure surprisingly appropriate for almost every political occasion, especially when enlivened with what you might call the LAWS of persuasive speech: *language, anecdote, wit,* and *support.*

But using all that well means absorbing some basic principles when it comes to *how* you persuade, *whom* you persuade, and how to find what you *need* to persuade.

You'll find these in the next three chapters.

chapter 2

Persuasion

"**H**ave you ever heard of Plato? Aristotle? Socrates?" asks the winningly evil Vizzini, played by Wallace Shawn in William Goldman's classic movie, *The Princess Bride.* "Morons!"

Vizzini is trying to impress Westley, disguised as the Dread Pirate Roberts, with his intellect. It's a sign of how much we still respect the Greeks that, 2,300 years after they died, Goldman still makes them Vizzini's yardstick for brilliance.

A lot has changed about speeches in the last half-century, much less since the days when Aristotle sat in the garden of his villa, transcribing student notes from his lectures into what became *Ars Rhetorica.* No doubt, some of why people venerate Aristotle comes from incredulity. How could someone living so long ago—before iPods!—possibly have any insight for people today? But the human psyche seems immutable. Whether wearing the chitons of the Athenian marketplace, the togas of ancient Rome, or the Brooks Brothers suits of Washington, D.C., politicians have persuaded crowds in much the same way. Aristotle's ideas form the basis for a lot of what twentieth-century rhetoric scholars urge—as well as this chapter. Yes, you can write a great speech without knowing Aristotle. If that tempts you to skip this chapter, the quicker to get to the nuts and bolts of writing, please don't. Knowing some theory and scholarship is a practical thing to do. Defining *persuasion,* dissecting its various kinds, learning the strategies and tactics that work in politics, and seeing how long they have worked for different cultures can make clear how and why they can work for you.

DEFINING PERSUASION

"Rhetorical study in its strict sense," Aristotle wrote, "is concerned with the modes of persuasion."[1] We looked briefly at what persuasion means in chapter 1: the attempt to *change or reinforce values, beliefs, or action,* as opposed to informative speech: the attempt to *convey knowledge and understanding.*

The difference can sometimes seem confusing. If speakers say, "We should ban stem cell research," don't they need to "convey knowledge" to persuade their listeners? Often, persuasive and informative speeches can cover the same information. How to tell the difference?

The key words are *we should.* Persuasive speakers use knowledge to *advocate* one position. If the same speakers say, "Here's why *the administration believes* stem cell research should be banned," that becomes informative. They are conveying information about a view without endorsing it.

Here is one clue as to which is more important in politics. When I write for corporate clients I often write informative speeches. No politician has ever hired me for anything but persuasion.

TYPES OF PERSUASION

It was Aristotle, using different words, who proposed dividing persuasion into questions of *fact, value,* and *policy.* Let's look closely at each one, using the celebrated and reviled speech that Secretary of State Colin Powell delivered to a February 2003 plenary session of the United Nations (UN).

AS DELIVERED

Colin Powell at the UN. In addition to the three kinds of persuasion, this chapter covers some traditional ways politicians can make their views more palatable. Watch to see how Powell delivers each excerpt. But watch the whole speech, too, noting which of the other techniques Powell uses. Could he have used more? Were they effective? How would you have done it?

http://college.cqpress.com/politicalspeech

Remember the context, much of which only emerged years later. The George W. Bush administration wanted to invade Iraq. Powell, we now know, opposed the attack but told the president he could support it if the United States invaded in partnership with other countries. He spoke to win their support. Out of Powell's anguished need to weigh skepticism against a life-long belief in loyalty to a commander in chief came a bitter conflict between State Department and CIA analysts to make sure the evidence Powell used was accurate and the reasoning valid. Later, Powell would call the speech a "blot" on his reputation, clearly feeling it didn't serve him or the country well.[2]

It serves you well, though. Powell's overall goal was to persuade the UN delegates about *policy.* But the 10,771-word speech demonstrates how, in order to do that, political speeches must provide answers to the other two questions, too.

QUESTIONS OF FACT

No, not Nadal! Federer did!

Who won Wimbledon in 2008? You can persuade others by looking it up. Questions of fact have *verifiable* right or wrong answers.

Did 2008 presidential candidate Mike Huckabee oppose teaching evolution in schools? Does making helmets optional increase the numbers of motorcycle deaths? Whether we have picked the right facts or definitions to persuade on those issues will spark passionately felt divisions. But because most people on either side *believe* they are verifiable, these are still questions of fact.

Persuading on questions of fact takes up much of Powell's speech. Early in the text, he raises one: Has Saddam Hussein tried to disarm? That is, does he still have the weapons of mass destruction (WMDs) the UN had ordered him to dismantle? Powell begins his answer this way:

> The facts on Iraq's behavior . . . demonstrate that Saddam Hussein and his regime have made no effort—no effort to disarm as required by the international community. Indeed, the facts and Iraq's behavior show that Saddam Hussein and his regime are concealing their efforts to produce more weapons of mass destruction. Let me begin by playing a tape for you. . . .

Powell plays two tapes so his audience can hear the evidence with their own ears. Then he summarizes them. "My colleagues," he says, "every statement I make today is backed up by sources, solid sources. These are not assertions." Not everyone listening believed that he'd verified his claim, but virtually everyone agreed that somewhere, *someone* knew the truth. Whether Iraq still had its WMDs was as verifiable as who won Wimbledon; Powell had tried to answer a question of fact.

QUESTIONS OF VALUE

Even if Powell was right, though, that would not by itself convince other countries to act. Powell's own country had similar weapons, and nobody was asking for sanctions against the United States. What made Iraq's dangerous? Powell must tackle another question: Is this good or bad?

Such a question involves judgment about what people *value*. That can mean what seems important to them—family, career, education, national security—or what kinds of behavior seem morally right or wrong. Since people differ about values, such questions can create vastly different answers.

Is Saddam a bad person? Powell first chooses to makes assertions involving moral judgments:

> Saddam Hussein has no compunction about using [WMDs] against his neighbors and against his own people. Saddam Hussein's inhumanity has no limits.

Later in the speech, Powell accuses Saddam of character traits everyone in the audience despises: selfishness, cruelty, and vengefulness. These charges are not verifiable; cruelty to one person might seem like a legitimate use of power to another. Powell is trying to convince the delegates that Saddam rejects their *moral values*: compassion, concern for others, and the need to protect their own citizens.

But Powell knows that even if his audience agrees about Saddam's moral turpitude, that won't be enough. Many delegates were already on record with their contempt for Saddam Hussein. They could argue that there are plenty of bad leaders in the world, and the UN can't go to war against them all. So Powell appeals to something else his audience values, the safety of their countries:

> Given Saddam Hussein's history of aggression, given what we know of his grandiose plans, given what we know of his terrorist associations, and given his determination to exact revenge on those who oppose him, should we take the risk that he will not some day use these weapons ... when the world is in a weaker position to respond?

Powell clearly believes he has proven these assertions. So far, he has used judgment and inference to persuade his listeners that because Saddam rejects their values, his WMDs are a bad thing.

But to Powell that's not enough. He has only paved the way for what he really wants from them: action.

QUESTIONS OF POLICY

The delegates know that UN Security Council Resolution 1441 requires Saddam to disarm. Should the UN force him to comply? This is a question of policy. Powell answers it this way:

> My colleagues, we have an obligation to our citizens, we have an obligation to this body to see that our resolutions are complied with. ... We wrote 1441 to give Iraq one last chance. Iraq is not so far taking that one last chance. We must not shrink from whatever is ahead of us. We must not fail in our duty and our responsibility to the citizens of the countries that are represented by this body.

Fact. Value. Policy. Powell's speech doesn't just illustrate all three but the way they intertwine. In order to persuade his listeners to act, Powell must persuade them about the *facts,* then demonstrate the danger to their *values.* Only then will they accept the policy he wants.

In virtually every political speech you can find some variant of that three-pronged approach. But to attempt to persuade your listeners about questions of fact, value, or policy is not to persuade them. What makes an argument persuasive? Again, we find an answer in Aristotle.

ELEMENTS OF PERSUASION: ARISTOTLE'S RULE OF THREE

> *Of the modes of persuasion furnished by the spoken word there are three kinds. The first kind depends on the personal character of the speaker [ethos]; the second on putting the audience into a certain frame of mind [pathos]; the third on the proof, or apparent proof, provided by the words of the speech itself [logos].*[3]
>
> Ars Rhetorica

Speechwriters learn early that there is a "rule of three" that you only break with caution. It's the rule that says you have three sections in a joke—a rabbi, priest, and minister walk into a bar. Four makes the joke drag. Two rushes things. In litanies, you also have a rule of three—three examples allow speakers to build to the climax, two make things too compressed.

Aristotle's rule of three is at the heart of effective persuasion. The extract above summarizes exactly what politicians need but don't always know: the three elements you should see in almost every speech they give: *logos* (reason); *pathos* (emotion); and *ethos* (character).

To see how politicians use all three we leave Powell's speech to examine three others in more frankly political settings: Arnold Schwarzenegger's immensely skillful 2004 Republican National Convention keynote, and the acceptance speeches by John McCain and Barack Obama at the Republican and Democratic conventions of 2008.

> ### AS DELIVERED
>
> ***Three Convention Speeches.*** Again, watch these speeches to see all three speakers deliver the excerpts—and how the crowd responds. But look further. This book's introduction and this chapter show ways Obama and McCain made similar appeals in their 2008 Democratic National Convention speeches. Can you see differences? As you watch all three, can you detect in yourself the reluctance to see flaws in your own candidate—or good things in the other side? Look up the term cognitive dissonance. How strong a factor is that in judging political rhetoric?
>
> http://college.cqpress.com/politicalspeech

LOGOS (REASON)

"My fellow immigrants, my fellow Americans, how do you know if you are a Republican? Well, I['ll] tell you how," says Arnold Schwarzenegger. "If you believe that government should be accountable to the people, not the people to the government, then you are a Republican."

Democrats might have a hard time accepting it, but Schwarzenegger's speech provides a perfect example of how reasoning works in politics. Bear with me as I condense a year-long logic course into a page. Such courses divide logic into two kinds: deductive and inductive. Deductive reasoning means you work from *general* to *specific*:

- All humans die.
- Socrates is human.
- Socrates will die.

Inductive reasoning works from *specific* to *general*:

- Socrates and everyone we know have died.
- All of them are human.
- All humans will die.

This is not the place to review the hotly debated controversies over whether inductive reasoning exists, or the interesting discussions of what makes a valid syllogism. For here is the good news: in politics, the embarrassingly simple truth is that almost *all reasoning is deductive.* In fact, it overwhelmingly uses variations of two forms:

- X policy is good.
- Our side has done (or believes in) X.
- We are good.

Or:

- X policy is bad.
- The other side has done X.
- The other side is bad.

Does that seem cynical? Take Schwarzenegger's example. Looked at logically, it would take this form:

- Government accountable to people (X) is good.
- Republicans believe in X (good).
- Believers in X are Republican.

Ah, says the resident Democrat, *but Democrats also believe in accountable government.* Good point. Apparently, Schwarzenegger has taken the first semester of logic, which involves creating a *valid* syllogism. But he hasn't taken the second semester, which deals with *truth:* the facts, brief or extended examples, or expert testimony that make listeners believe a point.

Powell's speech contains plenty of examples as evidence. Contrary to myth, so do campaign speeches. Obama, in his Invesco Field acceptance speech, uses one kind of evidence—a statistic:

> It's not change when John McCain decided to stand with George Bush 95 percent of the time, as he did in the Senate last year.

As a syllogism, that would look like this:

- Standing with George Bush is bad.
- John McCain stands with George Bush.
- McCain is bad.

If you want to read more about formal logic, consult this book's bibliography. But if you want to know enough to write persuasive political speeches responsibly, know this: worrying about both validity and truth is well worth doing, even in the heat of campaigns.

PATHOS (EMOTION)

English speakers still use the word *pathos* to describe the quality that produces emotion—usually sympathy—in an incident or image they observe. By pathos Aristotle meant an appeal to emotion. Here is Obama again:

> Maybe if he went to Iowa and met the student who works the night shift after a full day of class and still can't pay the medical bills for a sister who's ill [McCain would] understand that she can't afford four more years. . . .

Those details serve as evidence to support Obama's point (logos). But clearly the main reason Obama provides such concrete detail is to elicit emotion, too. *People are suffering. That's terrible. And McCain's doing nothing about it!* The audience is meant to sympathize with the student—and become furious with McCain.

Some researchers think the emotional appeal is more important in politics than ever. During the 2008 campaign, neuroscientist Antonio Damasio pointed out that in earlier times, voters could reflect on issues. "But now, with 24-hour cable news and the Web, you have a climate in which you don't have time to reflect," he said. "The amount and speed of information, combined with less time to analyze every new development, pushes us toward the emotion-based decision pathway."[4]

Whether or not he's right about the trend, evoking emotion is enormously important in politics. Because later chapters focus so intently on ways anecdote, wit, and use of language can move, anger, and inspire audiences, we won't examine examples of it now.

Instead, let's move to the third—and most misunderstood—of Aristotle's ideas: ethos.

ETHOS (CHARACTER)

In English, the word seems related to ethics. But ethics makes up only part of what Aristotle meant. While evidence and emotion are qualities of the *speech,* ethos refers to the qualities of the *speakers*—that is, the entire assembly of virtues and flaws that makes audiences trust them.

Aristotle apparently had skeptics among his students, because he felt compelled to defend this point. "It is not true," he wrote, "that the personal goodness revealed by the speaker contributes nothing to his power of persuasion; his character may . . . be . . . the most effective means of persuasion he possesses."[5]

What Aristotle valued in 350 B.C. politicians value today. They may demonstrate character by showing they share the audience's beliefs or by demonstrating virtues not related to belief: intelligence, humility, humor, and compassion. In their 2008 acceptance speeches, both Obama and McCain showed humility this way:

> I stand before you tonight because . . . what the naysayers don't understand is that this election has never been about me. It's been about you.
>
> Obama

> Cindy [McCain] said a lot of nice things about me tonight. But in truth, she's more my inspiration than I am hers. . . . I've been an imperfect servant of my country for many years.
>
> McCain

Obama praises the crowd, and McCain his wife. But both sound humble by minimizing their own virtue. Does either of them feel that way? They probably have a more complicated view.

Whatever they think, should qualities like evoking emotion or demonstrating virtue be relevant in political speech? Are audiences so weak that speakers have to tug at their heartstrings? Get listeners to favor their views because they like them as people? What's wrong with just using evidence? These are fair questions. Clearly, ethical persuasion must also involve marshalling evidence; and in chapter 12 we will discuss ways to do that.

But the essence of political life is realism. An enormous amount of research confirms that for American audiences, persuasion involves more than logic. Half of all adults in the United States believe in ghosts, almost a third in astrology, and more than a quarter in reincarnation. Meanwhile, voters choose candidates for strange reasons. In the 2000 presidential campaign, researchers found that Americans whose surname began with B were more likely to contribute to Bush—and to Gore if their names began with G.[6]

Late in the 2008 campaign, McCain's campaign manager, Rick Davis, made clear his view about what persuaded voters: "This election is not about issues," he said. "This election is about a composite view of what people take away from these candidates."[7] In their endorsement of Obama, the editors of *The New Yorker* magazine disputed Davis, but only up to a point. "The view that this election is about personalities leaves out policy, complexity, and accountability," they wrote. But they agreed that "what most distinguishes the candidates . . . is character." They just felt that Obama's was "the stronger of the two."[8]

STRATEGIES OF PERSUASION

Faced with an often nonrational audience, politicians must combine evidence with emotional appeals and displays of character. But it's not helpful only to describe the weapons of persuasion—logos, pathos, and ethos. How do we use them? We now move from describing those weapons to the strategies we map out to use them well.

APPEALING TO REASON

> We measure progress in the twenty-three million new jobs that were created when Bill Clinton was president—when the average American family saw its income go up $7,500 instead of down $2,000, like it has under George Bush.
>
> Obama

> Keeping taxes low helps small businesses grow and create new jobs. Cutting the second highest business tax rate in the world will help American companies compete and keep jobs from moving overseas. Doubling the child tax exemption from $3,500 to $7,000 will improve the lives of millions of American families.
>
> McCain

Even in their acceptance speeches, where emotions run high, both Obama and McCain appeal to reason—and with good, well . . . reason. Obama doesn't simply assert that Americans saw progress under the Clinton administration; he uses statistics for support. McCain doesn't only state that his proposals will help create jobs; he offers two brief examples and a statistic.

The appeals are not exactly the same; implied in each paragraph are ideological differences that traditionally separate the two parties: for the Democrats, that activist government actually creates jobs; for the Republicans, that cutting corporate taxes allows the private sector to create them.

But both candidates provide evidence. Sometimes, people accuse politicians of using "rhetoric," or "empty" rhetoric, by which they mean assertions that sound nice but lack support when you look at them more closely. Actually, almost all political speeches are built partly on appeals to reason, since they provide examples for each point. Whether the examples are relevant, timely, or true is another question.

Politicians provide their evidence to achieve three strategic goals. First, evidence *reinforces*. Obama and McCain's highly partisan crowds already agreed with their candidates. Providing evidence allowed the audience to believe it more strongly: *I thought that was true—but now I know it!*

Second, evidence *insulates*. Watching on TV, after all, are people who are skeptics. In the internal dialogue they carry on with a speaker, they may be thinking: *Oh really? You expect me to believe that?* Using evidence shields Obama and McCain from those who would dismiss their points without it.

Finally, evidence *convinces*. Whom does it convince? The undecideds, who are thinking, *I'd like to believe that. But is it really true?* They may not critically examine the evidence they hear. It may allow them to do what they really want—become partisans: *Okay. He sounds rational. I believe.* But others listen critically, evaluate, and, believe it or not, make a rational choice.

One of the problems with segmenting these strategies is that appeals to reason, emotion, and character don't appear in isolation. Early in his speech,

McCain compliments Obama, clearly an attempt to characterize himself as generous and principled:

> Despite our differences, much more unites us than divides us. We are fellow Americans, an association that means more to me than any other. We're dedicated to the proposition that all people are created equal and endowed by our Creator with inalienable rights. . . . And I wouldn't be an American worthy of the name if I didn't honor Senator Obama and his supporters for their achievement.

But isn't this an appeal through characterization *and* reason? McCain presents a premise ("More unites us than divides us"), and then offers two examples to support it before coming to his basically deductive conclusion. As we shall see throughout this book, just as our needs intertwine, so must our strategies.

APPEALING TO EMOTION

In the final week of the 2004 presidential campaign, candidate John Kerry published an op-ed in which he contrasted his politics of "hope" with the Republicans' politics of "fear"—similar to the way, four years later, President Obama used his inaugural address to announce that Americans had chosen "hope over fear." Each was catering to what voters always tell pollsters: they like optimism—hope—and detest tactics that appeal to their fears, like "negative" ads.

But why should "negative" appeals distort any more than "positive" ones? If the audience hopes the policies of one side succeed, won't it fear the policies of the other? The fact is that both are effective, and all politicians appeal to both. Let's see why.

Appealing to Fear

It begins with a girl standing in a meadow counting petals on a daisy. We hear a male voice counting down. The camera moves in until viewers see the girl's terrified eyes. "Zero!" A flash of light—and the terrifying mushroom cloud that during the cold war symbolized everyone's worst nightmare. "Vote for President Johnson on November 3," the voiceover intones. "The stakes are too high for you to stay home."[9]

It was called the "Daisy" ad, and Lyndon Johnson used it only once in the 1964 presidential campaign. But it has become a symbol of the way politicians use fear to motivate. Despite the distaste voters profess for them, negative ads motivate campaign workers and switch votes. Viewers saw that in the "Willie Horton" ad against Michael Dukakis in the 1988 presidential campaign, and in Hillary Clinton's "3 A.M." ad twenty years later. Echoes of the Daisy ad remain even in off-years. Here, for example, is George W. Bush on October 7, 2002, talking about the "clear evidence of peril" in Iraq:

> We cannot wait for the final proof—the smoking gun—that could come in the form of a mushroom cloud.

The Daisy ad appealed to the audience's need to feel safe. In politics, speakers appeal to fear in two ways: (1) reminding audiences of bad things the other side has *done, believes,* or *overlooks;* and (2) predicting dire events ahead if the other side gets its way. The first promotes not only fear but an equally useful emotion for speakers who want an audience to act: anger. The Obama and McCain acceptance speeches include lots of examples of both.

Reminding of Bad Things Done

John McCain's voted with George Bush 90 percent of the time.

Obama

We lost their trust when . . . both parties and Senator Obama passed another corporate welfare bill for oil companies.

McCain

Predicting Dire Things Ahead

His plan will force small businesses to cut jobs, reduce wages, and force families into a government-run health care system where a bureaucrat stands between you and your doctor.

McCain

Next week in Minnesota, the same party that brought you two terms of George Bush and Dick Cheney will ask this country for a third . . . we love this country too much to let the next four years look like the last eight.

Obama

Obama appeals to the voters' fears that they might get another George Bush, then the most unpopular president in decades. McCain appeals to their fear that they'll get a president who caters to oil companies and takes away their right to choose a doctor. One might think that the appeal to fear crops up only during campaigns, but that isn't so. Actually, listeners find such an appeal persuasive in any debate over policy. Later, we will look at the appeal to fear in a variety of speeches that focus only on issues.

But appealing only to fear can backfire. Researchers have found that simply scaring listeners makes them too uncomfortable to listen; they need to know that there are reasons for optimism. Therefore, political speech evokes another emotion.

Appeal to Hope

Taking advantage of the fact that his first hometown was Hope, Arkansas, Bill Clinton made "A Place Called Hope" the slogan of his first presidential campaign. He was smart to do it. Ignoring an appeal to hope is like leaving your cleanup hitter on the bench. In politics, persuasion means not just fixing the blame but fixing the problem. McCain and Obama evoked hope through similar tactics. Here's one.

Promising Solutions Ahead

> I will set a clear goal as president: I will . . . invest in clean coal technology and find ways to safely harness nuclear power.
>
> Obama

> My fellow Americans, when I'm president, we . . . will drill new wells offshore and we will drill them now. We will build more nuclear power plants. We will develop clean coal technology.
>
> McCain

Do some of these proposals sound discouragingly similar? Yes. McCain and Obama could each be telling the absolute truth while intending to spend 1 percent of U.S. resources on clear coal—or 50 percent. Of course, a close reading clarifies differences between the two. Obama's insertion of the word *safely,* for example, implies that nuclear power and safety have not yet been yoked together—a view McCain doesn't share. But these are nuances almost no listeners would absorb, because they don't matter to them. Audiences don't need to hear every detail in a plan as much as believe there *is* a plan. They've heard that, and it gives them hope.

Naturally, just stating a proposal, or reminding the audience of the other side's unpopular stance, aren't the only ways to appeal to hope and fear. Otherwise, the speeches would be too dry to arouse emotion. Stories, examples of "real" people, concrete details, and a variety of rhetorical techniques make such tactics work, as they do for the following way speakers appeal to audience needs.

APPEALING THROUGH CHARACTERIZATION

Mark Twain once described hearing a sermon in church. At the beginning, he was so enthusiastic he vowed to put $400 in the collection plate. But the preacher kept talking, the church was hot, and after a while Twain decided to give just $100. At the end, he said, "I stole ten cents out of it."[10]

Twain describes what textbooks call the three types of characterization: *initial, derived,* and *terminal,* meaning how much the audience trusts or respects you at the start, during, and after a speech.

Some speakers can alter that initial credibility if they give a good speech. When a dentist comes to a church men's club to talk about the value of implants, both dentist and subject may be unknown to most of the listeners. By the end, though, they all may want to call for an appointment.

It's harder for politicians. They are usually well known. Listeners tend to already have opinions about them and their issues. Cognitive dissonance—the discomfort you feel when you hear reasonable-sounding ideas that clash with others you hold—imposes limits on what speakers can do to change those initial views. In 2008, a group of Democrats would not have been likely to trust Vice President Dick Cheney no matter what he did or said in a speech, unless he announced a resignation.

Still, even hostile political audiences can change somewhat. Politicians can win them over by characterizing themselves in two ways. First, they can demonstrate *sympathy* to the goals of their audience. They do that by showing that they know about their problems, have personal experiences with them, or have actually tried to solve them perhaps in partnership with the group. Sometimes it's enough to mention that they take inspiration from the audience's heroes.

Decrying Problems

> I know some of you have been left behind in the changing economy and it often seems your government hasn't even noticed. . . . That's going to change on my watch. . . .
>
> McCain

Citing Real People

> When I hear a woman talk about the difficulties of starting her own business, I think about my grandmother, who worked her way up from the secretarial pool to middle-management despite years of being passed over for promotions because she was a woman.
>
> Obama

Mentioning Partnerships

> I work for you . . . I've fought to get million dollar checks out of our elections. I've fought lobbyists who stole from Indian tribes. I fought crooked deals in the Pentagon.
>
> McCain

> When I listen to another worker tell me that his factory has shut down, I remember all those men and women on the South Side of Chicago who I stood by and fought for two decades ago after the local steel plant closed.
>
> Obama

Taking Inspiration from Events or Figures the Group Loves

> The party of Lincoln, Roosevelt, and Reagan is going to get back to basics.
>
> McCain

> We are the party of Roosevelt. We are the party of Kennedy. So don't tell me that Democrats won't defend this country.
>
> Obama

Finally, and most irresponsibly, politicians show sympathy by redefining goals until they become impossible to oppose.

Redefining Goals

> What is that promise [of America]? It's a promise that says each of us has the freedom to make of our own lives what we will, but that we also have the obligation to treat each other with dignity and respect.
>
> Obama

> All you have ever asked of government is to stand on your side, not in your way.
>
> McCain

These goals aren't meaningless. But is that really the "promise of America"? Is that really all Americans "have ever asked of government"? Because both sides agree on them, they aren't relevant definitions. In an election, they are redefined so the audience thinks: *Yes! At least we can agree on that!* They are irrelevant—but effective.

The second way politicians characterize themselves is by exhibiting what this book will refer to as *personal virtue*. That is, character traits that transcend any specific issue—or beliefs that are so universal listeners associated them with character, not ideas. Common examples include the following.

Taking the Middle Ground

> We may not agree on abortion, but surely we can agree on reducing the number of unwanted pregnancies in this country. The reality of gun ownership may be different for hunters in rural Ohio than for those plagued by gang violence in Cleveland, but don't tell me we can't uphold the Second Amendment while keeping AK47s out of the hands of criminals.
>
> Obama

> Instead of rejecting good ideas because we didn't think of them first, let's use the best ideas from both sides. Instead of fighting over who gets the credit, let's try sharing it. This amazing country can do anything we put our minds to. I will ask Democrats and Independents to work with me . . . and I won't care who gets the credit.
>
> McCain

Tolerating the Other Side

> One of the things we have to change in our politics is the idea that people cannot disagree without challenging each other's character and patriotism. . . . I love this country, and so do you, and so does John McCain.
>
> Obama

> Finally, a word to Senator Obama and his supporters. We'll go at it over the next two months. . . . But you have my respect and admiration. Despite our differences, more unites us than divides us.
>
> McCain

Let's review. We have defined *persuasion,* described the types, presented the three elements, and explored some strategies.

Knowing that doesn't tell you how to approach any one speech, any more than knowing the principles of warfare tells generals everything they need to know to fight a battle. A speech, like a gun, missile, or battalion, is a means to an end. Like generals, speakers need to know the enemy before knowing what to do. In political speechwriting, the equivalent of an enemy army is the audience—even a friendly one. Before the often intuitive and unarticulated process of mapping out your strategies, you must learn where they are vulnerable.

Who are these people you hope to persuade? What exactly do they need? How do you find out whether they're concerned about roads, taxes, global warming, war in the Middle East, or jobs in the Midwest?

That's next.

The Speechwriter's Checklist: Persuasion

WHEN APPEALING TO REASON, HAVE I:

- ☐ Tried to persuade about questions of fact, value, and policy?
- ☐ Appealed to reason, emotion, and character?
- ☐ Reinforced views the crowd already holds?
- ☐ Insulated my boss against hostile questions?

WHEN APPEALING TO EMOTION, HAVE I:

- ☐ Appealed to both fear and hope?
- ☐ Demonstrated that the other side has done bad things—and will do more?
- ☐ Showed the audience that its solutions are my boss's solutions?

WHEN APPEALING THROUGH CHARACTERIZATION, WILL LISTENERS FEEL MY BOSS HAS:

☐ Shared the audience's goals?

☐ Cared about its problems—and worked to fix them?

☐ Admired some people the audience admires?

☐ Disagreed with at least one view of the audience's side, and conceded a point to the other?

☐ Possessed personal virtues the listeners like?

Audiences

In 1992, Bill Clinton had a problem. Black voters had become a passionate and indispensable part of his base. But a chunk of white voters resented African Americans, whether because of the high crime rates in black neighborhoods, hip-hop music, or a suspicion that black leaders like Jesse Jackson (a Clinton supporter) felt unreasonable hostility toward whites. Clinton thought he had to show those white voters his sympathy for black voters only went so far.

In May he found a way. He'd been invited to Jackson's Rainbow Coalition conference in Chicago, along with black hip-hopper and Rutgers University graduate Sister Souljah, who was on record with this quote:

> If Black people kill Black people every day, why not have a week and kill white people?[1]

Reporters quoting Sister Souljah had left out a key point: she was describing not her own views but those of gang members. No matter. Usually speakers lavish praise on other guests at an appearance, but in Chicago, Clinton criticized Sister Souljah by name, and treated her words as if they described her own ideas. "If you took the words *white* and *black* and reversed them," Clinton said, "you might think David Duke was giving that speech."[2]

By linking Sister Souljah with the most prominent racist in American politics, Clinton infuriated almost everyone in the hall. Later, his polling showed what to his campaign was the more important result: a measurable inroad into the white vote. And by creating what political consultants still call a "Sister Souljah moment," he had demonstrated one of the realities of political speechmaking: while most speakers have only one audience, politicians have many.

This chapter will focus mostly on four questions about audiences:

- What do they need?
- What characteristics make them unique?
- What shapes their attitudes—friendly, hostile, or neutral—toward political speakers?
- What strategies can work with each?

But as Clinton's Sister Souljah moment demonstrates, politicians and speechwriters must answer another question first: *Which audience is most important?*

PRIMARY AND SECONDARY AUDIENCES

Run your mental eye across a montage of people who speak: teachers in a classroom, lunchtime lecturers at the Rotary Club, or corporate officers talking to their managers. They rarely face a battery of microphones and cameras. For them, the audience that counts is usually the one seated before them.

Politicians need to worry about other audiences: reporters covering the event, or the readers who read, hear, or see the reporters' stories. Then there are audiences within those audiences: other legislators, fund-raisers, heads of nonprofits, lobbyists, and—oh, yes—voters. The fact that there may be no reporters in the crowd hardly ensures privacy. These days, even if there is no press coverage, a political speech can be on YouTube within the hour.

Textbooks sometimes urge considering the audience's needs before everything else. That's fine for the insurance broker informing a Rotary Club about long-term care. Politicians don't have that luxury. They meet the needs of the people in the seats to help meet their needs. They have to weigh the needs of the live audience against the audiences not there.

AS DELIVERED

George Allen Introduces Macaca. Here you can watch the offhand remark that destroyed a presidential campaign. See if you agree with the way Allen's critics interpreted what he said. What does that imply for speechmaking today?

http://college.cqpress.com/politicalspeech

Forgetting *one* audience is rarely fatal, but it has happened. In 2006, Virginia senator and presidential hopeful George Allen made what he thought was a harmless ad-lib to a friendly audience. Annoyed at the dark-skinned Indian American Democratic staffer who had been attending every speech in his reelection campaign for Senate armed with a camcorder, Allen said, "This fellow here over here with the yellow shirt, Macaca, or whatever his name is. He's with my opponent. . . . Let's give a welcome to Macaca, here. Welcome to America and the real world of Virginia."

Macaca, it turned out, is a racial slur used by French colonialists, derived from the name for a kind of monkey. The live audience thought Allen's remark was hilarious; the storm of outrage from *secondary* audiences who read and heard about it sunk both Allen's Senate campaign and presidential hopes.

This need for a multi-audience approach is not exactly a secret in politics. When Robert Gordon and James Kvaal of *The New Republic* complained about inconsistencies in presidential candidate John McCain's platform in the summer of 2008, they put it in this exasperated way: "The Arizona Republican is making diametrically opposed policy promises to different audiences *at the same time.*"[3]

Reconciling these different needs can be an awkward business. Placating antismoking advocates and tobacco farmers, or teachers' unions and parents, means walking a tightrope; but it's a fact of political life. Accommodating the plethora of political audiences involves two steps. First, it means figuring out which audiences will hear, and hear *of,* your remarks. That will allow you to decide whether what you say will offend others, and whether that's worth doing.

Second, it means identifying audiences you *want* to alert to your speech. These are the groups who won't hear about the speech unless you make sure they do. But if they hear it, they may like it. You're doing a floor speech on the excess profits tax bill? Most people in your district won't be watching on C-SPAN, and if you are a state legislator or on the city council the coverage will be small. But blast e-mails, newsletters, and direct mail can do what the media won't.

As part of that process, political speech can routinely include issues not relevant to the live audience. Talking to state legislators doesn't mean you can't talk about the Iraq war. They won't mind; no group is so narrow that it doesn't care about other issues. When it comes to speeches, even a state legislator, small-town mayor, or alderman should grab every opportunity to demonstrate that they know and care about more than stoplights and potholes.

"You know what the main difference is between your job and mine?" a Clinton speechwriter once asked me when I was working for Al Gore. "You care about the live audience." He was exaggerating, of course; even a president usually cares about the people in the seats. But he was right that for a president, watched by millions each night, the live audience can be a prop—an excuse to reach the wider audience. For almost everyone else, weighing primary and secondary audiences involves a careful balancing act that begins with the first of these four questions.

WHAT DO AUDIENCES NEED?

A good way to start to find out is by looking at Maslow's Hierarchy of Needs, shown in Figure 3.1. Developed by psychologist Abraham Maslow in 1943, the hierarchy, often depicted as the pyramid presented on page 34, ranked needs roughly in the order people want them satisfied. Maslow began at the bottom; people who are starving most likely won't care much about self-actualization.

It's easy to dismiss as psychobabble something so symmetrical about the messy business of human psychology. But when you look at political speeches, it's rare not to see them appealing to the needs on Maslow's pyramid. Two examples from McCain and Obama's acceptance speeches come straight from Maslow's fifth step (problem solving):

> I've worked with members of both parties to fix problems that need to be fixed. That's how I will govern as president.
>
> McCain

> What is that promise? . . . Ours is a promise that says government cannot solve all our problems, but what it should do is that which we cannot do for ourselves.
>
> Obama

In politics, where speeches are often cobbled together in frantic attempts to beat deadlines, speechwriters sometimes have to make educated guesses about

FIGURE 3-1 **Maslow's Hierarchy of Needs**

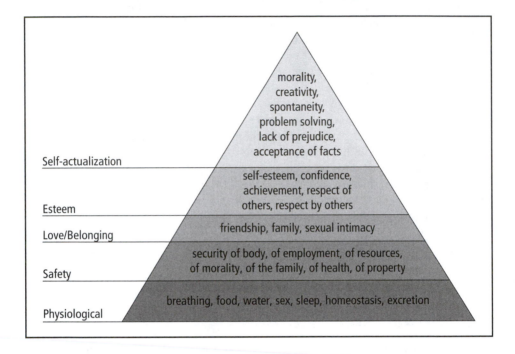

needs. After a while, they get good at making the right guess. If you're doing a keynote for the ACLU luncheon or a floor speech on the bank bailout of 2009, it doesn't take much to understand what listeners want to hear.

But every audience is unique. You can't just tape a copy of Maslow's pyramid to the wall and pick a few elements to include. Therefore, sensitive speechwriters try to find out the answer to the next question.

WHAT CHARACTERISTICS MAKE THE AUDIENCE UNIQUE?

For political speakers, this means finding out about four areas: *beliefs, values, interests,* and the grab bag consultants like to call *demographics.* Let's look at the questions you need to ask—and examples of speeches that take the answers into account.

BELIEFS

Does the audience believe in God or not? In a literal God? Does it believe life starts at conception or at birth? Is government an instrument for good—or an obstacle to markets? Does the audience fear a powerful government or favor it?

Does it favor a collectivist approach to solving problems or an individualistic one? All of these beliefs influence how an audience will react to a speaker's views on policy. Let's return to the Arnold Schwarzenegger keynote we examined in chapter 2 to see how his sense of their beliefs influences his approach to this friendly crowd at the 2004 Republican National Convention. He knows the delegates favor smaller government, but he also wants to reach the larger, less partisan audience at home. Well, both audiences suspect (1) government power; (2) "special interests"; and (3) high taxes. He redefines Republican beliefs to make them acceptable to both.

> How do you know if you are a Republican? Well, I'll tell you how.
>
> If you believe that government should be accountable to the people, not the people to the government, then you are a Republican.
>
> If you believe that a person should be treated as an individual, not as a member of an interest group, then you are a Republican.
>
> If you believe that your family knows how to spend your money better than the government does, then you are a Republican.

VALUES

What about abstract ideas that are not rooted in fact? How does the audience weigh freedom of speech against keeping a nation secure, keeping a check on the powerful against preserving incentive for entrepreneurs, or telling the truth against the right to privacy? All involve often unarticulated feelings not rooted in fact—but that influence an audience's reactions to speeches.

Like Schwarzenegger, Ronald Reagan faced a mixed audience in his 1989 farewell address from the Oval Office. His views about education wouldn't reach those who believed education should be "value neutral." He clearly decided to appeal only to viewers who believed schools—and entertainment—should directly reinforce values, including love of country.

> **AS DELIVERED**
>
> *Ronald Reagan's Farewell Address.* This is another speech we will examine many times. Aside from education, can you see other areas where Reagan appeals to values?
>
> http://college.cqpress.com/politicalspeech

> Those of us who are over thirty-five or so years of age grew up in a different America. We were taught, very directly, what it means to be an American. And we absorbed, almost in the air, a love of country and an appreciation of its institutions . . . you could get a sense of patriotism from the popular culture. The movies celebrated democratic values and implicitly reinforced the idea that America was special. But now . . . some things have changed. We've got to do a better job of getting across that America is freedom—freedom of speech, freedom of religion, freedom of enterprise.

INTERESTS

Interests in this context doesn't mean what critics sometimes call *special interests:* the powerful groups—like banks, unions, or oil companies—asking for favors the public thinks government grants because of their power. It means the audience's personal interest in issues affecting people's daily lives. Is a company outsourcing and threatening its jobs? Do members of the audience have relatives who are ill with cancer? These variables will influence their reactions when it comes to their own paychecks, or health care. In 2008, for example, the cost of health care and the forty-six million Americans with no health insurance gave audiences a direct interest in health care policy. And so John McCain must appeal to those interests, in a problem/solution approach that we will discuss later.

Problem — A future of hope and opportunity requires that all our citizens have affordable and available health care. When it comes to health care, government has an obligation to care for the elderly, the disabled, and poor children. But too many Americans cannot afford a health
Solution — insurance policy. And so tonight, I propose two new initiatives to help more Americans afford their own insurance.

DEMOGRAPHICS

How old is the audience? What percentage of it is male or female? Gay or straight? White, black, or brown? Catholic, Protestant, Jew, Muslim, or atheist? NRA members or ACLU members? Urban or rural? From North or South? All play a role in determining the audience's rhetorical needs. To the boisterously adoring crowd at this NAACP award acceptance, Bono appeals to a black audience by lavishly complimenting not only Martin Luther King Jr. but the international influence of the civil rights movement.

AS DELIVERED

Bono's Acceptance Speech at the NAACP Awards. Later we will examine other parts of Bono's acceptance speech, but here we focus on the interplay between ethnicity and values. Does it work? Can you tell from shots of the audience how they're reacting?

http://college.cqpress.com/politicalspeech

I grew up in Ireland, and when I grew up, Ireland was divided along religious lines, sectarian lines. Young people like me were parched for the vision that poured out of pulpits of black America, and the vision of a black reverend from Atlanta, a man who refused to hate because he knew love would do a better job.

These ideas travel, you know, and they reach me clear as any tune, lodged in my brain like a song. I couldn't shake that. The right to live, period. Those are the stakes in Africa right now.

Knowing the beliefs, values, interests, and demographics of your audience helps you map out strategy. But there's one more thing you have to find out.

It's a question that involves not beliefs, values, or race, though it is naturally an outgrowth of them all.

WHAT DOES THE AUDIENCE FEEL ABOUT THE SPEAKER?

Is the audience friendly, hostile, neutral, apathetic—or divided? That attitude, born mostly from some combination of its needs, unique characteristics, and what it knows about the speaker, helps determine which strategy you choose. It is where *your* skills and *the audience's* needs intersect.

Politicians love speaking to friendly crowds, but they can't do that all the time. When conservative Republicans avoid talking to the NAACP or liberal Democrats refuse to go on *The O'Reilly Factor,* they seem weak. Besides, few audiences are monolithic; there are undecideds in most crowds. And what about the most hostile of them? Isn't it possible to reach *some* people who hate their guts?

It is. A properly calibrated speech can alter attitudes somewhat before any group, which is why presidential speeches from the Oval Office invariably make approval ratings go up. Sarah Palin, speaking at the 2008 Republican National Convention, saw an overwhelmingly favorable crowd in the seats; but millions of voters watched on TV who ranged from bitterly hostile to completely indifferent. At the end of her speech, though, she won at least initial approval from 53 percent of independents and 22 percent of Democrats—not a trivial achievement.

Of course, celebrated speeches with big TV audiences create some unique effects. When the favorable crowd leaps to its feet cheering, that has an effect on neutral viewers at home: *Wow! She must be good!* Even the shrewdest attempts at persuasion won't win over everyone in a hostile crowd, or make partisans out of a neutral one. But politicians can accomplish a lot if they understand their limits, and learn the basic strategies researchers have worked out for the three main attitudes they confront.

FRIENDLIES

Friendly audiences don't need to be persuaded about issues. Speakers *can* make them see the urgency of what they believe. *I knew that,* they'll think, *but I didn't know it was so important.* By mounting a strong case, speakers reinforce beliefs just like you might reinforce a building to make it impervious to earthquakes. But politicians want more than belief from friendly audiences. William Jennings Bryan once pointed out that when Cicero spoke, people listened, but when Demosthenes spoke, people marched. For friendly crowds, politicians need to play Demosthenes. And in 1896 Bryan's "Cross of Gold" speech became one of the best-known examples of the Demosthenes approach, igniting the Democratic National Convention and winning him the presidential nomination. (In those days delegates actually went to a convention not knowing who would be the nominee.) Politicians want to make a friendly crowd march: vote, send a check, walk a precinct, or become advocates for a new law.

When listeners fervently believe, political speakers can get them to act in a variety of ways. In his passionate, skillful, and much-ignored speech to the Reform Party, accepting its 2000 nomination for president, Pat Buchanan combined appeal to principle with an appealing image: beleaguered people who would stick courageously to principle no matter what the odds because of what was at stake.

> Because there has to be one party that has not sold its soul for soft money. There has to be one party that will stand up for our sovereignty and stand by our workers who are being sacrificed on the altar of the Global Economy. There has to be one party that will defend America's history, heritage, and heroes against the Visigoths and Vandals of multiculturalism. There has to be one party willing to drive the money-changers out of the temples of our civilization.

RULE FOR FRIENDLIES: REINFORCE BELIEFS AND URGE ACTION

HOSTILES

Even by rebuking Sister Souljah, Clinton couldn't win over all the white voters hostile to him. It is asking too much to convert a crowd that looks on you as the enemy.

Researchers who examine audience attitudes suggest a different approach. "If listeners are strongly opposed to your viewpoint, you can consider your speech a success if it leads even a few to reexamine their views," says Stephen Lucas in *The Art of Public Speaking*, probably the most popular textbook on the subject.[4]

AS DELIVERED

Charlton Heston on Winning the Cultural War. As opposed to others in political life, Heston was an exceptionally talented actor. In addition to the ways his text accommodates this hostile audience, he works hard to deliver his speech effectively. Listen to the whole speech. Does his delivery add to his persuasiveness, or does it seem overprepared, or acted?

http://college.cqpress.com/politicalspeech

In 1999, Charlton Heston, not a public official but the newly elected president of the National Rifle Association, visited Harvard University to talk to the law school. It was a liberal crowd, almost entirely hostile to him. It's worth studying Heston's speech; he uses a number of techniques we reviewed in chapter 2 to mitigate hostility, particularly those of *characterization*. For if you doubt that an audience will accept your views, you can moderate its hostility by appearing likable.

Heston uses two ways to win over an audience sympathetic to civil rights.

Personal Examples

> I marched for civil rights with Dr. King in 1963—long before Hollywood found it fashionable. But when I told an audience last year that white pride is just as valid as black pride or red pride or anyone else's pride, they called me a racist.

I've worked with brilliantly talented homosexuals all my life. But when I told an audience that gay rights should extend no further than your rights or my rights, I was called a homophobe.

Admiration for Their Heroes

I learned the awesome power of disobedience from Dr. King . . . who learned it from Gandhi, and Thoreau, and Jesus, and every other great man who led those in the right against those with the might.

Did that work? Probably not much. News reports of the event described an audience still hostile after the speech. But in a political system where switching 1 or 2 percent means the difference between winning or losing, even reaching a few is worth doing. Heston's tactics showed his awareness of what was possible before a hostile crowd, and what wasn't. Heston may indeed have reached a few people. Maybe it was a coincidence, but a few years later a group of Harvard law school students founded the first gun club in the school's 350-year history.

RULE FOR HOSTILES: MITIGATE HOSTILITY

Most audiences are not neutral; even those who say they may lean one way or the other. For those who are not firmly in one camp or the other, though, persuasion is possible.

NEUTRALS

Is it likely that neutral listeners will leap into action the way friendlies will? No. But undecideds are not as set in their views as hostiles. Speakers can at least change some beliefs. They can switch them from undecided to weak supporters on election day. And little by little, weak supporters can become strong ones.

Since undecided listeners are by definition not extremists, they respond well to a strategy of moderation. Speakers seeming to take the middle ground or conceding error use tactics that can make those incremental gains.

When folksy, ad-libbing former preacher Mike Huckabee went to the Council on Foreign Relations in 2007, he faced a moderate audience that knew nothing about his views on foreign policy. Huckabee characterized himself as a moderate using the following tactics.

Criticize Your Own Side

This administration's bunker mentality has been counterproductive both at home and abroad. They have done as poor a job of communicating and consulting with other countries as they have with the American people.

Take the Middle Ground

> We can't export democracy as if it was Coca Cola . . . but we can
> nurture native moderate forces in all these countries where al Qaeda
> seeks to replace modern evil with medieval evil. . . . My goal in the
> Muslim world is to correctly calibrate a course between maintaining
> stability and promoting democracy. We have to support moderates
> with no favoring of Sunnis or Shiites. . . . It's past time to . . . reach
> out to moderates with both hands.

RULE FOR NEUTRALS: SEEK INCREMENTAL GAINS

This by no means exhausts the subject of audience attitudes. What about audiences who are apathetic? What about divided audiences? Later we will talk about ways to segment your appeals to reach both.

To know that you appeal to values, interests, and demographic information, to make decisions about which audiences are important to you—all that only gets you partway home. How do you find that information? No matter how sophisticated you are about persuasion, you cannot hope to weave together an effective speech without the dogged, time-consuming, and shrewd collection of the material from which you need to weave it. That is, research.

The Speechwriter's Checklist: Audiences

- ☐ How many audiences will this speech have?
- ☐ Which is most important?
- ☐ Which should be alerted?
- ☐ What makes the primary audience for this speech unique?
  - ☐ Values?
  - ☐ Interests?
  - ☐ Demographics?

- ☐ Have I adequately considered the attitude of the primary audience?
- ☐ For a friendly audience, what beliefs will the speech reinforce?
- ☐ For a hostile audience, what common ground will the speech help it find?
- ☐ For a neutral audience, what specific small gains are being made?
- ☐ If different audiences have conflicting needs, how does the speech acknowledge them?

chapter 4

Research

Picture this scene: It's afternoon. I sit in my office on the second floor of Old Executive Office Building, the enormous, ornate, gray behemoth just west of the White House that holds most of the White House staff.

It is a wonderful building, with marble, wide-tiled floors and ornate ceilings; offices with fat leather couches and thick oak doors with brass handles embossed with anchors that remind us that a hundred years ago it housed the Department of the Navy; and winding staircases with brass rails running along the banisters. William Howard Taft, legend has it, was so fat he had the rails installed so he could pull himself from step to step.

Sometimes, late at night, I love taking walks around the place, but right now I'm at my desk, looking at an invitation letter. It is mid-July 1995. Al Gore will give the keynote speech at a Women's Legal Defense Fund (WLDF) luncheon. I know vaguely who the group is, but what does it want? The letter tells me WLDF supports litigation dealing with women's issues: choice; pay discrimination; and, of course, the Family and Medical Leave Act, which President Bill Clinton signed into law two years before, allowing workers to take unpaid leave from their jobs to take care of sick relatives.

President George W. Bush had vetoed this bill in 1992, when I worked in the House of Representatives; the next year I had written Gore's remarks for Clinton's signing ceremony. Because the idea seemed so unobjectionable—how could a boss be so heartless as to deny an employee unpaid leave in a crisis?— the law has come to symbolize the difference between the two parties. Whatever I write, I know I'll have to highlight it.

But what else? How can I fill twelve pages with three thousand words— about twenty minutes of material—and get it in the briefing book for Gore before late evening, when he's going to look at it? Where to look? What to look for? It is the moment of truth, reminding me of what I sometimes think is my real title: speechresearcher.

Once, when I worked for House Majority Whip David Bonior, he came by my desk at about 11:45 in the morning and said, "I think I want to do a one-minute." One-minutes are the sixty-second speeches any member of Congress can deliver in the half hour after the House goes into session.

"Great," I said. "When?"

"Noon."

Not much time for research when you're typing as fast as you can, pulling a draft from the printer, and racing up the back stairs of the Capitol and onto the floor just before your boss goes to the well for this custom unique to political life.

But political speeches often need to get done yesterday. The speed of political life is one reason why political speechwriters should ignore much of what traditional speech texts urge when it comes to research: selecting a topic, narrowing it, investigating different views, and evaluating every source for VCR (*v*alidity, *c*urrency, and *r*eliability).

Not that research is unimportant; it is essential in political life, and much of what the textbooks urge gets done by someone, at some point, in a political office. But not by the person writing the speech.

This chapter covers the three main things political speechwriters need to explore regarding research:

- The event
- The ideas
- The poetry

It suggests what you should look for, and where to look for it. This is part of the overall point of this book: helping you think the way the best political speechwriters think, see the way they see, and do what they do. And one thing political speechwriters quickly learn is that the unique needs of politicians make research unique, too.

The uniqueness stems only partly from the speed that compresses every step in the leisurely process teachers like me can suggest on a campus. Students usually work alone; political speechwriters have people to help them. Student work should be original; speechwriters can borrow from other speeches. Students devote a lot of time to picking a topic; for speechwriters that decision has been made.

Still, there's plenty of research left to do. To see why, let's begin with the most basic step, looking at both what you need to find, and sources that help.

RESEARCHING THE EVENT

"Hey there."

You look up. Looming over you is the legislative assistant for health, the LA; or your boss's scheduler; or, depending on where you work, maybe the boss.

"Hey, Alice."

"Got a speech to some women's group. They put it on the schedule yesterday. Need it by tonight."

The ubiquitous "they." That's so you know complicating your life isn't Alice's fault. "No problem," you say, wondering what you'll have to cancel to get it done. Dinner? Certainly the softball game. "You got the invitation letter?"

And soon you do. It tells you the date, time, place, and maybe a half sentence about what the group hopes to hear. But you have questions the letter doesn't answer.

How large is the audience? Is it large enough that you can use text without seeming stiff, or do you go with talking points?

What's the male-female ratio? Racial makeup? Are there equality or discrimination issues worth mentioning?

Whom does this crowd admire? Will quoting them have particular resonance?

What's the setup of the room: dais with a podium, auditorium style, round tables? Will it be awkward for the speaker to go down into the crowd to shake hands and mingle? Or does the group expect that?

Does the group want a Q&A session? If so, what tough questions will members ask—and do you want to insulate your boss by dealing with them in the speech, where you can shape an answer the way you want?

Why did the group invite your boss? Is it happy about a vote—and should you write about that?

Important questions. They influence what issues to cover, as well as what format to use. If the audience is forty people, a text seems too formal. If it is a thousand, you might want to use a teleprompter.

SOURCES THAT WORK

Other Staffers

If your boss is even a state legislator, someone on staff or on the state party payroll has worked with this group. They will know why the invitation came, what the group cares about, and whether it wants Q&A. They will also know who can answer the questions that they can't. Call them. Beyond these specific questions they will want to be involved, and so will you. That will make it easier to use them for other things later.

The Group's Communications Directors

Always deal with communications directors. The odds are they can answer a lot of questions themselves, and if they refer you to other people, using their name will get you faster and more candid results. Meanwhile, since communications directors often have an eye for effective detail, you can pick up tidbits about the event that may find their way into the draft.

The Web Site

Often the group's Web site tells you important things about the event not included with the invitation: ticket prices, a picture of the hall, and other speakers. But exploring the Web site has many other uses, as well. Clicking through issues, speeches, or other links for a half hour should give you useful information.

RESEARCHING IDEAS

Like your family doctor, speechwriters can't know everything. That's what spe-cialists are for. In politics, every staffer is a specialist. Learn to use them. Speeches take a team effort. Even if you are listed on a staff roster as *the* speech-writer, you can't be under the illusion that you're on your own. Other staffers should know off the top of their heads what might take you a day to find out. And they can find material you should read buried somewhere on the piles of memos, bills, clips, and reports on their desks.

Equally important, political speeches shouldn't start from scratch. Whether you're writing a floor speech on a fisheries bill or a convention keynote on children's health, memos and white papers covering these issues already exist, either in your office or through the research services available for Congress, state legislatures, or executive agencies. Whether you are the one staffer for a small-town alderman or a legislative assistant for a U.S. senator, the times that nothing exists for you to use should be very, very rare. Your workload is just too great to ignore others who know a lot, or material you can reuse.

SOURCES THAT WORK

When you're researching for ideas and looking for a place to start, begin with these four.

Other Staffers

This section started with another staffer breaking the bad news to you. Depend on staffers for a lot more than delivering bad news. They know issues. They know how to find answers faster. They should know the audience better than you do. But like you, they are overworked. They love sitting down to talk about what should be in the speech, and handing over a stack of memos for you to read.

Depend on them for some things they may not love. It's not at all out of line to ask, "Would you mind writing a few pages that could work?" While you need to check to make sure there are no conflict-of-interest problems, you might even ask people from other agencies, or the media relations staff of the group that sent the invitation. To let them write the speech is both unethical and fraught with danger. To see what approaches they value makes good sense.

What they give you may be marginally useful, full of turgid boilerplate, or—worse—clichéd stabs at what they think is speech talk. Sometimes you'll hear speechwriters laugh at what policy staffers contribute. I'm ashamed to say I've done that myself. Resist. We speechwriters may know why active voice is a good idea in a speech about the stimulus package, but they know how the stimulus works.

Old Speeches

The story you'll find in this chapter's *Behind the Scenes* box is here not because it's an interesting bit of historical trivia. It's an object lesson for speakers and speechwriters, and one you'll find in later chapters. Like Martin Luther King Jr.'s aides in 1963, staffers sometimes complain about hearing the same old material.[1] Pay no attention. Powerful material doesn't grow on trees. Audiences haven't necessarily heard what staffers have. Finding something good, then discarding it, is like throwing out a great recipe for chocolate chip cookies because you've already made a batch. Furthermore, recycled material allows speakers to use their greatest hits—and, like any actor, get good at doing them. It lets them look out at the crowd and build smoothly toward a climax with the confidence that comes only from knowing the material. Political speech is one time when familiarity shouldn't breed contempt. Everyone in politics has seen candidates stammer over a stump speech at the start of a campaign—and become powerful before election day. Practice makes perfect. As you begin to amass the material you will use in a new speech, begin by looking back at old ones to see what's worth using again.

Going Online

In 1996 I used to routinely head for the library before beginning to write. Today I go to Google. Moreover, I use the Internet to research even issues and details I know well. To write from memory about, say, Hurricane Katrina is to deprive yourself of the best details. When you go to Images and spend a few minutes clicking through pictures of waves lapping against the tops of stop signs, or of splintered sailboats piled on top of one another, you come away with details that would elude even those with the best memories.

Outside Web sites—not just the one from the group inviting your speaker—have become rich with information. You cannot overlook them. Other staffers don't have a monopoly on the interesting idea or startling statistic that will make audiences sit up.

Of course, you can overdo this kind of research. Just as it wastes time to become an expert, for most political speeches it's a waste to spend hours wading through the tons of position papers you can click through. No matter how important they consider their own issues, most audiences don't expect to hear about them the entire time a speaker is at a podium. An audience of environmentalists is flattered if, in addition to what you think about Superfund and drilling in the Arctic, speakers talk about the broad issues it expects from someone in political life. Two or three minutes about its pet issues in a keynote are usually enough. The lesson for this step in research: skim, don't scrutinize.

The Speech Conference

You may notice that I haven't suggested what political staffers, nurtured on stories about Ted Sorensen's long hours spent with John F. Kennedy, sometimes imagine happening to them: speech conferences with the boss.

Yes, they are important. For one thing, they make the boss see you as a person. If you come armed with a perceptive comment—even one—it can help your career. Just ask Chris Brose. At a meeting in 2005, after Condoleezza Rice became secretary of state, Brose—then a junior writer—raised his hand and asked a question. "Who's that skinny, red-haired guy?" Rice reportedly asked her chief of staff. Soon Brose was her chief speechwriter, traveling around the world with her and offering advice on policy as well as language.[2]

But that kind of relationship is an exception. Speech conferences help when they happen. They allow speakers to bless the general thrust of a speech idea suggested by others. But in most cases, relatively little material comes from what staffers call "face time."

After all, think about what it's like for them. They get off the phone after twenty calls spent winning support for a vote on the floor to see a few people poking their heads in the door. "Speech conference about that Women's Legal Defense thing," someone says.

The boss struggles to remember. "How'd that get on the schedule?"

"You approved it."

"Okay. Come in."

Why the hell do I need this? But it's on the schedule. Can't just make it seem like my mind's a blank. The boss suggests a few lines. (*Do something about equality. You know. Title Nine.*) There might follow a half hour of conversation, during which you can ask a few questions that will help. (*Do you want to be partisan? Do you want to mention your vote on House Bill X?*) And then staffers

BEHIND THE SCENES

Wyatt Tee Walker

He has been a theologian, anti-apartheid activist, author, and pastor, but Wyatt Tee Walker is best known for being Martin Luther King Jr.'s chief of staff during the days of the March on Washington. In 2008, he told CNN what it was like to be behind the scenes.

It turns out King's staff was distressed that King was going for the same old speech. "The 'in' circle of Dr. King felt that the 'I have a dream' portion was hackneyed and trite because he used it so many times in other cities," Walker told CNN reporter Soledad O'Brien.

So, the night before the speech, they decided he should have a new ending. They called it "Normalcy never again."

Wyatt said, "I remember very vividly Andy Young and I going up and down the strips of the hotel taking drafts of what we thought should be a new climax."

King took the new speech with him to the Mall the next morning. He came to the new ending. And paused.

"I was out in the crowd somewhere," Walker remembered, "and when he swung into 'I have a dream,' I said, 'Oh [expletive deleted]' . . . after all that work.'"

Walker had forgotten what staffers often forget at their peril: That usually what they hear every day, what they find hackneyed and "trite," is fresh to almost everyone else.

Source: This *Behind the Scenes* box is based on Soledad O'Brien's interview for CNN's Special Investigations Unit entitled "MLK Papers: Words That Changed a Nation," which aired January 20, 2008. The transcript of the program can be found at www.cnnstudentnews.cnn.com/TRANSCRIPTS/0801/20/siu.01.html.

leave, with speakers convinced they've provided almost everything the writer needs—except for a bit of what they call "wordsmithing."

If speechwriters do their jobs, they will transcribe their notes and make sure to include the page of usable material the meeting produced; speakers will see their words and feel they haven't been ignored. Then they will go about the tough research: providing the material that will bring the boss's speech to life.

RESEARCHING THE POETRY

"Devote more time to the poetry than substance," Peggy Noonan says.[3]

She means that for a speechwriter, more important than the actual points you'll make are the stories, concrete details, examples, quotes, and yes, sometimes even poetry, that make speeches inspire, excite, move, and characterize.

She is absolutely right. Those who think about it all the time can hand you policy ideas. No one else is likely to suggest a clever analogy, inspirational story, or genuinely funny joke. Only the person writing the draft thinks about those things. I've been in lots of speech conferences where others in the room ask about nuances in a bill, or whether we're using "current numbers."

After a while, the speaker looks at me. *What do you need?* his face asks.

"Did you see Jon Stewart last night?" I ask. "He said something you could use."

Sometimes other staffers look at me like I'm trying to sabotage things. But as you will see, the "poetry" looked on as ornaments by other staffers is what audiences remember. It moves audiences to march. Because no one else cares about that material, the speechwriter must. Because there is no one else to help, it takes the longest time. It's not unusual to spend an entire day finding the right story or detail—then an hour to write the draft. That isn't a mistake; it's a sign you're doing things right.

SOURCES THAT WORK

Personal Contact

This does not mean getting on the boss's calendar. The best way to waste a half hour of politicians' time is to try pumping them for personal stories. "None come to mind," they'll say, and all you'll have done is make them feel guilty, a little foolish, and maybe resentful of you. Instead, seek out time to be there when they are talking with others, or are relaxed after an event. Then, without the pressure of a question, they may tell some story, never thinking it's at all relevant.

Once, when I worked for Lloyd Bentsen, the senator from Texas, I heard Bentsen tell someone else a story about how his father took him to get his tonsils out.

"Thirty-five dollars," the doctor said.

"Kind of steep," Bentsen's father replied. "If I had five kids could I get a discount?"

"You don't have five kids."

"My brother does."

The next day, Bentsen remembered, he and his cousins all came in, got their tonsils out, and Bentsen's father got a discount.

Bentsen thought he was telling a funny story. To me, the story was funny—and said a lot about the strides the country had made in health care. Furthermore, Bentsen could tell the story well, and it had the virtue of being true. The day after I heard that story it found its way into a speech about health care—and about ten speeches after that.

Web Sites

If this were a few years ago, it might still have been possible to put going online further down the list. Now, there is no question about its relevance. Over the last few years Google and other search engines have become versatile, and powerful. Meanwhile, the explosion of Web sites about everything under the sun makes them easily preferable to those antiquated research tools called "books." (Hint: add *PDF* to your query to rule out commercial sites and you will find useful material even faster.)

At the risk of alerting readers to a rival, speechwriters should make a daily stop at Stephen Lucas's www.americanrhetoric.com. There you will find hundreds of great speeches, many not just with text, but audio and video as well. Will you find a moving story to suit your immediate need? Not necessarily, but you can examine great speeches for structure and innovative approaches, and you'll run across stories and memorable lines to save for other days.

Next, Google "political jokes." Among the 781,000 hits, you'll see www. politicalhumor.com, www.ahajokes.com, and www.madblast.com. They are your resources for the best late-night jokes, cartoons, and a wealth of other items, most of them useless. Look for the one that isn't.

Finally, explore Web sites that post the kinds of material you need. For a Republican, the Republican National Committee Web site—or the party Web site of your state—should give you exactly the kind of readymade material politics demands.

Anecdote, Quote, and Joke Books

Okay, I was kidding about books. Despite the wealth of material on the Internet, there is still no substitute for them. Anyone speaking often—or writing speeches often—should amass a library of the immensely useful books of quotes, anecdotes, jokes, and other materials that can bring a speech to life.

There are some who look down their noses at these books, arguing that they allow speakers to fake erudition. That might be true if it were clear that audiences think about such things. Most don't.

Besides, without quote books you sacrifice the best way to find the wealth of pithy, insightful, and witty things others have said, or the moving—and often true—accounts of people whose stories can move, inspire, or illustrate your points. Among them: CQ Press's *Respectfully Quoted;* Lewis D. Eigen and Jonathan Siegel's *The MacMillan Book of Political Quotations;* any of the collections edited by James Humes, such as *Roles Speakers Play,* or *The Wit and Wisdom of Winston Churchill;* Clifton Fadiman's *Little Brown Book of Anecdotes;* Garrison Keillor's collections of *Pretty Good Jokes;* Mo Udall's classic, *Too Funny to Be President;* or any of the books published by former senator and presidential candidate Bob Dole. One particularly useful book: Ralph Keyes's *The Quote Verifier.* It's incredible how often the speaker who gets credit never uttered a famous line. You can still use the quote. And mentioning who really said it impresses the people listening.

Leafing through these books just before a speech is a sure way to strike out. At moments like that nothing looks funny. Remember: Babe Ruth struck out 1,330 times. He hit 714 home runs.

Reading the books when you have time is more useful. Leave them in the bathroom. Put sticky notes next to the quotes you might use. Even finding one in a book makes it worth the purchase price.

Daily Papers

For people living in Washington, D.C., pick up the front page of the *Washington Post.* Fully half the stories now use anecdotal leads relevant to some public policy issue. Often, these are issues politicians mention: jobs, health care, global warming, poverty, taxes. Steal them. Cite the *Post.* It will make clear that your boss doesn't just read position papers but—like everyone in the audience—the newspapers.

TV Late-Night Shows

"I see the Iraqis are writing a constitution," Jay Leno said once, as the Bush administration was beset with news about Abu Ghraib prison, not to mention its own illegal wiretaps. "Why not give them ours? Written by some smart guys, it's lasted for two hundred years—and we're not using it anymore."[4] Nan Aron, the president of Alliance for Justice, the nonprofit whose chief issues are judicial appointments, has been using that joke ever since. "Always gets a laugh," she says.[5]

The problem with humor in politics is this: it needs to be edgy—but not raunchy. Politicians love Chris Rock, but they can't quote anything he says. On the other hand, they *can* quote the late-night talk show hosts. And now it's easier than ever to use jokes from David Letterman, Conan O'Brien, Jay Leno, or some of the cleaner Jon Stewart routines. All are online.

Other Speeches

So many other speeches are now online. Regularly comb through them. Often, when politicians post speeches, staffers remove the jokes and clean up places that didn't work. They are useful, still. Why? Because they were prepared for people with exactly the same needs as your boss.

Of course, it's easy to generalize. As I was writing this tip on September 19, 2008, I decided to test it. I picked a Democratic senator at random—Chris Dodd. I went into his Web site and clicked on the first speech I saw, one for the Senate floor about granting retroactive immunity to companies that had taken part in the president's wiretapping program. After a page, Dodd quoted James Madison:

> There are more instances of the abridgement of the freedom of the people by gradual and silent encroachments of those in power than by violent and sudden usurpations.

"Silent encroachments." Not bad. If I were a Democratic politician, I could use that. I might find out the circumstances, and make it into a story. I'd certainly put it into a file and note it for future use. Test successful.

Personal File

Every time you use a joke, story, or interesting fact, you have found a bit of material with an important stamp of approval: yours. Whether you are a politician thinking about your own speeches or a staffer writing them for a boss, begin a file. Forty years ago, this would have meant a cumbersome system of note cards in a file drawer. Now it is easy to copy and paste each joke, quote, interesting litany, startling statistic, or even—it's possible—a thoughtful or clever line you have thought up yourself. Without the file, you'll never remember them.

Keeping those sources in mind, let's return to that WLDF luncheon. This was not a big event; Gore would barely remember it now. Rather, it was a *typical* event: aimed at a policy group; favorable toward Gore, as most of his audiences were; and, though it took place in the days when people used faxes and landline phones, still useful as a guide for us. Let's see how I spent the rest of that day, and whether or not it illustrates the ideas we've already covered.

Picture this scene:

Depend on the Kindness of Others: I should call over to WLDF and get someone to fax a list of its issues.

I also need to mention the administration's achievements on women's issues. I call over to the West Wing. Somebody there has a thick file on achievements.

Good. I'm getting hungry. I walk over to get the list, stopping to get some mango sorbet from the White House Mess—I only have carryout privileges there, a telling detail about the status of speechwriters in the White House. On the trip back across Executive Drive, I read through the list. There are lots of numbers: how many appointees have been women; how many judicial nominees were women; what the administration did to support RU-486.

Ready to write? Not yet.

Now I do call WLDF, taking notes while its communications director tells me how many people will be at the lunch, and who's coming. She mentions that a woman named Donna Lenhoff actually wrote the first draft of the Women and Family Leave legislation eight years ago, and faxes over a list of everything the group has accomplished since 1971. I read through that.

Okay. I know what WLDF has done. Enough of that.

Keep Research on Issues to a Minimum—and Recycle: What are Gore's issues? That is, what does the White House want Gore to mention?

Here, I don't have to research. I've sat through too many staff meetings not to know how worried everyone is about the confirmation hearings for their nominee for surgeon general, Henry Foster, and about affirmative action programs, which have been hamstrung by recent Court decisions. I need some details, naturally. What exactly has the administration done about affirmative action? I call some people for that, and wind up skimming some more overly detailed white papers. There is some language that's been used before. I can use it again.

Two hours gone. I'm worried. I have plenty of facts, and some applause lines. But while this Donna Lenhoff story looks promising, the rest of what I have is dry. I need to start what will take up the most time: finding material that makes this interesting.

Spend More Time on the Poetry: I spend about an hour, largely without success, looking for more. I need something about Hillary. These people are fans. Flip through the collection of jokes and anecdote books. Look through old speeches. Ask my intern. Nothing.

I'm getting worried, but I need a break. I pick up a newspaper. There's a cartoon on the editorial page. It shows two drunks in a bar.

"So we're angry white men?" one asks.

"Yeah," the second man says, "corporations are cutting our pay, exporting our jobs, and laying us off."

"So we're angry at corporations."

"No," the other one says, in the final frame, his face contorted with mottled fury. "HILLARY CLINTON!"

That's a start! Fold up the paper, add it to the pile. Back to work. I need more. What about something personal? This is too small an event to discuss with Gore. But the other day Gore and his wife, Tipper—along with the speechwriter and other runners on the staff—had run in the Race for the Cure, the giant 5K cancer fund-raiser that takes place in Washington each year. Running it was a pain in the ass; the streets were so crowded I couldn't even break into a jog for the first mile. But it was impressive how many people were there, all with signs saying they ran for their mother, their daughter, their sister. Could I use that?

I jot down a few notes. But I've been researching for almost four hours. I glance at the clock and feel a twinge of alarm. I'll have to plead with my wife to pick up the kids from day care so I can stay late.

What about this Donna Lenhoff? I should talk to her—sometimes people exaggerate these stories. I call back over to WLDF and get her on the phone. Sure enough, she had written that draft back in 1987. She describes what it was like to come back from the Hill after a meeting on maternity leave privileges and to sit down at the typewriter. It sounds dramatic. I could open with it—everyone there knows her. After coming up dry for hours I've found my lead! Maybe I can start writing.

Just then, someone comes in to show me an interview with Madeline Kunin, the deputy secretary of education. She had worked in the White House during the Carter years. In those days, she says, White House meetings meant she sat uncomfortably in the Roosevelt Room with only one other woman in a room full of men. Now, she says, "I went back to the Roosevelt Room not too long ago, and I couldn't get over it. Half the group was composed of women . . . and I thought, how can I ever have thought that this was such a masculine space and that I did not belong there?"

What about that? Isn't there an admission of insecurity there that's unusual but that would strike this group as true? Wouldn't Gore get credit for being sensitive enough to quote it? Into the pile.

It's late. Soon the briefing book people are going to be poking their heads in. Where's the draft? Got the draft yet?

Ready or not, it's time to write.

What should you make of this afternoon in the life of a speechwriter? Two thoughts. First, no matter how much you know about research tools, it can never be reduced to a science. There are times when you take a break, pick up the newspaper, and see the perfect detail jumping off the front page. There are times when for a routine speech you spend hours rejecting one piece of material after another—and for another, find everything you need in an hour. It's naive to advise holding off on writing until you're ready. When your boss calls and says, "Hey, where's the draft?" you gulp, say, "Forty-five minutes," and go with what you have. But only if you have no choice.

Second, don't just use other staffers. Cultivate them. That day I depended on at least four people for help. Be grateful. Show your respect. Go out of your way to help them if they need advice on how to phrase something. Then, when you need research, they will show theirs for you.

We'll come back to the WLDF speech in chapter 15. We now leave me nursing my melted mango sorbet, trying to suppress my annoyance about mess privileges, my worry about who will pick up the kids from day care, and my excitement that I'm shaping the words of someone who, in those days, I could imagine might some day be president of the United States.

So far in *The Political Speechwriter's Companion*, we've covered four areas: the special needs of the politician; the ways people have tried to persuade others for almost 2,500 years; the needs of those listening to them; and some steps regarding research.

Time to examine what goes into the speeches themselves. Soon we will cover the LAWS of political speech first mentioned in chapter 1: *l*anguage, *a*necdote, *w*it, and *s*upport. They are the elements that can do for a speech what brick, glass, stone, and metal can do for a building: make it exciting, moving, memorable, and persuasive—and, well, beautiful.

But the brick and glass of a building obscure something important: the skeleton of steel girders underneath. You can't have a building without that structure, though. Speeches need structure, too. And while there are many kinds of structures, we'll only focus on one, because of its incredible utility in politics.

The Speechwriter's Checklist: Research

RESEARCHING THE EVENT

- ☐ How large is the audience?
- ☐ What's the male-female ratio? Racial makeup?
- ☐ How will the room be set up?
- ☐ Does the speaker want a Q&A session?
- ☐ Will the speaker need a microphone? Teleprompter? Lectern?

RESEARCHING IDEAS

- ☐ Have I benefitted from other staffers' ideas?
- ☐ Have I talked to the communications staff of the group sponsoring the event?
- ☐ Have I looked at the group's Web site?
- ☐ Have I reviewed old speeches for elements I can recycle?

RESEARCHING POETRY

- ☐ Have I talked to my boss specifically about the stories, jokes, quotes, personal reflections, and other elements that add color?
- ☐ Have I looked through recent news stories for anecdotes?
- ☐ Have I asked other staffers for stories they might remember?
- ☐ Have I looked at speeches I admire?
- ☐ Have I checked my personal files and library for quotes, jokes, and anecdotes?
- ☐ Do I *feel* ready to write?

chapter 5

Structure

People knew Leland Stowe in the 1930s and 1940s as one of the first journalists to alert Americans to the Nazi threat. But one day, after World War II was over, Americans heard him speak of a different threat. It was 1948, and Stowe was talking on the radio about what he'd seen on a street corner in Athens. Here's his opening paragraph:

> I pray that I'll never have to do it again. Can there be anything much worse than to put only a peanut between a child and death? I hope you'll never have to do it and live with the memory of it afterward. If you had heard their voices and seen their eyes, on that January day in the bomb-scarred workers' district of Athens. . . . Yet all I had left was a half-pound can of peanuts. As I struggled to open it, dozens of ragged kids held me in a vise of frantically clawing bodies. Scores of mothers, with babes in their arms, pushed and fought to get within arm's reach. They held their babies out toward me. Tiny hands of skin and bone stretched convulsively. I tried to make every peanut count. In their frenzy they nearly swept me off my feet. Nothing but hundreds of hands, begging hands, clutching hands, despairing hands; all of them pitifully little hands. One salted peanut here, and one peanut there. Six peanuts knocked from my fingers and a savage scramble of emaciated bodies at my feet. Another peanut here, and another peanut there. Hundreds of hands, reaching and pleading: hundreds of eyes with the light of hope flickering out. I stood there helpless, an empty blue can in my hands. . . . Yes, I hope it will never happen to you.

Still powerful, decades later. But what's relevant to us is not Stowe's subject, but how he spoke about it. Or, more precisely, the structure he used—a five-step format designed for what, as you have already learned, politicians usually need to do: persuade about policy.

Because of his format, Stowe's address became a favorite example for Alan Monroe, the rhetoric professor who, while teaching at Purdue University in the 1930s, developed and popularized it so shrewdly you find it in virtually every public speaking text, as Monroe's Motivated Sequence (MMS). Oddly, because speechwriters learn their craft so often on the job, professional speechwriters usually don't know about it. In fact, for the last two years, I've asked about 125 speechwriters at a national speechwriters' conference if they've heard of it. Last year two hands went up.

They don't know it by name, though they use elements of it in their work. It's worth a close and systematic look; there are various ways to organize a persuasive speech, but none as tailored to the unique needs of American politics.

In Box 5.1, you'll see Monroe's terms first. Where it's appropriate, I include some commonly used alternates in parentheses.

Let's look at the rest of Leland Stowe's short speech and see how (1) after *opening dramatically,* Stowe (2) *describes the problem,* using statistics to show

---

BOX 5.1   **Monroe's Motivated Sequence**

1. **Attention.** Monroe argued that no matter how compelling your ideas are, you can't persuade people who aren't paying attention. Audiences are fickle. You should grab them as close to the first sentence as possible. After thirty seconds, they should be thinking: *Wow! This is fascinating!*

2. **Need (Problem).** Audiences will only care about policy if it meets their needs. Monroe's second step: show the audience not just that it needs a policy change but *really* needs it. This doesn't necessarily mean a personal need, like finding a job. It can mean helping others whose situation is so dire the audience couldn't live with its collective selves until that need was satisfied—or the problem solved. Their thoughts after step 2: *That is terrible! I had no idea things were this bad.* Or: *I knew things were bad. Here's someone else who does! I hope he can fix things!*

3. **Satisfaction (Solution).** Now the speaker satisfies that need—in other words, solves the problem. But presenting a solution doesn't mean just stating it. Speakers need to provide evidence to show that the solution works. At this stage, listeners should say: *Sounds like it could work. But will it?*

4. **Visualization.** It's not enough to present dry evidence to persuade audiences that you can solve their problem. To truly motivate them, Monroe advocated showing them how this idea would brighten their future. Let them visualize success, he argued, by imagining the future—or showing examples of success in the past. Thoughts: *If that could happen—and it seems possible!—our lives would be so great!*

5. **Action.** So far, MMS offers a format for persuasion of value. But now Monroe goes further. Why let your listeners off the hook? If they agree with you, get them to do something about it. Monroe suggested that speakers end by urging the crowd to act: *Yes!* (they should think). *I want to get involved. I want to do something now!*

his audience the scope of it; (3) *presents a solution,* using a variety of ways to persuade his audience it's a good one; (4) *shows his vision* of what will happen; and (5) asks his listeners directly to *act.*

Who would say that a child's life is worth less than a movie a week, or a lipstick, or a few packs of cigarettes? Yet, in today's world, there are at least 230 million children who must depend upon the aid of private agencies and individuals. From Amiens to Athens, from Cairo to Calcutta and Chungking, millions upon millions of waifs of war still hold death barely at arm's length. Their only hope rests in the private relief agencies which, in turn, depend entirely upon you and me—upon how much we care and what we give. — Problem

A world-wide campaign exists as a demonstration that the people of the United Nations do care. Our own branch of UNAC is American Overseas Aid—United Nations Appeal for Children, with headquarters at 39 Broadway, New York City. In February, American Overseas Aid makes its appeal to raise $60,000,000 from Americans. That's something to put peanuts forever in their place. Something big enough for every American to want to be in on. Every penny contributed to American Overseas Aid will help bring food, medical care, and new life to millions of child war victims. — Solution

If we could hear their voices and see their eyes, countless millions of children, now hungry and diseased or soon to die, would run and play and laugh once more. It only depends on how many of us hear and how many see. — Visualization

Look at their reaching outspread fingers and send your contribution to American Overseas Aid, 39 Broadway, New York.[1] — Call to Action

WHY MMS WORKS WELL IN POLITICS

Stowe's speech accomplishes much of what you have already seen most political speeches need: outlining problems, presenting solutions, and moving audiences to act. But it works for other reasons, too. That's why politicians used versions of MMS long before Monroe lent his name to it.

We see MMS, for example, in a short speech by an American president who won *attention* by reminding his listeners of an event "four score and seven years" earlier; then launched into his *problem*—the question of whether "any nation so conceived and so dedicated can long endure."

In that 1863 address at Gettysburg, Abraham Lincoln proposed a *solution*—that the "living be dedicated here to the unfinished work which they who fought here have thus far so nobly advanced"; called for *action* ("we here highly resolve . . ."); and ended with his *visualization* ("that this government, of the people . . .").

It shouldn't surprise you that those writing the best political speeches have used this structure even if they didn't know it had a name—like Molière's *bourgeois gentilhomme* who'd heard about this wonderful thing called "prose" and was amazed to find out he'd been speaking it all his life.

Today, though, because politicians speak so much, it is even more valuable for several reasons.

MMS IS VERSATILE

MMS fits so many different occasions. Take politicians on the stump. They get our *attention* fast, often with a joke, startling statement, or story. They present a *problem*—usually the other candidate—and a *solution:* electing the speaker. They outline their *vision* of what winning can bring, and *call* for help to get there.

Imagine them after the campaign is over. In speaking, say, to the Sierra Club, they still want to get *attention* fast, and outline a *problem.* In this case it might be global warming. The *solution* might be a bill. But a smart politician will also include a *vision* of what can happen once the bill becomes law, and *call* on the group to lobby for it.

Now imagine them on some weekday when the House is in session. They might argue on the floor for a bill—say, about the luxury tax on boats. They rush over to talk to an organization with a special interest—say, the American Boatbuilders Association. They might make a detour on the way back to talk to a group of school kids from their district. Once the House adjourns for the day, they're off to speak at a fund-raiser.

Different situations. But in each case, the audience is interested in the problems they outline—and their solutions. What about other occasions: toasts, tributes, introductions, awards, commencements, or eulogies? In each case—yes, even in eulogies, as you will see later—politicians do not ignore politics. They find ways of mentioning problems, and their solutions.

By combining the problem-solution contrast most political speeches need with the inspiration of its vision and call-to-action steps, MMS includes the elements most important to politicians, and allows speakers to accommodate the rest.

MMS IS COMPELLING

Researchers haven't—yet—established an edge for MMS when it comes to persuasion. But researchers have found a "significant" difference when it comes to *remembering* content. This shouldn't surprise anyone; MMS emphasizes compelling attention right away—and outlining needs that an audience finds urgent. No wonder the audience would listen to solutions with more attention than formats that neglect the attention step or the inspirational effect of a vision.

MMS IS FAST

Now imagine not just that member of Congress, but the poor writer who has to prepare the speech. Because political speeches need to be written fast, there's often no time to wrestle with structure. Modified MMS helps for the same reason you type your friends' phone numbers into your cell phones. When you have ten minutes to write a draft, being able to speed-dial a structure is a big help.

OBJECTIONS TO MMS

MMS is by no means the only structure for persuasive speech. Here are some others.

Problem-Cause-Solution

In this format you add a middle section exploring the roots or causes of your problem as a way of making your solution believable.

Comparative Advantage

This is useful when the problem is a given, but the audience needs to choose among solutions to decide which work best.

Refutation

Useful in debate, this four-step format allows you to (1) state the proposition you will refute; (2) rebut it; (3) outline yours; and (4) support that.

MMS says nothing about cause, comparative advantage, or rebuttal—or these four other tasks that are crucial in politics.

SAYING THANKS

Sometimes those thank-yous in political speeches seem endless. (*It's a pleasure to see Joe here tonight. Hi, Joe. And Alice. . . .*) Politicians need to do it, though. Political audiences are full of people who have knocked themselves out in campaigns, often as volunteers. When you see politicians wink, or jab an index finger at someone in the front row as though they're delighted to see them, you might think they look like the third-rate lounge singers of public life. Really, they often dislike that kind of tradition, cringe at seeing it on video, and know that mentioning everyone by name bores the rest of the crowd. But in the frenzy of campaign appearances, it's hard to think of a more graceful way to do it.

ESTABLISHING CREDIBILITY

This is the *I'm okay you're okay* part of a speech, which in its most hackneyed form goes like this:

> It's so great to be at a group that has done so much for [write in issue]. It's my issue too—and I remember working with your president on. . . .

Like thank-yous, this is also an often-parodied step that makes politicians appear more cartoonlike than they are. But there's no getting around it: politicians need to praise the people they are addressing, salute past achievements, and find ways to praise themselves without seeming fatuous.

Providing Background

Particularly in issue-driven speeches, politicians sometimes need to provide context: factual background that makes the audience understand the problem or solution better. That can be part of other steps, but sometimes it deserves a section of its own.

Sounding Smart

Believe it or not, introspection and reflection can form part of a political speech. So can analysis of an idea untrammeled by the need for sharp rhetoric.

ENDING WITH IMPACT

Who doesn't know instantly where these quotes came from? *Give me liberty or give me death! . . . Shall not perish from the earth . . . Do not crucify mankind on a cross of gold!* No line has more impact than the clincher—one of the last lines or the very last line of a speech. In political speech, a disproportionate amount of effort should go into making that line memorable.

MODIFYING MMS

Monroe never intended his formula to be all inclusive; like a rubber band, it is perfectly capable of expanding to include all those elements. For that reason, and because political life routinely demands more than Monroe's five steps, I use a modified version of MMS. It accommodates the need to thank people, praise the audience, provide the background that issue-centered speeches sometimes need, include the kinds of support solution steps need to win support, and end memorably.

Outlined, with Monroe's steps in bold, such a speech might look like this:

1. **Attention**

2. Praise: thank-yous, acknowledgments, praise for audience and self

3. Background

4. **Problem**

5. **Solution:** possible rebuttal and comparative advantage

6. **Visualization:** or other way to inspire

7. **Action**

8. Clincher

Throughout the rest of this book we will examine speeches that use MMS and excerpts—like openings or conclusions—demonstrating ways to use each step well. As a first step, though, let's look closely at an entire speech to see how the eight steps fit together: one that Barack Obama delivered on the Senate floor in 2005.

FLOOR STATEMENT OF SEN. BARACK OBAMA: SUPPORT FOR STEM CELL RESEARCH, JULY 17, 2006

Mr. President, a few weeks ago I was visited by two of my constituents— Mary Schneider and her son Ryan.   — Attention

Here Obama begins with the most attention-getting way to open: a story, told without preamble. Note that he chooses one with a personal dimension—people he has met. Personal stories add credibility to speakers, and demonstrate virtue—in this case, compassion. In chapter 8 we will look again at how and why that works.

When Ryan was just two years old, his parents and doctors noted severe delays in his motor and speech development, and he was diagnosed with cerebral palsy. His parents were devastated, as the prognosis for many children with cerebral palsy is quite grim, and given the severity of Ryan's condition, his doctors didn't have much hope for his improvement.

Yet, his parents had hope. Because when Ryan was born, his parents had saved his cord blood, a viable but limited source of stem cells. They found a doctor at Duke University who was willing to perform an experimental infusion with these cells to see if they might improve his condition.

They did. In fact, they seem to have cured him.

Within months of the infusion, Ryan was able to speak, use his arms, and eat normally, just like any other child—a miracle his family had once only dreamed of.

Ryan's story exemplifies the power and the promise of stem cells to treat and cure the millions of Americans who are suffering from catastrophic, debilitating, and life-threatening diseases and health conditions.

Like Leland Stowe, Obama has used anecdote to win attention. To show his listeners the scope of this problem, anecdote—no matter how moving—can't be enough. Again, like Stowe, Obama uses statistics to make sure they see that Ryan's story is not rare; that such illnesses affect all people.

Problem —————— Each year, 100,000 Americans will develop Alzheimer's disease. Over 1 million adults will be diagnosed with diabetes this year, which can lead to complications such as blindness, damaged nerves, and loss of kidney function. And there are far too many individuals with spinal cord injuries who are struggling to maintain mobility and independence.

Before explaining his solution—embryonic stem cell research— Obama needs to provide some history and developments in medical research.

Background ——— For most of our history, medicine has offered little hope of recovery to individuals affected by these and other devastating illnesses and injuries.

Until now.

Solution 1 ——— Recent developments in stem cell research may hold the key to improved treatments, if not cures, for those affected by Alzheimer's disease, diabetes, spinal cord injury, and countless other conditions.

Many men, women, and children who are cancer survivors are already familiar with the life-saving applications of adult stem cell research. Patients with leukemia or lymphoma often undergo bone marrow transplants, a type of stem cell transplant, which can significantly prolong life, or permanently get rid of the cancer. This therapy has been used successfully for decades, and is saving lives every day.

Yet this breakthrough has its serious limitations. Adult stem cells, such as those used in bone marrow transplants, can only be collected in small quantities, may not be a match for the patient, and have limited ability to transform into specialized cells.

Cord blood, like the kind Ryan used, has limitations as well. If, for example, young Ryan's condition should deteriorate or he should develop another illness, there simply are not enough cord blood cells left for a second use. His mother has told us that the few remaining cells would have to be cloned to get enough cells for future use, or they would have to obtain stem cells from another source.

There are actually two solutions in this speech: first, the promising avenue of embryonic stem cells; and second, the specific bill Obama supports. Obama now demonstrates the promise of the first, using concrete examples of promising research.

These and other difficulties are the reasons why scientists have started to explore other types and other sources for stem cells, including embryonic stem cell research.

Embryonic stem cells can be obtained from a number of sources, including in vitro fertilization. At this very moment, there are over 400,000 embryos being stored in over 400 facilities throughout the United States. The majority of these are reserved for infertile couples. However, many of these embryos will go unused, destined for permanent storage in a freezer or disposal. We should expand and accelerate research using these embryos, just as we should continue to explore the viability of adult stem cell use and cord blood use.

All over the country, exciting progress is being made in the area of embryonic stem cell research. At the University of Illinois, they're finding that stem cells have the potential to treat blood disorders, lung diseases, and heart damage.

At Johns Hopkins, researchers were able to use mouse embryonic stem cells to repair damaged nerves and restore mobility in paralyzed rats. One can't help but think that it's a matter of when, not if, this research will be able to one day help those who have lost the ability to walk.

Why believe Obama? How do you know he has any experience with this highly technical subject? Obama here praises himself—as he should—to demonstrate his long history of involvement when it comes to stem cell legislation—increasing both his credibility in debate and his approval by stem cell supporters following the debate.

Praise (for credibility) ———

For these reasons, I'm proud to be a long-term supporter of greater stem cell research. While I was a member of the Illinois Senate, I was the chief cosponsor of the Ronald Reagan Biomedical Research Act, which would specifically permit embryonic stem cell research in Illinois, and establish review of this research by the Illinois Department of Public Health.

Obama has talked about a general solution. But this is a floor speech, which often revolves around a piece of legislation. Obama shows listeners why the specific bill he supports will help.

Solution 2 ———

And I'm proud to be a cosponsor of the stem cell bill before us today. This bill embodies the innovative thinking that we as a society demand and medical advancement requires. By expanding scientific access to embryonic stem cells which would be otherwise discarded, this bill will help our nation's scientists and researchers develop treatments and cures to help people who suffer from illnesses and injuries for which there are currently none. But the bill is not without limits; it requires that scientific research also be subject to rigorous oversight.

Because the issue is so volatile, Obama chooses to rebut the objections of the other side, taking a stab at showing comparative advantage—and emphasizing the broad support it has from Republicans.

Rebuttal ———

I realize there are moral and ethical issues surrounding this debate. But I also realize that we're not talking about harvesting cells that would've been used to create life and we're not talking about cloning humans. We're talking about using stem cells that would have otherwise been discarded and lost forever—and we're talking about using those stem cells to possibly save the lives of millions of Americans.

Visualization, and Call to Action 1 ———

Democrats want this bill to pass. Conservative, pro-life Republicans want this bill to pass. By large margins, the American people want this bill to pass. It is only the White House standing in the way of progress—standing in the way of so many potential cures.

Like Stowe trying to get his listeners to imagine the children of Athens ("If we could hear their voices and see their eyes"), Obama calls up an image of the Schneider family. Meanwhile, this first call to action asks President George W. Bush to imagine them before vetoing the bill, an original and effective touch.

I would only ask that the president thinks about this before he picks up his pen to deliver his first veto in six years. I would ask that he thinks about Ryan Schneider and his parents, and all the other families who are sitting and waiting and praying for a cure—hoping that somewhere, a researcher or scientist will find the answer.

Often, visualization means imagining the future—as Martin Luther King did ("I have a dream"). It isn't the only way to inspire, as you will see in later chapters. We will cover other ways in detail through chapter 17. Here Obama looks back to get his audience to visualize success—a historical analogy—before moving into two more steps provided in our outline.

There was a time in the middle of the last century when America watched helplessly as a mysterious disease left thousands—especially children—disabled for life. The medical community worked tirelessly to try and find a cure, but they needed help—they needed funding to make their research possible.

With a world war raging and the country still emerging from depression, the federal government could have ignored their plight or told them to find a cure on their own.

But that didn't happen. Instead, Franklin Delano Roosevelt helped galvanize a community of compassion and organize the March of Dimes to find the cure for polio. And while Roosevelt knew that his own polio would never be cured by the discovery of a vaccine, he also knew that, at its best, government can be used as a force to accomplish together what we cannot achieve on our own.

And so the people began to care and the dimes piled up and the funding started to flow, and fifty years ago, Jonas Salk discovered the polio vaccine. —— Inspirational Close

Drawing his analogy, Obama provides a memorable sentence as clincher with antithesis, a technique we examine in chapter 7. He could have ended effectively with that sentence, contrasting today and tomorrow, but does what most politicians do on the floor: he ends by urging action once more.

Americans are looking for that kind of leadership today. All over the country, patients and their families are waiting today for Congress and the president to open the door to the cures of tomorrow. —— Clincher

He urges his audience to act as Americans did with polio—and urges the Senate to vote with him.

At the dawn of the twenty-first century, we should approach this research with the same passion and commitment that have led to so many cures and saved so many lives throughout our history. —— Call to Action 2

I urge my colleagues to support this bill. Thank you.

MMS IN PRACTICE

Obama's speech is not perfect. It could use shorter sentences and a less passive voice. But speeches don't have to be perfect to be terrific. If this one included thanking Obama's colleagues and cosponsors, it would cover every step of the modified MMS that politicians need.

To use MMS well, you will need to adapt it—not just adopt it. You'll also need to avoid some pitfalls. Here are some guidelines about avoiding pitfalls I've had to find out for myself.

KEEP YOUR BALANCE

MMS works best when you balance each element. You can't devote five minutes to the problem in a seven-minute speech. You can't take half the speech to open with a story, no matter how powerful it is. Even now there are times I'll open with an anecdote I know is way too long. Finish the draft, take a deep breath, pretend you never saw the speech before. Then nerve yourself to go through it, cutting ruthlessly to get the proportions right, and remembering what Justice Louis Brandeis once said: "There's no great writing. Only great rewriting."[2]

GET ATTENTION FAST

Political offices pressure writers to load up the first few minutes with acknowledgments. Resist. Audiences are fickle. As much as possible, fold in acknowledgments and other bits of rhetorical throat-clearing later in the speech. Don't begin with "It's a pleasure to be here." Everybody assumes that—you're talking to them! Choose the most gripping way to start, and begin your attention step as close to the first sentence as possible.

DON'T STINT ON VISUALIZATION

One virtue of MMS is that it emphasizes moving an audience. Yet the step that can be most moving—vision—is the one most often neglected. Don't do that. It worked very well for King. And while visualization doesn't always mean imagining the future, it usually implies hope for the future. There are few audiences who cannot be stirred by the concrete ways to inspire that research can uncover.

THINK ROADMAPS

A confused reader can go back and reread; listeners can't. That means speakers have to give them a roadmap for what's ahead. Later you will see a section on transitions—the statement of purpose, previews, internal summaries, and cuing tips that help audiences follow along. This book covers those ideas in the next chapter; it's not too early to start thinking about them now.

REFLECTIONS

Yes, Monroe created a formula. Does relying so much on formula stifle creativity? Even Shakespeare used formula in the structure of his thirty-seven plays. Originality isn't limited by your blueprint; you can be original in your language or in the details you juxtapose. Besides, even the modified MMS this chapter suggests shouldn't be accepted intact. Lincoln's speech flips the order of steps 4 and 5. Does that matter? Not at all. In fact, Ted Kennedy's 1980 Democratic National Convention speech, written by Bob Shrum, does the same thing to great effect.

MMS isn't the only format you'll ever need. Unfortunately, politics isn't that one-dimensional. But by the end of this book you should see that it can be your structure of default—that MMS provides a blueprint that can work for almost every kind of speech in politics, as well as accommodate the frenzy of political life.

Remember, though, that if MMS *by itself* could make speech moving, entertaining, or persuasive, the Cliffs Notes of *Hamlet* would be as effective as the play. It won't make your speech great, any more than a skeleton makes you human.

So now it's time to look at the flesh, brains, and ligaments that bring the Monroe skeleton to life: *l*anguage, *a*necdote, *w*it, and *s*upport. They make up the LAWS of political speech. In Part II we'll examine why.

The Speechwriter's Checklist: Structure

- ☐ Does this speech grab the audience's attention right away?
- ☐ Does it include the listener's roadmap: a fully fleshed-out statement of purpose?
- ☐ Does it have all five MMS steps?
- ☐ Have I used acknowledgments appropriately?
- ☐ Have I thought about the needs not part of Monroe: like establishing credibility?
- ☐ Has this speech met the balance test?
- ☐ Is the speech persuasive about both problem and solution?
- ☐ Does it include the often overlooked vision-of-success step?

PART II

WHAT TO DO

"But enough of levity."

Gahan Wilson. Published in *The New Yorker*, May 26, 2008

chapter 6

Language People Understand

In the 1940s, Franklin Delano Roosevelt wanted people working in federal buildings to start saving energy. According to James C. Humes, the speechwriter who has made a career collecting useful stories and quotes for political speeches, FDR ordered his staff to send out an order.

The first draft read: "Illumination must be extinguished when premises are not in use." "'Dammit,'" Roosevelt reportedly said, "why can't they say 'put out the lights when you leave?'"[1]

Humes's story makes this chapter's point: in politics, you speak so people understand. It makes another point as well. Language conveys more than literal meanings. Understanding means sensing subtext—the unarticulated meaning. That stuffy first draft of Roosevelt's order carried the message that that this was serious business befitting a president's order. Roosevelt's revision carried another: "Hey, I mean business." Just as necklaces are more than strings of beads—or pearls—so sentences are more than strings of words. Writers convey many meanings through the seemingly infinite choices of words, sentences, techniques, and strategies we call *style*.

WRITING FOR CLARITY

In one sense, style *is* content—that is, the language and sentence structure you choose become part of your message. To say, "We should vote against the measure" is not the same as saying, "Vote NO!"—though both statements urge the same step.

Still, you can make meaningful distinctions between style and content. If asked what the point was of those two sentences—the content—most of us would focus on the step they urged, not the language. But put yourself in the shoes of state senators getting a call from the party whip. To the first they might say: "Thanks, I'll consider it." To the second: "Yes, sir!"

Do you use imagery? Can you vary your tone—ironic at times, yet forceful at others? Do you want to speak in the balanced sentences and lofty diction people think of as "presidential" ("Illumination must be extinguished")? Or do you prefer the informal language of a city council candidate talking to a group of neighbors over coffee? Such choices convey not just the substance of what you say, but the kind of person you are. Style carries with it a kind of signature: Jesse Jackson's rhymes ("Hope in your brain, not dope in your veins!"); Ronald Reagan's "Well . . ."; or John McCain's "My friends."

We don't always consider stylistic signatures a virtue. They could mean a penchant for using the wrong words (George W. Bush) or talking too much (Joe Biden). Neither do we always recognize elements of style. In his book *Public Speaking: Strategies for Success,* Northwestern University professor David Zarefsky points out that people praise the Gettysburg Address for its absence of style, but fail to see that brevity and plain structure are also elements of style.[2]

Meanwhile, it is important to realize that politicians don't limit themselves to a single style. The George W. Bush of the 9/11 speech was a lot different than the George W. Bush on the stump.

Chapter 7 covers the stylistic choices that make speeches *memorable.* We begin our discussion of language, though, with the stylistic choices writers make often—but not entirely—among *individual* words to make speeches *clear.*

READING VERSUS HEARING

You're lost. You pull into a gas station and ask the attendant how to get to I-95. "Well, first go down, oh, five traffic lights," he begins. And you realize you don't have a pen.

Maybe you can just . . . remember it all. When he's done, you get back in the car. But was it five lights or six? Right or left? You're embarrassed. But you reach into the glove compartment for a pad, go back, and ask, "Could you run that by me again?" You've done the right thing—and demonstrated the difference between oral and written speech.

Listeners can't reread a speech, at least not while they're listening to it. That's why politicians need to make speeches simpler than, say, an op-ed. They need repetition, shorter sentences, and more hints to listeners about what's coming next. In the limited universe of political speech, ignoring these rules is dangerous. Those who point out that George Washington's farewell address made no such concessions forget that it was not an address at all. As Robert Schlesinger points out in his entertaining book *White House Ghosts,* the piece was written—largely by James Madison and Alexander Hamilton—for a Philadelphia newspaper to print.[3]

These days, politicians actually speak. They speak to hairdressers, mechanics, and bus drivers—as well as nuclear physicists and Internet entrepreneurs. Is one style appropriate for every occasion? Of course not. But in politics, you can never forget the difference between language to be read and language to be heard.

For those engaged in the partly conscious, partly intuitive, partly imitative way that writers choose words, clarity means making sure six things become as instinctive as breathing.

SHORT WORDS

Even at the most formal occasions, short words work best in politics. Chapter 1 previewed the virtue of using one-syllable words. Notice all the single-syllable words in these well-known phrases—written, as one speechwriter put it, when you're "reaching for marble":

Ask not what you can do for your country.

I have a dream.

Mr. Gorbachev, tear down that wall!

But speakers cannot limit simplicity to the occasional lines they hope to see engraved on federal buildings; it should be not the exception, but the rule. It's not, however. Politicians don't really speak in the fatuities you see in *New Yorker* cartoons, but they are surprisingly willing to tolerate speeches laden with big words and long sentences—profundity by abstraction. Take this typical example from a 2007 floor speech by Kansas senator Sam Brownback:

> Given the billions of dollars broadband access providers have invested in creating and maintaining Internet infrastructure, it is reasonable for them to request that content providers pay their fair share for the services they use.

That's a thirty-five-word sentence with sixteen two-syllable words. Why not say it this way?

> Broadband companies have spent billions creating the Internet. Now they want customers to pay their fair share for services they use. There's nothing wrong with that.

Twenty-six words, only eight of which are over one syllable. Subject both to the Flesch-Kincaid readability test described in chapter 1. Listeners need a twelfth-grade education to read the first, but a seventh grader could read the second. For political life, those five grades constitute a big advantage. If politicians find themselves saying "currently" instead of "now," or "utilize" instead of "use," it's time to rewrite.

CONCRETE WORDS

We've already seen how simplicity worked in the "Keep Hope Alive" conclusion to Jesse Jackson's famous 1988 Democratic National Convention speech. But adding to its impact was Jackson's use of concrete detail—the images and language that allow speakers not just to tell, but show. Jackson didn't just say he grew up in poverty. He put it this way:

> My mother, a working woman. So many of the days she went to work early with runs in her stockings. She knew better, but she wore runs in her stockings so that my brother and I could have matching socks and not be laughed at at school. . . . At three o'clock on Thanksgiving Day we couldn't eat turkey because mama was preparing someone else's turkey . . . around six o'clock she would get off the Alta Vista bus and we would bring up the leftovers and eat our turkey—leftovers, the carcass, the cranberries—around eight o'clock at night.

Jackson could have cut the name of his mother's "Alta Vista bus," a detail almost no one else would remember. But the bus, the runs in his mother's stockings, the turkey carcass, all give this passage the ring of truth. "Above all," Joseph Conrad wrote in a passage about writing novels, "make the reader see."[4] Listeners, too. Concrete detail makes the listeners see Jackson's life as a teenager, and moves them in a way abstract language can't. It makes writing vivid and meaning clear.

Sometimes writers think solemn occasions mean abstract language. Not true. Take President George W. Bush's speech in China, a month after the World Trade Center and Pentagon attacks. His writers could have had him express gratitude this way:

> We will not forget the way people all around the world showed solidarity with America's loss. We saw that in Canada, in Korea, in Japan and China.

Instead, they gave him this:

> We won't forget the American Stars and Stripes flying in solidarity from every fire truck in Montreal, Canada; or children kneeling in silent prayer outside the embassy in Seoul; baseball players in Japan observing moments of silence; a sign handwritten in English at a candlelight vigil in Beijing that read, "Freedom and justice will not be stopped."

Bush didn't say "athlete." He said "baseball player." He didn't say "written." He said "handwritten." Concrete detail is the secret to making your audiences see—and react.

ACTIVE VERBS

Speaking clearly means clearly conveying who's doing what. In active voice, the subject is the actor (*The girl threw the ball*). In passive, you leave the actor unnamed (*The ball was thrown*), or as the object (*The ball was thrown by the girl*).

Passive voice appears in speeches for several reasons. First, colleges mistakenly tolerate it as a tradition in scholarly writing. Second, the nonwriters who stumble into speechwriting in politics think it denotes seriousness. Finally, it allows writers to evade naming the people responsible for a blunder, like the often-ridiculed failure by Richard Nixon's press secretary to choose the active voice in his Watergate apology ("Mistakes were made").

Beyond clarity, of course, we find the issue of energy. Speeches larded with the passive voice make speakers sound lethargic and stuffy, as in this example from the swearing-in speech for Bush administration secretary of state Robert Gates:

> Afghanistan cannot be allowed to become a sanctuary for extremists again.

What if Bush's writers had rewritten it this way?

> We can't let Afghanistan become a haven for extremists again.

Passive voice reduced to zero. Understandable to eighth graders instead of twelfth graders. Meaning intact. The combination of simple language and active verbs alone makes a big difference.

APPROPRIATE WORDS

Now we move to more complicated choices. Simple words, active verbs, and concrete detail are virtues at any time. But language should change as audiences—and situations—change. Audiences expect, or at least tolerate, more complicated diction at a Council on Foreign Relations dinner than at a campaign rally. Thus, here are two examples from different speeches by Al Gore, the first at a fourth-grade level, the second clocking in at tenth grade:

At a Rally

> And the same people who opposed Family and Medical Leave and Motor Voter were fighting it tooth and nail.
>   Did they have a plan of their own?
>   AUDIENCE: NO!
>   Did they have a way to get America moving again?
>   AUDIENCE: NO!
>   But the president did.

At a Conference about Fatherhood

> A child does not learn to have an intimate, loving relationship with a father because once a week Dad awkwardly sets out on a walk around the block. Children don't learn from occasional efforts to help with homework or from looking up at the lacrosse game and seeing Dad still in his suit, up in the stands for the final period.

No, fatherhood becomes meaningful from the day-in-day-out experience of being home.

At one point in our culture, such involvement was considered beneath men. . . .

Appropriateness, too, is partly an issue of clarity. Words like *intimate* or *occasional* convey meaning with a precision that would strike the rally audience as odd. Each speech used language appropriate to the audience and the event.

But the differences are not as big as you might think. Check the percentage of one-syllable words in the first line of each. It's about 37 percent for the first, and almost 86 percent for the second. In fact, the fatherhood speech, laced with talk about homework and lacrosse games, is actually the more concrete of the two. Certainly, appropriate language can differ from event to event. But politicians forget the necessities of oral speech at their peril.

SENSITIVE WORDS

How do you know this speech wasn't given recently?

In no way have the value and manhood of the American Negro been more fittingly and generously recognized than by the managers of this magnificent exposition . . . when it comes to business, pure and simple, it is in the South that the Negro is given a man's chance. . . .

That's right. Nobody in political life would be so gauche as to talk about a "man's chance" or use the word *Negro* instead of *black* or *African American*. It was okay for Booker T. Washington in 1896. Not now.

But politicians can't wait a hundred years to develop sensitivity to race, ethnicity, and gender. It's possible to work up sympathy for those who are distressed at the exquisite distinctions necessary in finding such language. It's definitely a pain to find some substitute for *he* as a pronoun or find terms that don't offend audiences. (Hispanic or Latino? Black or African American?) Critics sniff at the PC needs of this new century.

Tough. Politicians are in the business of winning votes from African Americans, Jews, Native Americans, Asians, Latinos, and women. You don't do that by calling them Negroes, Hebrews, Indians, or Orientals, or by talking about a "man's chance."

This too raises an issue of clarity. You're making it clear that you accept the diversity and respect for groups traditionally excluded from much of American culture.

COLLOQUIAL LANGUAGE

So far, we've examined ways that single-word choices can clarify meaning. But clarity involves more than single words.

Colloquial speech involves choosing the kinds of words and expressions you might use in conversation. It includes a host of things, none of which you learn in academia: sentence fragments and contractions; the use of *and* and *but* as transitions instead of *furthermore, however,* and other, more cumbersome words you use in formal writing.

In part, colloquial speech matters to politicians because they need to show they are not above those who vote for them. But it also matters because people understand it instantly. Examine this breezy excerpt from Hillary Clinton's 248-word announcement of her candidacy for president in January 2007:

> So let's talk. Let's chat. Let's start a dialogue about your ideas and mine. Because the conversation in Washington has been just a little one-sided lately, don't you think? And we can all see how well that works. And while I can't visit everyone's living room, I can try. And with a little help from modern technology, I'll be holding live online video chats this week, starting Monday.
>
> So let the conversation begin. I have a feeling it's going to be very interesting.

AS DELIVERED

Hillary Clinton Announces Her Candidacy. Note how then-senator Clinton breaks with tradition. She is in a den, sitting in her chair—and makes her announcement online. What are the advantages and disadvantages of her one-on-one approach?

http://college.cqpress.com/politicalspeech

Written at a seventh-grade reading level, Clinton's speech opens sentences with words like *because, and,* and *so.* It uses sentence fragments, folksy expressions ("Don't you think?"), and comments ("We can all see how that works!") you might hear in a den like the one in which it was taped. Clinton is reading off a teleprompter. Her writers could have cut those first two sentences, which imply that she spoke off the cuff, and used a formal word (*talk*) before deciding to come down to earth with *chat.* They kept it in to give listeners the illusion that when she sits in a living room she talks, or chats, like the rest of us. It makes them feel that she not only talks to the people but is one of them.

You might argue that it is manipulative for someone who went to Wellesley and Yale to choose a style she could have handled when she was thirteen. But any style a speaker chooses is deliberate. It makes sense to select one that people understand. So in addition to the kinds of words that make speech colloquial, choose two other steps.

Keep Sentences and Paragraphs Short

In 2003, Securities and Exchange commissioner Paul Atkins gave a speech containing this twenty-nine word sentence:

> There will always be a natural tension between directors as business advisors—a vital role—and their role as monitors of management on behalf of the stockholders' ownership interests.

What happens if you use the tools this chapter covers: simple words, concrete words, active voice, and colloquial language—and make, say, five sentences out of it?

> Directors wear two hats. First, they advise managers. Second, they watch over them. The roles conflict. They always will.

You've cut ten words overall, and reduced the grade level from twelfth to sixth. While about a quarter of Americans would understand the first version, more than half would understand the second—about 10 percent of that increase simply from shortening sentences. Meanwhile, you have preserved meaning.

Research on audience retention shows audiences have a hard time understanding long sentences. But short sentences and paragraphs promote clarity by helping speakers, too. They often have a hard time saying long sentences, especially in the first few minutes, when nerves might rob them of breath control. For speakers who may not have read through the draft before getting up to speak, litanies—so obvious with single-sentence paragraphs—become tough to spot in time to perform them with power.

Meanwhile, short sentences are fully capable of carrying mature thought. Take this paragraph from Ronald Reagan's famous 1987 speech, written by Peggy Noonan, after the space shuttle *Challenger* exploded while millions of American children watched in school:

> They wished to serve, and they did. They served all of us. We've grown used to wonders in this century. It's hard to dazzle us. But for twenty-five years the United States space program has been doing just that. We've grown used to the idea of space, and perhaps we forget that we've only just begun. We're still pioneers. They, the members of the *Challenger* crew, were pioneers.

The sentences average about eight words each. Noonan wrote the speech at about a fourth-grade level. The thought that Americans take extraordinary things for granted was hardly childish; Noonan's choice of diction and short sentences simply allowed Reagan to say something interesting that children could understand.

Eliminate Clutter

Speechwriters can use fewer words in almost any draft. Once your draft is done, declutter it. Say, "Okay, I'll trim this by 10 percent." Then go to work, sentence by sentence. You will be amazed by how much you can lose—and how much you gain.

Decluttering doesn't work only for terrible speeches. Here's an example from this generally entertaining paragraph in Hillary Clinton's excellent 2001 speech at Yale University's class day, perhaps as she delivered it rather than what was in her text:

> When I arrived at Yale in 1969 it was the first year that women had been admitted to the college. Some of the students who I had

known at Wellesley actually transferred to Yale and they were on the front lines of integrating Yale. And it was a wonderful adventure for me to look at from the distance of law school. Because I had known that when I had graduated from high school, I and others of my gender could not have applied to Yale. We might have had A averages but we lacked a Y chromosome. And that was all that mattered in those days.

In my speechwriting class I use this extract as a class exercise to demonstrate the decluttering step. Here's one result:

I arrived at Yale in 1969—the first year women were admitted to the college. I had known some of those women at Wellesley. They transferred, and helped integrate this place. That was wonderful to see from the distance of law school. After all, when I had graduated from high school, women could not apply to Yale. We might have had A averages—but we lacked a Y chromosome.

The paragraph is 25 percent shorter. It is crisper, less heavy-handed, and—like a cleaned-up room—less cluttered.

Use Transitions

One public speaking text calls transitions the "neurosystem of speeches."[5] While this book doesn't cover outlining and other techniques taught in standard writing courses, transitions are vital to speechwriting—and essential for clarity. Remember: listeners can't reread. Just like road signs (*Democracy Boulevard, next light*), transitions can either look back to help listeners remember, or tell them what's ahead. Here are the most common:

- *Previews.* These warn listeners that the speaker is about to move to a new section or idea. For example, if after this definition I was to examine one preview, I might say, "Let's see how that works."
- *Internal Summaries.* Listeners need to get a brief look back for the rest of a speech to make sense. If I was lecturing on this chapter, I might say, "Simple words. Concrete words. Colloquial language. We've covered a lot."
- *Signposts.* Usually that means the single words listeners need to know (*First, second . . . next . . . finally . . .*) as speakers move from point to point.

Transitions do more than give clues to what's ahead. They can compare (*Similarly*), contrast (*On the other hand*), or show cause and effect (*As a result*). Important to remember as well: transitions in speech should be less formal than in prose. Here's an example of what composition courses call the "full-sentence transition":

Another way this bill violates the Constitution appears in section X, depriving citizens of habeas corpus.

For a speaker, you might write it this way:

Does it violate the Constitution in another big way? Absolutely. Take habeas corpus rights. Look at paragraph X.

SUMMING UP

So far, we've discussed how language can create clarity. But politicians need to be more than clear; they need to be memorable. That means they need to move, inspire, and excite listeners so the experience becomes unforgettable. It also means they need to be quotable. They need a line that print reporters will pick up for their stories and that TV reporters will show.

That's the point of chapter 7.

The Speechwriter's Checklist: Language People Understand

- ☐ Have I written a speech for the listeners in the audience?
- ☐ Have I aimed for short words, short sentences, and brief paragraphs?
- ☐ Have I used active verbs?
- ☐ Have I incorporated language that is concrete and colloquial?
- ☐ Have I used language that is appropriate to the event?
- ☐ Have I checked to make sure that the language used is sensitive to race, religion, gender, and sexual preference?
- ☐ Have I trimmed the text by at least 10 percent or tried to "declutter" it?
- ☐ Have I remembered transitions, not only to preview or recap, but to compare and contrast?
- ☐ Have I read the speech aloud before sending it on?

Language People Remember

He stood up in the Virginia House of Burgesses without a note; spoke, one witness wrote, until "the tendons of his neck stood out white and rigid, like whipcords"; and in the end uttered the lines we still learn in school: "I know not what others may do! As for me, give me liberty or give me death!"

Or did he? The only existing evidence of what Patrick Henry actually said in his famous speech in 1775 comes from an account of it written forty years later.[1] I'm old enough to know what it's like trying to remember a speech verbatim after four decades. The likelihood of that speech being close to what Patrick Henry really said is dim.

There's some evidence that the last line was his, though. Whatever the case, it is certainly one of those lines so memorable that if someone quotes the opening ("The only thing we have to fear . . ."; "A day that shall live in . . ."; "The content of their . . ."; "Make my . . ."; "Yes we . . .") many Americans can finish the rest.

MAKING LANGUAGE MEMORABLE

In politics it is not enough to be clear. It is not even enough to evoke emotion through story or concrete detail. If there was a rhetorical lesson in the 2008 presidential campaign, it was surely the incredible advantage enjoyed by politicians who can use language the crowd remembers and reporters will quote.

To find out how they did it you don't need Aristotle—only Quintilian, the Roman rhetoric teacher born about the decade Jesus died. Quintilian earned his entry to heaven by cataloging those things that make speech memorable— *figures of speech.* By the time of the Renaissance, a group of Quintilian's fanatical successors had uncovered and listed almost two hundred of them.[2]

Don't worry. In politics you can make your speeches quotable and exciting with about twenty. Among them you'll find the one that Patrick Henry may have used—and others did.

A note to those who have actually studied rhetoric. You won't see here the usual way textbooks present these devices. I used to insist students learn what *antimetabole* is until the day I found myself glancing down at my notes to remind myself. Much better to teach speechwriters and politicians what they need to speak effectively. I've divided them not into tropes and schemes and their various subdivisions but by the effects speakers want: language people remember because it is *vivid* and *rhythmic.*

MAKING LANGUAGE VIVID

"If we don't hang together we'll hang separately," Richard Penn said during the signing of the Declaration of Independence, a clever pun often attributed to Ben Franklin.[3] Penn used the word *hang* in one way, then surprised listeners by using it again with a different meaning.

Language often becomes memorable—in politics, read "quotable"—when you use words in a startlingly different way than usual. In Penn's line the different meaning is obvious. But what about Walter Mondale's line in the 1984 presidential campaign: "For a working person to vote for Reagan is like a chicken voting for Colonel Sanders."?

Usually, saying something is "like" something else means the two are similar. But simile and its cousin, metaphor, compare dissimilar things. To say, "The players fought like tigers," doesn't mean they are tigers in the usual sense—big members of the cat family with gold and black stripes. But in a different sense—ferocity—they are. Mondale doesn't really mean a working person is a chicken. But the audience sees the different sense of the word, and that surprises them into laughter.

Surprise links the figures of speech that follow, first defined, then illustrated. Because they surprise, they are memorable. Politicians use them because they can anger, amuse, move, and—most important—linger in the memory banks of those listening.

▶ **SIMILE AND METAPHOR:** *expressions that compare two essentially unlike things.*

Simile compares directly, often—but not necessarily—using *like, as if, more than,* or other explicit words of comparison ("They fought like tigers"). Metaphor implies comparison ("They were tigers"). Both surprise the audience by finding similarities in unlike things. One popular use in politics: similes with cultural references, like Mondale's, which use ads, movies, and celebrities that voters recognize from their daily lives. Here, for example, is a simile from Gov. Mike Huckabee's speech from the 2008 Republican National Convention:

> The reporting of the past few days have proven tackier than a costume change at a Madonna concert.

▶ **SYNECHDOCHE AND METONYMY:** *two similar techniques in which a part stands for the whole.*

Synechdoche and metonymy both surprise the audience with images that are not literally true. In this 1960 campaign speech example, Richard Nixon doesn't literally mean a "cold shoulder." He means the United States had demonstrated hostility in a way he doesn't want to spell out:

> In Europe we gave the cold shoulder to DeGaulle and now he gives the warm hand to Mao.

Similarly, Barack Obama, describing a 106-year-old voter in his 2008 victory speech, could use one telling detail to symbolize each of three events, allowing his listeners to visualize them in just nine vivid words:

> She was there for the buses in Montgomery, the hoses in Birmingham, a bridge in Selma.

▶ **PUN:** *words that surprise the audience by suddenly using a second meaning the audience had totally forgotten.*

While audiences usually associate puns with the groan-producing one-liners of older comedians ("Politics is like golf: you're trapped in one bad *lie* after another"), politicians use them often, and effectively. Puns can use a word in two different ways, like Richard Penn did, or by finding a word that modifies two incongruously different words, as Ronald Reagan does here, talking about diplomacy in his 1989 farewell address:

> If and when they don't, at first pull your punches. If they persist, pull the plug.

▶ **UNDERSTATEMENT:** *words that seem to minimize the significance of what you say—and surprise once the audience realizes the importance.*

Really, understatement is an often underused kind of humor. The speaker gets credit for dry wit, and the audience can congratulate itself for having the sophistication to appreciate it. It's even effective in serious matters from which you normally might shy away from humor, as in these grim lines uttered by George W. Bush in his CEO dinner in Shanghai, in 2001:

> I gave Taliban leaders a choice: turn over the terrorists or face your ruin. They chose unwisely.

▶ **IRONY:** *words that convey what the audience knows say the opposite of the literal meaning.*

The speaker says them seriously. Once the audience realizes the joke they laugh, seeing a detested enemy mocked. Here again is Governor Huckabee at the 2008 Republican National Convention, from a speech we will examine at the end of this chapter:

> I'd like to thank the elite media for doing something that, quite frankly, I wasn't sure could be done, and that's unifying the Republican Party and all of America in support of Senator McCain and Governor Palin.

▶ **HYPERBOLE:** *exaggeration, often for comic effect.*

Politicians often reserve hyperbole for campaign speeches—with good reason. Red-meat audiences love the mocking exaggeration they would usually acknowledge as untrue. Here is vice presidential candidate Sarah Palin's celebrated example during the 2008 campaign, also mentioned later:

> Our opponent . . . is someone who sees America it seems as being so imperfect that he's palling around with terrorists who would target their own country

▶ **RHETORICAL QUESTION:** *question that doesn't require an answer.*

Usually people ask a question they want answered. Rhetorical questions have the opposite effect. The act of asking makes the answer clear, or allows the speaker to answer. Why use a rhetorical question? To create the effect that last sentence hopefully did in you: a sense of anticipation (*And why will we win?*) or to make clear that the speaker thinks the answer is obvious. Nixon used this to great effect in his famous 1952 "Checkers" speech:

> Do you think that when I or any other senator makes a political speech, has it printed, [we] should charge the printing of that speech and the mailing of that speech to the taxpayer?

Figures of speech play a role in making speech memorable. American political rhetoric is filled with them. Each day politicians, consultants, and press secretaries devote hours to finding a figure of speech that will make it into stories, onto the evening news, and sometimes, into history.

But they make up only part of what makes audiences remember speeches. After all, each is effective only for the few moments it takes to utter them.

There is another way to make speeches memorable. That's the technique that allows speakers to build in excitement. It is the technique that lends speeches the pulsing rhythms that make audiences jump to their feet. It is the technique that succeeds not because of a single sentence but all of them.

And as you will see, it is the technique that infuses the paragraph you just read.

MAKING LANGUAGE RHYTHMIC

In elementary school I had a class that in retrospect must have been designed to let us blow off steam. Technically it was Music. The teacher would hand out cymbals, little drums, triangles, and sticks we could knock against each other. We could bang or shake whatever instrument we had in our hands. We could make as much noise as we wanted. But there was one rule. The teacher would put on a record. We had to bang in time to the music.

They called the class Rhythms. And that's how we learned that all music divides into patterns of repetitive sounds, usually in groups of two or three.

Rhythmic patterns aren't always mechanical successions of twos and threes. Sometimes composers take one rhythmic pattern and use it over and over with different instruments, speeds, and keys. For example, the three short and one long notes opening Beethoven's Fifth Symphony (Bu-Bu-Bu-*Baah*); or, in my day, the two weak, one strong, one weak pattern that made us all want to be Mick Jagger (I can't *get* no/Sat-is-*fac*-tion). Listeners find repeating those rhythmic patterns—*motifs*, in music—incredibly exciting.

And so we come to the first ingredient in making speech exciting.

▶ **REPETITION:** *repeated use of grammatical structure, words, or sounds.*

Like Beethoven, like Mick Jagger, speakers also repeat rhythmic patterns again and again. Take these famous words:

> We shall fight on the beaches.

By themselves, not much. What makes the line memorable stems from what happens when Winston Churchill, the Mick Jagger of oratory, begins repeating that pattern in June 1940, after the fall of Dunkirk:

> We shall fight on the beaches, we shall fight on the landing grounds, we shall fight in the fields and in the streets, we shall fight in the hills; we shall never surrender.

Note how repetition allows the listeners to be affected not just by what Churchill's words mean but how they sound.

Repetition is the best way speakers can create power—speech that evokes emotion. How can you not become excited even by merely reading Churchill's "we shall fight" clauses? You imagine him getting a little louder each time, until by the end every English family, listening on their radios, feels they will beat back the Nazis.

Repetition allows skilled speakers to raise their pitch, turn up the volume, and accelerate speed. They sound passionate, which creates passion in listeners. There's nothing unusual about recommending repetition in speech: every public speaking text does. But it is vital for political speech, because politicians need not just to persuade audiences but excite them.

You can use repetition as Churchill did, through "balanced construction." That means repeating the grammatical structure in each clause. Here are some examples.

▶ **PARALLELISM:** *parallel structure to present similarity.*

Speakers use parallel construction when they want to show their audience the bad things the other side has done, the good things the speaker has done, the number of people who have suffered, or a determination to succeed. Churchill's example is one. Here's another, from the Gettysburg Address:

> That these dead shall not have died in vain—that this nation, under God, shall have a new birth of freedom—and that government: of the people, by the people, for the people, shall not perish from the earth.

By creating three clauses with similar grammatical structure, similar because they each forecast success, Lincoln built a passage in which repeated rhythms created power.

▶ **ANTITHESIS:** *parallel structure to present contrast.*

Antithesis is one of the most popular means of being quotable. It succeeds because such contrast allows you, among other things, to urge one course of action and reject another. That's the secret of Patrick Henry's line ("Give me liberty or give me death!"). Antithesis makes what he accepts and rejects clear and easy to remember.

In politics speakers may use antithesis to reject pessimism and embrace optimism. They also use it to contrast their virtues with the other side's short-comings, as you can see in these lines from Bill Clinton and Sarah Palin, respectively:

> There's nothing wrong with America that can't be fixed by what's right with America.

> Americans expect us to go to Washington for the right reasons, and not just to mingle with the right people.

Like two sharply contrasting themes in music, the contrast of antithesis becomes memorable partly through rhythm: the *bah-bah-bah*-bah-*bah* in Palin's "for the right reasons" repeated in the "with the right people," though of course, it becomes more memorable by speechwriter Matt Scully's pun on *right*.

David Kusnet

Just after Christmas 1992, David Kusnet was home in Washington, D.C., when he got a call from President-elect Bill Clinton's campaign office. Father Tim Healy, the former president of Georgetown University and Clinton confidante, had died of a heart attack at Newark Airport. Medics had found a cassette in Healy's jacket pocket with a taped memo to Clinton suggesting a metaphor for his inaugural address.

At this point, Kusnet, Clinton's chief speechwriter in the campaign, was about to be named Clinton's first chief speechwriter in the new administration. He was working with another writer, Michael Waldman, on what would be Clinton's inaugural address. Kusnet turned on his fax machine—in those primitive days fax was the equivalent of e-mail—and soon Healy's notes came through page by page.

"There was something remarkable, even mystical, about it," says Kusnet, the author of five books about language, politics, and labor issues, of the memo from a man with whom he had spoken on the phone but never met.

The transcript took four pages, but the metaphor was this: "We hold this ceremony in the dead of winter. But, in another sense, by the words we say and the faces we show the world, we are indeed forcing the spring."

"It was very much in the spirit of what Clinton wanted the speech to say," Kusnet says of this example of a figure of speech we examine in this chapter. He had already written a first draft, including this sentence, which he thought up himself, and which you have just read: "There is nothing wrong with America that cannot be cured by what is right with America."

Kusnet and Waldman, along with Clinton adviser George Stephanopoulos, met with the president-elect in Little Rock. "He had just given a speech about how his election involved changing of the guard. But now he told us his message should be more than generational transition, that Americans had to do what no generation had done before—invest in the future while paying down massive debts."

Kusnet in Washington, and Waldman in Little Rock, went back to work, now leading with Healy's metaphor. "Many cooks had a hand in the concoction," Kusnet points out, mentioning other writers who contributed drafts. Working together at an improvised transition office in George Washington University, taking a line from one, a phrase from another, he and Waldman wove it all together.

The day and night before the inaugural, there was a marathon rehearsal and rewriting session involving Bill Clinton, Hillary Clinton, Al Gore, Rodney Slater, and two of Clinton's oldest friends, the historian Taylor Branch and the novelist Tommy Caplan. Kusnet and Waldman took turns at a computer taking everything down and making the changes.

"I thought it was graceful. Seemingly effortless," Kusnet says, remembering Clinton's delivery of the speech and the two months of intense effort that went into it. With the perspective of fifteen years, he points out another way of looking at Healy's metaphor, one having to do with the twin tasks Clinton had outlined. "The tension between the two became a defining theme—and an internal debate—for his administration," Kusnet says. "You could say that, in his first two years as president, he was indeed 'forcing the spring'—trying to do too much, too soon."

Kusnet takes pride in his role in writing the speech, including the quotable surviving line that is indubitably his. Above his desk he has framed an autographed copy of a New Yorker cartoon that Clinton sent him a few weeks after the speech. It portrays a doctor showing an X-ray to an anxious patient. The caption: "There is nothing wrong with you that cannot be cured by what is right with you."

Source: David Kusnet spoke with Robert A. Lehrman in April 2009.

Parallelism and antithesis may be the most common examples of balanced construction. Three other ways to use repetition surprise listeners with their novelty.

▶ **ANTIMETABOLE:** *repetition of words in reverse grammatical structure.*

> Mankind must put an end to war—or war will put an end to mankind.
>
> John F. Kennedy, United Nations, 1961

▶ **POLYPTOTON:** *repetition of words with different meanings.*

> The only thing we have to fear is fear itself.
>
> Franklin Delano Roosevelt, first inaugural address, 1933

▶ **ALLITERATION:** *repetition of words beginning with the same sound.*

> We shall not falter, we shall not fail.
>
> George W. Bush, speech to joint session of Congress after September 11 attacks, 2001

So far, we have looked at examples of repetition within a single sentence. But since 1960, probably because speakers began imitating John F. Kennedy and Martin Luther King, who used them extensively—there are nine in his "I Have a Dream" speech—we see and hear politicians use repetition through groups of sentences. You could call this by its formal name: a scheme of repetition employing three or more full sentences in parallel construction. But politicians use a shorter one.

"You know the litany," George H. W. Bush told the 1988 Republican Convention as he accepted the nomination for president, almost as if he was a little embarrassed to be using a rhetorical technique.

And then he used one.

▶ **LITANY:** *a repetitive recital.*

Derived from the Greek word meaning "plea," litany usually describes the kind of prayer in which priest and congregation alternate responses. George H. W. Bush's litany (it goes on longer than this excerpt) was one of accomplishment and brought something that doesn't happen in church—cheers from the crowd:

> Inflation was 13 percent when we came in. We got it down to 4. Interest rates were more than 21. We cut them in half. Unemployment was up and climbing and now it's the lowest in fourteen years.

In politics, "litany" has become the popular way to refer to the device Bush used, sometimes as an insult and sometimes just to describe it. It's a useful term: brief, imaginatively adapted from religion, and bearing a pedigree (nineteenth-century poet Philip Freneau's most famous poem, "A Political Litany"). This book will use the word *litany* for this kind of repetition so common in politics.

AS DELIVERED

George H. W. Bush's 1988 Republican National Convention Speech. As you saw earlier, President George H. W. Bush was aware of rhetorical techniques. So was his speechwriter, Peggy Noonan. This underrated speech is full of the humanizing touches that characterize Noonan's work. Watch the whole speech and see which lines stick out, and why.

http://college.cqpress.com/politicalspeech

Today, politicians use litany to excoriate the other side, praise their own, pledge change, rouse the audience to action—or, sometimes, add impact to a quiet passage.

Why does litany work? First, litany *clarifies.* It demonstrates how much evidence a speaker has. The most famous example of litany in American history is the Declaration of Independence—a long litany of complaints. When a speaker launches into a list, moving through two—three, five, ten!—items, each more terrible or wonderful than the last, crowds react: *This threat is dangerous! These solutions can work! This administration has been a success!* The sheer wealth of examples makes points convincing.

Second, litany *evokes emotion.* It reminds the crowd how urgent the issues are. Let's say Bush had phrased his point this way:

> We reduced inflation and interest rate. They're both way lower than a few years back. And while unemployment was high, it's now the lowest in fourteen years.

It wouldn't have been nearly as effective. Bush didn't just want to make his audience remember these three achievements. He wanted to make them see the larger point: that there were lots of them. He wanted to sound excited. Repeating the same grammatical structure, driving home the point again and again, made that clear.

Finally, litany *characterizes.* Speakers get louder. They get faster. *Hey,* the listeners think, *Bush isn't as dull as we thought!* The fact that Bush sounds excited about what the administration did for them makes them excited about backing him. In the opening of this book I mentioned that between them, Barack Obama and John McCain use litany a total of twenty-eight times in their two convention speeches.

Enough about why you use litany in politics. How do you create it? Let's look at three patterns. You can use them within single sentences, but now, let's examine only those using the groups of sentences so popular in politics, the first two dealing with *where* you use repetition in each sentence, the third with how you organize those sentences.

BOX 7.1 Learning to Write—and Love—the Sound Bite

How to create them? Sound bites—and their first cousin, applause lines—use a very narrow range of techniques. All involve kinds of parallel construction or imagery discussed either in this chapter or in chapter 9, on wit. Here are some of the most common figures of speech.

Analogy

> If criminals have a right to a lawyer, then I think working Americans should have the right to a doctor.
>> Harris Wofford, Pennsylvania senate campaign, 1992

Antithesis

> It's not a question of being ready on day one. It's a question of being right on day one.
>> Barack Obama, rally in Florence, South Carolina, February 2008

Same Word, Different Meanings

> Now is the time to bring the marines out of Beirut—not because it is right for the election, but because it is right for America.
>> John F. Kennedy, Alf Landon lecture

Repetition in Reverse Grammatical Order

> I am Giacomo, a lover of beauty and a beauty of a lover.
>> Danny Kaye, in the film *The Court Jester,* 1956

Metaphor

> You have a row of dominos set up; you knock over the first one, and what will happen to the last one is the certainty that it will go over very quickly.
>> Dwight D. Eisenhower, news conference, 1954

Hyperbole

> If Hitler invaded Hell I would make at least a favorable reference to the Devil in the House of Commons.
>> Winston Churchill, Parliament, 1941

"Political language . . . ," said George Orwell in his 1946 essay "Politics and the English Language," "is designed to make lies sound truthful and murder respectable, and to give an appearance of solidity to pure wind."[4]

In defending the much-maligned sound bite, I have to be careful not to claim too much. Even speechwriters writing for people they admire know there are times when they must oversimplify or defend what they consider bad policy. Sometimes summing up an idea in eight clever words can make audiences believe what they should discard. But that is no reason not to learn how to make memorable the points you believe.

Sound bites are morally neutral—as opposed to the policy they reflect. And they communicate substantive thought very well. For evidence, look at Orwell's quote. It contains parallel construction, asyndeton, and metaphor: a sound bite if there ever was one.

▶ **ANAPHORA:** *repetition at the beginning.*

Below, see the repetition of the phrases "People of the world" and "Look at Berlin" in Obama's address, standing before the Victory Column in Berlin:

> People of the world—look at Berlin!
> Look at Berlin, where Germans and Americans learned to work together and trust each other less than three years after facing each other on the field of battle.
> Look at Berlin, where the determination of a people met the generosity of the Marshall Plan and created a German miracle; where a victory over tyranny gave rise to NATO, the greatest alliance ever formed to defend our common security.
> Look at Berlin, where the bullet holes in the buildings and the somber stories and pillars near the Brandenburg Gate insist that we never forget our common humanity.
> People of the world—look at Berlin, where a wall came down, a continent came together, and history proved that there is no challenge too great for a world that stands as one.
>
> Barack Obama, Berlin, July 24, 2008

> **AS DELIVERED**
>
> *Barack Obama's 2008 Berlin Speech.* Watch Obama deliver the litany in which repetition comes at the start of each sentence. Then compare it with Ted Kennedy's speech, which we look at next. One is a litany of praise, the other of criticism. Does that influence structure? Do the effects of each differ? Could Kennedy and Obama have gotten the same emotional effect without repetition?
>
> http://college.cqpress.com/politicalspeech

The details in each of Obama's four sentences differ. Repetition comes in the first four words of each, except for the last, where he adds an opening phrase. But as you watch, note how repetition allows him to build in excitement about the most important idea: Berlin as a model for the future.

▶ **EPISTROPHE:** *repetition at the end.*

Repetition at the end of a sentence or comment is an especially useful way to allow speakers to raise their voices and signal to listeners that it is time for them to clap. In this speech, Ted Kennedy uses repetition to open each sentence, but he achieves his emotional effect by repeating his most important idea at the end: an excellent example of epistrophe.

> The same Republicans who are talking about the crisis of unemployment have nominated a man who once said, and I quote, "Unemployment insurance is a prepaid vacation plan for freeloaders." *And that nominee is no friend of labor.*
> The same Republicans who are talking about the problems of the inner cities have nominated a man who said, and I quote, "I have

included in my morning and evening prayers every day the prayer that the Federal Government not bail out New York." *And that nominee is no friend of this city and our great urban centers across this nation.*

The same Republicans who are talking about security for the elderly have nominated a man who said just four years ago that "Participation in social security should be made voluntary." *And that nominee is no friend of the senior citizens of this nation.*

AS DELIVERED

Ted Kennedy's 1980 Democratic National Convention Speech. Where else do you see litany in Kennedy's speech? What else do you notice about Kennedy's problem litany? (Hint: It's mentioned in this chapter.)

http://college.cqpress.com/politicalspeech

The same Republicans who are talking about preserving the environment have nominated a man who last year made the preposterous statement, and I quote, "Eighty percent of our air pollution comes from plants and trees." *And that nominee is no friend of the environment.*

And the same Republicans who are invoking Franklin Roosevelt have nominated a man who said in 1976, and these are his exact words, "Fascism was really the basis of the New Deal." *And that nominee whose name is Ronald Reagan has no right to quote Franklin Delano Roosevelt.*

Ted Kennedy,
Democratic National Convention, 1980

But exciting a crowd doesn't stem just from *where* repetition comes. Details matter—and so effective political speech means another step.

▶ CLIMACTIC ORDER: *repetition from least to most important.*

Here's a three-part rhetorical question litany, slightly condensed.

Who was not embarrassed when the administration handed a major propaganda victory in the United Nations to the enemies of Israel, our staunch Middle East ally for three decades . . . ?

Who does not feel a growing sense of unease as our allies, facing repeated instances of an amateurish and confused administration, reluctantly conclude that America is unwilling or unable to fulfill its obligations as leader of the free world?

Who does not feel rising alarm when the question in any discussion of foreign policy is no longer, "Should we do something?" but "Do we have the capacity to do anything?"

Ronald Reagan acceptance speech,
Republican National Convention, 1980

Notice the way Ronald Reagan moves from "embarrassed" to "unease" to the most extreme emotion: "alarm." Audiences sense when litanies leap to issues of greater and greater moment. It makes the speaker's growing excitement logical—and contagious.

Notice too that in litany speakers may vary the last line, using devices that make it more memorable and signaling to listeners that this is their punch line. That was true with Obama, who uses three clauses of parallel construction at the end; with Kennedy, whose tone about Reagan becomes noticeably harsher; and with Reagan, who ends with antithesis.

So many varieties! How do you pick and choose among them?

TO BE QUOTABLE: COMPARE AND CONTRAST

Reporters clearly like the witty comparison, often to some part of American culture. They also seem to like contrast and clever wordplay. All that argues for devices like *antithesis, simile,* or *reverse grammatical structure.* Here, for example, is one of Barack Obama's oft-quoted litanies from his 2004 Democratic Convention speech:

> Well, I say to them tonight, there is not a liberal America and a conservative America—there is the United States of America. There is not a Black America and a White America and Latino America and Asian America—there's the United States of America.

TO BE FORCEFUL: MOVE FROM LISTS TO LITANY

Let's say a sentence in your draft reads "We must do x, y, and z." Change that to *We must do x. We must do y. We must do z.* The difference, when heard, is enormous. In the "I Have a Dream" speech, watch the difference when instead of running his list of places together, King turns it into this:

> And so let freedom ring from the prodigious hilltops of New Hampshire.
> Let freedom ring from the mighty mountains of New York.
> Let freedom ring from the heightening Alleghenies of Pennsylvania.
> Let freedom ring from the snow-capped Rockies of Colorado.
> Let freedom ring from the curvaceous slopes of California.
> But not only that:
> Let freedom ring from Stone Mountain of Georgia.
> Let freedom ring from Lookout Mountain of Tennessee.
> Let freedom ring from every hill and molehill of Mississippi.
> From every mountainside, let freedom ring.

TO ACHIEVE BOTH POWER AND QUOTABILITY: VARY YOUR APPROACH

Often, the most memorable speeches use litany to create power—then end with one of the other figures of speech as a clincher. Here is an excerpt from Bono's 2007 speech accepting an award for his ONE campaign, a global advocacy and campaigning organization dedicated to fighting poverty and preventable disease, particularly in Africa. It's worth watching for the way, at the end, after struggling with a pedestrian draft, he adopts a technique sometimes called "attacking the absent enemy." That is, he rebukes someone not there but disliked by the crowd, in this case those who refuse to help the victims of AIDS. Bono uses a litany, laced with concrete detail. But he closes with antithesis:

> And to those in the church who still sit in judgment on the AIDS emergency, let me climb into the pulpit for just one moment, because whatever thoughts we have about God, who He is, or even if God exists, most would agree that God has a special place for the poor. The poor are where God lives.
>
> God is in the slums, in the cardboard boxes where the poor play house.
>
> God is where the opportunity is lost and lives are shattered.
>
> God is with the mother who has infected her child with a virus that will take both of their lives.
>
> God is under the rubble in the cries we hear during wartime.
>
> God, my friends, is with the poor, and God is with us if we are with them.

AS DELIVERED

Mike Huckabee's 2008 Republican National Convention Speech. How many of the techniques covered in this chapter can you spot without looking at the annotated copy? Because Huckabee didn't win, his speech won't make history books. But for grace and skill it was a stunning job both for writing and delivery.

http://college.cqpress.com/politicalspeech

Like flour, sugar, water, and spices, combinations produce more than the sum of their parts. To see how that works, let's examine not just a line but an entire speech: one of the best from the 2008 campaign by one its most consistently interesting speakers.

Sitting through a presidential nominating convention feels different than watching it in prime time. Most of the two hundred or so speeches at each are largely ignored by the audience. There's no guarantee that a defeated candidate will excite delegations caught up in their own politicking. But during his ten-minute speech the crowd interrupted Mike Huckabee twenty-three times with laughter or applause—and not just by his home state.[5] No wonder. He used short sentences, simple words, concrete detail, and almost every one of the techniques this chapter describes.

Thank you. Well, let me say that, as much as I appreciate this magnificent opportunity to speak tonight, I've got to be honest with you.

I was originally hoping for the slot on Thursday night called the acceptance speech. [LAUGHTER/APPLAUSE]

— Understatement

Huckabee doesn't say he was hoping to win, but he gets laughter by pretending he just wanted a speech so obscure he has to tell the audience what it's called.

But I want you to also know that I am genuinely delighted to be here to speak on behalf of my second choice for the Republican nomination for president, John McCain. [APPLAUSE]

John McCain is a man with the character and the stubborn kind of integrity that we need in a president.

But I want to begin by doing something a little unusual. I'd like to thank the elite media for doing something that, quite frankly, I wasn't sure could be done, and that's unifying the Republican Party and all of America in support of Senator McCain and Governor Palin. [APPLAUSE]

— Irony

Huckabee says the opposite of what he and the audience feels (fury at the media); he misdirects his listeners with "quite frankly," making them think he's really going to praise reporters, which makes his punch line more surprising.

The reporting of the past few days have proven tackier than a costume change at a Madonna concert. [APPLAUSE]

— Hyperbole

He uses a cultural reference, a singer the audience despises, to get this laugh.

I grew up at a time and in a place where the civil rights movement was fought. And I witnessed firsthand the shameful evil of racism. I saw how ignorance and prejudice caused people to do the unthinkable to people of color, and it wasn't so many years ago.

— Litany #1/
Anaphora

In his first litany, a now-serious Huckabee begins each sentence with "I," directly followed by a verb.

I want to say with the utmost of sincerity, not as a Republican, but as an American, that I have great respect for Senator Obama's historic achievement to become his party's nominee, not because of his color, but with indifference to it. [APPLAUSE]

— Antithesis #1
and #2

The first litany indicates that he is rising above party; the second makes sure the audience knows it's not just out of affirmative action that he respects Obama's achievement.

Alliteration ——————
Antithesis #3 ——————
Party or politics aside, as Americans, we celebrate this milestone because it elevates our country. But the presidency is not a symbolic job, and I fear that his election would elevate our taxes and our risk in a dangerous world.

Note the "not," which makes this officially antithesis; but the clever part is using "elevate" in two different ways: one moral and the other a tax increase.

Antithesis #4, ——————
used ironically
Now, Obama was right when he said that this election is not about him; it is about you. [APPLAUSE]
When gasoline costs $4 a gallon, it makes it tough if you're a single mom trying to get to work each day in a used car that you drive. You want something to change.

Litany #2/ ——————
Epistrophe
If you're a flight attendant or a baggage-handler, and you're asked to take the pay cut to keep your job, you want something to change.
If you're a young couple losing your house, your credit rating, and your piece of the American dream, you want something to change.
But John McCain offers specific ideas to respond to a need for change. But let me say there are some things we don't want to change: freedom, security, and the opportunity to prosper.

In that concrete litany of complaints aimed at the TV audience, Huckabee signals for applause by ending each clause the same way.

Hyperbole ——————
Barack Obama's excellent adventure to Europe . . . [LAUGHTER] . . . took his campaign for change to hundreds of thousands of people who don't even vote or pay taxes here.

Another cultural reference, this time to a movie.

Antithesis #5 ——————
But let me hasten to say that it's not what he took there that concerns me. It's what he brought back: European ideas that give the government the chance to grab even more of our liberty and destroy our hard-earned livelihood.

Campaign speeches are often based on antithesis, but not always this wittily.

Antithesis #6 ——————
The fact is, my friends, most Americans don't want more government. They want less government. [APPLAUSE]

"More ... less" contrasts are especially popular in campaigns.

It was—it was, in fact, the founder of our party, Abraham Lincoln, who reminded us that a government that can do everything for us is the government that can take everything from us. [APPLAUSE]

— Antithesis #7/ Parallel structure #1

Not every contrast uses parallel structure; that one does, by changing just two words.

Now, I get a little tired of hearing how the Democrats care so much for the working guy, as if all Republicans grew up with silk stockings and silver spoons.

You know, my hometown of Hope, Arkansas, the three sacred heroes were Jesus, Elvis, and FDR, not necessarily in that order. [LAUGHTER]

— Synechdoche, though if this were an exam and you put metonymy, you'd get full credit

Hyperbole

One of the biggest laughs of both conventions; as a minister, Huckabee's willingness to say that Jesus might not have been first qualifies as edgy for politics.

My own father, for example, held down two jobs, barely affording the little rented house that I grew up in. My dad was one of those guys, like so many of your dads.

He worked hard. He lifted heavy things. He got his hands dirty. In fact, the only soap we ever had in my house was Lava. Let me explain that. I was in college before I found out it isn't supposed to hurt when you take a shower. [LAUGHTER]

— Litany #3

Let me make something clear tonight. I'm not a Republican because I grew up rich. I'm a Republican because I didn't want to spend the rest of my life poor, waiting for the government to rescue me. [APPLAUSE]

— Antithesis #8

Again, a "change" litany of two.

John McCain doesn't want the kind of change that allows the government to reach even deeper into your paycheck and pick your pocket, your doctor, your child's school, or even the kind of car you drive or how you inflate your tires. [LAUGHTER]

— Litany #4/ Anaphora

A witty use of "pick" in two different meanings, to steal and to choose.

And he doesn't want to change the definition of marriage. And unlike the Democratic ticket, Senator McCain and Governor Palin believe that every human life has intrinsic worth and value from the moment of conception. [APPLAUSE]

And speaking of Governor Palin, I am so tired of hearing about her lack of experience. I want to tell you folks something. She got more votes running for mayor of Wasilla, Alaska, than Joe Biden got running for president of the United States. [APPLAUSE]

John McCain—John McCain is by far the most prepared, the most experienced, and truly the most tested presidential candidate. He is thoroughly tested.

Three clauses beginning with the same word.

When John McCain received his country's call to service, he did not hesitate and he did not choose the easy path. He sat alone in the cockpit, taking off from an aircraft carrier, to fly in the unfriendly skies, knowing that there was a good chance he might not make it back.

*Here it is again, two clauses, both beginning with
"he did not"; it's not alliterative, but note the echoes of
George W. Bush's "we shall not falter."*

And one day, he didn't make it back. He was shot down and captured, brutally tortured. He could have eased his own pain, even cut short his imprisonment, just by uttering a few simple words renouncing his country. But then, as now, John McCain put his country first. And he knew—he knew . . . [APPLAUSE] that to return with honor later was better than to return without it now. [APPLAUSE]

A contrast between "with" and "without."

Most of us—most of us can lift our arms high in the air so that we can signify when we want something. He can't even lift his arms to his shoulder, which is a constant reminder that his life is marked not by what he's wanting to receive, but rather by what he has already given. [APPLAUSE]

Let me tell you about someone I know who understands this type of sacrifice.

On the first day of school in 2005, Martha Cothren, a teacher at the Joe T. Robinson High School in Little Rock, was determined that her students would not take their education or their privileges as Americans for granted. And with the principal of her school's permission, she removed all the desks from her classroom on that first day of school, 2005.

Parallel structure #2

Parallel structure #3

Cultural reference—in contrast to the United Airlines ad

Antithesis #9

Antithesis #10—using "receive" and "given"

Now, the students walked into an empty classroom and they said, "Ms. Cothren, where's our desk?" She said, "You get a desk in my classroom when you tell me how you earn it."

Well, some of them said, "Making good grades." She said, "Well, you ought to make good grades in my class, but that won't earn you a desk." Another student said, "I guess we get a desk when we behave." Martha said, "You will behave in my classroom." [LAUGHTER]

But that won't get you a desk either. No one in first period guessed right. Same for second period. By lunch, the buzz was all over the campus. Ms. Cothren had flipped out, wouldn't let her students have a desk.

Kids started using their cell phones. They called their parents. And by early afternoon, all four of the local network TV affiliates had camera crews out at the school to report on this teacher who wouldn't let her students have a desk unless they could tell her how to earn it.

By the final period, no one had guessed correctly, so the students filed in. Martha said, "Well, I didn't think you would figure it out, so I'm going to tell you."

And with that, she went to the door of her classroom and motioned, and in walked over twenty veterans, some of them still wearing the uniforms from days gone by, every one of them carrying a school desk. And as they carefully and quietly arranged those desks in neat rows, Martha said, "You don't have to earn your desk, because these guys, they already did." [APPLAUSE]

These—these brave veterans had gone halfway around the world, giving up their education, interrupting their careers and families so that we could have the freedom that we have. Martha told them, "No one charged you for your desk, but it wasn't really free. These guys bought it for you. And I hope you never, ever forget it."

And I wish, ladies and gentlemen . . . [APPLAUSE] I wish we would all remember that being American is not just about the freedom we have; it is about those who gave it to us. [APPLAUSE] — Antithesis #11

And let me remind you of something. John McCain is one of those people who helped buy the freedom and the school desk that we had. John McCain helped me have a school desk.

And I want to tell you: I pledge myself to doing everything I can to help him earn a desk, and I'm thinking the one that's in the Oval Office would fit him very, very well. [LAUGHTER/APPLAUSE] — Understatement

Thank you. God bless you folks. Thank you. Thank you.

Later, we'll look at other achievements in Huckabee's unusual speech. Now it's enough to know that in ten minutes Huckabee used antithesis eleven times, litany four times, and nine of the other schemes and tropes covered in the previous chapter. He didn't need to know the classical names for any of them. He knew something more valuable: how to use them to relate to his audience.

The Speechwriter's Checklist: Language People Remember

- ☐ Have I incorporated vivid language?
- ☐ Have I created a balanced construction (for power)?
- ☐ Have I used parallel structure (for similarity)?
- ☐ Have I demonstrated antithesis (for contrast)?
- ☐ Have I created a litany that rises to a climax?
- ☐ Have I used alliteration? Or reversed grammar for quotability?

chapter 8

Anecdote

In *Hardball,* his witty and useful book about politics, Chris Matthews, now host of the MSNBC program with the same name, tells a no-doubt apocryphal story about Bill Bradley who, shortly after being elected senator from New Jersey, came to speak at a banquet.

Bradley is sitting at the dais when a waiter puts a pat of butter on his plate. Bradley says, "Can I please have another pat of butter?"

The waiter replies, "One pat per person."

The emcee overhears this. Embarrassed, he rushes over to the waiter and whispers, "Maybe you don't know who that is. Bill Bradley—the All-Pro Knick, Rhodes scholar, senator from New Jersey!"

The waiter says, "Well, maybe you don't know who I am."

"I guess I don't. Who are you?"

"I'm the guy who controls the butter!"[1]

It's a deservedly popular story among politicians because it allows them to segue neatly into a point they often need to make: the need for partnership. Here's how former Democratic majority whip David Bonior moved off the punch line of the "butter" story and into his point when he spoke to a medical society back in 1992:

> No matter how powerful you are, there's always somebody you have to deal with. Nobody—not even the president—will single-handedly decide the matter of health care. . . .

In other words, there's always somebody who controls something. However you look at this story, it lets speakers make a point about the importance of working together, and the folly of thinking you control everything. And it makes that point in a much more memorable and interesting way than simply stating it. That's why I, as Bonior's speechwriter, used it over and over.

WRITING TO TOUCH THE HEART

There are simply no more effective tools for political speech than anecdote and the off-ramps that lead speakers to the points they want to illustrate. For politicians, anecdotes provide a lot more than support. They amuse, move, inspire, and make audiences remember. Technically, the definitions of *anecdote* and *story* are a little different: an anecdote is entertaining and often biographical; a story is a longer narrative that may or may not be true. By those definitions, all anecdotes are stories, but not all stories are anecdotes. This book uses the term *anecdote* because stories in politics are short and, hopefully, entertaining.

Remember that entertaining doesn't have to mean funny. An episode of a dramatic TV show—say, *Lost*—is entertaining, but it isn't funny. The Martha Cothren anecdote that Mike Huckabee used at the end of his 2008 convention speech (discussed in chapter 7) is entertaining. Even the most gripping anecdotes, like suspenseful movies, entertain.

In politics, speakers use anecdote to clarify, compel attention, persuade or reinforce beliefs, inspire, and influence an audience's view of the speaker. Why do they work well? Three reasons.

ANECDOTE MAKES LISTENERS REMEMBER

As with Monroe's Motivated Sequence, we know the effects of story or anecdote partly through research. In 1998, two Dutch social scientists tried to measure the effect of anecdote on listeners. They had seen data showing that audiences make up their minds in under a minute about whether a speaker is worth listening to or not. So how should speakers best use that first minute?

Testing anecdote against other kinds of openings, the researchers found that anecdote "led to significantly higher ratings of . . . comprehensibility and interest as well as the speaker's credibility." It didn't even seem to matter what *kind* of anecdote audiences heard. After describing an experiment with stories that had nothing to do with the subject, the researchers allowed their surprise to creep into the abstract. "Oddly enough," they wrote, "the relevance of the anecdote did not seem to make a difference."[2]

ANECDOTE MAKES SPEAKERS BELIEVABLE

Note that the researchers mentioned not just comprehensibility and interest but also anecdote's impact on credibility. To speakers reading this chapter, I offer this reminder: Telling a story about a hero shows listeners you share the hero's values. Telling a joke about yourself shows them you have a sense of humor and a thick skin. Telling a story that inspires your listeners sends them the message that "I'm one of you, because this story inspired me, too." All increase credibility.

Anecdote Moves Listeners

But credibility and retention are side effects. They stem from the main reason speeches need anecdote: stories touch the human heart.

This is hardly a secret. The title of the *Newsweek* story about audience emotional appeal (discussed in chapter 2) was "Heard Any Good Stories Lately?" It cited a number of interesting examples of research. "A candidate's personal narrative might sway more voters than experience, positions on issues, and policy proposals," wrote science reporter Sharon Begley. "Blame the power of emotions."[3] Of course. Facts are important, but anyone who examines their responses to articles in a newspaper or during a movie can see the effect of story. Skillful political speakers understand this. At the 2008 Republican National Convention, Sarah Palin and John McCain both ended their speeches with the story of McCain's capture and torture during the United States' war with Vietnam. It moved the crowd both times.

So why do so few political speakers use anecdote? Why do you see it so seldom as you click through the *Congressional Record* (the journal of each day's events in Congress, including every floor speech) or go on the Web sites of politicians who post their outside speeches? Perhaps speechwriters are more comfortable researching and focusing on issues. Maybe they believe that stories diminish the appearance of substance, or that if they start using stories they'll have to hunt for new ones for each occasion.

It's certainly possible to write a great speech without stories. Standing in front of the Lincoln Memorial in 1963, Martin Luther King did not use a single one. But to ignore anecdote is to ignore a powerful tool that compels interest from the audience—and respect for the speaker.

Moreover, not every anecdote has to be a full-blown, richly detailed production to move people. In his 2004 Republican National Convention speech, Gov. Arnold Schwarzenegger talks about what it was like growing up in divided Austria after World War II under Soviet occupation—how afraid his family was crossing into the Soviet sector, and how he feared Soviet soldiers would take people from their cars to use as "slave labor." Then he tells the audience this:

AS DELIVERED

Arnold Schwarzenegger's 2004 Republican National Convention Speech. After watching to see the effect of the story we examine next, watch the rest of the speech to see the effects of Schwarzenegger's other three stories, mentioned in the accompanying profile of Landon Parvin, Schwarzenegger's speechwriter. What are the different strategic needs each fills? What are some of the unusual ways they characterize Schwarzenegger?

http://college.cqpress.com/politicalspeech

> My family didn't have a car—but one day we were in my uncle's car. It was near dark as we came to a Soviet checkpoint. I was a little boy. I wasn't an action hero back then, and I remember how scared I was the soldiers would pull my father or my uncle out of the car and I'd never see him again.

Even one who disagrees with his views can see how Schwarzenegger's anecdote prepares the audience for the emotional off-ramp that serves as his punch line:

> My family and so many others lived in fear of the Soviet boot. Today the world no longer fears the Soviet Union—and it is because of the United States of America!

BEHIND THE SCENES

Landon Parvin

The first time he went out to work with Arnold Schwarzenegger, he wound up staying two months. His wife had to send him boxes of clothes. But to write the governor's 2004 Republican keynote speech, Landon Parvin spent only a few days in Sacramento.

They were busy days for Parvin, who started out specializing in humor but is also known for writing serious speeches that blend policy with wit and story.

"If I have a contribution to speakers, I do take storytelling seriously," Parvin says, sitting in his office on the third floor of his rural Virginia house, surrounded by bookcases, and on the walls, horseshoes and a pencil drawing of his horse. "I frequently hear speechwriters talk about 'humanizing' politicians. Politicians *are* human."

While people think a speechwriter's job is to write, Parvin has a different idea: "It's to listen."

He did a lot of listening on that visit, including to Schwarzenegger's wife, Maria Shriver. "She told me Arnold could defend America better than anyone else—because he's not from here. You can see her influence from that."

Schwarzenegger talks directly to immigrants in his keynote, and he does defend America. But in addition to the one we examine in this chapter, he tells three others: one about the day the governor became a citizen; a second about the day he heard Richard Nixon speak and became a Republican; and finally, one about a wounded soldier. "That was all from one meeting," Parvin says. "I'd ask him things and stories would come out. I always do that, both to find out where the person wants to go and also to go in my own direction, which is the personal."

He would also include one line that was not story. Earlier that year, Schwarzenegger had accused California Democrats in the state house of being a bunch of "girliemen."

In just sixty-four words, Schwarzenegger's narrative accomplishes three things confirmed by those researchers in Holland. He compels attention, illustrates a point, and characterizes himself—in this case as a patriot with a sense of humor ("I wasn't an action hero back then"). It is a model for politicians at every level—and every ideological stripe.

Anecdotes may be long or short, true or hypothetical, as current as today or as old as recorded time. Later in this book we will examine more thoroughly where and how all kinds of anecdotes can enrich a speech. First, though, let's review some ways anecdote helps achieve those three goals Schwarzenegger and his speechwriter, Landon Parvin, accomplished so beautifully in 2004.

USING ANECDOTE WELL

You can characterize anecdotes by mood (funny, dramatic), time (historical, current), or whether or not they're true or fictional—like parables or scenes

"It drove Democrats and the press nuts," Parvin remembers. "We wanted him to use it again. The Bush people didn't want us to use it." Back in Virginia, Parvin went about writing the draft the way he usually does, jotting down notes for an outline. "I put things down, stories, arguments, kind of to see how they fit together best. Then I write."

Parvin writes his first draft fairly fast, then edits. A lot. "I spend four times more time editing than I do writing. Lots of people think [editing]'s an ordeal. It's easier."

When Schwarzenegger got the draft they went over it together, line by line. Then Schwarzenegger practiced, with the discipline he had once applied to lifting weights. "By the time he went on he probably rehearsed that speech a hundred times," Parvin says.

Parvin wasn't at the convention the night Schwarzenegger spoke. "We'd put the speech to bed. I'd only be there if something was wrong."

Whether to use "girliemen" had been touch and go till the end. Schwarzenegger did, and the crowd roared.

But to watch the speech now is to be struck by the stories. They are varied, self-deprecating, and—especially the first one, where Arnold uses humor to tell a grim story—moving. Even to Democrats.

I ask Landon if there's something about speechwriting he hasn't yet said.

We've been talking about ourselves at that point, but now he stops to think. "I guess it would be how little understood speechwriting is—even by speechwriters. Look. No one is going to trust what you say as a speaker until they trust you. How do they trust you? By knowing you. So you [the speechwriter] have to let the audience know the speaker."

And then, Parvin does precisely what he is about to advise: "The way you do that, is share and reveal," he says, sharing the approach speechwriters would do well to adopt.

Source: Landon Parvin spoke with Robert A. Lehrman in March 2009.

---

from a novel. Some illustrate. Others may symbolize. And of course, some fit into no neat category, or into many; each of the ones in this chapter fit more than one.

Later, this book covers various ways to use anecdote. For now, here's a sampling of the rich variety of what's possible. We see seven types: dramatic, funny, personal, symbolic, illustrative, historical, and parable.

DRAMATIC

Dramatic incidents can awaken listeners to the urgency of problems. They can also inspire them by showing stories of courage or sacrifice. In an October 2007 speech to the New Hampshire Democratic Party, Sen. John Kerry—then still a possible presidential candidate in the 2008 campaign—used this account to make his audience see the urgency of sticking to principle, and imply that he would do the same:

Sometimes, I remember people not because of what they could have achieved, but because of what they did. Like Austin Griffin.

I met him over twenty years ago. I was a prosecutor, going after the Mob.

A group of thugs from one of the most ruthless gangs—I mean killers—had walked into the Disabled Vets Hall Austin helped run. They told him, "We're putting in slot machines, here. We want protection money. Do this by Friday, or else."

They picked the wrong guy. Austin Briggs never wavered. Never. He testified, looking them in the eye. We broke up that gang. They're still in prison.

When he died in July, his daughter said, "My father had his values. He wasn't going to cave."

Fellow Democrats, *we* have values.

FUNNY

Funny stories characterize speakers not just as having a sense of humor, which might be mean or sarcastic, but as being able to laugh at themselves. They can also illustrate points memorably and provide a change of mood. At the 2004 Republican National Convention, Laura Bush wants to show the audience how much her husband values education. But she also wants them to see that she and her husband can laugh at themselves. Since she is identified with Bush, her poking fun at him is self-deprecating—even as she asserts her independence by being irreverent. She begins by telling the crowd how often people ask her why George W. Bush should be president:

> As you might imagine, I have a lot to say about that. I could talk about my passion: education. At every school we visit, the students are so eager. Last fall the president and I walked into an elementary school in Hawaii, and a little second-grader came out to welcome us and bellowed, "George Washington!"
> Close. Just the wrong George W.

PERSONAL

Like all anecdotes, personal stories focus attention, amuse, illustrate, and absorb. In addition, they have two unique advantages: they demonstrate personal knowledge of an issue, which makes speakers believable, and they allow audiences to see the private lives of people they usually view from a distance as celebrities. Such stories satisfy people's yen for gossip and make them feel more warmly toward the speaker. In this story from the Yale class day speech we discussed in chapter 6, Hillary Clinton demonstrates affection for Yale to a Yale audience; characterizes herself as a pioneer, undeterred by bigots who would block women from going to law school; and shows she knows what she's talking about when she says there has been progress.

> I thought about how I ended up at Yale Law School. It tells a little bit about how much progress we've made.
>
> I was trying to decide whether to go to Yale Law School or Harvard. . . . A young man I knew who was attending Harvard invited me to come to a cocktail reception to meet some of the faculty at Harvard. I was introduced to a professor who looked as though he just stepped out of the set of *Paper Chase* and . . . my friend said to professor so and so, this is Hillary Rodham. She's trying to make up her mind between us and our nearest competitor. And he looked down at me and he said, "First of all we don't have a nearest competitor, and secondly we don't need any more women."
>
> So I decided that Yale was by far the more hospitable place.

SYMBOLIC

Here, Ronald Reagan tells an anecdote with a larger meaning; he even underlines the point ("A small moment, with a big meaning") so the audience won't miss its symbolic importance. On the surface, this is a story about an ocean rescue. Really, it is about what America has come to symbolize around the world under the eight years of his watch. By praising an American sailor, he achieves yet another purpose: reminding his audience that since he was president in those years, he too deserves praise.

AS DELIVERED

Ronald Reagan's Farewell Address. You know why Reagan tells this story. What makes it effective? What makes you think it's true? Is there a moment where Reagan reveals personal emotion? What effect might that have on his various audiences?

http://college.cqpress.com/politicalspeech

> I've been reflecting on what the past eight years have meant and mean. And the image that comes to mind like a refrain is a nautical one—a small story about a big ship, and a refugee, and a sailor. It was back in the early eighties, at the height of the boat people. And the sailor was hard at work on the carrier *Midway*, which was patrolling the South China Sea. The sailor, like most American servicemen, was young, smart, and fiercely observant. The crew spied on the horizon a leaky little boat. And crammed inside were refugees from Indochina hoping to get to America. The *Midway* sent a small launch to bring them to the ship and safety. As the refugees made their way through the choppy seas, one spied the sailor on deck, and stood up, and called out to him. He yelled, "Hello American sailor. Hello, freedom man."
>
> A small moment, with a big meaning.

ILLUSTRATIVE

This kind of anecdote serves as evidence, convincing the audience that the speaker's solution is practical ("Mitigation works"). In this 1997 speech, James Lee Witt, then director of the Federal Emergency Management Agency, doesn't do anything as crass as saying "under my direction"; he simply says "we." But everyone knows who was in charge. Note that this doesn't focus on an individual; only in the last sentence does the audience glimpse a real person. But anecdote can be about groups as well as individuals. And in making a funny reference to the Maytag repairman, Witt shows that he has a nice sense of, well . . . witt:

> Mitigation works. How do we know? Just ask the people in Grafton, Illinois. After that 1993 flood, 403 residents and businesses applied for disaster aid. Then the property acquisition program went into effect. We moved people out of danger. Two years later, floodwaters hit the same areas.
> Disaster applications? Eleven. The mayor said he felt like the Maytag repairman; the phone wasn't even ringing.

HISTORICAL

Historical stories inspire audiences, making them feel like they too are involved in great events. In this 1982 speech to the British Parliament, Reagan uses a story about Winston Churchill to inspire his audience. In doing so, he allies himself with a legendary British hero. Note the clever one-word switch in the quote when it recurs:

> During the dark days of the Second World War, when this island was incandescent with courage, Winston Churchill exclaimed about Britain's adversaries, "What kind of a people do they think we are?" Well, Britain's adversaries found out what extraordinary people the British are.
> But all the democracies [of that time] paid a terrible price for allowing the dictators to underestimate us. We dare not make that mistake again.
> So let us ask ourselves, "What kind of people do we think we are?"

PARABLE

Delivered solemnly by speakers who seem overly proud of their own profundity, parables can carry a whiff of pomposity that reduces their effectiveness. But this one, a favorite of litigators before juries, seems to work. Listeners enjoy the way the wise man outwits the prankster. More important, the story fits nicely into one theme politicians like to stress: that the solution to our problems lies in—well, you figure it out.

> There's an ancient story about an old wise man who could answer any riddle of life.
>
> One day a young boy decided to play a trick on the old man.
>
> "I will capture a bird," he told his friends, "hold it cupped in my hands, then ask whether it is dead or alive. If he says 'Dead,' I'll let it fly away. If he says 'Alive,' I'll crush it before opening my hands."
>
> Holding the bird, the boy went to the old man and asked: "Is the bird I have dead or alive?"
>
> The old man replied: "The answer . . . is in your hands."

This chapter doesn't present an exhaustive list of the different ways to use anecdote. It only tries to demonstrate the variety of anecdotes and the varied ways politicians can put them to use.

In Part III we look more thoroughly at those ways. Meanwhile, the ones we have just examined suggest three things that contribute heavily to making anecdote effective.

Use Stories with Punch Lines

Examine the parable on the previous page. It has a narrative question: Will the boy succeed? It then narrates three connected events: The boy has an idea. He visits the old man and gives him an ultimatum. The old man responds. That's the punch line. Brief as it is, the parable creates suspense. Just like *The Lord of the Rings,* the audience wants to know what happens next. In looking for stories, make sure yours create suspense, too. That will both move your listeners and keep them listening.

Be Truthful

About a decade ago, a U.S. senator told his home-state audience an old political story as if it had happened to him. It hadn't. He left. The other senator from that state came in and opened with the same story, also as if it had happened to him—thus dismaying supporters of both.

Why do that? In this era of YouTube and cell phone cameras, the risks of getting caught are too great. Mentioning that a story is apocryphal doesn't make it less effective. Admitting something is an "old story" or one you heard somewhere else makes you more credible, not less.

Give Stories Room

Sometimes you don't have much time to tell a story. In a three-minute speech, a sixty-second story doesn't allow you enough time to make an argument. But don't rush things. Concrete detail makes stories believable. Feeling the stories are true makes audiences find them moving. The richness in Reagan's anecdote about the sailor or in Schwarzenegger's about Soviet-occupied Austria contribute to the effects they can have. Fight for every second without destroying balance.

SUMMING UP

George Schultz, Reagan's secretary of state, liked to talk about the time he showed Reagan a speech that he'd drafted. Reagan said it was "satisfactory." Then he paused and said, "Of course, if I were giving that speech, it would be different. . . . You've written this so it could be read. I talk to people." And taking the text, Reagan began editing. He made four or five edits, then put a caret in the margin and wrote "story," Schultz recalled. "He had completely changed the tone of my speech."[4]

It is not surprising that people called Reagan the "great communicator." The reason was not how he said things, though he was a skillful deliverer of speeches. It was his eye for what moved people. His insight gave speechwriters, though they rarely talked to him, the license to find stories that could move a crowd. He had the wisdom to use them.

Anyone who writes speeches for a living should know how often the stories you use are the only things people remember, and what it's like to see a listener drift off, glance at his watch, or punch furiously at a Blackberry—then snap to attention when the speaker tells an anecdote.

We need to remember what Reagan said to Schultz: "I talk to people."

You do too.

The Speechwriter's Checklist: Anecdote

- ☐ Have I used anecdote throughout the draft?
- ☐ Do the stories used in the speech support or illustrate a point? Are they believable?
- ☐ Will the stories inspire, entertain, or move this audience?
- ☐ Have I given the stories room to breathe?
- ☐ Do the stories have punch lines?
- ☐ Have I been honest? Did I attribute quotes or lines if necessary? Have I avoided pretending that imagined stories happened to me/my boss?

Wit

March 2007. Arizona senator and presidential candidate John McCain, campaigning in New Hampshire, gets up to speak at what a reporter calls "a mansion, a heroic place with exposed beams, a fireplace the size of your kitchen, and chairs so huge and heavy that if you sat in one you might get lost for a week."[1]

"Thank you for welcoming all of us into this middle-income tract home," he begins. A little later, in the course of a twenty-minute speech, McCain tells what the reporter calls a "favorite joke."

The reporter mentions just the punch line. A lot of politicians will recognize it because they've used the joke so often themselves. It's about two Irishmen in a bar who seem to be strangers discovering similar things about each other, each discovery (*Y'don't say! I'm from Cork, too!*) making them cackle with glee—and call for a drink.

Finally, the bartender gets a call from his wife. She asks who's in the bar. He says, "Just the O'Reilly twins getting drunk again."[2]

McCain has demonstrated two basic kinds of political humor: the apparently spontaneous quip and the "evergreen"—a joke that never grows old. He has also shown his mastery of a great asset at all levels of political life: the ability to crack a joke.

WRITING TO MAKE THEM LAUGH

Why is humor so important in political speech? The most obvious reason is to win attention. But there are three other reasons that are crucial to speechwriting.

HUMOR MAKES A POINT

Take this joke, used by New York Democratic representative Charlie Rangel and Missouri Republican senator Kit Bond. It's about the man who orders rabbit stew at a restaurant and complains to the manager that it tastes like horsemeat. The manager confesses he did put some horse meat in the stew.

"How much?"

"It's equally divided. One horse, one rabbit."

Why do politicians like that joke? Not just because it's funny. Rather, it illustrates a situation that happens all the time in politics: the unequal compromise. If you think the other side has proposed a bill that gives your side only a little bit and theirs a lot, this kind of story, combined with the right off-ramp, can make the point in a devastating way.

HUMOR CHANGES PACE

Sometimes, you've been ranting for five minutes about the other party, or wading through some heavy State Department boilerplate about the nettlesome issues of trade. You sense the audience needs variety. You pause. Take a drink of water. Smile to yourself, as if you've just remembered something. And tell a joke.

Your listeners need that. They can't take constant hectoring, and neither can you.

HUMOR CHARACTERIZES

American audiences like speakers with a sense of humor. They especially like those willing to make fun of themselves. Self-deprecating humor is particularly appealing to people because it shows speakers can be modest as well as witty.

And so, two weeks before election day 2008, viewers could tune into *Fox News*—and later on YouTube—and see both Barack Obama and John McCain, seated a few feet from each other at the Alfred E. Smith Memorial Foundation Dinner, an annual charity fund-raiser held at the Waldorf-Astoria Hotel in New York.

It is a time when McCain has been criticized for not remembering Obama's name in a debate. Obama, in turn, has accused him of being a George W. Bush clone. Meanwhile, Republicans have attacked Obama for his visions of grandeur: endorsements by celebrities like Oprah Winfrey, an outdoor address to a crowd of two hundred thousand in Berlin, and an acceptance speech in front of Greek columns at Invesco Field in Denver. Because he has served on a board with William Ayers, former cofounder of a group that bombed public buildings in the 1960s, Sarah Palin has accused him of "palling around" with terrorists.

McCain begins by recalling the campaign's early days. "It began so long ago," he says, "with a man heralded by Oprah Winfrey as 'the one.' Being a friend and colleague of Barack, I just called him 'that one.'"

He waits for the laughter to die down. "He doesn't mind at all. He even has a pet name for me. George Bush."

AS DELIVERED

Obama and McCain at the 2008 Alfred E. Smith Dinner. Look at the entire speech for both Obama and McCain. How do they soften the barbs they toss at each other? Among the kinds of wit we've examined—one-liners, puns, hyperbole, irony—how many can you find?

http://college.cqpress.com/politicalspeech

The crowd roars. Obama has a big grin. He's laughing, nodding, applauding. Then it's his turn.

"There is no better crowd in America I would rather be palling around with right now."

Now McCain is laughing hard.

"I feel right at home here because it's often been said that I share the politics of Alfred E. Smith—and the ears of Alfred E. Newman," Obama says. "I was originally told we could move this venue outdoors to Yankee Stadium." He looks around. "Can somebody tell me what happened to the Greek columns I requested?"

The crowd loves them both.

Both McCain and Obama have good material. But they are effective because both obey the two maxims of political humor.

Make Fun of Yourself

Remember, politicians need to be likable. In the heat of a campaign, politicians can sometimes ridicule opponents. In the 2004 Republican National Convention, Sen. Zell Miller's hyperbolic ridicule of candidate John Kerry's ability to keep America strong ("With what? Spitballs?") brought the audience to its collective feet.

Usually, though, that kind of edgy ridicule makes political audiences uncomfortable. Much safer is self-deprecatory humor; politicians who can laugh at themselves have picked the right target. When Obama makes fun of his ears or his reputation for having a big ego, and McCain makes fun of his memory lapses, they come off as nice. This is not to say that they can't make fun of each other. In fact, they've been doing that all night. This is a roast, after all.

"It is an honor to be here with Al Smith," Obama says at one point, looking around at the 1928 presidential candidate's great-grandson. "I obviously never knew your great-grandfather—but from everything John McCain tells me the two of them had a great time together—before Prohibition."

Everybody is laughing, especially McCain.

But even there, Obama needs to make sure he doesn't sound mean. "Wonderful stories," he adds, a softening touch.

In doing so, he obeys the second mantra of political joke writers.

Singe, Don't Burn

In politics, today's enemy may be tomorrow's ally. The thickest-skinned politician will resent being belittled in front of a crowd. People who need to work with each other take great risks when they ridicule each other. The gentler approach works best.

Sometimes, speakers or their speechwriters despair of their ability to provide this element that audiences want. How, they ask, do comedy writers make up jokes? There is no shortage of books on the subject. They describe the process—clustering, the search for exaggeration, and the "joke dump" from which you cull the eventual keepers. They describe formulas: the definition joke (*Or, as Mark Sanford puts it* . . .); the rule of three (*A rabbi, a priest, and a minister walk into a bar* . . .); or acronyms (*FEMA—which means For Emergencies Must Avoid*). Such advice is beyond the scope of this book. I suggest readers try it, though. You might surprise yourself.

But my colleague Eric Schnure, profiled in this chapter, points out one way in which wit differs from every other element in effective political speech. You don't have to make it up; you can steal it.

This approach to humor is completely bipartisan. Here, for example, is a joke that was popular among Democrats in 2007:

> President Bush is out jogging one day, and doesn't notice a bus barreling right towards him. Three boys jump off the sidewalk and push him out of the way, saving his life.
>
> Bush is grateful. "I'm president of the United States," he tells the kids. "You saved my life. I'd like to reward you. What can I give you? Anything at all!"
>
> The kids huddle. One says, "We'd like three plots in Arlington Cemetery."
>
> Bush says, "Funeral plots? Why?"
>
> "We're Democrats. When our dads find out what we did— they'll kill us!"

I first used that joke in 1988. It was old even then. Who invented it? No one knows, but no one expects a source for these jokes—and they still work.

Even if you can't invent a joke to save your life, there are many ways to find humor, and many different kinds. There are the arcane literary stories for use on college campuses, like this one about the author of *Gulliver's Travels*, Jonathan Swift—more quote than narrative—from John F. Kennedy's commencement speech at Syracuse University in 1957:

> Dean Swift regarded Oxford . . . as truly a great seat of learning: for all freshmen were required to bring some learning with them in order to meet the standards of admission—but no senior, when he left the university, ever took any learning away; and thus it steadily accumulated.[3]

There are animal stories, campaign stories, sarcastic stories for partisan events, and rueful ones for people who have lost campaigns. Where to find them? The nearest Borders bookstore will have so many joke books you could go broke buying them. Are most of the jokes useless? Of course. But if you find

Eric Schnure

To the Bush White House in 2002, Senate Majority Leader Tom Daschle was public enemy number one. Angry Republicans called him an obstructionist and blamed him for blocking their agenda. By March the attacks were working so well that even some Democrats had begun avoiding Daschle as if he had a contagious disease.

Enter Eric Schnure and Jeff Nussbaum, with a tough assignment: craft a speech to change the tone. A former White House speechwriter for Al Gore, Schnure had his own speechwriting business and sometimes worked with Nussbaum, then Daschle's speechwriter, on the "roasts" that are a Washington tradition. This time they were writing for the most venerable roast of all, the one put on for the political press by the Gridiron Club.

A Washington institution since 1885, Gridiron is a white-tie dinner staged by the establishment print media. It attracts the most powerful people in the city, including the president, for an evening in which drinks flow and reporters sing songs lampooning American leaders. For politicians, performing well at the Gridiron roast is so important that the event is often called the "invisible primary."

"We knew we had to deal with this criticism," Schnure recalls. But when he, Nussbaum, and a friend sat down to write Daschle's Gridiron speech, they rejected the analogy of Daschle having a disease.

"More like an addiction," one of them said.

Hmm. Long evening, that Gridiron. Everybody's drinking.

"AA meeting," someone said.

"Hi. My name is Tom. And I'm an obstructionist."

Schnure typed it into his laptop.

"This is my first meeting."

Okay, what else do people say at AA? They say they how long it's been since their last drink, right?

"I haven't obstructed anything in the last twenty-four hours."

Weeks later, after many drafts and many rehearsals, Bush was sitting just a few feet away on the dais as Daschle delivered those lines and continued: "Well, actually, just a couple of minutes ago, the president asked me to pass . . . the salt. I wanted to, I tried to. I just can't bring myself to pass anything."

The crowd loved it. "Classic political humor," Schnure says. "Singe, don't burn, true to the Gridiron's motto. We could include lots of jokes about others, but the whole premise was Daschle was poking fun at himself."

The speech, reprinted in the appendix of this book, bolstered Daschle's reputation—not to mention Schnure's and Nussbaum's. The two formed a company called the Humor Cabinet, have collaborated on dozens of such events, and been called by one reporter "the go-to-guys for political humor in Washington."

For people in positions of power, Schnure says, self-deprecating humor is the safest kind. "People want to know you can laugh at yourself, that you don't take yourself too seriously." Still, he says, in politics, "The main point is not just getting laughs; it's being liked." He thinks a bit. "And getting votes."

Source: Eric Schnure spoke with Robert A. Lehrman in February 2009.

one joke in a book and use it again and again, you've spent your money wisely. Web sites—especially of the late-night talk shows—are useful because they are timely. Speakers don't have to steal them; to say, "Jon Stewart said last night" signals an audience that a joke is coming. Finally, listen to other political speeches. The jokes in them have the advantage of already being scrubbed for political life. Also, with those nobody minds if you fail to attribute them, for they were undoubtedly stolen from someplace else.

WIT: FROM QUIPS TO QUOTES

Let's look at the kinds of humor that work most often in politics.

QUIPS

These are the asides, sometimes just a sentence fragment long, whose aim is to get a mild chuckle. It's unclear what George W. Bush, in Shanghai in 2001, meant by what happened in 1975—probably his own well-documented wildness. But even a puzzled audience can see that he is poking fun at himself and perhaps his mother, the kind of self-deprecating humor that works best.

> I want to thank our hosts. I was telling Chairman Yu that I was [in Shanghai] in 1975 with my mother. Shanghai has finally recovered.

ONE-LINERS

Longer than quips, often carefully worked out, designed to be quoted—and not always original. This Ronald Reagan one-liner, from a 1983 speech in New York, is so old he doesn't need to cite a source. Note the strategic value of it. Reagan not only makes the audience laugh but characterizes himself as a skeptic about Washington, a stance that characterized his entire career:

> I've learned in Washington that that's the only place where sound travels faster than light.

STORY-JOKES

These can be used to poke fun at someone or make a point relevant to the speech. They can be short or very long. Here's a short one, used by Sen. Joe Lieberman when he accepted the nomination for vice president from Al Gore:

> Reminds me of the story about the taxidermist and the veterinarian, who went into business together. They put up a sign saying "Either way you get your dog back."

This joke has been a staple of Republican and Democratic speeches for at least a decade. Why? First, there's an edge to it—dead dogs! Second, it fits nicely into a point politicians love to make, which is that it does make a difference how you vote, or what party is in power. Usually, the on-ramp for this joke is something like, "There are those who say there's no difference between Democrats and Republicans."

Here's a longer story-joke, used by Reagan Treasury secretary Jim Baker at a Gridiron dinner. Baker is making fun of Paul Volcker, then chair of the Federal Reserve Board:

> I had a terrible dream last night: I dreamed the three most powerful Americans—the president, the Speaker of the House, and the chairman of the Federal Reserve—suddenly passed away. All three appeared in St. Peter's waiting room.
>
> A voice came over the intercom telling the president to go to Room One. He went inside and found himself with a huge gorilla. The voice then said, "Ronald Reagan, you have sinned, and you must spend eternity with this gorilla."
>
> The voice over the intercom then sent Tip O'Neill to Room Two, where the Speaker found a mad dog. "Mr. Speaker," the voice on the intercom said, "You have sinned, and must spend eternity with this mad dog."
>
> Then the voice sent Paul Volcker to Room Three. He went in, and to his surprise, he found himself with Bo Derek. Then the voice came over the intercom and said, "Bo Derek, you have sinned. . . ."

You could also use this joke to make the point that the Federal Reserve had been hurting America, simply by prefacing it this way: *I don't agree that the Fed should refuse to cut interest rates. In fact, I had a terrible. . . .* In that way the joke both makes a point and characterizes Baker as someone who can poke fun at people in either party.

HYPERBOLE

We've already seen hyperbole in Mike Huckabee's 2008 convention speech. Here's one that doesn't use pop culture. Unlike his earlier joke, George W. Bush's target is his mother, known for being a parent who speaks her mind. But he pokes fun with a light touch (singe, don't burn), and the implication that he may be a little intimidated (self-deprecating). Either way, the speech was perfectly attuned to this YMCA picnic audience in 2001, making them laugh after both the second and third lines:

> Part of respect is to respect your mom and dad. So to the campers here, my advice is, listen to your mother. [LAUGHTER AND APPLAUSE] In my case, I don't have any choice. [LAUGHTER]

ANALOGY

More about analogy in the next chapter. It has its uses in supporting serious points, but it is a staple of comedy. Republican senator S. I. Hayakawa's analogy to rescue efforts has survived for decades in the speeches of other politicians. Here it is in two versions: the first from Texas senator Lloyd Bentsen on the Senate floor in 1990; the second from Wisconsin representative David Obey, criticizing a 2006 labor bill on the House floor. Both versions demonstrate how you can tailor jokes to the time you have:

> Most of us remember our former colleague Senator Hayakawa's way of summing up the difference between Democrats and Republicans. If Republicans saw a drowning man fifty feet from shore [he said], they'd throw [him] a thirty-foot rope and tell him swimming the rest would build character.
>
> Democrats would throw a hundred-foot rope—then walk away looking for other good deeds. By their logic, throwing a ten-foot rope to someone in a twenty-foot hole is okay because it's better than a five-foot rope. The problem is it still won't get the job done.

QUOTES

The world has gone through centuries in which people have tried to be funny. Some were pretty good at it—like Voltaire, Mark Twain, Winston Churchill, or Bob Hope. And people have made money by compiling these lines in big books that you should buy. In them, you can find your very point made with more wit than you can supply, especially during the hectic routine of drafting a political speech.

Quotes can amuse the audience; show that speakers have a literary background, which is not always an advantage; and make your point memorable, as in this rueful and well-known example that Adlai Stevenson used after losing his 1952 race for president against Dwight Eisenhower:

> Someone asked, as I came in, down on the street, how I felt, and I was reminded of a story that a fellow townsman of ours used to tell—Abraham Lincoln. They asked him how he felt once after an unsuccessful election. He said he felt like a little boy who had stubbed his toe in the dark. He said that he was too old to cry, but it hurt too much to laugh.

CONCLUSION

Reviewing the types of humor politicians use—there are others, naturally—doesn't tell you how to use them. That's for later in the book. But no matter what your purpose or what kind of humor you use, four principles just about always apply.

USE IT THROUGHOUT

Politicians shouldn't reserve wit for roasts. It's useful in every speech—and every part of a speech. Speakers who open with a joke, then ignore humor for the rest of their speech, seem both obvious and clumsy. It's as if they say, *Okay, I've shown you I can be funny. Don't have to do that anymore.* More important, they ignore a powerful tool that has many uses. Would a carpenter put away a hammer after the first blow? Jokes are appropriate at every stage in a speech, including the very last line, as we shall see.

USE IT WITH OFF-RAMPS

Even if your main goal is to change pace, wit shouldn't appear jammed into a speech. Make it relevant. Audiences will remember the joke—and the point it illustrates. Craft on- and off-ramps with care.

USE IT WITH TASTE

There are those who make fun of politicians because, with some exceptions, their jokes are bland. It's true. Raunchy, sexist, or racist jokes are inappropriate for speeches, precisely because characterization is so important.

When Jesse Jackson used the word *Hymietown* in private conversation, and when George W. Bush was caught on a live mike calling a *New York Times* reporter an "asshole," they created a furor among people who would never object to such language in their own conversations.[4]

In political speech you have to amuse a broad audience, not offend it. Audiences for Chris Rock or Sarah Silverman attend *because* they find them funny. That's not the crowd at a church pancake breakfast.

USE—AND REUSE

Sometimes politicians—or their staff—demand new jokes for each speech. *We did that already,* they'll say disdainfully. That's a mistake. Political speakers do need some new material tailored to the event—and there are certainly jokes about current events that have a shelf life of only a few days. But most audiences rarely hear a political speaker; the jokes that bore the speaker and his staff are new to them.

The comedian David Brenner once confessed that he would never use a line on the *Tonight Show* unless he'd used it in his act for at least six months. If it takes a professional comedian six months to perfect his timing, inflection, and language, why should a politician think he or she can do it in ten minutes? Politicians constantly on the prowl for new jokes run the risk of stumbling over punch lines, and defeating the very purpose they want to accomplish.

Humor is a weapon. Like hand grenades, jokes can win a battle—but they can explode in your hand. In politics you can't always say publicly what you would say in private. This makes politicians no different than anybody else who has to swallow an urge to tell off a boss, a parent, a spouse, or an exasperating child.

But sometimes—sometimes—humor allows you to admit truth you can admit in no other way. Mo Udall, the Arizona Democratic representative and presidential candidate whose book *Too Funny to Be President* is still essential reading for political speechwriters, would sometimes end speeches to trade associations with this line: "Well, them's my views. And if you don't like 'em—I'll change 'em."[5]

Actually, he was always notably unwilling to change any of his views. But by including himself as a participant, he could satirize one of the least savory aspects of politics without offending listeners. Even an audience that devoutly hoped he would change his views could give him credit for wit.

Udall's kind of wit teaches a valuable lesson. His jokes were rarely original, never offensive, usually funny, and invariably made a serious point. They helped him stay popular during a long career.

The Speechwriter's Checklist: Wit

☐ Have I followed the political humor rule of thumb: singe, don't burn?
☐ Have I given the speaker an opportunity for self-deprecatory humor?
☐ Have I avoided offending or insulting listeners?
☐ Will the jokes play well in both the room and in tomorrow's papers?
☐ Do they make a point?
☐ Do my off-ramps make those points clearer?
☐ Do I use humor throughout?
☐ Do I use new jokes only if the speaker practices?

chapter

10

Support

About two weeks after the 2004 elections, while Americans were still debating about the vote totals in states like Ohio, an obscure Food and Drug Administration scientist named David Graham took his place in front of the Senate Finance Committee and set off a debate about an entirely different set of numbers.

Those numbers revolved around Vioxx, Merck's popular anti-inflammatory drug that by 2004 had been prescribed for over eighty million patients around the world. Graham told the Finance Committee that people using Vioxx instead of other drugs were four times as likely to suffer heart attacks and strokes. Did that mean Americans had actually had those heart attacks and strokes? "From 88,000 to 139,000 Americans," said Graham. "Of these, 30 to 40 percent probably died."[1]

That might have been alarming enough. But Graham had also come armed with some eye-popping analogies, one aimed at the committee chair, Sen. Chuck Grassley, R-Iowa:

> How many people is 100,000? For Iowa it would be 5 percent, for Maine, 10 percent, for Wyoming, 27 percent. I'm sorry to say, Senator Grassley, but 67 percent of the citizens of Des Moines would be affected, and what's worse, the entire population of every other city in the state of Iowa.

Then Graham used another way to put things in perspective:

> Imagine that instead of a widely used prescription drug, we were talking about jetliners [with] an average of 150 to 200 people on an aircraft. This would be the rough equivalent of 500 to 900 aircraft dropping from the sky . . . 204 aircraft every week, week in and week out, for the past five years. If you were confronted by this situation . . . what would you do about it?[2]

Thousands of people testify each year, in Washington and state capitols. They rarely make news, but Graham did. He had given the senators not only a clinic in the dangers of a popular drug but also a lesson in how to persuade.

So far this book has examined ways to make listeners understand, remember, sympathize, and laugh. Now we enter a new area.

WRITING TO MAKE THEM BELIEVE

Figures of speech, anecdote, and wit often become nonrational ways to persuade. Responsible persuasion must also support points with evidence—especially facts, the data that help politicians support their points using reason.

In a country where about a third of the population believes in ghosts, political audiences clearly include many people for whom evidence is only part of the picture. But they also include people who care *only* about it. To reach them, politicians mostly use three kinds of factual evidence: *statistics, examples,* and *testimony.* They also use *analogy,* a tool of reasoning. This chapter defines these terms, shows you how politicians use them, and explains how they can use them effectively. But too often, political speech misuses evidence. Because you should not only learn how to argue well but to avoid ways of arguing badly, we'll end by examining the most common fallacies in politics, and how avoiding them can be easier than you think.

Before we move along, though, it's worth mentioning that supporting points rationally doesn't mean sounding dull. Like each of the other elements, evidence does more than persuade, and that includes evoking emotion.

There's no better example than Graham's testimony. He doesn't just provide numbers. He puts them in context. As Graham makes his listeners visualize airliner after airliner falling to Earth, who wouldn't find themselves growing angry?

In addition to evoking emotion, the way you use facts can characterize, and not just because reeling off a string of statistics makes listeners think speakers are smart. In the Colin Powell speech we examined in chapter 2, there's a point where Powell wants to support his assertion that Saddam Hussein never meant to comply with the UN mandate. He puts it this way:

> Iraq's goal was to give us, in this room, to give those of us on this council the false impression that the inspection process was working.
>
> You saw the result. Dr. Blix pronounced the 12,200-page declaration, rich in volume, but poor in information and practically devoid of new evidence.
>
> Could any member of this council honestly rise in defense of this false declaration?

Powell gives the audience more than a dry recitation of facts. He cites Dr. Hans Blix, no friend of the United States, but trusted by the audience.

He shows indignation ("us, in this room, to give those of us on this council") that Saddam had lied. Finally, he finishes with a question that needs no answer. In other words, he shows passion, integrity, and a willingness to trust someone the crowd respects. Whatever listeners think of his argument, they may think better of him.

As we look at statistics, examples, and expert testimony, keep in mind those other dimensions important to politicians.

▶ **STATISTIC:** *quantified evidence that summarizes, compares, and predicts things, from batting averages to birthrates.*

The *New Yorker* once ran a cartoon of a politician examining a speech as his speechwriter stands waiting. "It's vague, noncommittal," the politician says. "I like it!"

People often think political speech is vague, but the real problem is often the reverse: speeches are far too cluttered with facts, especially statistics. It's easy to see why. First, statistics seem conclusive—how can you argue with a number? Second, politicians are comfortable with statistics because the issues that occupy their time require them. They vote on issues involving millions or billions of people. How much will a road cost? How many people will use it? How many will get hurt? You can't muster a persuasive argument about these issues without some numbers.

Politicians generally use statistics in three ways: to *summarize, compare, and predict.* And so, on a typical day, February 13, 2009, while members of Congress were getting up to speak about the economic collapse and newly elected president Barack Obama's stimulus package to fix things, Rep. Ed Perlmutter, D-Colo., used raw numbers to *summarize:*

> The facts are we lost 600,000 jobs last month . . . and some 3.6 million jobs last year.

Rep. Frank Pallone, D-N.J., used statistics to *compare:*

> Madame Speaker, last month the unemployment rate increased from 7.2 percent to 7.6 percent.

And Rep. Dennis Kucinich, D-Ohio, used a combination to *predict:*

> According to Moody's Economy.com, the measure before us [will] create perhaps only 2.2 million jobs by 2010, leaving unemployment hovering at about 10 percent.

Statistics provide a way to indicate the scope of a problem or the likely effects of a solution. They allow politicians to compare their ideas with the other side. *He voted with George Bush 90 percent of the time!* Just hearing that a politician knows them—even when they read from a script the audience assumes they do—reassures a crowd. *She has the statistics. Must know what she's talking about.* As long as they are accurate, relevant, up to date, and attributed, they are central to arguing ethically, since the scope of the problems politics tries to solve are too large to do so through reasoning.

▶ **EXAMPLE:** *factual material that illustrates, clarifies, or describes in order to support a point.*

Overloading a speech with statistics is a mistake not just because listeners can't absorb all those numbers but because voters expect more. They want politicians to use concrete detail and to see the human side of problems. Thus the importance of examples, or types of factual support that don't involve numbers. Examples clarify, humanize, show competence, and satisfy the different needs of those in the audience. We use three kinds: brief, extended, and hypothetical.

Brief

Here is Barry Goldwater at the 1964 Republican National Convention, arguing that the Democrats have failed in foreign policy. Note that while Goldwater's examples are concrete, his language is not neutral. There is nothing wrong with that. Words like "blot," "infest," and "haunt" express his contempt for Democratic policy, illustrated by these five examples that take up no more than a few words each, and are, thus, brief:

> Now failure cements the wall of shame in Berlin; failures blot the sands of shame at the Bay of Pigs; failures marked the slow death of freedom in Laos; failures infest the jungles of Vietnam; and failures haunt the houses of our once great alliances and undermine the greatest bulwark ever erected by free nations, the NATO community.

Extended

The extended example may be a story; in chapter 8 we examined stories that illustrate points. But stories involve a sequence of events. We may illustrate points by describing the acts or remarks of real people at some length that don't fit the definition of story. Extended examples about individuals cannot demonstrate scope, but they humanize, illustrate, and keep an audience listening the way no other kind of support can.

At the Democratic Convention in 1984, New York governor Mario Cuomo used an extended example to illustrate the virtues of ordinary people: his father.

> That struggle to live with dignity is the real story of the shining city. And it's a story, ladies and gentlemen, that I didn't read in a book, or learn in a classroom. I saw it and lived it, like many of you. I watched a small man with thick calluses on both his hands work fifteen and sixteen hours a day. I saw him once literally bleed from the bottoms

of his feet, a man who came here uneducated, alone, unable to speak the language, who taught me all I needed to know about faith and hard work by the simple eloquence of his example. I learned about our kind of democracy from my father.

Twenty-four years later, at the 2008 Republican National Convention, John McCain used examples of three people to illustrate a different point:

> I fight for Americans. I fight for you.
>
> I fight for Bill and Sue Nebe from Farmington Hills, Michigan, who lost their real-estate investments in the bad housing market. Bill got a temporary job after he was out of work for seven months. Sue works three jobs to help pay the bills.
>
> I fight for Jake and Toni Wimmer of Franklin County, Pennsylvania. Jake works on a loading dock, coaches Little League, and raises money for the mentally and physically disabled. Toni is a schoolteacher, working toward her master's degree. They have two sons; the youngest, Luke, has been diagnosed with autism.
>
> Their lives should matter to the people they elect to office. They matter to me.

> **AS DELIVERED**
>
> *John McCain's "Real People."* McCain uses three examples of "real people" in his 2008 Republican National Convention speech. Which is the most effective? Why?
>
> http://college.cqpress.com/politicalspeech

Real-life examples need not be people. In politics you use them to allow listeners to visualize problems, solutions that work, inspirational events, praise, and anything else that needs illustration. They may delight, compel, entertain, anger, thrill, or bore. By themselves they cannot show scope, so they can't "prove" a point. But if you pick them well, and use details that resonate with listeners, they are powerful tools to persuade.

Hypothetical or Imagined

Most people don't think of made-up examples as a kind of evidence, and it's true that hypotheticals don't carry the full force of facts. But sometimes the perfect real-life example doesn't exist or is hard to find. If speakers pick the right details for their imagined example, as in this example from Al Gore's 1994 "fatherhood" speech, they can persuade by evoking a shock of recognition—the same reaction that makes novels feel true.

> Fatherhood becomes meaningful from the day-in-day-out experience of being home.
>
> Ask your daughter if anything special happened at school, and she may only look sullenly up and say, "No." But if you are around a little later, putting dishes away or folding laundry, suddenly the words spill out and you hear story after story about band practice or the new teacher or a fight with her best friend.

▶ **TESTIMONY:** *opinions or firsthand accounts of others, whether expert or not, usually in their exact words.*

"It's important to note that this range does not depend at all on the data from our Kaiser-FDA study," said Graham in his Senate testimony. "Indeed, Dr. Eric Topol at the Cleveland Clinic recently estimated up to 160,000 cases of heart attacks and strokes due to Vioxx, in an article published in the *New England Journal of Medicine.*"

Why is such testimony important? John F. Kennedy didn't quote experts in his inaugural address. Martin Luther King didn't quote anyone to prove integration was right (though he did quote the Declaration of Independence and "America the Beautiful" for other reasons). Ronald Reagan didn't quote anyone in his farewell address, nor did Lincoln in the Gettysburg Address.

Still, testimony has been essential for political speakers since the time of Demosthenes. Politicians quote the words of others in their day-to-day speeches for six main reasons: (1) to bolster credibility because of the expertise of the speaker; (2) to make audiences remember the speech because of the pithiness of the quote itself; (3) to persuade because of the reputation or power of the person they quote; (4) to undercut the arguments of the other side by using the words of opponents against them; (5) to remind the audience of the experiences of ordinary people; and (6) to draw parallels between the events surrounding the quote and today.

On May 23, 2000, as the Clinton administration wound down, Congress debated one of the most controversial issues of the year: "normalizing" trade relations with China. I remember watching the debate, and noticing the unusual quantity of impassioned and skillful speech. There was a lot of quoting in that debate as well. Following are examples of four, taken from the *Congressional Record* for that day.

Expertise

Here, Rep. Ron Kind., D-Wis., quotes a source not because of the source's language, which is unexceptional, but because of the source's knowledge and experience:

> And perhaps the foremost human rights activist in China today, Martin Lee, had this to say . . . : "bring China into the international forum and hold her to the agreement rather than exclude her."

Pith

Here's Representative Kind again, this time from a source whose use of antithesis is pithy and memorable:

> I also believe in what former secretary of state Cordell Hull was famous for saying, and that is, "When goods and products cross borders, armies do not."

Status

Often in politics, both the expertise of the speaker and the words and ideas in the quote are less important than who said it. Rep. Jim Ramstad, R-Minn., uses a quote that is neither pithy nor by someone with expertise, but happens to have been said by the popular governor of Ramstad's home state:

> My governor, Jesse Ventura, is not one to mince words; and he talks plain talk. He put it like this. . . . "This will be one of the most important votes of the century in Congress . . . Congress will be doing more to expand our economy and create jobs than anything else we could possibly do."
> My Chairman, the governor of Minnesota got it right. . . .

Quoting the Opposition

Here is Rep. George Miller, D-Calif., persuading people to oppose the motion. Again, there is nothing exceptional in the language; what's important is that Miller has found the other side agreeing with him.

> Even the Clinton administration's own briefing book in favor of PNTR [permanent normal trade relations] for China says, "China denies or curtails basic freedoms, including freedom of speech, association, and religion."

So far, we've examined the garden varieties of evidence—that is, the factual things that convince crowds that what a speaker says is true. But now we move to the one kind of reasoning used so often as evidence it probably doesn't seem like reasoning at all.

▶ **ANALOGY:** *inferences or conclusions drawn from things most people know in order to help them understand or believe in something new.*

Analogy is a type of reasoning through comparison—in this case by detecting similarities. We've already examined several kinds of analogy in chapter 7: metaphor, simile, and hyperbole. Now let's dig deeper.

In 1996, commenting on a landmark same-sex marriage trial, Sen. Charles Robb, D-Va., said this:

> Until 1967, sixteen states, including my own state of Virginia, had laws banning couples from different races to marry. When the law was challenged, Virginia argued that interracial marriages were simply immoral. Today we know that the moral discomfort—even revulsion—that citizens then felt about legalizing interracial marriages did not give them the right to discriminate thirty years ago. Just as discomfort over sexual orientation does not give us the right to discriminate against a class of Americans today.

Robb's analogy doesn't prove his case the way factual evidence does. He hoped that audience might reason something like this:

- We should have struck down the ban on interracial marriage.
- Banning gay marriage is similar to the ban on interracial marriage.
- We should strike down the ban on gay marriage.

It's a syllogism. And it is indispensable in politics. Politicians use analogy to remind their audience of precedent, citing historical events ("Four score and seven years ago"). They use analogy to clarify arguments by demonstrating similarity, as Robb did. And they use it to ridicule, as Huckabee did with his analogy about the media and Madonna.

Political speeches use two kinds of analogy: literal and figurative.

Literal

Literal analogies directly compare one real-life situation with another in hopes that the audience agrees on one and so will agree about the other. Robb is marshaling a substantive argument, using a kind of analogy that works only if the audience feels as he does about interracial marriage.

Sometimes politicians use analogies not to demonstrate that something is wrong but to inspire their listeners with hope. Here, for example, is Barack Obama ending his inaugural address:

> In the year of America's birth, in the coldest of months, a small band of patriots huddled by dying campfires on the shores of an icy river. The capital was abandoned. The enemy was advancing. The snow was stained with blood. At a moment when the outcome of our revolution was most in doubt, the father of our nation ordered these words be read to the people:
>
> "Let it be told to the future world ... that in the depth of winter, when nothing but hope and virtue could survive ... that the city and the country, alarmed at one common danger, came forth to meet [it]."
>
> America, in the face of our common dangers, in this winter of our hardship, let us remember these timeless words. With hope and virtue, let us brave once more the icy currents, and endure what storms may come.

AS DELIVERED

Barack Obama's Inaugural Address. Obama's inaugural address was criticized for not having the kind of inspirational quality that marked Obama's campaign speeches. Why does it seem more subdued than the close of the election day speech in Chicago? Would you have done something differently?

http://college.cqpress.com/politicalspeech

We'll look at that technique in chapter 11. For right now, it's enough to know that analogy can be stunningly effective, and in more than one way.

Figurative

These analogies compare something real to something imagined; they often begin with "It's as if." You see this kind of analogy most often in partisan speeches. Some examples:

Oliver North, protesting the 1987 congressional investigation of his role in the Iran-contra affair:

> This is a strange process that you are putting me and others through. It's sort of like a baseball game in which you are both the player and the umpire. It's a game in which you call the balls and strikes and . . . determine who is out and who is safe.

MAKING EVIDENCE MEMORABLE

In politics, the problem with using the evidence you need to support your point is that it might clash with our other needs: being compelling, inspiring, and exciting. Nothing makes a crowd's eyes glaze over faster than a string of numbers. It's difficult to bring an audience to its feet when you have to explain an idea in all its nuances, or demonstrate the historical context that makes audiences agree about policy.

Difficult, yes. Impossible, no. Analogy provides one way of keeping audiences interested. At one point in that 2000 debate over China, Rep. Dana Rohrabacher, R-Calif., wanted to make the point that embracing China through trade would not force that country to restore human rights to its citizens. He might have presented his idea this way:

> To think we restore human rights in China by bringing them into the World Trade Organization is naive. You don't make allies of those who oppose your ideas by being nice.

A former speechwriter, Rohrabacher knew how to argue effectively. He put it this way:

> We do not make a liberal by hugging a Nazi.

More economical. More memorable.

Analogy is especially useful when it comes to making audiences pay attention to the most mind-numbing form of evidence: statistics. One rule of thumb: never provide numbers without some way of setting them in context, often by comparing or contrasting them.

Analogy, after all, was one thing that made David Graham's testimony so compelling. Here's another. Speaking in 1998, former surgeon general C. Everett Koop tells the audience that five hundred million people around the world will die from smoking by 2025. "That's a numbing figure," he says. "So let me put it in other terms for you." See how he ignores the "rule of three" limit speakers often impose to make no less than six comparisons in this litany of analogies:

> That's a Vietnam War every day for twenty-seven years. That's a Bhopal every two hours, for twenty-seven years. That's a *Titanic* every forty-three minutes for twenty-seven years.
>
> If we were to build for those tobacco victims a memorial such as the Vietnam Wall, it would stretch from here [Koop is speaking in Washington, D.C.] one thousand miles across seven states to Kansas City. And, if you want to put it in terms per minute, there's a death every 1.7 seconds, or about 250 to 300 people since I began to speak to you this afternoon.

Analogy isn't the only way to make audiences sit up with statistics. Some are so clichéd it may be time to retire them (*As dollar bills it would stretch from here to the moon*). Here are three other—and still useful—ways to provide context.

SHOW WHAT IT MEANS FOR ONE PERSON

This speech, from October 27, 1964, is so old the numbers seem hard to believe. (Was there a time when tuition was that low?) Ronald Reagan knows that the large amount Washington spends on the "war on poverty" means little to most people. He demonstrates what it means for one person, then mocks it by comparing it to another use his listeners can understand:

> AS DELIVERED
>
> *Ronald Reagan's "A Time for Choosing" Speech.* This speech is what made "the great communicator" famous for his politics. Can you see the rhetorical similarities to the Ronald Reagan who became president? How many kinds of support can you spot throughout this speech? Are they concrete? Are they aimed at audiences outside the hall?
>
> http://college.cqpress.com/politicalspeech

> Now we declare "war on poverty" . . . we are going to spend each year just on room and board, for each young person that we help, $4700 a year! We can send them to Harvard for $2700!

SHOW WHAT IT MEANS FOR ONE DAY, HOUR, OR MINUTE

In this 1993 speech in Memphis, Bill Clinton knows his listeners might hear anecdotes about violence in schools but not know the scope of the problem. He uses the bigger number, but just for one day, to make them feel urgency:

> One hundred and sixty thousand children stay home from school every day because they are scared they will be hurt in their school.

TRANSLATE INTO WHAT IT COULD BUY

Clumsily phrased but clear to the audience, Walter Mondale's speech at the 1984 Democratic National Convention doesn't use a number at all, but makes the crowd angry by comparing what tax cuts for the rich would buy for the rich, compared to what the tax cuts for average folks would buy for them:

> They cut their taxes enough so the very rich can buy a new Mercedes-Benz, and they cut your taxes enough to buy a hubcap.

ARGUING RESPONSIBLY

Arguing responsibly means using current, relevant evidence from reputable sources, and at least in your own mind justifying the conclusions you draw from it. It need not be the death of interesting speech. The conflicting needs of political speech mean you have to work harder to do both.

No chapter on support would be complete without examining how to minimize the ways political speech distorts, misleads, and sometimes includes outright lies. To see how often this happens, you need only read a sampling of the entries on www.factcheck.org, the incredibly useful site that in the 2008 campaign examined the truthfulness of claims made by the presidential candidates.

Should audiences hold candidates and officeholders to the same standards that they expect from scholars? In the court of public opinion, aren't speeches more like legal briefs, presenting whatever arguments the jury—voters—will buy?

A political speech is not a doctoral dissertation. But in my experience, political speeches reflect far too cavalier an attitude about truth. I've argued over the years with sincere, principled people with years in politics who believe political life makes some fallacies necessary. They argue that the other side will do it, that people accept in politics what they wouldn't in other parts of their lives, and that knowingly using fallacy creates such a clear political advantage that it outweighs the need to argue ethically.

I don't agree. You'll find a more responsible view in the interview with David Frum that appears below, included here because he talks about the need for speeches that can "stand scrutiny." Standing scrutiny is a virtue. It's possible for politicians to give up falsehoods, distortions, evasions, and shoddy reasoning without losing a single vote. In the process, we just might increase the credibility and lessen the suspicion people have of them.

That's why, in addition to Behind the Scenes, this chapter closes with a section describing the common fallacies of political speech and arguing against them.

David Frum

For a brief moment in 2002, White House speechwriter and author David Frum became, to his own surprise, the most famous person in Washington. It happened on his last day, as he was in his office across from the West Wing, packing up the few boxes of personal things the White House allows departing aides to take home.

"Bob Novak is talking about you on TV," someone told him.

Novak was claiming that Frum had been fired because Frum's wife had leaked the fact that Frum authored of one of President George W. Bush's most controversial lines: the "axis of evil" phrase in his 2002 State of the Union address.

Frum *had* written a version of that memorable line, though Novak's story wasn't true. But that it should even be a news story was ironic. The reason Frum had come to the White House had nothing to do with writing memorably. Since the 1980s the Canadian-born Yale and Harvard Law graduate had developed a reputation as a political conservative who wrote perceptively about complicated questions of policy. The White House had offered him the job to write Bush's economic speeches.

"If you read Sarah Palin's speech, that's how most political speeches work," he says now, careful to emphasize that he admires Matt Scully's work creating her 2008 Republican acceptance speech. "Here I am, love me. But once in a while you have to persuade. Your speech has to make sense as a coherent, constructed argument."

Frum's job would be to write not for average voters but sophisticated ones—the ones who know policy issues and could analyze them.

Frum was tempted by the job. "I live in Washington," he says. "I'd walk by the [White House] gates, stand at the rail, and look in. Now, maybe I'd stand inside and look out."

But once there, he was frustrated. Like many administrations, the Bush presidency had to square some contradictory campaign pledges: the promise to raise skill levels of the American workforce, for example, with the promise of a guest worker program that would lower them.

"I developed great ingenuity reconciling these," he says, with a wry smile.

I ask him for a speech he remembers with satisfaction. The most important ones, he says, were the ones Bush never gave. He describes one aimed at the Detroit Economic Club. Peggy Noonan had once told Frum that speechwriters see problems before anyone else because actually writing a draft exposes weaknesses staffers in a speech conference can overlook. As he wrote the one for Detroit, Frum saw what she meant.

"This was a speech for boards of trade, members of the [House] Appropriations committees. Smart people with smart staffs." But the more other staffers reviewed the Detroit draft, the more coherence seemed out of reach. "It became a rally speech," Frum says.

He is quick to point out that this was not a dilemma only for the last administration; Barack Obama has just given an economic speech at Georgetown University that Frum feels exposed

FALLACIES

On June 5, 2005, Secretary of State Condoleezza Rice strode onstage at the Washington meeting of the Organization of American States General Assembly, and, putting in a plug for the virtues of democracy, began this way:

similar inconsistencies, though he acknowledges the people writing for Obama might dispute that.

But for much of his time in the White House, Frum became a kind of speech doctor. "A lot of my time was devoted to finding good anecdotes and stats. You'd find some example of how existing tax law caused disincentives."

At one point, Novak took Frum to lunch and asked if he would become a source for information about the administration. Frum wasn't happy with his job, but he said no, and wouldn't let Novak pick up the lunch check, either. It was to retaliate, Frum believes, that Novak tried to embarrass him.

"The lesson is, don't retaliate," Frum says. On the day he was packing up, he had thought it might be time to activate his law degree and maybe do some work on Wall Street. When he got home the phone was ringing off the hook. Novak's revenge actually did him a favor; it gave Frum the chance to become a pundit.

Today, Frum talks about the dilemma he saw inside the White House. Politicians, he points out, need to reach more than moms and dads. "A policy that says disregard the best-informed people and those who care most, and focus on those less informed and care least, can work for a short interval. But the speeches you write can't stand scrutiny."

Frum is raising one of the most difficult issues for political speechwriters, not to mention politicians: the group of interlocking questions that revolve around telling the truth. The purely logical: Have you found relevant, appropriate evidence to support your points? The political: Can you satisfy the need to govern after election day without going back on what you said before it? The ethical: Is it right to fudge?

Frum sees the need for speeches that inspire. But not his speeches. "I'm a lawyer. For me, the satisfactions of speechwriting are not literary. In fact," he says, perhaps allowing himself a moment of hyperbole, "it's dangerous if your satisfactions are literary."

The month before our conversation Frum had written a *Newsweek* cover story urging Republicans not to become dominated by the "politics of Limbaugh." In it he mentioned how angry his views make some of his conservative friends. "He keeps shooting us in the back. . . . Hey, Frum: you're a putz!" said one radio host.

Eight years, many articles, and three books after Frum's role as a White House speechwriter put him at the center of controversy, Frum's words still engender debate. But now he chooses what to say and when to say it, no longer has to reconcile the irreconcilable, and writes material that can stand his own meticulous scrutiny. A writer who experienced the power of working inside the White House gates has found what others have before him: You may have more power when you're back outside.

Source: David Frum spoke with Robert A. Lehrman in April 2009.

As recently as 1999 the two million Cubans in the United States earned a combined income of $14 billion. Now compare that with Castro's Cuba, a country of eleven million citizens and a GDP only slightly larger than $1 billion.

Already, we have a problem, though not with her reasoning. Rice was using statistics to compare, and the difference certainly seems large. She has her figures wrong; Cuba's GDP was about $25 billion. But her 14:1 ratio is the same as the per capita GDP difference between the two countries. Let's assume some staffer got the numbers wrong and no one caught it. Not a big deal.

But then Rice drew this conclusion: "The lesson is clear: When governments champion equality of opportunity, all people can prosper in freedom."

Is that the lesson? That equal opportunity is the only reason Cuban Americans prospered more than the people they left behind? Were there no other reasons? Natural resources? Military might? Crippling effects of a decade-long embargo on Cuba? Were all governments that championed "equality of opportunity" prosperous?

Secretary Rice uses concrete data. Her last sentence might very well be true, especially with the qualifying word *can*. But she draws her large conclusion from such a small amount of evidence that alert listeners—and at an OAS General Assembly there were bound to be a lot of them—should reject it, noting an example of the reasoning from too few facts: the fallacy of "hasty generalization."

A political speech like that one becomes persuasive not just by adopting the best qualities of argument but by avoiding the worst. Among the worst is fallacy.

First, some definitions. Rhetoric scholars usually distinguish between two kinds of fallacy. The first is the fallacy of *matter,* or false statements, which include misstatements, half-truths, lies, or misstatements, like Rice's about Cuba's GDP. In a class on logic we'd call that a fallacy of matter, even if it was an honest mistake.

When politicians don't prove or support a statement, does that mean they have committed the sin of fallacy? Not at all. People accept statements all the time without proof. When you say "All men are created equal," nobody would expect you to provide evidence. That's not because the statement can't be questioned. (*Equal in what? Intelligence? Wealth? And who says they were created? And why only men?*) It's because speakers know that for most Americans it is a given.

Because few politicians consciously misstate facts, this chapter examines the second kind of fallacy: that of *form,* or invalid reasoning. In politics, some basic fallacies of reasoning crop up again and again. Consult the bibliography for books that explore them in more detail than this book can afford.

How can you avoid fallacies? Before discussing that, let's look at some examples. You've seen the one Secretary Rice used in 2005. Here's one even more common in politics.

STRAW MAN

Yes, the term originated in the sexist days when people used the word *man* to include women. Straw man carries with it the image of the scarecrow in *The

Wizard of Oz, outfitted with pants and a hat, designed to look formidable to crows or thieves, but really made of straw. In this fallacy, a speaker creates a convincing rebuttal—not to the opponent's muscular, real argument but to a weak, straw-filled one easy to destroy. It's like watching the Nationals beat the Yankees, not realizing the losing team was made of imposters wearing Yankee uniforms.

One way politicians do that is to inaccurately paraphrase the other side. Instead of rebutting an actual quote, they rebut their paraphrase. It's easy to do. Here, John McCain does exactly that. He summarizes Barack Obama's ideas on education, then dismisses them:

> Senator Obama wants our schools to answer to unions and entrenched bureaucracies. I want schools to answer to parents and students.

It's a clever idea, but where had Obama ever said that these were his views? Answer: nowhere. No politician in his right mind would want schools to answer to "entrenched bureaucracies." To examine McCain's paraphrase even for a moment is to see how absurd it is, and why he should get no credit for rebutting it.

AD HOMINEM

Another sexist term too common to replace, *ad hominem*—meaning "to the man"—involves dismissing someone's ideas by attacking them personally. *That may sound good,* you might say, *but you know what a liar he is.*

Of course, in politics, character—biographical details and the presence or absence of virtues like honesty, courage, or intelligence—presents a legitimate subject for debate. To attack an opponent's character does not by itself constitute a fallacy. Attacks only become ad hominem when you use personal attack to discredit an opponent's views.

Here, for example, is then Senate Majority leader Bill Frist at the 2004 Republican National Convention, rebutting opposition to the Republican prescription drug benefits plan:

> Now, some of our opponents don't want seniors to get this card. They don't want seniors to know that our plan [cuts] the cost of their medicines. They'd rather play politics than help patients.

You could argue that by summarizing unnamed opponents, Frist is committing the sin of straw man. But speakers who use straw-man arguments usually delight in rebutting them, using evidence. Frist doesn't rebut the "opponents" at all; he only dismisses them by asserting that they have an unworthy motive.

Like most campaign years, 2008 was full of ad hominem attacks. The entertaining blog "Stifled Mind" pointed one out in late July. It occurred during a conversation between ABC anchor George Stephanopoulos and John McCain about the senator's proposed "gas tax holiday":

> **Stephanopoulos:** Not a single economist in the country said it'd work.

> **McCain:** Yes. And there's no economist in the country that knows very well the low-income American who drives the furthest, in the oldest automobile, that sometimes can't even afford to go to work.

"This is a pretty good example of the fallacy of ad hominem," the blog's author wrote, then made clear why by framing McCain's statement as a syllogism:

- "Economists claim that the gas tax holiday will not benefit the public.
- Economists are not part of the lower class who struggle to pay for gas.
- Therefore the claim that the gas tax holiday will not benefit the public is false."[3]

Let's say McCain had answered this way:

> Yes, but maybe most economists don't know what it's like for low-income Americans. They drive the furthest, in the oldest automobile. They sometimes can't even afford to go to work. It may be that they're too small a group to show up on economists' calculations. But we have to fight hardest for those who struggle the most.

He still makes his personal attack, qualifying it with a "maybe." But he also would have rebutted his opponents' ideas by calling into question the way they collected data. And he wouldn't have given Stifled Mind that pretty good example.

APPLES AND ORANGES

People compare apples and oranges all the time—in nutritional value, for example. This kind of comparison becomes the fallacy sometimes called *false analogy*—when you find similarities between things whose differences are more important, and vice versa. In politics, politicians often find similarities in an opponent's plan to ones voters don't like, but they ignore much more important differences. For example, here's Mike Huckabee comparing health care and military costs in September 2007:

> The reality is, with a $2 trillion-a-year health care budget, we're spending more on health care, nearly 17 percent of our gross domestic product, versus 3.8 percent of GDP on the entire military budget.

The problem: Huckabee was comparing total spending by Americans, public and private, against Department of Defense–only spending on military programs. Politifact.com's truth-o-meter titled its examination "Apples and Oranges," pointing out that when you just compare federal spending for each budget, the result becomes an undramatic 5.5 percent for health versus 4.2 percent for defense.

FALSE CAUSE

This is the political tactic that labels something as the cause of a problem when it is not, or when it's only a small part of the cause. You see this when politicians take credit where they don't deserve it or blame others who don't deserve it.

In the second of the three 2008 presidential debates, Obama tried to find examples of education issues where he agreed with McCain. He answered this way:

> Charter schools—I doubled the number of charter schools in Illinois despite some reservations from teachers' unions.

As some critics quickly noted, the bill applied not to Illinois but just to Chicago, so Obama clearly overstated its effect. But you see false cause in his words "I doubled." That would be true only if Obama thought up the idea, was solely responsible for introducing or passing the bill, or was the critical vote. In fact, he did not originate the idea and was just one of a number of sponsors. The bill would have passed without his work on it. "There's no 'I' in team," said Jack Morris after reporters asked how "he" beat the Braves in the 1991 World Series seventh game.[4] Obama was just part of the team.

AS DELIVERED

The Second Presidential Debate, 2008. Is this a speech? Actually, in debate prep, candidates study from binders full of mini-speeches designed to cover every issue. Does this kind of inaccuracy matter outside of the small audience of policy wonks? Before looking at the last page of this chapter, see how you could edit Obama's response to avoid "false cause."

http://college.cqpress.com/politicalspeech

EITHER-OR

This fallacy presents a false choice by ignoring other options. In November 2006, President Bush directed this comment to American allies:

> Over time it's going to be important for nations to know they will be held accountable for inactivity. You're either with us or against us in the fight against terror.

Whether or not you sympathize with the president's anger, there were more than two options in deciding on a response to 9/11, not to mention nuances within those options. One might ask whether Patrick Henry's use of antithesis ("Give me liberty or give me death!") was also false choice. The answer is no. If he actually said that line, Henry was expressing his personal view. For him, there may have only been two choices. The quest for reasoned ways to persuading about policy is another matter. Bush was not simply expressing a feeling; he was urging a policy decision by others that would make them active allies of the United States. In fact, by warning them that they would be "held accountable for inactivity," he was close to using a fourth method of persuasion, not mentioned by Aristotle: the "do it or die" technique formally known as persuasion by coercion.

SLIPPERY SLOPE

The most famous example of this fallacy in American politics is certainly President Dwight D. Eisenhower's 1954 "domino" analogy, which makes the point that if the United States did not defend Vietnam it would see "the loss of Indochina, of Burma, of Thailand . . . of the Peninsula, and Indonesia."

> You have a row of dominoes set up, you knock over the first one, and what will happen to the last one is the certainty that it will go over very quickly.

The fallacy? In dominos, one falling domino will topple the rest. In war, there are too many possibilities to predict with such certainty. Often politicians use "slippery slope" to argue not that something might happen, thus reflecting the complexity of world events, but that it certainly will.

AD POPULUM

The Latin name is pretty easy to understand: rebutting an argument by labeling it with a term that people generally hate, or supporting it with a term they love. Common examples for praise: *patriotic, American, God-fearing, working people, free enterprise.* For candidates on the attack: *socialism, elite, big business, special interests.*

In rebutting Obama's remark to Joe the Plumber, caught on video, that he would like to "spread the wealth," Republican vice presidential nominee Sarah Palin could have chosen many ways to discredit him. To argue ethically, she would have had to present evidence, as conservative economists have done in great detail, that spreading the wealth would be dangerous. By choosing instead to endorse the view of those who labeled it "socialism," she gave her audience a handy example of ad populum:

> Senator Obama said he wants to, quote, spread the wealth. What that means is he wants government to take your money and dole it

out however a politician sees fit. Barack Obama calls it spreading the wealth. But Joe the Plumber and Ed the Dairy Man, I believe that they think that it sounds more like socialism. Friends, now is no time to experiment with socialism.

Hasty generalization. Ad hominem. Straw man. Apples and oranges. Either-or. False cause. Slippery slope. Ad populum. The definitions are not always cut and dried. Is Palin's quote really just ad populum? Why isn't it also slippery slope? In fact, it is. But a book covering the basics must omit some complexities—as well as a discussion of other fallacies with colorful names, like "begging the question," "red herrings," and "reducing to absurdity."

Isn't it possible to argue that adopting strict standards for political speeches takes the fun out of them? Isn't part of the fun of politics making arguments in ways both sides know are wrong, but which they accept because they have germs of truth in them—and allow audiences to jump to their feet and cheer lustily?

No. You needn't eliminate the hyperbole that, properly used, makes politics fun. With a little work, speechwriters could argue more ethically and still have fun.

Let's say that instead of saying:

> Senator Obama wants our schools to answer to unions and entrenched bureaucracies. I want schools to answer to parents and students.

McCain had said:

> Too often, Senator Obama's plan would have entrenched bureaucracies control our schools and schools answer to unions. I want schools to answer to parents and students.

Or if instead of saying:

> I doubled the number of charter schools in Illinois despite some reservations from teachers unions.

Obama had said:

> I helped double the number of charter schools in Chicago, despite some reservations from teachers unions.

It's hard to imagine that adding such nuances would have lost these candidates a single vote. The arguments might still have been wrong, but they would have been more ethical.

Yes, in the heat of a campaign ethics is not front and center in the minds of either candidates or campaign managers. But isn't that precisely when politicians should be the most ethical? Speechwriters, not always the most powerful campaign aides, have the power to help simply by adding nuance. Use facts and examples that are true, relevant, and come from unbiased sources. Use real quotes from opponents. Make sure attacks on character do not become the sole way to rebut. Take pleasure every time you see a legitimate argument escape unscathed.

SUMMING UP

And with that, we reach the end of our description of the elements of speechwriting. We have looked at one kind of structure for the political speech, which contains many of the elements you need. We've looked at the different ways political speeches use language, anecdote, wit, and support. We've also looked at some ways politicians argue that you should try to avoid.

In the preface to this book I suggested that the LAWS of speechwriting were a little like the strokes in tennis. They are the tools you use in building a speech. You've learned the strokes. How do you use them in a match?

Answering that question is the point of Part III.

The Speechwriter's Checklist: Support

☐ Have I varied the evidence presented in this speech? Do I include facts, examples, testimony, and analogy?

☐ Have I created an effective argument? Does this argument include:
  ☐ Statistics in context?
  ☐ Concrete examples?
  ☐ Pithy quotes?

☐ Have I created an ethical argument? Are the facts current, relevant, and responsibly sourced?

☐ Are the facts appropriate for this audience?

☐ Of the fallacies, have I avoided:
  ☐ Forming hasty generalizations?
  ☐ Making an ad hominem attack?
  ☐ Presenting a false cause?
  ☐ Constructing a straw man?

PART III

HOW TO DO IT

"More wiggle room."

Bernard Schoenbaum. Published in *The New Yorker*, November 4, 1996.

Beginnings

In August 1914, Sir Ernest Shackleton, the Antarctic explorer, placed an ad in a London newspaper. "Men wanted for hazardous journey," it read. "Small wages, bitter cold, long months of complete darkness, constant danger, safe return doubtful. Honor and recognition in case of success."[1]

Seventy-six eventful years later, an Arizona Republican senator named John McCain began a speech to the Greater Omaha Chamber of Commerce by quoting that ad and telling what happened next:

> Twenty-eight men answered the ad and began a twenty-two-month endurance trial under the most miserable circumstances of ice, snow, and bitter cold to make the first crossing of the Antarctic by foot. Their mission failed, but Shackleton and his men left a record of honor and courage that endures to this day.
>
> One can't help but wonder, who among us today would answer Shackleton's ad? How many of us would volunteer to serve in a cause greater than ourselves . . . ?

McCain was off to a good start: a story dramatic enough to evoke the image of courage to people who remember reading about Shackleton in high school and an ad droll enough ("safe return doubtful") to undercut what might seem like melodrama. As Monroe's Motivated Sequence urges speakers to do, McCain won attention, even from listeners full of food and whiskey sours. You'd think politicians would open that way as a matter of course.

They don't. Much more common are openings like these, the first taken almost at random from the February 26, 2009, *Congressional Record,* from a speech by Florida representative Kathy Castor; the second from a 2008 National Defense College speech by Defense Secretary Robert Gates.

> Mr. Speaker, I rise today in strong support of the Helping Families Save the Home Act. This act throws a lifeline to families who are fighting to stay in their homes during this economic crisis.
>
> This morning, I'd like to discuss some of the ideas and analysis, as well as points of contention, behind the National Defense Strategy—and then offer my perspective on its institutional implications.

The most common opening in politics, in other words, is not story but a flat statement of purpose. (*I rise today to speak . . . ; This morning I'd like to discuss . . . ; I am sad to report . . . ; It's a pleasure to be here. . . .*) Some speech textbooks find this acceptable, arguing that getting right to the point characterizes the speaker as too substantive to worry about the frippery of rhetoric. There may very well be moments so important it sounds slick to open anecdotally. Here is one from George W. Bush's address to the nation on October 7, 2001:

> Good afternoon. On my orders, the United States military has begun strikes against al Qaeda training camps and military installations of the Taliban regime in Afghanistan.

Right after 9/11, trying for interest might have seemed like spinning. Bush didn't need to work hard to win attention; he had it.

Usually, though, this kind of opening just represents a failure of imagination. In fact, even during those months after 9/11, Bush's graceful speechwriters found ways to use antithesis to make those flat openings artful, as in his October 20, 2001, speech in Shanghai:

> We meet today with recent memories of great evil—yet great hope for this region and its future.

Even floor speeches, where legislators may have only thirty seconds to make their listeners pay attention, don't have to open so mechanically. And in longer speeches, which often open with interminable acknowledgments, false flattery, and sanctimonious generalizations, skillful speakers and speechwriters can ignore those traditions, as well. This chapter examines how the elements we've covered so far can make openings not just interesting but urgent.

Politicians, like most speakers, need to accomplish four things as they begin: win attention, build credibility, create goodwill, and preview the speech. Here's how that worked in one classic example, the immensely skillful speech Gov. Arnold Schwarzenegger delivered to the 2004 Republican National Convention:

What a greeting. What a greeting. Wow! This— this is like winning an Oscar. As if I would know!

> Attention/Joke #1: Schwarzenegger wins attention with three jokes

Speaking of acting, one of my movies was called *True Lies*. And that's what the Democrats should have called their convention.

> Joke #2

You know, on the way up here to the podium, a gentleman came up to me and said, "Governor, you are as good a politician as you were an actor." What a cheap shot. Cannot believe it.

> Joke #3

Anyway, my fellow Americans, this is an amazing moment for me. To think that a once scrawny boy from Austria could grow up to become governor of the state of California and then stand here—and stand here in Madison Square Garden and speak on behalf of the president of the United States. That is an immigrant's dream. It's the American dream!

> Goodwill #1: Schwarzenegger compliments his listeners by expressing his pride at the honor of speaking to them

You know I was born in Europe and I've traveled all over the world, and I can tell you that . . . there is no place, no country, that is more compassionate, more generous, more accepting, and more welcoming than the United States of America.

> Credibility: He reminds people of his international experience to make them believe what comes next

> Goodwill #2: He praises his listeners by praising their country

As long as I live—as long as I live, I will never forget the day twenty-one years ago when I raised my right hand and I took the oath of citizenship. You know how proud I was? I was so proud that I walked around with the American flag around my shoulder all day long.

> Attention/Credibility: He tells a personal story emphasizing his patriotism and love of America

Tonight, I want to talk to you about why I'm even more proud to be an American—why I am proud to be a Republican, and why I believe that this country is in good hands.

> Preview: He gives the audience the roadmap for the rest of his speech

Schwarzenegger's opening has the four opening gambits many skillful political speeches use to begin:

- opening jokes (attention);
- praise for the group (goodwill);
- opening story (attention and credibility); and
- statement of purpose (preview).

His jokes do more than make the crowd laugh; they characterize him as someone who can laugh at himself. His praise does more than make his listeners feel good; it characterizes him as respectful of them. His story does more than make them pay attention; it characterizes him as patriotic. His statement of purpose does more than offer the roadmap; it makes clear that his beliefs are their beliefs.

Each step of a speech's beginning serves a strategic need important to politicians. Let's look at those needs, and how language, anecdote, wit, and support serve them.

THE OPENING JOKE

In *Too Funny to Be President,* Mo Udall's compendium of the jokes he'd used throughout his long career, Udall includes the story of a minister who sells a mule to his neighbor. The minister says, "Remember. Be kind to the critter."

A few days later the minister sees the mule hitched to a plow, and his exasperated neighbor gently trying to coax him to move. The mule won't budge.

"I'll get him going," the minister says. He picks up a two-by-four and smacks the mule between the eyes. The mule sets off.

The farmer yells back, "You said treat him kindly!"

"First you have to get his attention."[2]

STRATEGY

Lots of politicians know enough about getting attention to start with a joke—just the way I've done. But jokes also have strategic importance because of the messages they send. That's important, because even in the first minute of a speech, audiences size the speaker up. You already know that in politics, jokes *characterize,* and that *self-deprecating* jokes make speakers likable. They also tell the audience things like:

I'm one of you.

The speaker doesn't have a swelled head; is tolerant of the vices you also have, like drinking; or hates the same people you do.

I know about you.

The speaker has taken the trouble to find out about you.

Schwarzenegger's jokes are the first kind. *See, like you, I have weaknesses. I'm not too full of myself to know my weaknesses. I know I'm not a great actor. And like you, I know how scurrilous the Democrats are.*

He knows that opening jokes shouldn't just win laughs, they should win friends. In the different ways to "open funny" that follow, that absolutely essential goal for people running for office remains the same.

QUOTES

In this 1996 farewell speech to his fellow senators, Bob Dole began his reminiscences by quoting the self-deprecating way Hubert Humphrey had made fun of his own long-windedness. Dole made himself likable by satirizing himself. And by quoting someone from the other party, Dole made himself even more engaging:

> Hubert Humphrey once said about his own speeches, "I didn't think they were too long. I enjoyed every minute of them." Well, in that spirit, I enjoyed my time in the Senate.

HOWDAHELLS

A term invented by speechwriter Eric Schnure, *howdahells* mean the local references that show the listeners their speaker has taken the trouble to learn about them. In George W. Bush's 2005 Calvin College commencement speech, he pleases the crowd by mentioning a particularly rigorous professor—then turns it into a self-deprecating joke about one of his most satirized difficulties:

> I bring a great message of hope and freedom to Calvin College Class of 2005: There's life after Professor Vanden Bosch and English 101. [LAUGHTER] Some day you will appreciate the grammar and verbal skills you learned here. [LAUGHTER AND CHEERS] And if any of you wonder how far a mastery of the English language can take you [LAUGHTER] just look what it did for me.

IRONY

Irony—saying the opposite of what you mean—often gets a bigger laugh than you might expect because you deliver it with a straight face, which increases the crowd's surprise. In this 2008 National Press Club speech to a nerdy group, Louisiana governor Bobby Jindal pokes fun at his own nerdiness:

> I have to tell you, I will never be as colorful or interesting as Reverend [Jeremiah] Wright. So if that's what you came to see, I suggest you get another cup of coffee. In fact, I am less interesting and less colorful than any Louisiana governor you have ever met. I told my staff the very first day I was sworn in that was one of my goals.

FUNNY PERSONAL ANECDOTE

Personal story builds credibility. Here, Hillary Clinton at Yale uses this story about herself—and an understated last line—to make people laugh; implicitly praise Yale; and characterize herself as someone who, like the audience, dislikes people hostile to women's rights:

> As Nick was speaking I thought about how I ended up at Yale Law School. It tells a little bit about how much progress we've made.

> I was trying to decide whether to go to Yale Law School or Harvard. . . . A young man I knew who was attending Harvard invited me to come to a cocktail reception to meet some of the faculty at Harvard. I was introduced to a professor who looked as though he just stepped out of the set of *Paper Chase* and . . . my friend said to professor so and so, this is Hillary Rodham. She's trying to make up her mind between us and our nearest competitor. And he looked down at me and he said, first of all we don't have a nearest competitor, and secondly we don't need any more women.
>
> So I decided that Yale was by far the more hospitable place.

PUBLIC SPEAKING ANECDOTES

You'll find them in collections of stories like James Humes's *Roles Speakers Play*.[3] Some are corny, many are dated—and some still work. This one has a slight edge—it's basically about two famous people being mean to each other. That's useful when speakers risk sounding bland. Pay attention to the off-ramp to see how National Endowment for the Humanities chair Bill Ferris, speaking to an audience of scholars who still remembered George Bernard Shaw, made this anecdote relevant:

> I enjoyed being with you last year. I'm honored that you wanted me back.
>
> You can never take second appearances for granted, you know.
>
> I'm reminded of that story about the time George Bernard Shaw had one of his plays opening up. He sent Winston Churchill a note, saying, "Here's two tickets to the play. Bring a friend—if you have one."
>
> Churchill wrote back: "Sorry, I'm busy. I'll come for the second performance—if there is one."
>
> So, here I am, back for a second performance.
>
> And while I didn't bring a friend, I see a lot of friends, whether it's . . .

COMBINATIONS

Don't stop with just one! There are a number of things to note in the four jokes that open Barack Obama's 2005 Knox College commencement speech. First, a dig at the fiftieth-anniversary class, combining a wink at their drinking (*one of you*) with the softening touch of his congratulations (*singe, don't burn*). Second, his gentle self-mockery, which reminds students he was recently one himself (*one of you*). Third, his acknowledgment that, while some in the crowd didn't vote for him, he is willing to forgive (*singe, again*). And finally, a joke that needs no explanation, the Pumphandle (*howdahells*).

Good morning President Taylor, Board of Trustees, faculty, parents, family, friends, the community of Galesburg, the class of 1955—which I understand was out partying last night, and yet ——— Smile and wink
still showed up here on time—and most of all, the class of 2005. Congratulations on your graduation, and thank you—thank you for the honor of allowing me to be a part of it. Thank you also, Mr. President, for this honorary degree.

It was only a couple of years ago that I stopped paying my ——— Self-deprecating #1
student loans in law school. Had I known it was this easy, I would have run for the United States Senate earlier.

You know, it has been about six months now since you sent me to Washington as your United States senator.

I recognize that not all of you voted for me, so for those of ——— Self-deprecating #2
you muttering under your breath "I didn't send you anywhere," that's okay too.

Maybe we'll hold—What do you call it?—a little Pumphandle ——— Howdahells
after the ceremony. Change your mind for the next time.

The opening joke—and the other examples of wit in political speech—are important. They make politicians likable, give crowds something they can repeat later, and make points memorable. But the opening joke is an ornament, not the building. "People don't want a Comedian-in-Chief," Schnure points out.[4] Be quick—in-and-out—and move on.

PRAISE

Was McCain's Shackleton opening interesting?

Very. The trouble is, that was not how McCain really began. First, at a time when they were still friends, he felt it necessary to praise Sen. Chuck Hagel, R-Neb., and two other people being honored that night in language like this:

> Chuck Hagel is the model citizen, the one who inspires us to be better Americans. So, too, I might add, do your other two honorees tonight, David Sokol and Charles Durham. Regrettably, I cannot claim the privilege of a close friendship.

And on.

These are the dreaded acknowledgments, the eye-glazing ritual of compliments, thank-yous, and praise for the audience politicians feel they must utter before any big speech.

STRATEGY

Politicians can't skirt the need to thank individuals. First, that helps them win support. Second, it expresses sincere emotion: politicians *do* feel grateful to people who have helped them. But that doesn't mean they need to thank all twenty people on the lists overeager staffers suggest. Three suggestions.

Follow a Rule of Three

If speakers feel uncomfortable without some acknowledgments, thank the three most important people in the room for thirty seconds, and get on with the speech. Usually political events don't end with the speech. A warm thanks, clap on the back, and a question (*How're the kids?*) as they work the rope line can do a lot.

Acknowledge throughout the Speech

Instead of lumping all the acknowledgments in at the beginning, leave them for the moments when what they've done is most relevant. (*Nobody's done more than Joe Jones to remind us of this: We must control our energy needs—or they will control us!*) People applaud for two reasons, and everybody's happy.

Be Funny

There's no rule that acknowledgments have to be dull. (*Thanks to my old friend Joe, who's helped in so many ways. Thanks, Joe.*) You can be funny. Here's how Lloyd Bentsen once acknowledged three old friends at a Women's National Democratic Club meeting: Bob Strauss, former Democratic National Committee chair; Pamela Harriman, longtime Democratic fund-raiser and fabulously wealthy diplomat; and Jack Valenti, well-known aide to Lyndon Johnson and lobbyist. After Strauss introduced him, Bentsen began this way:

> It's a pleasure to hear such an objective introduction. In Texas, we don't say you're getting a song and dance—we call it a Strauss waltz.
> And Jack Valenti, my old friend, a man who can talk for two hours about any subject—four if he knows about it.
> And Pamela—who recently gave that magnificent Van Gogh still life "Roses" to the National Gallery. When I read about that, I said to [my wife], "That's great. Is there anybody who doesn't appreciate a Van Gogh?"
> She said, "You mean—is there a Van Gogh that doesn't appreciate?"
> Really, after all she's done for the Democratic Party we should be sending *her* roses.

Notice that Bentsen winds up on a warm, somewhat sycophantic note; friendship notwithstanding, he wouldn't have been comfortable making even a veiled reference to Harriman's money without ending that way. He essentially combined this rule of three with the need to open funny, then got on with his speech.

The other part of lavishing praise doesn't have to be dull, either: thanking or praising the entire audience, a step that establishes both *credibility* and *goodwill*. This is the step, of course, that makes outside observers laugh at political speech, since it can sound so fatuous with its fulsome praise of people the speaker can't stand. Politicians aren't idiots; if candidates talk at a pancake breakfast, they know the deputy mayor lied about support in the last campaign, the hardworking precinct captain is a moron, and the county chair plans to run against them in the next primary. But what's their option?

> *County Democrats! You've done some good work, though not lately. That's partly because Frank is scheming against me, Joe is a moron, and Alice is a total liar. On the other hand, Andy works pretty hard.*

Sometimes acknowledging reality just won't do. Speeches are job interviews, and at job interviews we pretend. We laugh at the interviewers' jokes, funny or not; praise the company whether we think it's a great place or not; and talk about how we relish "challenges," even if we shrink from them. As for the submerged tension and hostilities? Such emotions exist among the closest friends, not to mention family members. You still praise your kids and—sometimes—parents. Why should political life be any different?

Like the opening joke, praising the audience has strategic importance. It helps the politician become likable, by winning credibility and building goodwill. Whether politicians use the inclusive "we" or the more generous-sounding "you," here are the things they praise:

Beliefs shared. Political audiences usually believe they stand for something larger than themselves. Praise for their views meets the need for self-actualization that Abraham Maslow put at the top of his hierarchy (see chapter 3).

Things accomplished. It may be a bill. It may be an election. It may be the successes their party has had over the years. Democrats like to hear about Franklin Roosevelt's New Deal, and Republicans about Ronald Reagan's call to "tear down this wall." Reminding them about accomplishments, including those from history books, makes them swell with pride.

Bad things overcome. Politics is a competitive, brutal business fought out by people who really do think people on the other side are a nasty bunch. Even issue groups appreciate praise not just for winning a victory but beating back the bad guys.

Personal virtue. In calmer moments, political people will acknowledge that neither the United States nor the parties have cornered the market on courage, intelligence, tolerance, or hard work. No matter. Political audiences like praise for those qualities, and it is a virtual tradition to praise "Americans" for being more hardworking and more innovative than anyone else in the world.

Finally, one thing that stands alone.

Praising the other side. In mixed audiences, or on TV, the single most effective way to boost credibility is to praise the other side. It characterizes politicians as broadminded. And on the floor it becomes necessary because the next day politicians will need to work with them.

That's *what* to praise. Let's look at some innovative ways politicians have used language, strategy, anecdote, and analogy to help. In this section, language becomes more important. You'll see a variety of techniques highlighted for each element.

METAPHOR

Clearly a "we" example with praise for *beliefs* shared, this celebrated 1984 Democratic National Convention speech brought Mario Cuomo attention not just because he praised the crowd but because of the way he used language:

Metaphor — Republicans believe that the wagon train will not make it to the frontier unless some of the old, some of the young, some of the weak are left behind by the side of the trail.

We Democrats believe that we can make it all the way with the whole family intact.

Analogy — Ever since Franklin Roosevelt lifted himself from his wheelchair to lift this nation from its knees. Wagon train after wagon train.

ANTITHESIS

Giving the response to Barack Obama's first speech to Congress, Louisiana governor Bobby Jindal started out with two problems. His party had been crushingly defeated a few months before, and he was speaking right after the still-popular new president. Jindal used antithesis in two ways. First, he praised Obama (and America) for *obstacles overcome:*

Tonight we witnessed a great moment in the history of our Republic.

Antithesis #1 — In the very chamber where Congress once voted to abolish slavery, our first African-American president stepped forward to address the state of our union. . . .

Antithesis #2 — Regardless of party, all Americans are moved by the president's personal story—the son of an American mother and Kenyan father, who grew up to become leader of the free world.

Next, he used it to praise his own party's *beliefs* and Louisiana voters to the rest of America:

> Republicans are ready to work with the new president to provide these solutions.
>
> Here, in my state of Louisiana, we don't care what party you belong to if you have good ideas to make life better for our people. We need more of that attitude from both Democrats and Republicans in our nation's capital.

— Antithesis

REPETITION WITHIN SENTENCES

In his celebrated 1962 speech at Rice University, John F. Kennedy opened forcefully with his repetition of "noted," then a second trio beginning with "in an." Note the double use of "rule of three" and the climactic ordering from small portions of time to large:

> We meet at a college noted for knowledge, in a city noted for progress, in a state noted for strength, and we stand in need of all three, for we meet in an hour of change and challenge, in a decade of hope and fear, in an age of both knowledge and ignorance.

— Rule of three #1

— Rule of three #2 and climactic order

HYPERBOLE

Fulsome praise for the other side in his 1948 Democratic National Convention speech made Hubert Humphrey famous. Humphrey's support for civil rights led Strom Thurmond and other southern delegates to walk out. But as much hatred as there was in the hall on both sides, Humphrey needed to compliment his racist opponents. He would deal with them later in life—and had to try to block the walkout that eventually occurred. He couldn't praise their views, but he could praise their *personal virtues:* "sincerity . . . courtesy . . . and forthrightness." Believable? No. Necessary in politics? Absolutely.

> I realize that there are those here—friends and colleagues of mine, many of them—who feel as deeply as I do about this issue and who are yet in complete disagreement with me.
>
> My respect and admiration for these men and their views was great when I came here. It is now far greater because of the sincerity, the courtesy, and the forthrightness with which they have argued in our discussions.

— Antithesis #1

— Antithesis #2, of "great" and "greater"

ALLITERATION

Again, here is a "we" litany of praise for both *accomplishment* and *obstacles overcome,* made forceful by a last sentence. Ronald Reagan's speech at the Republican National Committee 1994 gala was one of the last he ever gave. Read the last sentence out loud and you'll see that, though it merely strings two clichés together, its four words starting with the letter "B" create a memorable sound for listeners:

> So together we got the government off the backs of the American people. We created millions of new jobs for Americans at all income levels. We cut taxes and freed the people from the shackles of too much govern-
>
> Alliteration ——— ment. . . . [we] brought America back—bigger and better than ever.

LITANY OF ANALOGY

Another interesting way to use litany is this "you" praise for *accomplishment:* Bill Clinton's appearance before a group of five thousand black ministers at the podium where Martin Luther King gave his last speech before being assassinated. Clinton imagines King issuing them a report card—which has the added value of making it clear that he, too, reveres King:

> If Martin Luther King were to reappear by my side today and give us a report card on the last twenty-five years, what would he say?
> You did a good job, he would say, voting and electing people who formerly were not electable because of the color of their skin. . . . You did a good job, he would say, letting people who have the ability to do so live wherever they want to live, go wherever they want to go in this great country. You did a good job, he would say, elevating people of color into the ranks of the United States Armed Forces to the very top or into the very top of our government. You did a very good job, he would say. . . .

LITANY OF BRIEF EXAMPLES

This "we have seen" litany praising *personal virtue*—courage, love, generosity—becomes forceful because the examples are concrete, and because George W. Bush's writers gave him an imaginative antithesis in the final five words:

> We have seen it in the courage of passengers who rushed terrorists to save others on the ground—passengers like an exceptional man named Todd Beamer. And would you please help me to welcome his wife, Lisa Beamer, here tonight.

We have seen the state of our Union in the endurance of rescuers, working past exhaustion. We have seen the unfurling of flags, the lighting of candles, the giving of blood, the saying of prayers—in English, Hebrew, and Arabic.

We have seen the decency of a loving and giving people who have made the grief of strangers their own.   — Antithesis

LITANY OF CLIMACTIC ORDER

Among the stunning uses of language that characterized Obama's 2008 election night victory speech is this example of praise for accomplishment. It clearly rises to a climax, moving from "it was built" to "it grew strength" to "proved." It also demonstrates a variety of techniques:

Our campaign was not hatched in the halls of Washington—it began   — Antithesis/
in the backyards of Des Moines and the living rooms of Concord and   concrete detail
the front porches of Charleston.

It was built by working men and women who dug into what   — Climactic order
little savings they had to give five dollars and ten dollars and   quote
twenty dollars to this cause. It grew strength from the young people who rejected the myth of their generation's apathy; who left their homes and their families for jobs that offered little pay and less sleep; from the not-so-young people who braved the bitter cold and scorching heat to knock on the doors of perfect strangers; from the millions of Americans who volunteered, and organized, and proved that more than two centuries later, a government of the   — Clincher
people, by the people and for the people has not perished from this Earth.

This is your victory.

Does it seem like overkill to devote so much time to what seems like pandering? Actually, the way one praises an audience says a lot to the crowd. When Obama piles on example after example, rich in concrete detail, the audience begins to believe (*Obama really means it!*). Even if the details came out of the hours spent researching by a speechwriter, Obama gets credit for being willing to say each line.

And in running your mental eye over each example, you see that in each way that politicians praise the accomplishments of the audience, they make their listeners remember that the speaker was part of those events, too. In expressing how much they admire the audience, they remind their listeners that they should like their speaker. And that will be true for what comes next.

WINNING ATTENTION

In the winter of 2007, well before the disclosure of his affair with a campaign aide would make presidential politics a part of his past, John Edwards got up to speak at one of the big party gatherings featuring all the Democratic candidates. He didn't tell a joke. He didn't praise the audience. Here is how he began:

> We're all here together—but why are we here?
>
> We are here because somewhere in America . . . a little girl who ought to be drawing pictures and learning multiplication cries herself to sleep, praying that her father, who has been out of work for two years, will get a job again. It doesn't have to be that way.
>
> We are here because somewhere in America . . . , a young man folds a college acceptance letter and puts it in his drawer because even with his part-time job and his mother's second job, he knows he cannot afford to go. It doesn't have to be that way.
>
> We are here because somewhere in America a mother wipes her hand on a dishcloth to go answer a knock on her door . . . and opens it to find an army chaplain and an officer standing there with solemn faces and her boy's name—her patriotic son who enlisted after September 11—on their lips. It doesn't have to be that way.

STRATEGY

A "somewhere in America" litany is not original; Googling the phrase gives you eight million or so book titles, rock lyrics, TV shows, and political speeches. Still, it is a fitting example to begin the second, vastly more important way to fulfill Monroe's first step: winning attention—this time in a way appropriate to the seriousness of the speech.

Jokes certainly win attention. But when you're about to talk about war and peace, poverty, justice, education, or the environment, why settle for openings that mildly interest the crowd? Be compelling.

Edwards's opening was compelling. It offered a *montage* of brief examples designed to quickly evoke a place or time—as montage does in movies. There is no denying the power that results from this combination of concrete detail, repetition, and *epistrophe,* or repetition at the end of paragraphs ("It doesn't have to be that way").

There are other ways to achieve power: quotes, hypotheticals, startling statistics, the symbolic object—and, once in a while, simple description. But as with opening jokes and praise, a close look at these attention steps shows you more than technique. It shows you what the technique is used *for.* You use serious attention-getters to remind the audience of:

- problems everybody shares;
- evil on the other side;

- personal trustworthiness;
- significance of the group or event; and
- importance of the topic.

In each, the serious attention-getter opening carries an unspoken message: the speaker's own virtues, including an understanding of the audience's problems, determination to beat back those who have caused them, and passionate concern for finding solutions. That's not very different from the reasons for praise, or even for telling a joke.

Unlike what has come before it, though, the serious attention-getter can evoke emotion through the device that consistently tests as most absorbing to audiences because it includes a human dimension and narrative question, story, or anecdote.

"'Thou shalt not' might reach the head," writes the novelist Philip Pullman, "but it takes 'Once upon a time' to reach the heart."[5]

THE ANECDOTE

Dramatic

In this opening story in Ronald Reagan's speech for the fortieth anniversary of D day, you see what a dramatic story can do. A moment to contrast the quiet of the moment, and then—like the sharp cut of a flashback—you are there with the soldiers

> AS DELIVERED
>
> *Ronald Reagan's Speech on the Fortieth Anniversary of D Day.* Beginning about thirty-six seconds into the speech, this section is not just notable because it narrates a battle. What else about Reagan's language helps listeners see the events of forty years ago? And would the speech be strengthened or weakened if the first paragraph of the speech came later or were cut?
>
> http://college.cqpress.com/politicalspeech

Reagan had come to honor. Note that this is a story—complete with climax and an enlarging sentence to put it in perspective.

"I wanted American teenagers to stop chewing their Rice Krispies for a minute and hear about the greatness of those tough kids who are now their grandfathers," said Peggy Noonan, who wrote Reagan's speech.[6] No doubt, many did.

> We stand on a lonely, windswept point on the northern shore of France. The air is soft, but forty years ago at this moment, the air was dense with smoke and the cries of men, and the air was filled with the crack of rifle fire and the roar of cannon. At dawn, on the morning of the 6th of June, 1944, two hundred and twenty-five Rangers jumped off the British landing craft and ran to the bottom of these cliffs.
>
> Their mission was one of the most difficult and daring of the invasion: to climb these sheer and desolate cliffs and take out the enemy guns. The Allies had been told that some of the mightiest of

these guns were here, and they would be trained on the beaches to stop the Allied advance.

The Rangers looked up and saw the enemy soldiers at the edge of the cliffs, shooting down at them with machine guns and throwing grenades. And the American Rangers began to climb. They shot rope ladders over the face of these cliffs and began to pull themselves up. When one Ranger fell, another would take his place. When one rope was cut, a Ranger would grab another and begin his climb again. They climbed, shot back, and held their footing. Soon, one by one, the Rangers pulled themselves over the top, and in seizing the firm land at the top of these cliffs, they began to seize back the continent of Europe.

Two hundred and twenty-five came here. After two days of fighting, only ninety could still bear arms.

Infuriating

Ernie Green is an icon in the civil rights movement for something he did when he was seventeen—agree to be one of the Little Rock Nine, the nine teenagers who in 1957 integrated Little Rock Arkansas Central High School. In this speech, written to celebrate the fiftieth anniversary of *Brown v. Board of Education,* he begins by taking the audience back to what those days were like, not by talking about himself but about the risks endured by one of the less famous plaintiffs in that case:

> On the day before Christmas, in 1950, a man named Harry Briggs reported to the gas station where he worked in Clarendon, South Carolina. Pretty soon his boss called him in. Harry Briggs thought there might be trouble.
>
> He had been angered by a school system in Clarendon that spent $179 for every white student—but $43 for every black one. Why shouldn't he be angry? He'd fought for democracy in World War II. Why shouldn't he want to see democracy in his own home town?
>
> The Briggs family was one of twenty families signing a suit against the school board. His boss hadn't done anything at the time. But now, as Briggs came in, the man gave Briggs a Christmas present—a carton of cigarettes. Then, he fired him.
>
> "Harry, I want me a boy," he said.

Heart-wrenching

From the Al Gore speech for a conference about fatherhood, already cited in chapter 10. I remember being worried about this opening because it begins in the middle of the action, not even naming the subject until the second sentence—something more common in feature writing. It taught me that this could work in speeches, too:

He was nine years old when his mother first described the father who had deserted him. When he was a student at South Boston High, Marcellus Blanding wrote an essay about his reaction—and what he planned to do. He was going down South to see his father. He had some questions to ask him.

Then he listed them.

"What did you do after you got divorced? Was you thinking about my mother and me? Do you regret what you did you still love her? What made you leave her? Do you want her back?

"What did you do all those years I didn't hear from you? Are you proud I'm your son?"

And one more.

"Wanna play me one on one in basketball?"

Personal

At the 2004 Republican National Convention, Sen. Bill Frist needed to highlight what George W. Bush had done for health care. He builds credibility not just by reminding the crowd that he is a doctor—but that it was a family tradition to hold "healing" as a mission:

> Ten years ago, on my first day as a senator, my dad, a family doctor in Tennessee for fifty years, paid me a visit in my new office. He said, "Son, the nameplate on your door reads William Frist. Always remember you're committed to healing and helping people. It really should read, William Frist . . . M.D." Well, today, the door of my Capitol office reads just that—William Frist . . . M.D. It's a constant reminder of my dad's advice . . . to better the life of every individual American.
>
> And that, my friends, is what President George W. Bush has done, particularly when it comes to health care.

Message

Leticia Shahani, president of the Philippine Senate but in 1996 a potential candidate for United Nations secretary general, is anxious to appeal not to the big blocs but the Third World. Here, telling the story of one of the most successful secretary generals in UN history, Shahani makes the point that she, like Dag Hammarskjöld, would be the prisoner of no single ideology:

> Once, at the height of the cold war, during some heated debate about one of the issues separating the two blocs, reporters grew exasperated with the taciturn responses of Dag Hammarskjöld.
>
> "Could you say," one of them demanded, "whether the compass points left or right? East or West?"
>
> Hammarskjöld said, "It points forward."

Period

Sometimes opening with a story gives listeners more than narrative. On the twenty-fifth anniversary of the *Apollo 11* landing, Gore also tries to give his audience a feel for the bitter period in American history at the moment Neil Armstrong first stepped on the moon.

> 1969.
>
> It was the year of Charles Manson, of music in the rain at Woodstock, and the My Lai massacre in Vietnam. At Harvard, where I was a senior, we went to class and heard lectures and wrote papers and talked and fell in love—and argued passionately about the war. . . . It was not a happy time.
>
> But then, in July, while one-quarter of the world watched on live television, Neil Armstrong brought *Eagle* down to the Sea of Tranquility, slowly climbed down a ladder, and pressed his left boot into the untrod surface of the moon—and for a brief time, humans inhabited two worlds.

"Story should be your default opening," a speechwriter friend of mine said recently. But it isn't the only way to open compellingly. Here are others.

THE ANALOGY

We know John F. Kennedy's 1962 speech on space exploration at Rice University for one line. But there are imaginative things throughout, including its opening, where after a joke and his praise quoted earlier in the chapter, he uses this analogy between the long stretch of human history and a fifty-year version. His purpose: give listeners a sense that what he urges—putting a man on the moon—places them squarely in the accelerating and beneficial string of human achievement:

AS DELIVERED

JFK at Rice University. Does this opening, similar to leads in popular science magazines, work here? If so, why? Why should condensing the span of human knowledge to fifty years compel attention? And what does finishing just before midnight add to Kennedy's eventual message?

http://college.cqpress.com/politicalspeech

[C]ondense, if you will, the fifty thousand years of man's recorded history in a time span of but a half a century. Stated in these terms, we know very little about the first forty years, except at the end of them advanced man had learned to use the skins of animals to cover them. Then about ten years ago, under this standard, man emerged from his caves to construct other kinds of shelter. Only five years ago man learned to write and use a cart with wheels. Christianity began less than two years ago. The printing press came this year.

And then less than two months ago, during this whole fifty-year span of human history, the steam engine provided a new source of power. Newton explored the meaning of gravity. Last month, electric lights and telephones and automobiles and airplanes became available. Only last week did we develop penicillin and television and nuclear power.

And now if America's new spacecraft succeeds in reaching Venus, we will have literally reached the stars before midnight tonight.

THE QUOTE

Floor speeches often limit speakers to a minute or two. But even in a few seconds, a brief quote—in this case, a headline—can attract attention, as in this 1991 speech by the Democratic majority whip, David Bonior. No opening joke. No praise. Bonior goes right into his serious attention-getter:

> Mr. Speaker, a top White House aide says that George Bush does not need to pay attention to the home front because, there is not, and I quote, "anything that can be done right now."
>
> Nothing to be done?
>
> Let me read a few headlines: "Economic ills." "Economy weaker." "Economy absolutely stalled."
>
> Nothing to be done?

THE EXAMPLE

Sometimes, politicians can startle audiences simply by letting them see their private feelings. To most people, politicians exist in a world of wealth and power. They find hearing a president wish he wasn't so walled off from them incredibly appealing. Making that believable, though, takes skill. Here's how Peggy Noonan used concretely detailed examples to make Ronald Reagan believable in the opening to his farewell address. First, she has him confess to a longing to connect with people he sees from a distance. Then she has him attempt to make that connection by describing examples from his daily life:

> One of the things about the presidency is that you're always somewhat apart. You spend a lot of time going by too fast in a car someone else is driving, and seeing the people through tinted glass—the parents holding up a child, and the wave you saw too late and couldn't return. And so many times I wanted to stop and reach out from behind the glass, and connect.
>
> Well, maybe I can do a little of that tonight. . . .
>
> You know, down the hall and up the stairs from this office is the part of the White House where the president and his family live. There are a few favorite windows I have up there that I like

AS DELIVERED

Ronald Reagan's Farewell Address. What details in this opening make you believe Reagan is telling the truth? Does it matter if he is? Is there anything in this passage about the frustration of public life that you can apply for people holding smaller offices?

http://college.cqpress.com/politicalspeech

to stand and look out of early in the morning. The view is over the grounds here to the Washington Monument, and then the Mall and the Jefferson Memorial. But on mornings when the humidity is low you can see past the Jefferson to the river, the Potomac, and the Virginia shore. Someone said that's the view Lincoln had when he saw the smoke rising from the Battle of Bull Run. I see more prosaic things: the grass on the banks, the morning traffic as people make their way to work, now and then a sailboat on the river.

I've been thinking a bit at that window. I've been reflecting on what the past eight years have meant and mean.

I've been in those motorcades—you do notice people staring, and wonder about their lives, and wish you could talk to them. Noonan accomplishes that by being concrete. She doesn't write "Lincoln looked out of this window" but "that's the view Lincoln had when he saw the smoke rising from the Battle of Bull Run." She doesn't just write "I see more prosaic things," but lists things the audience can see—grass, traffic, a sailboat.

Did Reagan really do what he said in the speech? Who knows? It doesn't matter. Noonan shows us a public figure in a way most people never see—rich with detail. The effect is startling, and yes, compelling.

It should be obvious that while this chapter treats the openings of political speeches as if they begin in the same unvarying way, not every speech should. As we've already seen, John Edwards opens with a dramatic question, then a montage-like series of concrete details, and no story. Reagan's farewell doesn't include a joke, and doesn't need one. Bonior's one-minute speech begins with a headline and a sarcastic rhetorical question. I don't urge you to begin every speech in the same way. I'd like you to see the elements that make beginnings effective, then choose whether to use one or all, and in what order.

And then, having caught the audience's attention, speakers must lay out their roadmap for what's ahead. Skillful political speeches do that economically. But that tiny portion of the speech makes an incredible difference to listeners. Because without some warning of what's ahead, listeners—like motorists—may find themselves hopelessly lost.

STATEMENT OF PURPOSE

Listeners should remember the jokes and moving story in Arnold Schwarzenegger's opening speech at the 2004 Republican National Convention. How many would remember this one, thirty-six-word sentence that comes next?

Tonight, I want to talk to you about why I'm even more proud to be an American—why I am proud to be a Republican, and why I believe that this country is in good hands.

Not many. But this "statement of purpose" affected them, nevertheless. Schwarzenegger had provided them the rhetorical equivalent of MapQuest. Telling the audience what lies ahead is even more important in a speech than in, say, an op-ed. Why? Not just because—as this book emphasizes—listeners can't reread.

The reason goes to the heart of what most political speech is about: policy. Political speakers detail problems, outline solutions—and ask for support. What rhetoric books call the central idea, or thesis statement (*Switch grass is an often overlooked way to make the United States less dependent on foreign oil*) becomes far too narrow for the journey that lies ahead. Like the warnings you get from that wonderful woman living inside your own personal GPS (*In two hundred feet turn left onto highway*), a statement of purpose (SOP) warns listeners of the various twists and turns in the rhetorical road ahead. Often, that means three elements common to many political speeches: what is wrong, what will solve it, and how the audience can help. In the real world of political speech, the statements of purpose differ. Here, for example, is the lead for George W. Bush's 2001 Shanghai speech. See how he moves from praise into his two-part SOP.

I can't tell you what a startling difference it is—Shanghai is today than what it was in 1975. It's a great testimony to the Chinese people and the leadership of Shanghai. . . . — Praise

I also want to say that I'm proud to be accompanied by our great secretary of state who is doing such a fantastic job for the United States of America, Colin Powell. — Praise for self; indirect, because Powell works for him

We meet today with recent memories of great evil—yet great hope for this region and its future. — SOP: preview theme

Bush does not spell out what the evil is, or why he has hope for Shanghai's future. But the listener now knows to watch out for both themes. He's given them his roadmap for what's ahead. They know he's about to enter the on-ramp leading to the main road.

So are we, in this journey that may not be quite as dangerous as Shackleton's but at least promises honor in case of success.

The Speechwriter's Checklist: Beginnings

☐ Do I win attention from the very first sentence?

☐ Do I build goodwill by praising the audience? Is the praise offered for shared beliefs, accomplishments, and personal virtues?

☐ Do I fully preview what's ahead?

☐ Do I acknowledge the minimum of people and try sprinkling them throughout the speech?

☐ Do I use wit that characterizes my speaker in an appealing way?

☐ Is my speaker credible by demonstrating personal connection to the audience and its issues?

☐ Will my speaker demonstrate a sense of humor?

☐ Is my speaker likable?

☐ Is my opening story one that is gripping—and relevant to the audience's issues? If I didn't use an opening story—is there a compelling need for one?

☐ Do I quote people who are not only famous but intrinsically memorable?

Presenting the Problem

They met early in Philadelphia, early in June 1776, and the first order of business was deciding who should write the damn thing.

"You should do it," Thomas Jefferson said.

"I will not," John Adams said.

"Why?"

"Reasons enough."

"What can be your reasons?"

"I am obnoxious, suspected and unpopular. [And] you can write ten times better than I can."[1]

That's how Adams remembered the conversation as an old man, writing it down in a letter to Timothy Pickering almost fifty years afterwards. But if he didn't get the words they spoke exactly right, there's no question about his reaction a few weeks after that conversation, once Jefferson finished the final draft of what they would call the "Declaration of Independence." Adams loved it. "I was delighted with its high tone and the flights of oratory with which it abounded," he wrote.[2]

He admitted one reservation, though. Jefferson had characterized King George as a tyrant. "I thought this too personal," Adams wrote, "for I never believed George to be a tyrant in disposition and in nature; I always believed him to be deceived by his courtiers on both sides of the Atlantic, and in his official capacity, only, cruel."[3] But Adams never objected. He accepted the idea that persists to this day, that in politics it's sometimes necessary to caricature the other side. The Continental Congress approved Jefferson's draft of the document we now see only under glass, and which among other things contains the most famous example of what we discuss in this section—a list of problems, presented as litany:

> He has obstructed the Administration of Justice, by refusing his Assent to Laws for establishing Judiciary powers.
>
> He has made Judges dependent on his Will alone, for the tenure of their offices and the amount and payment of their salaries.

He has erected a multitude of New Offices, and sent hither swarms of Officers to harass our people, and eat out their substance. . . .

The language of the Declaration isn't what audiences today would call colloquial. But remember: it was primarily meant to be read. Whether for readers or listeners, the litany of complaints Jefferson found necessary to rouse the populace in 1776 is just as necessary today.

Naturally, litany isn't the only way to describe problems. But by now in this book it should be clear that presenting a list whose sentences march along in parallel construction, one after the other, allows speakers to be forceful. That's true even when it's done badly; bland abstractions still win applause lines. Some crowds will cheer anything.

When done well, though, a litany of problems—or *challenges,* as politicians often prefer to call them, with its implication that they are solvable—can arouse anger, fear, sadness, hope for solutions, and the urge to act.

STRATEGY

Well, either you're closing your eyes
To a situation you do not wish to acknowledge
Or you are not aware of the caliber of disaster indicated
By the presence of a pool table in your community.
Ya got trouble, my friend, right here,
I say, trouble right here in River City.
Trouble with a capital "T,"
And that rhymes with "P" and that stands for pool![4]

In politics we talk about problems for the same reason Harold Hill in *The Music Man* did: to alert listeners so they'll take action, usually one costlier than a boy's band.

For listeners already aware of the problems they face, politicians reaffirm their views; for those who don't know, they alarm them. But as we've already discussed, politicians can't stop there. Making people aware of the caliber of disaster is only the motivating prelude to getting involved.

As speakers outline problems, each of the elements we've reviewed plays a different role. Concrete detail, litany, and imagery make points memorable; anecdote humanizes them; wit, and often sarcasm, allows people to feel united in their hostility to the other side; and the various ways speechwriters use evidence can turn mildly partisan listeners into followers.

In this chapter we look at how strategic needs fuse with each element to make this part of political speech effective, beginning with decisions about three things: how to define the problem, how to contrast problem and solution, and how to find the clincher—the line that makes audiences clap, cheer, and remember.

ISSUE OR CULPRIT: DEFINING THE PROBLEM

Is it global warming? Or an obstructionist president who refuses to sign the Kyoto Protocol? High crime rates? Or liberal judges who let criminals go free?

All policy speeches are driven by issues. But in campaigns, or before highly partisan crowds, politicians identify a culprit: often—though not always—the other party, candidate, or administration. Since Democrats and Republicans differ over many issues, politically driven speeches use what you might call the *one-person/many issues* litany, attacking one opponent by listing the many bad policies he or she favors. When Sarah Palin took the stage to accept her 2008 vice presidential nomination, she attacked one person—Barack Obama—with this "he wants" litany:

> Victory in Iraq is finally in sight and he wants to forfeit. Terrorist states are seeking nuclear weapons without delay; he wants to meet them without preconditions. Al Qaeda terrorists still plot to inflict catastrophic harm on America and he's worried that someone won't read 'em their rights?
>
> Government is too big. He wants to grow it. Congress spends too much money. He promises more. Taxes are too high and he wants to raise them.

Most political speeches, though, are not so partisan. Politicians speak before plenty of audiences who consider themselves primarily *issue-driven*. A month before Palin's speech Obama went to speak in Berlin, hoping to demonstrate the kind of broad global vision that voters want in someone who might become president. He used many examples to illustrate a single problem: that events in one country can cause problems thousands of miles away, what you might call the *one issue/many examples* litany:

> The terrorists of September 11th plotted in Hamburg and trained in Kandahar and Karachi before killing thousands from all over the globe on American soil. . . .
>
> Poorly secured nuclear material in the former Soviet Union or secrets from a scientist in Pakistan could help build a bomb that detonates in Paris. The poppies in Afghanistan become the heroin in Berlin. The poverty and violence in Somalia breeds the terror of tomorrow. The genocide in Darfur shames the conscience of us all.

But deciding whether the problem is issue or culprit only leads to a second dilemma. After all, many political speeches offer both problem and solution. How do you contrast them?

DIRECT OR DELAYED

In *direct contrast*, you compare problem and solution at each step. Here is one example from Democratic senator Zell Miller's controversial keynote speech at the 2004 Republican National Convention, where the problem was John Kerry's views and the solution, those of George W. Bush:

> John Kerry wants to re-fight yesterday's war. President Bush believes we have to fight today's war. . . .
>
> George W. Bush wants to grab terrorists by the throat and not let them go to get a better grip. From John Kerry, they get a "yes-no-maybe" bowl of mush. . . .

Direct contrast sharpens the differences between candidates in political speech. In issue-driven speeches it lets the audience know right away that speakers have solutions for each problem they raise.

Delayed contrast means listing all the problems right away, leaving solutions for later. In this example, also from Miller's speech, the Georgia Democrat is criticizing the Democratic Party. Here he simply lists the errors of its ways, one after the other, making no attempt to offer the right views:

> They don't believe there's any real danger in the world except that which America brings upon itself through our clumsy and misguided foreign policy. . . .
>
> They claimed Carter's pacifism would lead to peace—they were wrong.
>
> They claimed Reagan's defense buildup would lead to war. They were wrong.
>
> And no pair has been more wrong, more loudly, more often than the two senators from Massachusetts, Ted Kennedy and John Kerry.

As the examples pile up, delayed contrast makes listeners feel either that the other side has been wrong a monumental number of times or, in issue-driven speeches, that the problem is cropping up everywhere.

FINDING THE CLINCHER

It's possible to simply list complaints, and plenty of politicians do. It's not the best way, though. To prompt applause, the most effective problem sections use a litany of climactic order, finishing with a *clincher* more memorable than what has preceded it. Here is an example from Democratic vice presidential nominee Geraldine Ferraro, running in 1984:

> Ronald Reagan visited a black family . . . but dragged his feet on the Voting Rights Act.
>
> Ronald Reagan plans to dedicate a monument to the great nature photographer, Ansel Adams. But in environmental affairs worked against everything Ansel Adams loved.
>
> I want an administration that takes polluters to court, not out to lunch.

Ferraro uses antithesis three times. Her last one, though, points to a solution—leading gracefully into the applause that followed.

It's useful to know those different ways to construct a problem section, in the same way a carpenter needs to know the different hammers or drill bits. But structure isn't the only area that offers options. Next, we'll look at others: the language we use, the stories we tell, the jokes we include, and the support we offer.

LANGUAGE

Language plays several different roles in talking about problems. Naturally, using litany with clauses or sentences in parallel construction allows speakers to be forceful. Showing example after example of problems, especially if done concretely, makes audiences see problems as urgent.

But there are subtle differences in the ways you can use the same devices. Note in the examples that follow how repetition at the end allows you to do different things than repetition at the beginning—for example, the way Sojourner Truth's final sentence comments on what had gone on before.

Rhetorical questions also add power to problem litanies. And finally, note how imagery, similes, or antithesis can sum up a passage, making the audience eager to applaud.

REPETITION AT THE BEGINNING

Repetition at the beginning may be the most common kind of problem litany. As you've already seen, it emphasizes similarity. In 1995 Hillary Clinton, then first lady, wanted to make the point that abusing women was not just a problem for women but for everyone. (Read more about that in this chapter's Behind the Scenes section.)

Examine how she links that opening repetition to seven different examples of abuse. The mounting effect of repetition ("It is a violation of human rights when . . .") coupled with suspense, as listeners wonder which horrific example comes next, allows her to build until the end. There, using *antimetabole*, the reverse order we examined in chapter 7, she draws the conclusion that—as speechwriter Lissa Muscatine describes—made the speech memorable. An excerpt:

> It is a violation of *human* rights when a leading cause of death worldwide among women ages fourteen to forty-four is the violence they are subjected to in their own homes by their own relatives.
>
> It is a violation of *human* rights when young girls are brutalized by the painful and degrading practice of genital mutilation.
>
> It is a violation of *human* rights when women are denied the right to plan their own families, and that includes being forced to have abortions or being sterilized against their will.

If there is one message that echoes forth from this conference, let it be that human rights are women's rights and women's rights are human rights once and for *all.*

REPETITION AT THE END

You've already seen one classic use of repetition, or epistrophe—Ted Kennedy's 1980 convention speech, discussed in chapter 7. Just as you often save your most important points for the end, as in climactic order, epistrophe allows speakers to comment on the examples they've used. Here, abolitionist and former slave Sojourner Truth, in an 1851 speech sometimes disputed for authenticity, uses it after each example to rebuke those who think women aren't as capable of working hard and enduring pain as men:

> That man over there says that women need to be helped into carriages, and lifted over ditches, and to have the best place everywhere. Nobody ever helps me into carriages, or over mud-puddles, or gives me any best place! And ain't I a woman?
>
> Look at me! Look at my arm! I have ploughed and planted, and gathered into barns, and no man could head me! And ain't I a woman?
>
> I could work as much and eat as much as a man—when I could get it—and bear the lash as well! And ain't I a woman?
>
> I have borne thirteen children, and seen most all sold off to slavery, and when I cried out with my mother's grief, none but Jesus heard me! And ain't I a woman?[5]

ANTITHESIS

Antithesis can use contrast to make audiences mad. Here, former Clinton official Robert Mallett contrasts treatment of those with wealth with those who have none to remind a left-leaning think-tank audience what has angered them about the Bush administration. Each antithesis drives home the contrast between helping the rich and neglecting the poor. Mallett uses antithesis again in his broadening clincher, a generalization earned by the concrete detail he has used so far:

> But you cannot tell me that we can spend $700 billion only when Fannie Mae and Lehman Brothers are going under—and can't afford to insure the forty-five million Americans who don't have health care.
>
> You cannot tell me we can only help the companies who devised risky subprime mortgage schemes—and not the millions of families who face foreclosure because of them.

> You cannot tell me we can spend three trillion dollars on a war in Iraq, and cannot wage war on illiteracy in the crumbling schools in Detroit, or Cleveland, or Washington, D.C. . . .
>
> You cannot tell me that we must spend so much wealth on the wealthy—and so little on those who worked to create it.

CONCRETE DETAIL

To interest audiences, provide shock of recognition, and evoke anger, be concrete. At the National Press Club in 2003, activist actor Tim Robbins had a strategic need: evoke sympathy for victims and anger at the intolerant. He used a litany of concrete detail (marred by too much passive voice) in this series of five brief examples illustrating his belief that harassment of those against the war in Iraq is no isolated phenomenon:

> A teacher . . . is fired for wearing a T-shirt with a peace sign on it. And a friend of the family tells of listening to the radio down South as the talk radio host calls for the murder of a prominent anti-war activist. Death threats have appeared on other prominent anti-war activists' doorsteps for their views. Relatives of ours have received threatening e-mails and phone calls. And my thirteen-year-old boy, who has done nothing to anybody, has recently been embarrassed and humiliated by a sadistic creep who writes—or rather scratches his column in the dirt.[6]

RHETORICAL QUESTION

In 2000, Alliance for Justice president Nan Aron used this litany of questions about who speaks for the powerless not simply to list injustices, but to praise this audience of nonprofit officers who lobby to be the spokespeople she describes. They don't have to answer her questions. Mentally, they should be thinking at the end of each sentence: *We do!*

> When there are those who would cut school lunch programs, who is there to speak for those children sitting in the cafeteria?
>
> When the corporate lobbyists are working to end affirmative action, who is there to speak for African Americans, Hispanics, Native Americans—who need a break?
>
> When there are those who lobby to curb federal legal services, who is there to speak for those who are at the mercy of a slumlord . . . or who can't afford a divorce?

CLIMACTIC ORDER

Republican presidential candidate Mitt Romney rebuts the other side's denial of a problem by pointing to those who have suffered from it. His 2007 "Tell

BEHIND THE SCENES

Lissa Muscatine

It was a diplomatic minefield.

First Lady Hillary Clinton had agreed to give the keynote speech at the 1995 UN World Conference on Women in Beijing. In June, however, China arrested an American human rights activist named Harry Wu as he entered China with a valid visa. "The left and right were united," Lissa Muscatine remembers. "They didn't want her to go."

After fifteen years as a reporter, Muscatine had gone to work for both Clintons as a speechwriter. She received firsthand experience on the first lady's views of women's rights: she'd been offered the job just after learning she was pregnant—with twins—and called the Clinton office to tell them she understood if they didn't want to hire someone in her situation.

Clinton had other ideas, though. If the White House couldn't have a workplace friendly to women, she told her staff, who could? They gave her help so she could work at home during the last six weeks of pregnancy, then extended maternity leave until she could return to work.

By 1995, Muscatine had spent so much time with Clinton she knew what the first lady wanted to say about women's rights in Beijing: that the world could not make progress when half the population was denied the same rights as the other half. But now it was unclear whether or not there would even be a speech in Beijing. Muscatine couldn't wait for an answer. She set to work.

She knew how it should open: "Simple, direct, evocative in examples. Tactile," Muscatine remembers. She wanted to find images from every continent—images concrete enough for the audience to think they were unique yet recognize they were universal. "When people heard about women in Indochina, [they'd] say, 'That's not me, but I get it.'"

She knew she had to stress Clinton's view that women's rights were in no way separate from other issues about social justice. Listing problems in an early draft, Muscatine added the line: "Human rights are women's rights, and women's rights are human rights."

For weeks, the debate about whether Clinton should go went back and forth. But then, China decided to expel Wu. The trip was on.

that" litany begins with small, faraway countries; moves to Europe; and then finishes with the most important locations of all: cities attacked recently, or during 9/11. But look how much it adds for him to say not "The people of Indonesia know that," but "Tell that. . . ." He expresses anger, characterizing himself as someone who doesn't just see injustice but is passionate about ending it:

> John Edwards says there is no War on Terror—it's just a bumper sticker.
> Tell that to the people of Indonesia, Malaysia, and Bali.

On a military plane travelling from Andrews Air Force Base to Hawaii, Muscatine worked on the draft. She met the Clintons there, where Bill Clinton critiqued it. Then she went with Hillary to Beijing. Helped by both Clintons, then–UN ambassador Madeleine Albright, and other staffers, she worked throughout the nine-hour flight. By the time they touched down, Clinton was happy with the speech.

Clinton's memoir describes the reaction in Beijing: a standing ovation; the delegates rushing up to thank her or "grab her hand"; the *New York Times* editorial calling it "her finest moment in public life"; and maybe the greatest compliment of all: China's blackout of her speech from the conference broadcast.[a]

Muscatine, though too modest to talk about the speech's reception, does mention with surprise the way the litany that included her one line would take on iconic status: "Women still come up to [Clinton] with copies of the speech, saying 'women's right are human rights, human rights are women's rights.'"

After an eight-year hiatus from speechwriting, Muscatine now sits in a State Department office, again writing speeches for now–Secretary of State Clinton. This time Muscatine has a staff, which she trains to understand the special needs of foreign policy. "If you're working for someone interested in substance, that's not something speechwriters do by themselves," she says. "You have to drill down to really know these issues. You have to work with others. And you have to understand how to make these issues emotional. Challenging."

She has no doubt about her boss's interest in "substance." Remembering that 1995 ride over the Pacific, she describes printing out her final draft, somewhere between Guam and Beijing.

"Almost everyone was asleep on the plane," she says. "It was one of those moments where all the lights are out except yours." But Clinton was awake. "I went up and handed it to her. She said, 'I just want to push the envelope as far as I can on women's rights.' I was *so* proud," says Muscatine, remembering the diplomatic minefield she helped Clinton travel—as she prepares for the minefields ahead.

Source: Lissa Muscatine spoke with Robert A. Lehrman in April 2009.

a. Hillary Rodham Clinton, *Living History* (New York: Simon and Schuster, 2004).

Tell that to the people of Tanzania, Kenya, and Spain.

Tell that to the people of London, Washington, and New York City!

ANECDOTE

No matter how many litanies of brief examples and cleverly chosen statistics speakers use, there is no substitute for story. Anecdotes can move audiences the way no other element can. Note in this section how choosing different kinds of stories to illustrate problems produces different effects.

PERSONAL

The problem: terrorism. At the 2004 Republican National Convention, former New York mayor Rudolph Giuliani uses a personal story, not just to dramatize his speech but to increase his credibility. He breaks the rule of short sentences, without losing a thing. He's not certain what floor the person was on, or how long it took. He makes no attempt to hide his lack of knowledge. He ends by repeating the same thing twice in different words. The lack of polish adds to the authenticity, making it clear he is still stunned by the events he witnessed on 9/11:

> On that day, we had to confront reality. For me, when I arrived there and I stood below the North Tower [of the World Trade Center], and I looked up, and seeing the flames of hell emanating from those buildings, and realizing that what I was actually seeing was a human being on the 101st, 102nd floor that was jumping out of the building, I stood there—it probably took five or six seconds; it seemed to me that it took twenty or thirty minutes—and I was stunned and I realized, in that moment, in that instant, I realized we were facing something that we had never, ever faced before. We had never been confronted by anything like this before.

DRAMATIC

In this 1986 speech, Democratic representative Dick Gephardt uses varied evidence—a stat, a brief example, and then a story from a Jonathan Kozol book on literacy. Notice how he gives the story room at the end to move his audience. To close with the stat would have destroyed the emotional impact and made him seem cold-blooded.

> Twenty-five million American adults cannot read the poison warnings on a can of pesticide.
>
> [But] it is the stories of people in Kozol's book that have remained with me more than the figures.
>
> Of the New Yorker, for example, who buys a *New York Times* every day and keeps it folded neatly next to his desk at work to hide the fact that he can't read it.
>
> Or the woman talking about her son and whether it matters to be illiterate. "Donny wanted me to read to him," she said. "I tried it one day, reading from pictures. Donny looked at me. He said, 'Mommy, that's not right.' He's only five. He knew I couldn't read."
>
> Oh, it matters.

HISTORICAL

Often, political rhetoric tries to demonize the other side. But look at Elie Wiesel become more credible with this "tale" illustrating the problem of indifference we examined earlier. Here he provides an example of Franklin Roosevelt, a figure admired by his audience, to acknowledge the goodness in those who are guilty of it:

> The depressing tale of the *St. Louis* is a case in point. Sixty years ago, its human cargo—nearly 1,000 Jews—was turned back to Nazi Germany. And that happened after *Kristallnacht*, the first state-sponsored pogrom, with hundreds of Jewish shops destroyed, synagogues burned, thousands of people put in concentration camps. And that ship, which was already in the shores of the United States, was sent back. I don't understand. Roosevelt was a good man, with a heart. He understood those who needed help. Why didn't he allow these refugees to disembark? A thousand people—in America, the great country, the greatest democracy, the most generous of all new nations in modern history. What happened? I don't understand. Why the indifference, on the highest level, to the suffering of the victims?[7]

WIT

It's rare in politics to use long story-jokes amid problem sections. More common are the quip, aside, quote, analogy, or very short story-joke. Politicians use them to poke fun at the other side—or at themselves to appear likable. In campaigns they use sarcasm, hyperbole, and other devices to caricature opponents.

QUIPS

Some of the cleverest lines from the 2008 presidential election came from Mike Huckabee's speech at the Republican National Convention. See, for example, his section on the *problem* with Democrats, particularly his rebuttal of the Democrats' caricature of his party, where this minister and hero of the religious right makes himself seem human to mainstream voters by admitting (gasp!) that Elvis might have been more important than Jesus. And note how effectively he surprises with a punch line in his last five words, especially by the gentling touch of that nicely placed "necessarily."

> Now, I get a little tired of hearing how the Democrats care so much for the working guy, as if all Republicans grew up with silk stockings and silver spoons. You see, in my hometown of Hope, Arkansas, the three sacred heroes were Jesus, Elvis, and FDR, not necessarily in that order.

ASIDES

In his 2007 State of the Union address, George W. Bush only needed six words to get a laugh from a crowd of friends and fierce enemies. He acknowledges a *problem:* that both sides indulge in secrecy. He lightens the tone, since the culprits are in his audience; characterizes himself as one who can see humor in serious situations; and makes listeners remember his point:

> Next, there is the matter of earmarks. These special interest items are often slipped into bills at the last hour—when not even C-SPAN is watching.

SUPPORT

I never tire of pointing out that there actually are people in political audiences who listen hard and evaluate evidence. But in the following excerpts, note that speakers don't just provide brief and extended examples, or testimony, or numbers. They combine them imaginatively with tools of language and structure.

BRIEF EXAMPLE

Ronald Reagan's 1987 "Tear down this wall" speech uses dramatic examples that Reagan organizes by geography. Why geography? Because of Reagan's strategic need: to demonstrate how all of Germany suffered.

But note how other devices make this passage effective. His writers use climactic order—Reagan's final example is Berlin, where the speech takes place. They infuse it with concrete detail (the "gash of barbed wire"); invert traditional grammar ("Behind me stands a wall"); and provide metaphor in paragraph four and in his simple final line. These ingredients work together in a way no formula can provide.

> Behind me stands a wall that encircles the free sectors of this city, part of a vast system of barriers that divides the entire continent of Europe.
>
> From the Baltic South, those barriers cut across Germany in a gash of barbed wire, concrete, dog runs, and guard towers.
>
> Farther south, there may be no visible, no obvious wall. But there remain armed guards and checkpoints all the same—still a restriction on the right to travel, still an instrument to impose upon ordinary men and women the will of a totalitarian state.
>
> Yet, it is here in Berlin where the wall emerges most clearly; here, cutting across your city, where the news photo and the television screen have imprinted this brutal division of a continent upon the mind of the world.
>
> Standing before the Brandenburg Gate, every man is a German separated from his fellow men.
>
> Every man is a Berliner, forced to look upon a scar.

EXTENDED EXAMPLE

Extended example often means anecdote. Here's one that's not. Sometimes speakers shy away from too much detail about one example, but staying on one for a while can give the audience time to see what you're talking about. When Rep. Duncan Hunter, R-Calif., talked to the Conservative Action Conference in March 2007, he used a single object—his podium—to illustrate the many problems disturbing him about the Chinese economy. Look closely to see how cleverly he uses a variant of the "And there's more!" structure of TV hucksters. Also study how he puts a policy into dialogue, as if the Chinese government is a person. In the next chapter we'll look at how that can make complex ideas accessible to audiences.

> China is cheating on trade.
>
> And let me tell you how they're doing it.
>
> If this podium was made in China and exported to us here in the United States and it was $100 when it goes down to the water's edge to be exported to us, the government of China walks over and gives its exporter all their taxes back, something we can't do under the trade law we signed, incidentally. They give them back $17, all their VAT taxes. So the cost of this is now down to $83.
>
> When we send the same product over to them, they give us a bill for $17, thereby making us noncompetitive.
>
> And just to make sure that the Americans never win in a competition, they devalue their currency by 40 percent. And that means that if this product is sitting in a showroom floor somewhere around the world, and sitting next to it is a product made in China, it's the equivalent, and they're both tagged at $100 and somebody's trying to decide which one to buy, the Chinese government in effect walks by and says, "We just had a markdown in aisle 5. Our product is now $60. Won't you buy it over the American product?"

TESTIMONY

Of the many ways testimony helps in presenting problems—quoting opponents, citing experts, using the pithy words of others—this one becomes effective because of what surrounds it. Mary Fisher, an AIDS victim, uses the testimony of one victim of Nazism to persuade delegates to the 1992 Republican National Convention to confront the issue of her disease. Pastor Niemöller's quote is almost too well known to be effective, but by prefacing it with her own version she gives it force. Then she finishes with a two-sentence clincher that uses antithesis twice, the second made more effective by the chilling understatement of her final two words.

> Because I was not hemophiliac, I was not at risk. Because I was not gay, I was not at risk. Because I did not inject drugs, I was not at risk.

My father has devoted much of his lifetime guarding against another holocaust. He is part of the generation who heard Pastor Niemöller come out of the Nazi death camps to say, "They came after the Jews, and I was not a Jew, so, I did not protest. They came after the trade unionists, and I was not a trade unionist, so, I did not protest. Then they came after the Roman Catholics, and I was not a Roman Catholic, so, I did not protest. Then they came after me, and there was no one left to protest."

The lesson history teaches is this: If you believe you are safe, you are at risk. If you do not see this killer stalking your children, look again.

FACTS/STATISTICS

As you saw in chapter 10, never be content just to cite a number. In his 1988 Democratic National Convention speech, Jesse Jackson makes clear the urgency of what he believes are problems facing America with a litany that surrounds each number with context. He uses repetition ("I just want . . .") at the start of each step to demonstrate similarity—a lack of common sense. Then he uses antithesis to contrast what he considers foolish policies with the facts that demonstrate why.

I just want to take common sense to high places. We're spending $150 billion a year defending Europe and Japan forty-three years after the war is over.

I just want to take common sense to higher places. If we can bail out Europe and Japan, if we can bail out Continental Bank and Chrysler—and [Chrysler CEO Lee] Iacocca makes $8,000 an hour—we can bail out the family farmer.

I just want to make common sense. It does not make sense to close down 650,000 family farms in this country while importing food from abroad subsidized by the U.S. government.

FINAL WORDS

As we finish our chapter on presenting the problem, two caveats.

First, on the need for combinations. In the last few examples, you've seen how different techniques work together to make audiences see the urgency of problems. Only longer excerpts can make clear how many devices can work together in a short space. Isolating rhetorical techniques to see how they help present problems is a useful teaching convention. But in real life, they need to work together. Here's Ernie Green, for example, illustrating the problem of racism in his speech celebrating the fiftieth anniversary of *Brown v. Board of Education,* first mentioned in chapter 11. In one minute of text, he uses brief example, rhetorical question, balanced construction, and a quote, in a single litany:

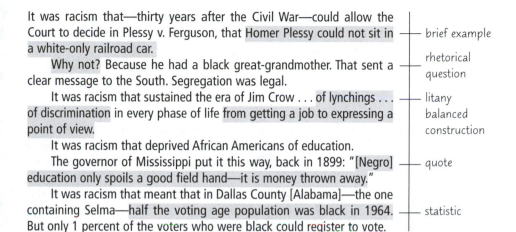

It was racism that—thirty years after the Civil War—could allow the Court to decide in Plessy v. Ferguson, that Homer Plessy could not sit in a white-only railroad car. — brief example

Why not? Because he had a black great-grandmother. That sent a clear message to the South. Segregation was legal. — rhetorical question

It was racism that sustained the era of Jim Crow . . . of lynchings . . . of discrimination in every phase of life from getting a job to expressing a point of view. — litany / balanced construction

It was racism that deprived African Americans of education.

The governor of Mississippi put it this way, back in 1899: "[Negro] education only spoils a good field hand—it is money thrown away." — quote

It was racism that meant that in Dallas County [Alabama]—the one containing Selma—half the voting age population was black in 1964. But only 1 percent of the voters who were black could register to vote. — statistic

Second, politics is not just, well, politics. There are times when politicians need to mount a substantive argument that makes few concessions to the audience. In the 2008 presidential campaign, Hillary Clinton decided to lay out her health care plan in detail. Here's a *very* brief section:

> We spend 16 percent of our gross domestic product—$2 trillion—on health care. And by 2016, health costs are scheduled to exceed $4 trillion, or almost 20 percent of GDP. That means that within less than ten years, 20 cents out of every dollar produced in America will be spent on health care. No other country spends more than 12 percent, a difference of more than $500 billion. All other wealthy countries spend even less. We spend $5,711 per patient. The next highest spending country, Switzerland, spends $3,847 on patients. Yet, they cover every single one of their citizens and have an average life expectancy that is three years longer than ours.
>
> Now, how have our costs spiraled out of control like this? Well, about 30 percent of the rise in health care spending is linked to the doubling of obesity among adults over the past twenty years. In other words, if our obesity levels had remained at 1990 levels, we would be spending 10 percent less on health care today—a savings of $220 billion. About two-thirds of the rise in health care spending is associated with a rise in the prevalence of treatable disease—like diabetes, asthma, and heart disease. Seventy-five percent of all health care spending—roughly $1.5 trillion—is associated with the 4 to 5 percent of patients who have multiple chronic illnesses and require ongoing medical management over a period of years, or even decades. And 10 to 12 percent of the total health care budget is spent on end of life care.

Her health care speeches were tough to follow, crammed with numbers, and loaded with passive voice (35 percent in this passage alone). She wasn't alone, either. Other candidates used similarly dense speeches and position papers to detail positions. They give the lie to those who think political speech must be free of substance.

Does it seem like a lot of work to find these different ways to talk about problems? Actually, the problem sections of political speeches are usually the easiest to write. After all, neither Democrats nor Republicans disagree on the existence of poverty, disease, unemployment, or war. (They do on others, like global warming.) It's when they propose solutions that arguments begin, especially when they detail solutions enough to make clear the role government would play or how much the solutions would cost. Still, that is what politicians must do.

It's no accident that in February 2009, as the members of the new administration settled into their new jobs, reporters described two of them in the following ways. First came a *Washington Post* profile of White House budget director Peter Orszag, quoting White House chief of staff Rahm Emanuel: "He doesn't come in and say, 'I've got a problem.' . . . He says, 'I've got a problem, and here's my idea for a solution.'"[8] Next came this headline about a more anonymous Obama staffer: "For Obama's Political Knots, He's the 'Fixer': Low-Profile Aide Jim Messina Has Tackled Tough Problems."[9]

When it comes to policies, the public expects politicians—helped by staff—to do more than outline problems. They are the fixers. Voters expect them to offer solutions.

This means that after racing through their problem litanies, politicians change pace. They may lower their voice, take a sip of water, and lean over the podium. Then, they may say something as simple as, "Terrible problems. How do we fix them?"

Let's see.

The Speechwriter's Checklist: Problems

- ☐ Have I described problems that are relevant to the audience?
- ☐ Have I used problems in the three ways that are useful in politics: reaffirming beliefs, alerting the audience, and motivating people?
- ☐ Have I made a conscious decision between direct and delayed contrast of problem and solution?
- ☐ Have I used clinchers for each issue?
- ☐ Have I made good use of litany?
- ☐ Have I described problems concretely?
- ☐ Are problems listed in climactic order?
- ☐ Are problems supported by varying evidence—including story, example, testimony, and fact?
- ☐ Was I able to find room for humor?

chapter **13**

Solutions

At one point in *What I Saw at the Revolution,* Peggy Noonan's interesting memoir about writing speeches for Ronald Reagan, she describes a "bureaucrat from State," assigned to work with the National Security Council on the annual economic summits. He would refer to himself and his colleagues as "we substantive types," and to the speechwriters as "you wordsmiths."

"He was saying," Noonan writes, "'we do policy and you dance around with the words.' We would smile back. Our smiles said, 'The dancer is the dance.'"[1]

That's an allusion to the William Butler Yeats poem that asks, "How can you tell the dancer from the dance?" But Yeats wasn't talking about the White House. The fact is, neither Noonan nor her bureaucrat needed to feel superior to the other. Policy people are not dull, plodding, or unimaginative, and it can certainly take as much imagination to fashion a welfare policy as a short story. Both she and the policy person were dancers. But Noonan was right to resent the "substantive types" for patronizing her—and right to mind something else about them: however creative their solutions or well-meaning their attempts, the language that policy people try to shoehorn into speeches tends to deaden them.

Well . . . of course. People with doctorates in economics have spent years thinking about economics. They're equipped to think up ideas, not package them for people with a seventh-grade reading level. But that doesn't mean they shouldn't try. They're right to care intensely about how speakers propose solutions, including the strategic decisions that govern the words you choose. Should you be confrontational or collegial? Do you want to appease your base or run to the middle? Should you sharpen your differences with the other side or soften them? Are you talking to supporters or appealing to the undecideds? Are you speaking to Americans in Idaho—or Muslims in Afghanistan? Those questions can be maddeningly uncertain for politicians and their staff, especially in campaigns. They shouldn't be left just to speechwriters.

Luckily, despite the detailed Hillary Clinton example we discussed at the end of chapter 12, speeches usually don't provide detailed solutions. In campaigns, candidates need to cover too many issues to do more than touch on them. In office, they can offer more detail during debates on the floor, or in keynotes to issue groups. But even then their speeches don't contain what anyone would confuse with groundbreaking substance.

In part, that is because, for most people, the detail of legislation is *dull,* which is why *The West Wing,* for all the seriousness with which it treated politics, rarely showed any of it. Aaron Sorkin's scripts had characters arguing out complex issues in a ten-second debate walking out of the Oval Office instead of the way they are in real life: through fifty-page memos, white papers, and six months of grindingly dull negotiations.

But that's not the only reason. Another is that most political speeches are too short for much detail; a keynote speech to, say, the Council on Foreign Relations may run twenty minutes and involve several issues. That leaves little room for outlining a *solution* in any detail. As I write this, I have on my desk Barack Obama's massive, 7,400-word 2009 speech on health care to the American Medical Association (AMA). Fidel Castro no longer gives speeches that long. But even for the AMA, Obama can only give a few paragraphs to issues about which people write books.

And if length were no obstacle, Obama wouldn't have enough knowledge to do more than read material he didn't really know. Despite the ease with which the word "expertise" is bandied about, most politicians are generalists. The chairs of Senate Foreign Relations committees aren't experts when it comes to foreign policy. Traditionally, they've been lawyers with an interest in the area. Those writing their speeches, usually staff aides in their twenties, are very smart, but hardly people likely to create truly substantive material.

Finally, political life itself works against candor and nuance. Truly nuanced discussion involves careful consideration of the most sophisticated arguments of the other side, of points where the other side may be right, of uncertainty, and of one's own mistakes. No politician can do that in public, especially since solutions are often the results of compromise, supported by a coalition of interests. It's uncomfortable sounding enthusiastic about every part of a bill when your real reason for supporting it is that half a loaf is better than none.

This isn't as dispiriting a picture as it seems. Audiences generally don't expect nuanced discussions from political speakers. Even somber audiences at think-tank panel discussions content themselves with a bare-bones outline with code words—timetable for withdrawal or single-payer—that tell them what they need to know. But it does mean that even when those in political life are experts, nuance is in short supply. The occasional long policy speech might devote only a few hundred words to argument, usually reflexively defensive of party positions.

Does that mean offering solutions in politics is a cynical business? No. Politicians believe in the policies that they offer—and so do their staffers. And since policy proposals basically offer solutions, it is for the solution part of a speech that they weigh most fervently. This creates an obstacle for speechwriters interested in writing well.

For example, Noonan's "substantive types" wanted their language accepted intact. This was my experience, too, especially in foreign policy. How many times in the White House did I round off a number, or change a sentence from "It is hoped" to "We hope," only to see the foreign policy aides shake their heads?

Well, that's not quite right.

What's not right?

We don't necessarily hope.

I thought we did.

Well, we do. But you can't say that. That locks us in.

Well, who's doing the hoping?

That's the thing. Say "It is hoped." Then nobody's locked in.

Diplomacy.

Right. Diplomacy.

I didn't like accepting passive voice. On the other hand, read through that typical—though made up—dialogue again. Policy wonks object to language not because they are insensitive clods with tin ears for grace—some are—but something more reassuring: they believe that diplomacy isn't necessarily a bad idea.

SOLUTIONS AND STRATEGY

The fact that speeches don't present solutions in all their complexity doesn't mean you avoid them. Even brief discussions carry weight in the charged atmosphere of political life where reporters comb through speeches looking for a single word that hints at something new.

In a few pages we'll look more closely at a variety of ways to present solutions responsibly without turning listeners off.

But before looking at how to write them, speakers and speechwriters need to decide how they think about them. By that, I don't mean what they think of the merits of a plan, but how they characterize themselves. Are they fighters or compromisers? Nerds or visionaries? Principled or practical? Because in politics the battle is so often about solutions, that decision has enormous ramifications.

CHARACTERIZING YOUR SPEAKER

Take the 2009 debate about health care that prompted President Obama's AMA speech. Let's say you're a member of Congress who favors "single-payer" health care—the proposal that government pay all the bills for an individual's health care. You might want listeners to know you'll battle for it. Or if you're pessimistic about the outcome, you might want to just say you believe in it. Or open the door to compromise. You might characterize yourself differently in 2009, depending on whether you were Democrat or Republican, talking to doctors or a union local, on the floor or back in the district.

Is this a tough decision? No. And you don't have an infinite number of choices. Usually, politicians pick from about five.

▶ **THE ACHIEVER:** *Present solutions by pledging the attempt to achieve them.*

Pledging to achieve specific things is risky; a year later people might ask why you haven't come through. But it signals boldness, and the will to stake your personal credibility, too. One famous example:

This much I swear to you—these things you shall have:

AS DELIVERED

Willie Stark's Speech, All the King's Men. How much of what Willie Stark says could a governor do today? Can you see him appealing to hope? Expressing humility? And finally, what in his speech could politicians not do?

http://college.cqpress.com/politicalspeech

I'm going to build a hospital, the biggest that money can buy, and it will belong to you. And any man, woman, or child who is sick or in pain can go through those doors and know that everything will be done for them that man can do: to heal sickness, to ease pain. Free!

Not as a charity, but as a right. And it is your right. Do you hear me? It is your right.

And it is your right that every child should have a complete education.

That any man who produces anything can take it to market without paying toll.

And no poor man's land or farm can be taxed or taken away from him.

And it is the right of the people that they shall not be deprived of hope.[2]

Okay, that one comes from a 1949 movie, *All the King's Men.*

The speaker: Gov. Willie Stark, played by Broderick Crawford. Films rarely include complete speeches, of course; no movie audience would stand for it. But movie speeches often offer ways to make speech sections interesting. Stark's use of repetition—and enlarging clincher—finds parallels in modern politics.

As they do in this example from real-life politics: the "pledge" section from John F. Kennedy's 1961 inaugural address. Kennedy segments his litany of promises by audience, beginning each section with "To those who," an often-imitated technique. In this two-sentence example he uses the repetition of "help" and two skillful examples of antithesis, including the memorable assertion of his "If" clincher.

> To those peoples in the huts and villages of half the globe struggling to break the bonds of mass misery, we pledge our best efforts to help them help themselves, for whatever period is required—not because the Communists may be doing it, not because we seek their votes, but because it is right. . . .
>
> If a free society cannot help the many who are poor, it cannot save the few who are rich.

AS DELIVERED

John F. Kennedy's Inaugural Address. Like Stark, Kennedy pledges as well, segmenting his audience and ending memorably. How do the speeches differ from each other? And while you're at this site, examine the excerpt on pages 196–97 of this chapter to see how Kennedy uses a "third way" approach to appeal to different audiences at once.

http://college.cqpress.com/politicalspeech

But also note what Kennedy actually promises: his "best efforts." In this way he differs from the fictional governor Stark. Politicians support, urge, call for, acknowledge need for, pledge to work toward—but they rarely promise immediate success ("These things you shall have"), and with good reason. Passing a bill—even introducing one—is too uncertain a proposition to warrant falling into that trap. Sports psychologists urge parents not to focus on winning because it's not something you can control. Rather, they say, focus on doing your best. It's not much different in politics.

▶ **THE BELIEVER:** *Present solutions as matters of belief the crowd shares.*

Sometimes you want to offer solutions without pledging anything, especially when you might lose. While Mike Huckabee did well in the February 5, 2008, "Super Tuesday" primary, he was still a long shot. His victory speech didn't promise success. He used a "we're here tonight" litany of solutions as a way of reminding supporters that the victory wasn't about him but the beliefs for which he was a voice.

> We're here tonight and winning states across the South because we've stood for the idea that mothers and fathers raise better kids than governments do. And government ought to undergird a family, not undermine a basic family's right to raise their own kids. . . .
>
> We're here tonight because people want to know that the president is going to secure our borders and make it so it's not more difficult to get on an airplane in your hometown than it is to cross the international border. . . .
>
> And we should uphold the sanctity of human life because it is a cornerstone of our culture of life.

And ladies and gentlemen, tonight I believe that one of the things you're seeing across the nation is that people are saying the conservatives do have a choice because the conservatives have a voice.

▶ **THE FIGHTER:** *For partisan crowds, make clear you'll fight for what's right.*

When the crowd is spoiling for a fight, speakers should present solutions as if they are, too. One way to do that: challenge the other side with a technique we haven't discussed so far. Apostrophe means speaking to the absent enemy. There are famous examples, among them "Mr. Gorbachev, tear down this wall." Here are two others. This time we'll open with another movie speech, Michael Douglas's in the 1995 hit *The American President.* Note his use of anaphora (repetition at the beginning of litany), rhetorical question, and sentence fragments. And afterwards, you will see another interesting example:

> America isn't easy. America is advanced citizenship. You've gotta want it bad, 'cause it's gonna put up a fight.
>
> It's gonna say, "You want free speech? Let's see you acknowledge a man whose words make your blood boil, who's standing center stage and advocating at the top of his lungs that which you would spend a lifetime opposing at the top of yours.
>
> You want to claim this land as the land of the free? Then the symbol of your country cannot just be a flag. The symbol also has to be one of its citizens exercising his right to burn that flag in protest."
>
> Now show me that, defend that, celebrate that in your class-rooms. Then you can stand up and sing about the land of the free.[3]

Too melodramatic for the real world of politics? Examine the often-cited but rarely quoted 2002 speech by the (then) obscure Illinois state senator Barack Obama, in which he impresses a fiercely antiwar crowd by addressing not it but the president. Note *his* use of anaphora, rhetorical question, and sentence fragments.

> So for those of us who seek a more just and secure world for our children, let us send a clear message to the president.
>
> You want a fight, President Bush? Let's finish the fight with Bin Laden and al-Qaeda, through effective, coordinated intelligence, and a shutting down of the financial networks that support terrorism, and a homeland security program that involves more than color-coded warnings.
>
> You want a fight, President Bush? Let's fight to make sure that . . . we vigorously enforce a nonproliferation treaty, and that former enemies and current allies like Russia safeguard and ultimately eliminate their stores of nuclear material, and that nations like Pakistan and India never use the terrible weapons already in their

possession, and that the arms merchants in our own country stop feeding the countless wars that rage across the globe.

You want a fight, President Bush? Let's fight to wean ourselves off Middle East oil through an energy policy that doesn't simply serve the interests of Exxon and Mobil.

Those are the battles that we need to fight. Those are the battles that we willingly join. The battles against ignorance and intolerance. Corruption and greed. Poverty and despair.

Did Obama consciously or unconsciously imitate Michael Douglas? Who knows? But this should remind you that in the search for models, you shouldn't be above looking to Hollywood.

▶ **THE HARMONIZER:** *Present solutions using ideas from both sides.*

"A communicator is likely to be perceived as more . . . trustworthy," writes persuasion expert Daniel O'Keefe, "if the advocated position disconfirms the audience's expectations about the communicator's views." One example he uses: "a lifelong Democrat speaking for a Republican candidate."[4]

This can mean Democrat Zell Miller speaking for George W. Bush at the 2004 Republican National Convention. It can also mean the strategy of John McCain when in 2008, with an unpopular Republican in the White House, he criticized his own party for "letting Washington change us." The solution he offered: bringing his own party "back to basics."

But confounding an audience's expectations doesn't mean just criticizing your own side. It can mean acknowledging that the other side's views have merit. That's why in 1996 Bill Clinton, under attack from the right, adopted policies that allowed him to be, as one aide put it, "more Republican than Republicans" about issues such as welfare reform, free trade, and tax cuts. In 2009, when Barack Obama gave his controversial commencement speech at the University of Notre Dame, the "pro-choice" president did something similar. Facing an audience that included many "pro-lifers," Obama offered solutions designed to reconcile, or harmonize, the two sides of one of the most bitter debates in American politics. Note how his last line, echoing Willie Stark ("These things you shall have"), differs from Stark in a way that points to the difference between politics in the movies and the more constrained politics of real life.

> When we open up our hearts and our minds to those who may not think precisely like we do or believe precisely what we believe—that's when we discover at least the possibility of common ground.
>
> That's when we begin to say, "Maybe we won't agree on abortion, but we can still agree that this heart-wrenching decision for any woman is not made casually, and it has both moral and spiritual dimensions."

So let us work together to reduce the number of women seeking abortions.

Let's reduce unintended pregnancies.

Let's make adoption more available.

Let's—Let's provide care and support for women who do carry their children to term.

Let's honor the conscience of those who disagree with abortion, and draft a sensible conscience clause, and make sure that all of our health care policies are grounded not only in sound science, but also in clear ethics, as well as respect for the equality of women.

Those are things we can do.

▶ **THE VISIONARY:** *Present solutions as vision of the future, allowing you to avoid commitment or timetable.*

Sometimes politicians want neither to promise nor to simply express solutions as beliefs. They want to inspire audiences with the vision of what might happen. They can't say "I have a dream"; that approach has been taken. But they can cast solutions as a kind of wish list. In this speech to the nonprofit youth organization Girls Inc., Hillary Clinton does that with a three-step "I would like to see" litany. It promises nothing, but it shows where her heart is.

But there is so much more we can do.

I would like to see us forgive portions of student loans for college students who volunteer as tutors and mentors for children in poor communities.

I would like to see us try to match every child in foster care, all five hundred thousand of them, with a responsible adult, starting with college students and giving those young people the reward of working with and serving someone else.

I would like to see us begin to do more through AmeriCorps and National Service to help young people navigate through school. We lose too many youngsters too early. By third grade, experienced teachers can tell us who's going to make it and who isn't. We need a little more support, we need a person, a real live person, to be there when someone falters or falls, to send the message that there are those of us behind you—come on, get up, you can keep going. . . .

People say to me all the time, "But isn't that expensive?" Yes, and so are the consequences of not providing that kind of launching pad for children who are otherwise going to be left out and left behind.

CREATING SOLUTIONS THAT INSPIRE

Here is how you don't inspire.

Trade brings better jobs and better choices and better prices. Yet for some Americans, trade can mean losing a job, and the federal government has a responsibility to help. I ask Congress to reauthorize and reform trade adjustment assistance, so we can help these displaced workers learn new skills and find new jobs.

From its impossible-to-disagree-with first line through its abstraction-laden call to action, this paragraph from President Bush's 2008 State of the Union address typifies what not to do. It isn't Bush or his writers' fault. The State of the Union, with its need to include dozens of solutions, inevitably produces boilerplate.

One reason is that even when politicians present solutions in the passive, polysyllabic voice of the bureaucracy, lightning doesn't strike. The speech ends, and people applaud. They even congratulate the speaker. But why settle for that? Solutions can be powerful, interesting, and applause-worthy—and not just the ritual applause of audiences conditioned to clap their hands when they hear "we must," but applause that comes spontaneously from—gasp!—genuine excitement.

In the next section we'll examine some ways to create excitement, first through language, then by using a format that allows you to combine that with story, wit, and support.

LANGUAGE

In solutions, litany should be your technique of default. Politicians urge solutions in litanies that use a variety of openings, all meeting slightly different strategic needs. They can set the tone even in the first two words.

- *To create urgency:* We should.
- *To create urgency:* We must, we need, or we should.
- *Something that can't wait:* Now is (the time).
- *For use after mentioning a problem:* That's why.
- *To evoke the need for partnership:* Let us.

One writer about campaign rhetoric suggests two other words: *if* and *then* (*If we do X . . . then Y will follow*), which can at least suggest why the plan is good.

But language achieves more than tone. Litany and concrete detail make speakers compelling. They persuade even when speakers offer little support for their solutions. That's the case in the following common approaches.

▶ **BETTER THAN WHAT WE HAVE:** *Use a "we can do better" litany—to suggest solutions.*

At the end of this February 2005 floor speech, Obama uses *repetition* and *concrete detail* to rebut supporters of the Bankruptcy Abuse and Prevention Act of 2005. He uses three concrete "we can do better" sentences about problems, then switches to a "we can give" clincher to offer his solution. His solution is vague, but he achieves impact by using repetition again—the two "you may" clauses in his clincher.

> But we can do better than one bankruptcy every nineteen seconds. We can do better than forcing people to choose between the cost of health care and the cost of college. We can do better than big corporations using bankruptcy laws to deny health care and benefits to their employees. And we can give people the basic tools and protections they need to believe that in America, your circumstance is no limit to the success you may achieve and the dreams you may fulfill.

▶ **BETTER THAN THE OTHER GUY:** *Use repetition at the end to contrast with the other side.*

In George H. W. Bush's 1988 acceptance speech, his clever litany directly contrasts his opponent's solutions to his own. Notice that Bush uses repetition at the end (epistrophe) to emphasize his view, not Michael Dukakis's. By ending with "I say yes," he insures the applause line.

> Should public school teachers be required to lead our children in the Pledge of Allegiance? My opponent says no—and I say yes.
> Should society be allowed to impose the death penalty on those who commit crimes of extraordinary cruelty and violence? My opponent says no—and I say yes.
> And should children have the right to say a voluntary prayer, or even observe a moment of silence in the schools? My opponent says no—and I say yes.

▶ **BETTER THAN DOING NOTHING:** *Use rhetorical questions not just to suggest solutions but to speak with passion.*

People remember this 1961 speech by Federal Communications Commission chair Newton Minow for one phrase—his assertion that TV is a "vast wasteland." But look how effectively he uses repetition. He recites a litany of rhetorical questions, great for sounding forceful, to outline solutions in this "fighter" speech challenging an audience of TV executives who have created the problem. By repeating "Is there no room" four times, Minow drives home his point: that there must be room for each solution. If listeners accept that, they will accept his call-to action clincher.

> What about your responsibilities? Is there no room on television to teach, to inform, to uplift, to stretch, to enlarge the capacities of our children? Is there no room for programs deepening their understanding of children in other lands? Is there no room for a children's news show explaining something to them about the world

at their level of understanding? Is there no room for reading the great literature of the past, for teaching them the great traditions of freedom? There are some fine children's shows, but they are drowned out in the massive doses of cartoons, violence, and more violence. Must these be your trademarks? Search your consciences and see if you cannot offer more to your young beneficiaries whose future you guide so many hours each and every day.

▶ **BETTER THAN WHAT WE'VE DONE:** *Combine "let us" with antithesis to suggest that your solutions apply to everyone.*

To say "Let us" implies partnership; it is a less arrogant way of presenting solutions or—the second way it's used—urging action. In this litany from his inaugural address, John F. Kennedy avoids blaming Russia, trying to pave the way for negotiation and suggesting that "both sides" have created problems. Note other language choices in these four sentences: antimetabole (the reversal of two words in their different meanings) and alliteration (the repetition of initial sounds in neighboring words or syllables). Kennedy uses both.

> So let us begin anew—remembering on both sides that civility is not a sign of weakness, and sincerity is always subject to proof. Let us never negotiate out of fear, but let us never fear to negotiate.
>
> Let both sides explore what problems unite us instead of belaboring those problems which divide us.
>
> Let both sides, for the first time, formulate serious and precise proposals for the inspection and control of arms. . . .
>
> Let both sides seek to invoke the wonders of science instead of its terrors.

To say a solution is better than nothing, or better than what we have, is not to demonstrate its worth. That doesn't make these statements meaningless; the audiences knew what Kennedy meant by "fear to negotiate," and what Minow meant by "reading the great literature."

But while this chapter has emphasized the limits on how much support politicians can provide for solutions, that doesn't mean they shouldn't offer some. It's perfectly possible to use evidence and some detail about how your solutions can work without being dull. Especially through a structure this book calls the Three Ps.

PROPOSAL, PERSUASION, PUNCH LINE: A STRUCTURE THAT WORKS

> We've got to do a better job of getting across that America is freedom—freedom of speech, freedom of religion.

So we've got to teach history based not on what's in fashion but what's important—why the Pilgrims came here, who Jimmy Doolittle was, and what those thirty seconds over Tokyo meant. You know, four years ago, on the fortieth anniversary of D-Day, I read a letter from a young woman writing to her late father, who'd fought on Omaha Beach. Her name was Lisa Canatta Henn, and she said, "We will always remember, we will never forget what the boys of Normandy did." Well, let's help her keep her word.

If we forget what we did, we won't know who we are.

What is Ronald Reagan—and his speechwriter, Peggy Noonan—up to in this section about two-thirds of the way through his farewell address? They are offering a solution to what the departing president saw as a problem with education: that Americans no longer learn patriotism from school and the popular culture the way they did in the past. What's his solution?

He offers a proposal, some persuasion, and a punch line: the Three Ps. After Reagan states his solution, he gives his listeners brief examples of how that would work, illustrates with a story and testimony, then closes with an idea that sums up his argument: that his solution will allow us to do something Americans value. All the techniques of language he uses, including colloquial language, repetition, and antithesis, fit within that useful framework. Let's examine the speech again—this time with the elements labeled.

	PROPOSAL:
Repetition and rule of three	We've got to do a better job of getting across that America is freedom—freedom of speech, freedom of religion.
	PERSUASION:
Antithesis	So we've got to teach history based not on what's in fashion
Concrete detail and rule of three	but what's important—why the Pilgrims came here, who Jimmy Doolittle was, and what those thirty seconds over Tokyo meant.
Anecdote/quote	You know, four years ago, on the fortieth anniversary of D day, I read a letter from a young woman writing to her late father, who'd fought on Omaha Beach. Her name was Lisa Canatta Henn, and she said, "We will always remember, we will
Antithesis and repetition	never forget what the boys of Normandy did."
Deliberately colloquial	Well, let's help her keep her word.
	PUNCH LINE:
Antithesis	If we forget what we did, we won't know who we are.

Like any structure, the Three Ps can be done well or miserably. Many elements work together to make this passage effective. Note its simplicity—of 122 words, 91 are one-syllable. Note, too, the way Reagan uses "You know" and "well" to create

AS DELIVERED

Ronald Reagan's Farewell Address. Though we haven't covered delivery yet, note how skillfully Reagan uses voice and tone to evoke emotion, particularly in the last line, where he shows his own emotion.

http://college.cqpress.com/politicalspeech

a nonstuffy persona, and the way he includes the woman's name, which persuades the audience that the letter he describes is real.

Do you only have time for such detail in Oval Office speeches? What about the highly partisan arena of a campaign? From the other side of the aisle, here's an example of a Three P solution in the more compressed, hyperbolic language of a rally—Al Gore at an August 2000 AFL-CIO convention in Iowa.

And the gun lobby doesn't have the right to play God with our safety. ——|—— Proposal

I come from a state of hunters. So do you. But you don't need .50 caliber sniper rifles . . . to hunt pheasant in an Iowa cornfield. There's a ——|—— Persuasion flood of guns in this country going to people who shouldn't have them and Republicans are protecting those who make it possible.

The gun lobby doesn't need more protection. . . . Families do. ——|—— Punch Line

Such an approach at least makes a stab at nuance, leads into an applause line, and can work for the statesmanlike approach of a president leaving office, or the partisan rally of a campaign.

What about a floor speech?

Here is John McCain, introducing a lobbying reform bill in 2005. McCain is the fighter here, calling for an end to "business as usual." He uses the Three P structure: a sarcastic proposal and a "they" litany of brief examples and metaphor, all leading to an "If-then" clincher.

The bill I am introducing today seeks to address business-as-usual in the ——|—— Proposal nation's capitol.

How these lobbyists sought to influence policy and opinion makers is a case study in the ways lobbyists seek to curry favor with legislators and their aides.

For example, they sought to ingratiate themselves with public ser- ——|—— Persuasion vants with tickets to plush skyboxes at the MCI Center, FedEx Field, and | with litany Camden Yards for sports and entertainment events. | of brief

They arranged extravagant getaways to tropical islands, the famed | examples golfing links of St. Andrews, and elsewhere.

Metaphor —————— |
Punch line —————— |

They regularly treated people to meals and drinks. Fund-raisers and contributions abounded.
This bill casts some disinfectant on those practices by simply requiring greater disclosure.
If there is nothing inherently wrong with such activities, then there is no good reason to hide them from public scrutiny.

The Three Ps approach works even in wonky, overdetailed substantive speech. Hillary Clinton's health care speech, again, is full of traditional support: statistics, background, brief personal example, story, and a punch line using antithesis. All help lift this section above boilerplate.

Proposal ——————

In a system of universal coverage insurance companies cannot as easily shift costs through cherry picking and other means.

Persuasion/statistic ——

In fact, according to a recent McKinsey report, insurance companies in America spend tens of billions a year figuring out how not to cover people—doing complicated calculations to figure out how to cherry pick the healthiest persons, and leave everyone else out in the cold.

Background ——————

That is how they profit: by avoiding insuring patients who will be "expensive"—and then trying to avoid paying up once the insured patient actually needs treatment.

Personal example ——

I see this all the time.

Story ——

For example, a father called me from northern New York—his son had a rare illness. Now he and his son were well insured. He'd worked for many years for the same employer who provided a good policy. But when his son needed a special operation—that could only be performed at one place in the country—the insurance company said, sorry, that's out of network, we're not going to send you to have that done.

So my office intervened. And in the end they got permission for the operation.

Punch line ——————

But I don't think people should have to go to their United States Senator to get their insurance company to give them what they've paid for.

SOLUTIONS: THE NEED FOR VARIETY

Let's be clear. The Three Ps are not the only way to make solutions effective. But variety is. Let's see how that works in two very different excerpts, one short, the other long.

In accepting the 2000 Reform Party nomination, commentator-columnist Pat Buchanan doesn't use evidence to support his proposal at all. His "plague-on-both-your-houses" approach mocks both major candidates, asserts his idea, then uses a six-word clincher. And, of course, his ridicule of George W. Bush is unfair—nobody who speaks in public all the time can avoid making silly mistakes. But look how many elements combine in this short section: *story,* then *apostrophe* to rebut his view with a *fact* about the president's home state. He rejects both major party candidates and appeals to shared belief with one sentence using *antithesis, alliteration,* and *hyperbole;* then he closes with a short, punchy clinching sentence *in parallel structure,* which is all the more effective because it contrasts with the long one it follows.

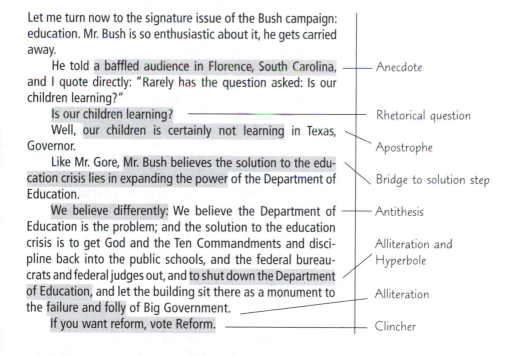

Let me turn now to the signature issue of the Bush campaign: education. Mr. Bush is so enthusiastic about it, he gets carried away.

He told a baffled audience in Florence, South Carolina, — Anecdote
and I quote directly: "Rarely has the question asked: Is our children learning?"

Is our children learning? — Rhetorical question

Well, our children is certainly not learning in Texas, Governor. — Apostrophe

Like Mr. Gore, Mr. Bush believes the solution to the education crisis lies in expanding the power of the Department of Education. — Bridge to solution step

We believe differently: We believe the Department of — Antithesis
Education is the problem; and the solution to the education crisis is to get God and the Ten Commandments and discipline back into the public schools, and the federal bureaucrats and federal judges out, and to shut down the Department of Education, and let the building sit there as a monument to the failure and folly of Big Government. — Alliteration and Hyperbole / Alliteration

If you want reform, vote Reform. — Clincher

Different devices have different effects. Sometimes you want to use more evidence, sometimes you want to rouse an audience to anger with rhetorical questions, and sometimes you want the power of repetition. We've examined short excerpts to see how the Three Ps work. To see what is possible, here's part of a longer speech Ted Kennedy used at the Alf Landon lecture series at Kansas State University in 1985. It is completely forgotten, a lesson in how what makes speeches memorable is much more than the text itself. But it offers an extraordinary variety of ways to build support for solutions.

Rhetorical question	In the face of all this how will the loyal opposition react?
Note repetition of "we must"—there are five	First, we must challenge ourselves not to accept the conventional terms of the economic debate.
Repetition of "can and should"	We can and should do more than brood about the deficits—and with courage, we can and should advocate the tax increases and military cuts necessary to reduce them. . . .
Proposal	
"There are some" for purpose of rebuttal	There are some who suggest that Democrats cannot be trusted to deal with federal deficits, because we have had too many of our own. But the present deficits are the greatest in the history of the nation; they make the most imprudent Democrat look positively parsimonious.
Hyperbole	
"Alternate use" statistic	The deficit for this year alone would pay for a national health insurance plan five times over.
Hyperbole as punch line	If Franklin Roosevelt had ever hinted at a budget so out of balance, Alf Landon would have carried Maine and Vermont and every other state as well.
Rhetorical question	When the administration renews its call for a balanced budget constitutional amendment we must reply: How dare they advance such a proposal again when they themselves are the biggest deficit spenders in American history?
Punch line	How can they ask the Constitution to balance the budget, when the president cannot do it himself?
	When the administration demands a line-item veto on spending we must ask: What items would they like to veto?
Apostrophe—modified	A responsible economic policy is also the key to putting profit back into agriculture.
Quote and humor	The Texas agriculture commissioner was right when he said, "Ronald Reagan's idea of a good farm program is 'Hee Haw.'"
	We must speak for the homeless, the hungry, and the middle-class families driven into deprivation.
Parallel compound object	Where is the economic recovery for those who are sleeping in the snow and the cold of our streets? Where is the economic recovery for the black teenagers who are out of school and out of work?
Using enemy rhetoric to rebut	The president says we must break the bonds of dependency.

But I do not believe in liberating people to live without shelter, without food, without health, and without hope. . . .

— Ascending order of importance, alliteration

Finally, we must reject the standard wisdom that foreign policy is never a decisive issue in a national campaign. Today, we are involved, directly or indirectly, in two hot wars and one cold war—and that is three wars too many.

— Rebutting the conventional

Rather than their empty calls to endless talks, I call on the administration to negotiate seriously, and at once, with the Soviet Union for an immediate, mutual, and verifiable freeze on the production, testing, and deployment of nuclear weapons.

— Rebutting of opponent
— Issue challenge
— Concrete proposal

I am talking about more than a plank in a party platform; a negotiated halt to the arms race must be the first priority of a new foreign policy and the first priority for the future of our planet.

— Not business as usual
— Note repetition in ascending order again

In the Middle East, our marines at the airport in Beirut have become the hostages of 1984. They are hunkered down and bunkered in below the ground.

— Literal analogy
— Parallelism and rhyme

They do not patrol; they do not seek out terrorists; they do not man checkpoints in the city. . . .

— Choppy repetition/rule of three

We sent them there to keep the peace, but there is no peace to be kept.

— Antithesis

We give up nothing of any diplomatic value by withdrawing combat troops that have no combat purpose. . . .

And as the last marine departs, I would advise any terrorist killer, and Druze artillery gunner, any Iranian, any Syrian, any Soviet leader who doubts our commitment—I would tell them to look offshore, and see the battleship U.S.S. *New Jersey.*

— Concrete detail
— Extended list
— Implied threat

Now is the time to bring the marines out of Beirut—not because it is right for the election, but because it is right for America, and not another marine deserves to die.

— Most urgent of all, with echo of King
— Antithesis/use of "not" to set off "because"

FINAL WORDS

Ronald Reagan always thought his best film was *Kings Row,* the 1942 tearjerker in which a surgeon amputates both his legs. Reagan's character doesn't know the surgeon is going to amputate. He wakes up, looks down the bed, and asks: "Where's the rest of me?"

Reagan later made that the title of his autobiography. It's such an appropriate question in political life, because the public so rarely sees politicians whole. But politicians do more than argue, posture, and speak in sound bites. They have doubts. They have personal experiences that don't lend themselves to two-minute intros. They can be funny, thoughtful, and reflective. If you're a politician, why sacrifice the chance to show listeners the rest of you? Why not put those qualities on display?

You can do that in the *bridge:* the moment between solution and conclusion.

CREATING THE BRIDGE

If you have presented a long list of solutions, phrased in a way that gets applause, audiences can use a change of pace. You have time to sound reflective, wise, and funny. You can reminisce, tell a moving story, or reflect on an idea. At this point you have a chance to show the side audiences rarely see.

Sometimes you can see right away how those passages could lead gracefully into the material you've reserved for a conclusion. But the creative process isn't always so cooperative. You may just hit on something moving or interesting and not know exactly where it leads. Try it; the odds are you will be able to find a way.

In George W. Bush's speech to the joint session of Congress after the events of September 11, his writers gave him a long litany ("We will come together to . . ."). Then, before the call to action that would end his speech, urging Americans to stay determined ("We must not lose our resolve"), they gave him this graceful bridge:

> After all that has just passed—all the lives taken, and all the possibilities and hopes that died with them—it is natural to wonder if America's future is one of fear. Some speak of an age of terror. I know there are struggles ahead, and dangers to face. But this country will define our times, not be defined by them. As long as the United States of America is determined and strong, this will not be an age of terror; this will be an age of liberty, here and across the world.
>
> Great harm has been done to us. We have suffered great loss. And in our grief and anger we have found our mission and our moment. Freedom and fear are at war. The advance of human freedom—the great achievement of our time and the great hope of every time—now depends on us.

One might quarrel about some of the reasoning here; it's certainly a little melodramatic to say that human freedom depends "on us." But, given the moment, that's forgivable. Meanwhile, the reflective tone, enhanced even by the passive verb ("Great harm has been done") lends the speech, and Bush, a reflective quality the public rarely saw. To me, it was the strongest moment in that speech.

We've examined a number of important things in this chapter: the special difficulties of talking about solutions, the different ways speakers can characterize themselves, how techniques of language and structure can help, the importance of variety, and ways to characterize speakers through a bridge into conclusions. Just as Bush's bridge paved the way for what he would say next, this bridge paves the way for what's next for us: ways to move from persuading listeners to inspiring them.

The Speechwriter's Checklist: Solutions

- ☐ Have I decided on these solutions with other staffers or my boss?
- ☐ Are these solutions supported both by speaker and audience? If not, why not?
- ☐ Does the audience want good ideas to fight for—or bad ideas to fight against?
- ☐ Have I presented a middle-ground approach to appeal to undecideds?
- ☐ Have I locked my speaker into a timetable or allowed flexibility in the solution?
- ☐ Have I persuaded as well as presented?
- ☐ Have I showed why the solutions are practical? Better than others?
- ☐ Have I used litany in presenting solutions?
- ☐ Have I used the Three Ps to build toward applause?
- ☐ Have I supported with varied evidence?
- ☐ Have I created a bridge into the conclusion?

14

Writing Conclusions

It's faintly comical to read Wyatt Tee Walter's account in chapter 4: how exasperated Martin Luther King Jr.'s aides were when their boss paused, looked up from his notes, and started that hackneyed ending of a speech they'd heard a thousand times.

According to Taylor Branch in his biography of King, he wasn't just dissatisfied with what he saw. From behind, he heard singer Mahalia Jackson say, "Tell 'em about the dream." That may have influenced him. [1]

Whatever the reason, it was then that, standing on the steps of the Lincoln Memorial on August 28, 1963, before 250,000 people massed on the Washington Mall, King began the peroration of the most-remembered speech of the twentieth century—ending so powerfully that even John F. Kennedy, always alert for interesting rhetoric, said, "He's damn good," and afterwards greeted King by saying, "I have a dream." [2] Why has the "I have a dream" section of King's speech become the one you see on TV over and over again; the passage textbooks reproduce more than any other; the one everyone cites when you ask them what speech they remember? It is in part King's passionate delivery and rich baritone; in part the importance of the moment, a turning point in the history of civil rights; in part the language.

From a speechwriter's point of view, it is also the selection of rhetorical technique, carefully studied from the moment King took his first homiletics course at divinity school. No rule of three here: King repeats the word *dream* ten times; his vision section is a mix of concrete detail ("the red hills of Georgia"), parallelism, alliteration, metaphor, quotes from Scripture and the secular scripture, and the Declaration of Independence. The basic device, of course, is litany.

You shouldn't overlook a point this book has stressed before and will mention later: the virtue of material King had used before. In fact, King had

---

AS DELIVERED

"I Have a Dream." There is little new to say about this most-commented-on speech of the twentieth century. But notice that once he starts the "dream" section, King no longer has to look at his text. And ask: When he repeats his "dream" line as if it is the end of one section, but it turns out to be the beginning of the next—why does he do that? And notice how many examples he uses. Doesn't ignoring the rule of three pay off?

http://college.cqpress.com/politicalspeech

used it to great success in Detroit a few months before, and in Chicago a week earlier. It's a little eerie to read that language in Branch's biography ("I have a dream that one day, right down in Birmingham, Alabama, where my good friend Arthur Shores was bombed just last night, white men and Negro men, white women and Negro women, will be able to walk together as brothers and sisters. I have a dream . . .").[3] It is as if King were plagiarizing, though of course it was his own language, and Chicago came first.

Performing lines you have used before allows you to look up, to get the accents right, to speak with a passion difficult when you are seeing a text for the first time.

But in addition to delivery and techniques of language, the "dream" section worked because showing people a vision of success is a great way to inspire them. That's why Alan Monroe made it step four of his famous sequence.

It is a step worth incorporating in any persuasive speech—and especially in the peculiar and narrowly focused needs of political speech. Speeches aren't legal briefs. Those that leave emotion only for the end are poorer for it; you have seen examples of story and detail that move audiences at every stage. Still, politicians really do try to use speeches that sound credible, provide varied evidence, and demonstrate the reasonableness of their solutions.

But as we move into the conclusion—the subject of this longest chapter of the book—it is time to leave reason behind. At this moment, evoking emotion is not one goal: like King in 1963, it is your chief goal.

That doesn't mean every speech should sound like his. On the other hand, speakers at every level can learn from his speech how to shape their own. For if his "dream" ending seems unique, the pattern it follows is not. It's similar to many of the most evocative contemporary political speeches. Not always in the same order, not always in the same proportions, and not always containing all of the elements, it involves variations of four steps. Because it's so immensely useful in politics, we'll look only at that versatile structure. In this chapter we will:

- Define that four-part close.
- Illustrate it.
- See why it is so useful in politics.
- Examine different ways to write each step effectively.

Because it helps to see how the steps work together, we look at longer examples than we have in most of the chapters so far, and end with a very long one. But we begin with one people watched just two and a half years earlier than King's, also standing on the Mall in Washington, facing not east, but west.

THE FOUR-PART CLOSE

He looks down—there were no teleprompters in those days—and begins the familiar final lines. One's eyes shift elsewhere: to Jackie, sitting composed, in a red dress; to Lyndon Johnson, legs crossed, gazing up attentively; to a man in a top hat, looking in contrast to the hatless president like a refugee from another age.

He's gesturing with a closed fist a little above the podium, looking out at the crowd now, but not smiling during the last few words. The applause begins. Not thunderous, but it'll do. He picks up the speech binder and puts it back on his seat, then turns around again as Johnson jumps up to grab his hand; Richard Nixon darts briefly into the frame, pumping Kennedy's hand. The camera pulls back; you see them all in hats and cloth coats, clapping and smiling, blissfully unaware of what will happen in the years ahead—or that they've just heard one of the most quotable speeches of the century.

Meanwhile, not on camera, high up behind the podium, sitting with his sister, relieved that there was finally applause at all, was the staffer who wrote the thing: Ted Sorensen.

Kennedy's inaugural speech—along with King's—has been analyzed in great detail. Here we look only at the conclusion, as full of famous lines as a Shakespearean soliloquy.

Sorensen's conclusion clearly relies on the devices of language we reviewed earlier, especially litany and antithesis. And like King's, it follows the four-part structure so useful for speech, which seeks to inspire an audience to act. Read through this annotated version to see how they fit together. Then listen to it, using the link on page 205.

INSPIRATIONAL EXAMPLE

It might be a quote, story, series of examples, montage, or poem. Often taken from history, an inspirational example might feature sacrifice, or someone succeeding against odds. As Kennedy's example of sacrifice, Sorensen chooses the graves of American soldiers to remind the audience that other generations fought to keep America free:

> Since this country was founded, each generation of Americans has been summoned to give testimony to its national loyalty. The graves of young Americans who answered the call to service surround the globe.

LESSON DRAWN

Having moved the audience, speakers draw a lesson from it—an analogy, making the example relevant for today. Sometimes the lesson may mean you should imitate the example. (*What they did we can do!*) Sometimes speakers will pose a question or paint two views of the future, thus creating a moment of suspense. (*Will we choose correctly?*)

Kennedy's lesson: We must act like those brave "young Americans." The "trumpet" that summoned them, he says, summons us to "defend freedom." Note how this step intertwines with Monroe. Kennedy asks his listeners if they will join him (but doesn't urge—that comes later). Then he outlines a vision of the success that can—not will—happen if they do.

> Now the trumpet summons us again. Can we forge against these enemies a grand and global alliance, North and South, East and West, that can assure a more fruitful life for all mankind? Will you join me in that historic effort?
>
> In the long history of the world, only a few generations have been granted the role of defending freedom in its hour of maximum danger.
>
> The energy, the faith, the devotion which we bring to this endeavor will light our country and all who serve it—and the glow from that fire can truly light the world.

CALL TO ACTION

What next? As Monroe suggests, don't let your audience off the hook. Make the sale. What is it you want your audience to do? Having asked if they will join him, Kennedy launches into a third step, a call-to-action litany appealing to what alert or obsessive readers will remember formed the highest step in Maslow's pyramid: self-fulfillment.

> And so, my fellow Americans, ask not what your country can do for you—ask what you can do for your country.
>
> My fellow citizens of the world, ask not what America will do for you, but what together we can do for the freedom of man. . . .
>
> Finally, whether you are citizens of America or citizens of the world, ask of us here the same high standards of strength and sacrifice which we ask of you.

Could he end there? It would seem abrupt. And so this four-part close involves a final step—the very last line.

CLINCHER

Clinchers usually remind listeners of the larger implications of their actions. By now speakers have moved beyond the mundane issues of which bills to pass or which candidates to support. They end by urging audiences to take action *because* that action will bring a noble end. And what is that noble end? Often it's freedom, the American dream, a better future for our children, or some other abstraction Americans value. Kennedy's is unusual—he promises only one "sure reward"

> With a good conscience our only sure reward, with history the final judge of our deeds, let us go forth to lead the land we love, asking his

blessing and his help, but knowing that here on earth God's work must truly be our own.

The language of Kennedy's clincher is less concrete than other sections, and more hackneyed ("the land we love"). Kennedy is careful to hew to the prerequisite of important political speeches by invoking God, which he refers to as a male. But his final sentence remains unusual in political life for three things he doesn't do. Kennedy doesn't promise success. He doesn't assure his audience of the right-

> **AS DELIVERED**
>
> *John F. Kennedy's Inaugural Address.* Note the presence of all four steps. And try to imagine how they can be effective in much smaller events.
>
> **http://college.cqpress.com/politicalspeech**

ness of their actions, since "history" is the final judge. And while invoking God, he doesn't simply say what has become the fashion today (*God bless you, and God bless America!*). Instead, he takes sides in one of the great debates of contemporary religion, reminding his listeners that good works, not just faith, will save them.

But by inverting the usual grammatical structure to create suspense, by using alliteration, repetition, and antithesis, his clincher surprises his audience, becomes memorable, and justifies its position as Kennedy's final sentence.

An invention of twentieth-century rhetoric? No. In fact, the Gettysburg Address uses this four-part close as well, if you allow Lincoln a little grammatical license.

The brave men, living and dead, who struggled here have consecrated it far above our poor power to add or detract. The world will little note nor long remember what we say here, but it can never forget what they did here. — Inspirational example

It is for us the living rather to be dedicated here to the unfinished work which they who fought here have thus far so nobly advanced. — Lesson learned

It is rather for us to be here dedicated to the great task remaining before us—that from these honored dead we take increased devotion to that cause for which they gave the last full measure of devotion—that we here highly resolve that these dead shall not have died in vain, that . . . this nation under God shall have a new birth of freedom, and that government of the people, by the people, for the people shall not perish from the earth. — Call to action / Clincher

Today, almost a half-century after Kennedy's inaugural and almost 150 years after Gettysburg, this four-part close remains popular, regardless of ideology or decade, or how celebrated the speaker. Let's look at a variety of more recent examples: from a president, a Nobel Peace Prize winner, and two 2008 presidential candidates.

Ronald Reagan: 1982 Speech to British Parliament

In this slightly condensed version, Reagan *inspires*—not just by quoting Winston Churchill, but by giving the audience context. Next, he draws his *lesson,* the analogy he sees between Churchill's time and the present. He moves into his one sentence "call." Finally, he offers the larger purpose for action as his *clincher.* Note that, like Kennedy, he also uses suspense in his clincher, presenting the reason before letting his listeners know what they must do.

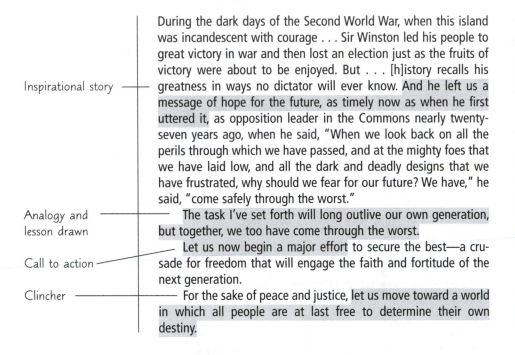

Inspirational story

During the dark days of the Second World War, when this island was incandescent with courage . . . Sir Winston led his people to great victory in war and then lost an election just as the fruits of victory were about to be enjoyed. But . . . [h]istory recalls his greatness in ways no dictator will ever know. And he left us a message of hope for the future, as timely now as when he first uttered it, as opposition leader in the Commons nearly twenty-seven years ago, when he said, "When we look back on all the perils through which we have passed, and at the mighty foes that we have laid low, and all the dark and deadly designs that we have frustrated, why should we fear for our future? We have," he said, "come safely through the worst."

Analogy and lesson drawn

The task I've set forth will long outlive our own generation, but together, we too have come through the worst.

Call to action

Let us now begin a major effort to secure the best—a crusade for freedom that will engage the faith and fortitude of the next generation.

Clincher

For the sake of peace and justice, let us move toward a world in which all people are at last free to determine their own destiny.

Al Gore: 2008 Nobel Peace Prize

Gore, in Norway, *inspires* with a Henrik Ibsen quote before drawing the *lesson* for today: Some day, others will hold us accountable. He gets listeners to imagine two possibilities; shows a flash of wit, calling political will a renewable resource; then compresses his *call to action* ("Let us renew it") and *clincher* into that single final sentence, writing it as a pledge to be uttered together—one more way of making the audience realize action is up to them.

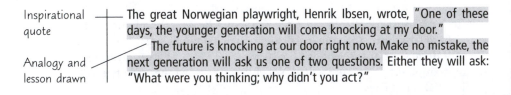

Inspirational quote

The great Norwegian playwright, Henrik Ibsen, wrote, "One of these days, the younger generation will come knocking at my door."

Analogy and lesson drawn

The future is knocking at our door right now. Make no mistake, the next generation will ask us one of two questions. Either they will ask: "What were you thinking; why didn't you act?"

Or they will ask instead: "How did you find the moral courage to rise and successfully resolve a crisis that so many said was impossible to solve?"

We have everything we need to get started, save perhaps political will, but political will is a renewable resource.

So let us renew it, and say together: "We have a purpose. We are —— Call to action/clincher
many. For this purpose we will rise, and we will act."

Joe Biden: 2007 International Association of Fire Fighters Convention

Don't expect polish in this example; Biden, then still running for president, isn't talking from a text, and he's one of the most voluble people in public life. But he is also the only speaker to actually talk about the author he quotes, making it more credible that he knows the quote rather than just reads something a speechwriter wrote. Biden also uses a quote as *inspiration*. He begins his *call to action*, and then—almost as if he remembers what he's supposed to do—*draws the analogy and lesson*. Since he was a long-shot candidate, it would seem immodest to predict victory. Biden chooses the more modest option, a *call* for his audience to "look me over." And his *clincher* includes his vision of the future: "we will change this nation."

There's a—my favorite modern Irish poet is a guy named Seamus Heaney and he won the Nobel Prize for poetry back in the mid-'90s. And he had a poem called "The Cure at Troy." There's a stanza in there that I think summarizes where the heart of the American people are right now, whether they're Democrats, Republicans, independents, where I think they are, what they're ready for.

And the stanza goes like this. It says, "History teaches us not to —— Inspirational quote
hope on this side of the grave. But then, once in a lifetime, that longed-for tidal wave of justice rises up and hope and history rhyme."

Join me. Join me. —— Call to action

We have a shot to make hope and history rhyme. It's totally within —— Analogy and lesson drawn
our power to change this nation now. The public is ready.

And you—you—are the ones who can lead the charge because you are the ones who can play the most significant role in the union movement in who's likely to be the next nominee for the Democratic Party because of your involvement in the states that are involved, and because how up-front you've been in the past.

All I ask you is, look me over. If you like what you see, help out. If —— Call to action
not, vote for the other guy or woman. But look me over, because, folks, I guarantee you, we will change this nation, and we'll change it now. —— Clincher

Mike Huckabee: 2007 Family Research Council Meeting

This former pastor has the most unusual approach: in an election where the influence of religion is an issue, Huckabee uses as his first *inspiration* a rousing, richly detailed litany of biblical examples, before drawing the analogy and *lesson for today* ("Stand by our stuff"). Next, he provides a second inspiration, this time historical. Finally, in one crammed, next-to-last sentence, Huckabee compresses *analogy, lesson,* and *three-part call to action* ("true . . . right . . . eternal"), before ending with his three-word *clincher.*

Litany of biblical inspiration — You see, I was led to believe that it was a lot better to be with David—that little shepherd boy with five smooth stones—than it was with Goliath with all his heavy armor.

I was taught that it was better to be Daniel than it was a whole den full of lions because Daniel would come out better off than those lions. It went to sleep before it was all over.

I was taught that it was better to be one of the three Hebrew children than it was to be the fiery flames of the furnace, because with God's power those flames couldn't even leave the smell of smoke on the lives and the clothes of those three Hebrew children.

I was taught to believe that it was better to be Elijah with an altar that had been soaked not once, not twice, but three times with water than it was to be 850 prophets of Ba'al screaming and yelling all day long for the fire to fall on Mount Carmel.

I was led to believe that we serve a God who stood in the middle of a boat in the Sea of Galilee in the midst of a storm and said for the storm to stop and it did, or a Jesus who took mud and put it in the eyes of a blind man and he could see again. And one who could take two little fish and five biscuits and feed a crowd of five thousand people and have enough leftovers that it would make the disciples realize that there was never an end to the supply of what our God could do when our people had faith—a savior who in fact could even go to the tomb of a dead man named Lazarus, so dead that the Scripture says he already was stinking—that's pretty blunt, folks [LAUGHTER]—and he made him live again.

Analogy and lesson drawn — I don't want ever for us to let expediency or electability replace our principles as the new value.

The new value needs to be the old value. We believe in some things. We stand by those things. We live or die by those things. [APPLAUSE, CHEERS]

And, ladies and gentlemen, I want to say with all my heart: this today, I understand, is not a rally for one party or another, but many of us are affiliated with a political party, as am I. But I want to make it very clear that for me, I do not spell G-O-D, G-O-P. [APPLAUSE] Our party may be important, but our principles are even more important than anybody's political party. Stand by our stuff.

Nearly 250 years ago, fifty-six very brave men took a pen and signed the document that would forever change the history of the world and would set a course that each of us today are able to live because of.

Those brave men, when they affixed their signatures to the Declaration of Independence, did not say I sign here as long as everything is going well. I sign here with the hopes that King George will listen to us and maybe negotiate a little bit with us and ease up on us a little bit. I sign here so that I can have a little seat at the table and be tossed a few of the king's crumbs from time to time.

These men signed understanding full well what they were doing. And they said on this day we pledge our fortunes, our families, our lives, and our sacred honor.

Ladies and gentlemen, it is time for those of us who call ourselves values voters to pledge our lives, our families, our fortunes, and our sacred honor to that which is true, which is right, and which is eternal.

Let us do it.

Inspiration #2: historical parallel

Lesson drawn, call to action

Clincher

The similarities in these endings, from very different politicians, go beyond structure. In fact, each step often has the same specific functions. They:

Motivate

The inspirational example may take different forms, whether a quote, story, or montage, but usually they motivate with examples of sacrifice for noble ends, whether soldiers who died (Kennedy, Lincoln), or revolutionaries signing the Declaration of Independence (Huckabee).

Define

The lesson learned *defines* the task ahead for listeners, as Kennedy does (fighting "these enemies"), emphasizing urgency so when speakers ask for action there should be little doubt about the right course.

Ask

Everyone who does political fund-raising knows about the "ask"—the moment you explicitly request money. Here, the "ask" is usually about something else. Having defined the cause as noble, and inspired us by reminding us of our own heroes, how can listeners say no when speakers call for us to do the same? Every speaker *asks* listeners to enlist, whether to "lead the land we love," to "take increased devotion to that cause," to demonstrate "moral courage," or other ways to become heroes as well.

Elevate

What should ring in our ears as they finish? Clinchers *elevate* our gaze, striking a number of common themes, all reminding us of the larger purpose.

Are these four steps the only ways to end a speech? Of course not. Sometimes politicians may not want to inspire—especially in floor speeches, which have the give-and-take flavor of a debate. On the floor, they may want to end by: (1) rebutting the other side, or (2) suggesting another approach and ending just with a call to vote yea or nay.

Does the four-part close always include these elements in the same order? Also, no. Sometimes speakers combine them in a single sentence, as Huckabee did. They use the call to action in different ways. Some command (*Dare to dream!*). Others suggest (*We must . . .*). They may replace the call to action with a simple assertion of optimism. The reasons to vary this approach aren't always rational; sometimes speakers are too inhibited to do a long, rousing litany. Sometimes speakers will be so entranced with inspirational quotes that they will use not one but two.

Often, though, you will see all four steps, and in this order, whether on the floor, in a stump speech, in a keynote, or even in informal remarks at a fundraiser, not because speakers or their writers have studied them in a book, but because, like Monroe's Motivated Sequence, they reflect common sense. What politician wouldn't want to inspire an audience—and, by reminding them of the noble ends that drove most of them into politics in the first place, put them to work?

In such endings, some ideas recur again and again:

- the uniqueness of America, which is rarely called the "United States";
- a reminder that the progress won't be easy; and
- confidence that there are better days ahead.

Yes, these are clichés. But one is a necessary caution audiences interpret as realism, and the other two satisfy a need for optimism basic to politics. Politicians ignore them at their peril.

Like Monroe, the four-part close is skeleton, not flesh. Speakers and speechwriters should be flexible enough to adapt it, for reasons that involve the interplay of personality, skill, and the occasion. And as you examine various ways speakers and speechwriters have used language, anecdote, wit, and support for each of these four steps, you should keep in mind that there are also ways no one has yet invented.

THE FOUR-PART CLOSE: APPLYING THE ELEMENTS

This section includes not just examples of what politicians do but examples of what they've done well. That means excerpting speeches where the inspirational example may be unusually effective but the rest of the conclusion mediocre. Those of you who want to find where you can read each speech in its entirety should consult the bibliography. I divide the examples into three sections: inspiration and the lesson learned, call to action, and clincher.

A warning about what lies ahead. As we have looked at openings, problems, and solutions, it has made sense to show how language, anecdote, wit, and various kinds of support contribute. Except for the inspiration step, other issues will prove to be more useful. As we review steps 3 and 4 we'll abandon the usual format to examine them.

Finally, you've seen URLS for many of these speeches throughout the book. Remember: Speeches are meant to be heard. I suggest reading the excerpt first, taking advantage of your ability to reread. Then watch.

INSPIRATION AND THE LESSON LEARNED

For these first two steps, some techniques of language play a relatively small role, as do varying kinds of support—like statistics. But note how concrete detail and colloquial language contribute in these different ways to use three elements essential to inspiring listeners: anecdote, example, and quotations.

ANECDOTE

Inspire through Stories of Heroism: Sarah Palin, 2008 Republican National Convention.

More effective than McCain's own use of his POW experience, this story of heroic suffering for what the audience believes is a noble cause opens the close to Sarah Palin's 2008 Republican National Convention acceptance speech. Why is it better than McCain's version? First, because it comes not from McCain himself, so it doesn't carry the whiff of self-praise; but also because it is economically told and contains the concrete detail—real names and the "pinhole" in the door—that rings true. In this case, Palin's *lesson* defines the traditional task for campaigns: his heroism then means we need him as president, now.

> **AS DELIVERED**
>
> *Sarah Palin's 2008 Republican National Convention Speech.* Watch through to the end. If you like, click on John McCain's acceptance speech. Both use the story of his imprisonment. Which do you think is more effective? Why? Note that Palin's call to action is one sentence long. Why doesn't she need more? What keeps the audience listening?
>
> http://college.cqpress.com/politicalspeech

To the most powerful office on earth, he would bring the compassion that comes from having once been powerless . . . the wisdom that comes even to the captives, by the grace of God . . . the special confidence of those who have seen evil, and seen how evil is overcome.

A fellow prisoner of war, a man named Tom Moe of Lancaster, Ohio, recalls looking through a pin-hole in his cell door as Lieutenant Commander John McCain was led down the hallway, by the guards, day after day.

As the story is told, "When McCain shuffled back from torturous inter-rogations, he would turn toward Moe's door and flash a grin and thumbs up"—as if to say, "We're going to pull through this." —— Anecdote

My fellow Americans, that is the kind of man America needs to see us —— Lesson through these next four years. drawn

Inspire with Heroism of Ordinary People:
Al Gore, 1994 Family Reunion

Gore has described the obstacles—and solutions—to being an effective father. Now he wants to inspire his listeners by reminding them how much having a good father means to children, with a man so anonymous we don't even know his name. Gore's *lesson* draws an analogy not with the father but with the way the son remembers him. Note the litany of three examples in his "lesson learned" section. You don't have to keep the lesson brief.

Anecdote ——— A few months ago I read an interesting story about the Baseball Hall of Fame, up in Cooperstown, New York. Some workmen were renovating, and when they removed a display case, a snapshot fell out.

There was no name on it. It was a picture of a man in a Sinclair oil baseball uniform, holding a bat and smiling.

On the back was this note:

"You were never too tired to play catch. On our days off you helped build the Little League field. You always came to watch me play. You were a Hall of Fame Dad. I wish I could share this moment with you. Your son, Pete."

The curators debated what to do with it. They thought about putting it on display. They thought about launching a search to find out who the man was. But in the end they decided to put the picture right back where it was, wedged under the display case, a secret memorial to every parent who has taken the time to play baseball with his kids.

Lesson drawn ——— The world we must work toward is a world in which children grow up wanting to model their own attempts at parenthood on these kinds of memories: of fathers not afraid to say "I love you"; of fathers who feel blessed to have created children; of fathers who are the air in the ball of life; of Dads who belong in their children's personal Hall of Fame.

Inspire with Stories of Personal Selflessness:
Mother Teresa, 1979 Nobel Peace Prize

The four-part close is borrowed by politicians from religion—often through the influence of Martin Luther King. For Mother Teresa, the great cause is helping the poor. She draws a *lesson* politicians usually don't—the need to "love one another." But her structure is exactly the same.

Anecdote ——— The other day I received fifteen dollars from a man who has been on his back for twenty years, and the only part that he can move is his right hand. And the only companion that he enjoys is smoking. And he said to me: I do not smoke for one week, and I send you this money. It must have been a terrible sacrifice for him, but see how beautiful, how he shared, and with that money I bought bread and I gave to those who are hungry with a joy on both sides, he was giving and the poor were receiving.

This is something that you and I—it is a gift of God to us to be able to share our love with others.

And let it be as it was for Jesus. Let us love one another as he loved us.

Lesson drawn

EXAMPLE

Story is one way to inspire, unmatched for dramatic effect. But drama isn't the only way to inspire. Examples can be moving, too. We looked at this one earlier. Here we see how it contributed to the rest of Cuomo's conclusion.

Inspire through Personal Example: Mario Cuomo, 1984 Democratic National Convention

Polished, full of the rhetoric politicians are expected to say is about parents, Mario Cuomo's extended example of his father becomes memorable because of its intensity, and detail concrete enough to ring true. But Cuomo's example demonstrates not just his father's nobility, but the nobility of the "democratic process." And because his audience believes the democratic process has been thwarted by the incumbent (Ronald Reagan), the *lesson* Cuomo draws is that this kind of democracy can be restored on election day.

It's a story, ladies and gentlemen, I didn't read in a book or learn in a classroom. I saw it and lived it, like many of you.

Example

I watched a small man with thick calluses on both hands work fifteen and sixteen hours a day. I saw him once literally bleed from the bottoms of his feet, a man who came here uneducated, alone, unable to speak the language, who taught me all I needed to know about faith and hard work by the simple eloquence of his example.

I learned about our kind of democracy from my father.

And I learned about our obligation to each other from him and from my mother.

And they asked to be protected in those moments when they would not be able to protect themselves. This nation and its government did that for them.

And that they were able to build a family and live in dignity and see one of their children go from behind their little grocery store in south Jamaica on the other side of the tracks where he was born to occupy the highest seat in the greatest state in the greatest nation in the only world we know, is an ineffably beautiful tribute to the democratic process.

And ladies and gentlemen, on January 20, 1985, it will happen again.

Lesson drawn

Inspire with Brief Examples of Hopes That Came True: Barack Obama, 2004 Democratic Convention

This montage of brief examples, from the 2004 speech that made Barack Obama famous, exemplifies hope. Note how carefully he picks them: slaves who would someday be free; willing immigrants who would find prosperity; a lieutenant in Vietnam who would run for President, and a self-deprecating description of himself keynoting a convention. The *lesson* for today: We too should be audacious enough to hope for better days.

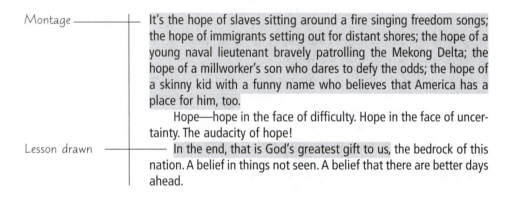

Montage

It's the hope of slaves sitting around a fire singing freedom songs; the hope of immigrants setting out for distant shores; the hope of a young naval lieutenant bravely patrolling the Mekong Delta; the hope of a millworker's son who dares to defy the odds; the hope of a skinny kid with a funny name who believes that America has a place for him, too.

Hope—hope in the face of difficulty. Hope in the face of uncertainty. The audacity of hope!

Lesson drawn

In the end, that is God's greatest gift to us, the bedrock of this nation. A belief in things not seen. A belief that there are better days ahead.

Inspire with Examples of Sacrifice: Ronald Reagan, 1986 Speech to the Nation on Campaign against Drug Abuse

Reagan and Obama strike the same theme: the need to have hope. But Reagan's examples are not just those who hoped for better days but who took risks. He uses an unusual repetition—"they came" four times, then "they all came" to sum up. He draws an unusual *lesson*, too: as opposed to Lincoln, who asks us to honor those who went before, Reagan motivates listeners by saying that drug use dishonors those from "whence we came."

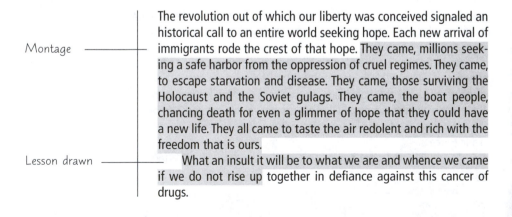

Montage

The revolution out of which our liberty was conceived signaled an historical call to an entire world seeking hope. Each new arrival of immigrants rode the crest of that hope. They came, millions seeking a safe harbor from the oppression of cruel regimes. They came, to escape starvation and disease. They came, those surviving the Holocaust and the Soviet gulags. They came, the boat people, chancing death for even a glimmer of hope that they could have a new life. They all came to taste the air redolent and rich with the freedom that is ours.

Lesson drawn

What an insult it will be to what we are and whence we came if we do not rise up together in defiance against this cancer of drugs.

Inspire with an Object Symbolizing Heroism: George W. Bush, 2001 Speech to Congress after 9/11 Attacks

Bush inspires his audience by describing the heroism of a police officer. But he makes it concrete by holding up his shield, making an abstraction like heroism concrete. Pay special attention to his graceful way of drawing the lesson. Its antithesis, similar to so many of those you've already seen, defines what he will ask as the natural response to heroes who have already sacrificed.

It is my hope that in the months and years ahead, life will return almost to normal. ——— Inspirational vision

We'll go back to our lives and routines, and that is good. Even grief recedes with time and grace. But our resolve must not pass. Each of us will remember what happened that day, and to whom it happened. We'll remember the moment the news came—where we were and what we were doing. Some will remember an image of a fire, or a story of rescue. Some will carry memories of a face and a voice gone forever.

And I will carry this: It is the police shield of a man named ——— Inspirational object

George Howard, who died at the World Trade Center trying to save others. It was given to me by his mom, Arlene, as a proud memorial to her son.

This is my reminder of lives that ended and a task that does ——— Lesson drawn

not end.

I will not forget this wound to our country or those who inflicted it.

QUOTATION

Why do the words of others inspire? Sometimes because they say things so well. But there are other reasons. They may inspire because they come from revered figures, or anger because they come from someone despised. They may have the patina of words listeners have heard all their lives, or dramatic scenes they know well.

Inspire by Quoting Revered Figures: Martin Luther King, 1957 "Power of Nonviolence" Speech

In his address to a Los Angeles temple, King draws on an Old Testament figure as well as Jesus and the founding fathers. This rich speech, full of humor, is too long to quote in full here. King mocks those who talk about the "maladjusted," inspiring his audience with the maladjusted who have turned out to have vision. His *lesson:* We too should be as maladjusted as Jesus.

Inspirational quotes ————

Lesson learned ————

Modern psychology has a word that is probably used more than any other word in psychology. It is the word maladjusted.

But . . . I say to you that I am absolutely convinced that maybe the world is in need for men and women who will be as maladjusted as the prophet Amos who in the midst of the injustices of his day would cry out in words that echo across the centuries: "Let justice roll down like waters and righteousness like a mighty stream";

as maladjusted as Abraham Lincoln who had the vision to see that this nation could not survive half slave and half free;

as maladjusted as Thomas Jefferson who in the midst of an age amazingly adjusted to slavery would etch across the pages of history words lifted to cosmic proportions: "We hold these truths to be self evident, that all men are created equal, that they are endowed by their Creator with certain inalienable rights and that among these are life, liberty and the pursuit of happiness";

as maladjusted as Jesus of Nazareth who said to the men and women of his day: "Love your enemies, bless them that curse you, pray for them that despitefully use you."

And through such maladjustment we will be able to emerge from the bleak and desolate midnight of man's inhumanity to man into the bright and glittering daybreak of freedom and justice.

Stories, examples, quotes, personal examples, or montage. Within the narrow strictures of political speech exist a wide variety of examples to inspire an audience, preparing them for the next step.

CALL TO ACTION

Here—as advertised—we depart from the format earlier chapters use. It's not as if a call to action can't be influenced by story, wit, or evidence—or the language you choose. It can. But more often than not, the call to action takes the form of a litany. Other elements important in the rest of political speech become less useful.

On the other hand, that doesn't mean every call to action looks the same. Speakers have inspired the audience, and defined the task ahead. Now it's time to ask for help. But how? Some speakers command listeners to act. Others suggest, or imply. Some just assume listeners will join them—that they don't really have to persuade anyone. Let's look at some examples.

COMMAND

Command Them to Adopt Attitudes: Hillary Clinton, 2003 Stanford Commencement Address

Following what is often the custom before younger audiences when policy seems inappropriate, Clinton commands her daughter's classmates to adopt some absolutely unobjectionable attitudes.

> Just as this is a special time in your lives, it is for me as well because my daughter will be graduating in four weeks.
> And I leave these graduates with the same message I hope to leave with my graduate.
> Dare to compete. Dare to care. Dare to dream. Dare to love. Practice the art of making possible. And no matter what happens, even if you hear shouts behind, keep going.

Command Them to Take Concrete Action: Charlton Heston, 1999 Harvard Law School Address

Heston's call to action to his hostile Harvard crowd is effective for its wealth of concrete detail.

> When your university is pressured to lower standards until 80 percent of the students graduate with honors . . . choke the halls of the board of regents. When an eight-year-old boy pecks a girl's cheek on the playground and gets hauled into court for sexual harassment . . . march on that school and block its doorways. When someone you elected is seduced by political power and betrays you . . . petition them, oust them, banish them. When *Time* magazine's cover portrays millennium nuts as deranged, crazy Christians holding a cross as it did last month . . . boycott their magazine and the products it advertises.

Command Them to Join the Battle: John McCain, 2008 Republican National Convention

Note that McCain first offers a *pledge*—that he will fight—before commanding the audience to do the same.

> I'm going to fight for my cause every day as your president. . . .
> Fight with me. Fight with me.
> Fight for what's right for our country.
> Fight for the ideals and character of a free people.
> Fight for our children's future.
> Fight for justice and opportunity for all.
> Stand up to defend our country from its enemies.

Stand up for each other; for beautiful, blessed, bountiful America.

Stand up, stand up, stand up and fight. Nothing is inevitable here. We're Americans, and we never give up. We never quit. We never hide from history. We make history.

Command the Absent Enemy: Ronald Reagan, 1964 Republican National Convention

Reagan not only suggests a message from the "next president" but phrases it in a way similar to William Jennings Bryan's "cross of gold" passage, a command to those he thinks are enemies of the United States.

> If there is one message that needs to be sent to all the nations of the world by the next president, it is this: "There will be no more Taiwans and no more Vietnams, regardless of the price or the promise, be it oil of Arabia or an ambassador sitting in Beijing, there will be no more abandonment of friends by the United States of America."

SUGGEST OR IMPLY

To command sounds forceful. To the right crowd it can be exciting. On the other hand, it sounds kind of bossy. Speakers can also motivate listeners in less preemptory ways. As you read through these samples, ask yourself whether speakers and their writers made the right choice.

Use "We Must" to Suggest Importance of Action: Barry Goldwater, 1964 Republican National Convention

There are ways of urging action less preemptory than the command. To say "we must" is not the same as saying "you must." But it does imply that there will be serious consequences if the audience doesn't get moving. Goldwater's 1964 call to action is far too abstract to be effective, but it's true to his stubborn insistence on the urgency of the philosophical ideas in his rhetoric.

> In our vision of a good and decent future, free and peaceful, there *must* be room, room for the liberation of the energy and the talent of the individual. . . .
>
> We *must* assure a society here which while never abandoning the needy, or forsaking the helpless, nurtures incentives and opportunity for the creative and the productive.
>
> We *must* know the whole good is the product of many single contributions.

Use "Let's" to Imply the Speaker Is Not Exempt: Mother Teresa, 1979 Nobel Peace Prize

The terms *let's* or *let us* include the listeners instead of ordering them. It's the difference between saying "Let's go to the movies," and "Go to the movies, now!" They imply partnership, but permit passion. Mother Teresa uses "let us" to create a gentle appeal and, after a digression, she uses one final "let us" in her clincher.

Let us love Him with undivided love. ————————————————— Call to
    And the joy of loving Him and each other—let us give now—that   action
Christmas is coming so close.
    Let us keep that joy of loving Jesus in our hearts. And share that joy with
all that we come in touch with.
    And that radiating joy is real, for we have no reason not to be happy
because we have no Christ with us. Christ in our hearts, Christ in the poor that
we meet, Christ in the smile that we give and the smile that we receive.
    Let us make that one point: That no child will be unwanted, and also —— Clincher
that we meet each other always with a smile, especially when it is difficult
to smile.

Ask, Don't Tell: Sarah Palin, 2008 Republican Convention

No one should mistake the measured, reflective way Palin finishes for lack of partisanship. The understatement of "I ask you to join" in this skillful close allows her to build in excitement, repeating "join" twice before finishing her clincher. Note the parallel construction as Palin contrasts Obama and McCain to set up an "if-then" litany of reasons before making her request.

> For a season, a gifted speaker can inspire with his words. For a
> lifetime, John McCain has inspired with his deeds.
>   If character is the measure in this election . . . and hope the
> theme . . . and change the goal we share, then I ask you to join our
> cause.
>   Join our cause and help America elect a great man as the next
> president of the United States.

Use "Ask" with Litany of Pledges to Create Audience Response: Bill Clinton, 1993 Martin Luther King Day Speech

In the conclusion to this speech, mentioned elsewhere in the book, Clinton inspires his listeners by quoting Scripture; draws his lesson; invokes King's memory in an interesting way; then calls for action by asking his audience to join him in an unusual series of pledges, which leads directly into his clincher, appropriate for a church audience sitting in the pews. There isn't space to include it all, but the last few minutes of this speech provide a particularly rich example of the four-part close we study here. It's worth reading along and listening to the audio (www.americanrhetoric.com/speeches/wjclintonmemphis.htm) to see how what's written allows Clinton to build excitement.

> So in this pulpit, on this day, let me ask all of you in your heart to say we will honor the life and work of Martin Luther King.
> We will honor the meaning of our church.
> We will somehow, by God's grace, we will turn this around.
> We will give these children a future.
> We will take away their guns and give them books.
> We will take away their despair and give them hope.
> We will rebuild the families and the neighborhoods and the communities.
> We won't make all the work that has gone on here benefit just a few.
> We will do it together by the grace of God.

Imply Call to Action by Asserting Belief: Barack Obama, 2004 Democratic National Convention

Each example so far asks, however diplomatically, for action. It isn't always necessary to be so explicit. Sometimes you assume (*Now we join together*), implying the audience needs no persuasion. Sometimes you pledge (*I'll work as hard as I can*), implying the speaker doesn't want to be so impolite as to pressure the crowd. In 2008 Obama effectively implied action with the phrase "this is our time," combining it with the optimism of "Yes we can." Later, we will examine that ending in detail.

But right now, note this call to action from Obama's 2004 Democratic National Convention keynote. Obama does not call or ask for action. His litany asserts a theme he has used with remarkable consistency: that "we can" succeed—and that if his audience "feels" the same way, if they do what they "must do," success will come.

> I believe that we can give our middle class relief and provide working families with a road to opportunity.
> I believe we can provide jobs to the jobless, homes to the homeless, and reclaim young people in cities across America from violence and despair.
> I believe that we have a righteous wind at our backs, and that as we stand on the crossroads of history, we can make the right choices, and meet the challenges that face us.
> America! Tonight, if you feel the same energy that I do, if you feel the same urgency that I do, if you feel the same passion that I do, if you feel the same hopefulness that I do—if we do what we must do, then I have no doubt that [vision] all across the country, from

Florida to Oregon, from Washington to Maine, the people will rise up in November, and John Kerry will be sworn in as president, and John Edwards will be sworn in as vice president, and this country will reclaim its promise, and out of this long political darkness a brighter day will come.

And now, the very end of the speech: the clincher.

CLINCHER

It's safe to say that while contemporary politicians and speechwriters use the four-part-close format, few have any idea that this is what they've done. But Martin Luther King, trained in homiletics, may have known he was imitating a grand tradition. The end of his "Dream" speech illustrates it well. He *inspires* by quoting the lyrics of "My Country 'tis of Thee," written by an Andover student in 1831; draws his *lesson;* moves into his famous "So let freedom ring" *call to action;* and closes with his traditional "when that happens" *clincher.* Let's start by examining this four-part close to see how naturally King's influential clincher grows out of what precedes it.

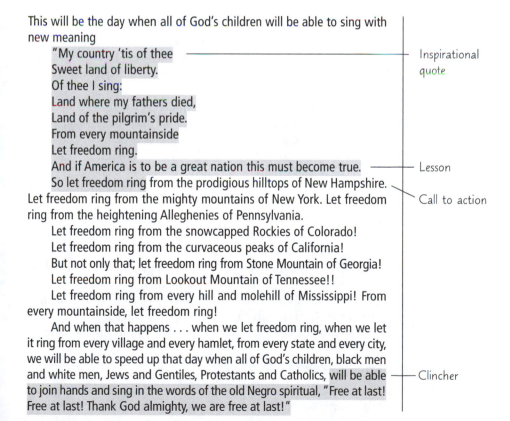

This will be the day when all of God's children will be able to sing with new meaning

"My country 'tis of thee ————————————————— Inspirational
Sweet land of liberty.   quote
Of thee I sing:
Land where my fathers died,
Land of the pilgrim's pride.
From every mountainside
Let freedom ring.
And if America is to be a great nation this must become true. ——— Lesson
So let freedom ring from the prodigious hilltops of New Hampshire.
Let freedom ring from the mighty mountains of New York. Let freedom —— Call to action
ring from the heightening Alleghenies of Pennsylvania.
Let freedom ring from the snowcapped Rockies of Colorado!
Let freedom ring from the curvaceous peaks of California!
But not only that; let freedom ring from Stone Mountain of Georgia!
Let freedom ring from Lookout Mountain of Tennessee!!
Let freedom ring from every hill and molehill of Mississippi! From every mountainside, let freedom ring!
And when that happens . . . when we let freedom ring, when we let it ring from every village and every hamlet, from every state and every city, we will be able to speed up that day when all of God's children, black men and white men, Jews and Gentiles, Protestants and Catholics, will be able —— Clincher
to join hands and sing in the words of the old Negro spiritual, "Free at last! Free at last! Thank God almighty, we are free at last!"

Profound? Of course not. Even rhetorically, King's call to action is unexceptional—a list of landmarks characterized with oddly extravagant adjectives ("Prodigious hilltops"? "Curvaceous peaks"?). One imagines King chuckling as he uses a word in those days used for actress Jayne Mansfield. Original? Also, no. The accusation that King borrowed this ending from his friend Archibald Carey Jr.'s speech to the 1952 Republican National Convention is mostly true. Carey's ending:

> We, Negro Americans, sing with all loyal Americans: My country 'tis of thee, Sweet land of liberty, Of thee I sing. Land where my fathers died, Land of the Pilgrims' pride. From every mountainside Let freedom ring!
>
> That's exactly what we mean—from every mountainside, let freedom ring. Not only from the Green Mountains and White Mountains of Vermont and New Hampshire; not only from the Catskills of New York; but from the Ozarks in Arkansas, from the Stone Mountain in Georgia, from the Blue Ridge Mountains of Virginia—let it ring not only for the minorities of the United States, but for the disinherited of all the earth—may the Republican Party, under God, from every mountainside,

But King's speech was meant not to stretch minds or conform to academic requirements; it was meant to move hearts. Because nothing follows the clincher except—hopefully—applause, it must be memorable. Because it can go beyond the speech's subject, it has the ability to surprise, as does the last line in Kennedy's inaugural address.

Finally, because audiences need a final reminder of why their actions are so important, clinchers should make sure listeners see that final, elevating purpose. King ended by echoing one of the most common themes in political speeches: the prediction that by acting we will usher in freedom.

Political clinchers are not always about freedom. But their range is not vast. Whether for audiences large or small, Democrat or Republican, partisan or nonpartisan, the following themes dominate American politics: freedom, a bright future, the uniqueness of America, winning, change, peace, hope, and "the American dream"—a phrase used in various ways but usually meaning the ability to achieve some combination of economic and political freedom. Only speakers with more limited subjects—for example, safe toys, or fatherhood—return to those narrower subjects, and even then, not always.

Let's look at how speakers strike these themes in their very last sentence. And we'll finish by seeing how often one technique of language occurs again and again because of its capacity to both surprise and become memorable.

Predict a Brighter Future

In chapter 12 you read the selection from AIDS activist Mary Fisher's speech at the 1992 Republican National Convention, with its memorable line about those who "do not dare whisper the word AIDS." Because secrecy seems so destructive, it's appropriate that in a "referral ending"—a format that refers to a line or image planted earlier, she imagines a brighter future when people "may not need to whisper it at all." Worth noting, too: even though Fisher imagines a better future in her last line, hers is an incredibly sad speech, made more moving by the pledge to her children that precedes it—a reminder that ending with optimism doesn't always preclude honesty.

To my children, I make this pledge: I will not give in, Zachary, ——— Pledge
because I draw my courage from you. Your silly giggle gives me
hope; your gentle prayers give me strength; and you, my child,
give me the reason to say to America, "You are at risk."
        And I will not rest, Max, until I have done all I can to make
your world safe. I will seek a place where intimacy is not the prelude to suffering. I will not hurry to leave you, my children, but
when I go, I pray that you will not suffer shame on my account.   Clincher—act so
        To all within the sound of my voice, I appeal: Learn with me   the future will be
the lessons of history and of grace, so my children will not be   better
afraid to say the word "AIDS" when I am gone.
        Then, their children and yours may not need to whisper it ——— Vision of a
at all.   brighter day

Assert the Greatness of America

In his classic farewell speech, Reagan ends reflectively with an extended meta-phor: America as a woman, like the Statue of Liberty—he echoes Emma Lazerus's famous line, "I lift my lamp beside the golden door"—nurturing and strong, then ends with a prediction of success to justify his belief in America's "eternal" greatness:

> Her heart is full; her door is still golden, her future bright. She has arms big enough to comfort and strong enough to support. For the strength in her arms is the strength of her people. She will carry on in the '80s unafraid, unashamed, and unsurpassed.
>   In the springtime of hope, some lights seem eternal. America's is.

Assert America's Special Place in the World

Anton Chekhov once wrote that in drama, if you put a gun on the wall in Act I, you must discharge it in Act III.[4] He might also have said: Plant the gun in Act I to add impact in the end. Referring back to something you have planted in the beginning of the speech lends the speech unity, thus intensifying the feeling of closure. It also has impact because the audience experiences the shock of recognition from having heard it before.

We have already seen one example: Mary Fisher's "whisper" referral. Here, you'll see all four steps of George W. Bush's 2001 inaugural address conclusion, in order to see how his writers created that effect.

Inspirational example	After the Declaration of Independence was signed, Virginia states-man John Page wrote to Thomas Jefferson: "We know the race is not to the swift nor the battle to the strong. Do you not think an angel rides in the whirlwind and directs this storm?"
Lesson	Much time has passed since Jefferson arrived for his inaugura-tion. The years and changes accumulate. But the themes of this day he would know: our nation's grand story of courage and its simple dream of dignity.
	We are not this story's Author, who fills time and eternity with His purpose. Yet His purpose is achieved in our duty, and our duty is fulfilled in service to one another.
Call to action	Never tiring, never yielding, never finishing, we renew that purpose today, to make our country more just and generous, to affirm the dignity of our lives and every life.
Referral clincher	This work continues. The story goes on. And an angel still rides in the whirlwind and directs this storm.

CLINCHERS AND ANTITHESIS

In this chapter, we have already seen a great variety of the techniques of language: metaphor, simile, parallel construction, short sentences, and others.

With limited space, let's examine just one device that can accommodate so many needs memorably: *antithesis*.

Using it to end a speech is hardly new. Here's one famous (italicized) example from 1630, John Donne's final sermon:

> There we leave you in that blessed dependency, to hang upon him that hangs upon the cross, there bathe in his tears, there suck at his wounds, and lie down in peace in his grave, till he vouchsafe you a resurrection, and *an ascension into that kingdom which He hath prepared for you with the inestimable price of his incorruptible blood.*

Not exactly a political speech. But in contrasting the bloody sacrifice of Jesus to the glorious Kingdom awaiting those who accept him, Donne fore-shadows the ways secular politicians now use antithesis.

In general, politicians use antithesis to: (1) celebrate the arrival of brighter days; (2) predict their coming; (3) urge sacrifice to ensure them; (4) remind the listeners that the days will be even brighter than they imagine; and (5) assure their audience that their goal is worthwhile. In striking those themes they find some contrasts that are especially valuable in politics, with its constant need for optimism. Here we see some different ways antithesis can draw contrasts to make the very last sentence memorable.

Past/Future

In his1994 speech about a "clean-car" initiative, Bill Clinton uses it to show how Americans blend tradition with innovation:

> We'll have the kind of car that is only a vision now, and people will trace it back to this partnership, between Americans willing to preserve what was best of our past—and work together for the future.

Small/Large

John Kerry, in his 2006 commencement speech at Kenyon College, contrasts "small" with "enormous" in this referral ending, mentioning stories and details he used earlier to assert the greatness of this moment:

> At some point you'll see that this small campus that changed you has produced enormous change in the world.
>
> And you will see that it came from what you learned here: from a class so compelling you were awake at the crack of dawn . . . from that night Teresa and I will never forget when you waited patiently till 4:15 at a polling place in Gambier . . . or from a coach who knew that her mission was to teach you how to win on and off the field.

Standing Still/Progress

Note the alliterative antithesis ("marking . . . made") in Reagan's ending to his farewell speech, in which he implies contrast between the previous administration and his own:

> My friends: We did it. *We weren't just marking time. We made a difference.* We made the city stronger; we made the city freer; and we left her in good hands. All in all, not bad—not bad at all.

Defeat/Victory

In his Oval Office speech after 9/11, George W. Bush contrasts the bleakness of that day with the determination to bring about the brighter days "we will" bring about this time. He uses antithesis twice, here—once to contrast past and present, the other to contrast tragedy and triumph:

> America has stood down enemies before, and we will do so this time. None of us will ever forget this day, yet we go forward to defend freedom and all that is good and just in our world.

Might/Right

The always useful "not-but" antithesis dominates this 1962 JFK speech about choice. Notice that alliteration, rhyme, and ascending order in the climax all contribute to the rich language.

> Our goal is *not* the victory of might, *but* the vindication of right—
> *not* peace at the expense of freedom *but* both peace and freedom,
> here in this hemisphere, and, we hope, around the world.

Effective endings don't rely on one device; they need a lot. We close this chapter by looking at one of the most original endings in political speech. Obama's conclusion on November 4, 2008, was notable for many things: the unusual length he allowed his inspirational example; his concrete detail; the way he fused the woman he described with the history of the twentieth century; and, certainly, the way he quietly brought back the theme. It wasn't just a YouTube moment.

Let's look at it, and see how many techniques he used.

Inspirational example	This election had many firsts and many stories that will be told for generations. But one that's on my mind tonight's about a woman who cast her ballot in Atlanta. She's a lot like the millions of others who stood in line to make their voice heard in this election except for one thing: Ann Nixon Cooper is 106 years old.
Parallel construction	She was born just a generation past slavery; a time when there were no cars on the road or planes in the sky; when someone like her couldn't vote for two reasons: because she was a woman and because of the color of her skin.
Antithesis and alliteration	And tonight, I think about all that she's seen throughout her century in America—the heartache and the hope; the struggle and the progress; the times we were told that we can't,
Epistrophe and first use of "yes we can"; expression of optimism	and the people who pressed on with that American creed: Yes we can.
	At a time when women's voices were silenced and their hopes dismissed, she lived to see them stand up and speak out and reach for the ballot: Yes we can.
"When" litany; antithesis	When there was despair in the dust bowl and depression across the land, she saw a nation conquer fear itself with a New Deal, new jobs, a new sense of common purpose: Yes we can.

When the bombs fell on our harbor and tyranny threatened the world, she was there to witness a generation rise to greatness and a democracy was saved: Yes we can.

She was there for the buses in Montgomery, the hoses in Birmingham, a bridge in Selma, and a preacher from Atlanta who told a people that "we shall overcome": Yes we can.

A man touched down on the moon, a wall came down in Berlin, a world was connected by our own science and imagination.

And this year, in this election, she touched her finger to a screen, and cast her vote, because after 106 years in America, through the best of times and the darkest of hours, she knows how America can change: Yes we can.

America, we have come so far. We have seen so much. But there is so much more to do.

So tonight, let us ask ourselves—if our children should live to see the next century; if my daughters should be so lucky to live as long as Ann Nixon Cooper, what change will they see? What progress will we have made?

This is our chance to answer that call.

This is our moment.

This is our time, to put our people back to work and open doors of opportunity for our kids;

. . . to restore prosperity and promote the cause of peace;

. . . to reclaim the American dream and reaffirm that fundamental truth, that, out of many, we are one; that while we breathe, we hope.

And where we are met with cynicism and doubt and those who tell us that we can't, we will respond with that timeless creed that sums up the spirit of a people: Yes we can.

Annotations (right margin):
- "When" litany; antithesis
- Synecdoche
- "A" litany
- Lesson learned
- "Done much," "more to do" litany
- Choice litany as rhetorical questions
- Implied call to action
- "This" litany
- Clincher of optimism, apostrophe, alliteration—and antithesis

In a chapter this long, it's worth a look back to see what we've covered. It included:

- The four steps of one common ending in political speech
- Examples of how these steps motivate, define, ask, and elevate.
- The themes common to those endings
- And the attitudes—command, suggest, imply—speakers adopt.

You have looked at the elements of political speech. You have seen how they work in each step of the most common format for persuasion about policy. But a speech is more than an assortment of techniques—and more than a series of steps.

The Speechwriter's Checklist: Writing Conclusions

☐ Have I evoked genuine emotion in this audience?

☐ Have I made my speaker demonstrate leadership?

☐ Have I broadened my conclusion to include larger themes?

☐ Have I offered "choice" or "referral" endings?

☐ Have I closed on a note of hope?

☐ In using the four-part close, have I:

    ☐ found material that will inspire these listeners?

    ☐ drawn a parallel they will accept?

    ☐ asked, commanded, or implied action in a way that will make them respond?

    ☐ made my last line memorable?

Delivery

He strides to the podium at the 2004 Republican National Convention, puts his hands on each side of the lectern, the very slowness of his movements exuding confidence, then thrusts his shoulders back and his chin out, nodding as if to say, "Yes, I deserve this."

You've seen him in *The Terminator,* covered with blood and dirt. Tonight he wears a black suit, starched white shirt, and yellow tie. Black, consultants say, is a power-suit color; yellow implies friendliness. He hasn't started speaking yet, but already he's sent signals about who he is and why he's worth listening to. For now, never mind what you'll hear. You're caught up by what you see.

In chapter 8, Landon Parvin mentioned how important rehearsal has been to Arnold Schwarzenegger. He may make fun of his own acting abilities, and like any other speaker, he needs rehearsal. But don't let Jay Leno's jokes about him obscure the truth: Schwarzenegger is an effective speaker. You should learn from him.

For in politics, speaking skills count. While this book focuses most intently on how to write speeches, you can't ignore how to deliver them. Without these skills, as learnable as playing tennis or guitar, or how to change a flat tire, you can make a well-written speech sound dull. With them, you can make a mediocre speech terrific. So it is baffling that people who speak so much devote so little time to learning them.

That they don't is evident to anyone who chooses to sit through an afternoon of debate in the U.S. House of Representatives, where, eyes wedded to the text, hands gripping the lectern, member after member drones through material.

True, politicians are often too rushed to rehearse. Anyone who's worked in the White House knows the experience of seeing the president or vice president walk to the motorcade or out to the Rose Garden ten minutes before an event, reading a draft for the first time.

Politicians usually manage to rehearse for the big speeches—but most speeches aren't big. In this chapter, we analyze how to deliver material compellingly, so you can apply the best speakers' techniques to your own speeches, whether they're major or routine.

There is one big difference between this chapter and the rest of the book. While the others aim equally at speaker and speechwriter, this chapter contains suggestions that only the speaker can carry out.

Those tips begin with the three basic elements of effective delivery: *appearance, movement,* and *voice.* Then we'll see how these elements combine to influence the three types of speeches most common in politics—*extemporaneous, impromptu,* and *text.* But to describe the basics of public speaking isn't enough; most career politicians understand them. The problem is that they ignore in practice what they understand in theory. So the final section covers the ways you *prepare* to speak.

For the most important point about delivery is not technical. It is this: *Great delivery comes not from what you do at the podium, but from what you do away from it.*

ELEMENTS OF DELIVERY

David Demarest, one of George H. W. Bush's communications directors, once said of his boss that a belief in being a good "orator" just "wasn't in Bush's DNA."[1] Sorry. To value speaking skills is not genetic. Every politician can not only improve as a speaker but excel. After ten years of teaching public speaking to undergraduates, I know that the lure of a good grade can turn undergrads into good speakers. Winning elections can, too. And that begins with three things.

APPEARANCE

If you didn't know it already, watching Schwarzenegger's convention speech should convince you: appearance counts. It is a fact of political life that taller candidates have an advantage over shorter ones, candidates with hair over bald ones, and better-looking ones over the less attractive. But you can overrate the significance of those things. "Politics," people in Washington say, "is Hollywood for ugly people." There's truth to that. Plenty of successful politicians weigh too much, and the political talk shows are filled with people whose wizened faces would win no beauty contests. Most politicians are in office not because of how they look but because of how and what they think.

Still, they need to do the best they can with what they have. In the studiedly cautious words of researchers who have looked into the subject, physical attractiveness "enhances one's effectiveness as a social influence agent." The research shows that before speakers say anything, audiences have formed some impressions of them.[2] In other words, delivery begins before speakers utter their first word. Here are three areas to think about as you help create your audience's first impression.

Stand Straight

"Listeners perceive speakers who slouch as being sloppy, unfocused, and even weak," Jo Sprague, Douglas Stuart, and David Bodary advise in the 2008 edition of their excellent *Speaker's Handbook*.[3]

But while most politicians know enough to stride briskly to the podium and look out at the audience as they start, it's not unusual as the speech progresses to see them slouching, crossing legs at the ankles, leaning on the lectern, or committing other sins of body language that in small, subtle ways risk lessening credibility or likability.

As your mother always said, stand up straight. And whether you move around the stage or stay behind the lectern, keep standing straight for as long as you're up there.

Dress Better Than Your Audience

Over seventy-five years ago, Dale Carnegie, then America's guru of public speaking, put it this way, in words chosen to express contempt:

> If a speaker has baggy trousers, shapeless coat and footwear, fountain pen and pencils peeping out of his breast pocket, a newspaper or a pipe and can of tobacco bulging out of the sides of his garment, I have noticed that an audience has as little respect for that man as he has for his own appearance. Aren't they very likely to assume that his mind is as sloppy as his unkempt hair and unpolished shoes?[4]

That was then. Have we made progress since the days of Calvin Coolidge? Not much. The fashion consultant David Wolfe points out that for job applicants, "dressing down . . . could mean you don't need the job."[5] Politicians, whose every speech before constituents is a job interview, can't risk creating that impression.

We have moved beyond the days when politicians had to live in a dark suit and dress shoes. But even if you are in an Iowa living room talking to farmers in overalls, the rule is to dress somewhat better than your audience. If a male speaker is wearing slacks and an open shirt, they should be pressed and—face it—expensive-looking. Do speakers need $400 haircuts? No. But they usually need a blow-dryer—and for candidates who shake thousands of hands a year, a manicure.

Look Younger

Politicians get wrinkled, go bald or gray, and lose their teeth. They gain weight, move with the stiffness of arthritic joints, and get liver spots on their hands. It is tempting to argue that the usual remedies for these universal conditions symbolize the posturing of so much of political life: Let your hair go gray! Wear those worry lines proudly!

Don't believe it. Audiences don't want their politicians to look twenty-two, and certainly once people are in public life for a long time they have assets like name recognition that overcome wrinkles. But appearance affects credibility *and* a speaker's mood. "Speakers who feel attractive are more self-confident," Steven Brydon and Michael Scott argue in their public-speaking text *Between One and Many.*[6]

For politicians, this means that within the limits of what culture finds acceptable, you should aggressively attack and mask the effects of aging. Some things don't work: obvious toupees, wretched comb-overs, or a full set of perfectly white implants in a politician over seventy. Few would claim that Sen. Joe Biden's hair plugs won him the vice presidency. But for all his ability, it is hard to imagine Gov. Mike Huckabee running for president if he hadn't lost one hundred pounds.

Politicians at the highest levels already know that appearance counts. In 2006, the average woman in the U.S. Senate was fifty-eight; only one had gray hair.

MOVEMENT

In the 1988 Democratic primary, Gov. Bruce Babbitt of Arizona was intelligent, thoughtful, and knowledgeable about the issues. Yet he made little headway as a presidential candidate. One small but hard-to-ignore reason: the facial tics he could not control during the early debates, leading one of his consultants to recommend "eyebrow pushups" as a way to stop blinking.

As governor and later secretary of the interior, Babbitt did have a successful career in politics. But even a tic can hurt. People in political life increase their effectiveness as speakers by doing systematic work to eliminate movements that distract—swaying, shifting, jutting out a hip, blinking, licking lips, playing with hair, and a variety of others.

You won't see movement problems much at national conventions, where speech coaches thoroughly rehearse speakers before sending them onstage to a podium flanked by teleprompters. It's more common at coffees or town hall meetings, where politicians sway, slouch, and stick their hands in their pockets; or in rarely rehearsed floor speeches, where they might look down nearly the whole time they're speaking.

In small gatherings—say, a living room—politicians don't have to stay behind a lectern. But they can learn to limit their movement so it doesn't seem as distracting as John McCain's in the second 2008 presidential debate, when he seemed to be wandering back and forth as if lost. Don't sway. Don't shift. Such movements signal that the speaker isn't comfortable. That means the audience won't be, either. And while you work on eliminating movements that distract the audience, focus on three areas that help you express your thoughts.

Use Appropriate Facial Expressions

You don't have to smile all the time. Watch Schwarzenegger later in that 2004 speech, telling a story of a soldier's sacrifice. His face is somber. Only at the end does he allow himself a smile as he lightens the moment with a joke. But certainly in the beginning of a speech, smiles signal that you're confident, happy to be speaking, and pleased to see the people in front.

Like posture, facial expressions count throughout the speech. It's important not only to watch for inappropriate expressions but also to monitor what all your expressions communicate. In the 2008 vice presidential debate, after Biden had choked up while talking about his late wife, Sarah Palin could have demonstrated sympathy with a pause and a compassionate nod. By launching right into her talking points, though, she showed the opposite—and the tracking monitors of CNN's sample audience measured an immediate drop in approval.

Maintain Eye Contact

In 1966, during Jimmy Carter's run for governor of Georgia, an Atlanta reporter named Achsah Nesmith noticed something odd: whenever Carter spoke he would look not at his listeners but above their heads. He seemed to be hunting for an exit.

One day when Carter asked Nesmith her impressions of his speech, she told him. "He looked hurt," she said later, "and I rather regretted it." But Carter stopped his overhead glances. And ten years later, he'd forgiven Nesmith enough to hire her as a speechwriter.[7]

Americans trust people who look them in the eye. Looking at your audience also allows you to see what they're feeling. If they're yawning, chatting, or devoting full attention to their cheesecake, it may be time to cut the speech short. And on the floor? Do the empty seats in front of you mean nobody's watching? Think again. Most speeches in the House are given to an empty chamber, but a hundred thousand people might be watching on TV. Whether reading from a text, talking points, or a note card, political speakers need to master the art of looking up.

And when you do look up, make sure you also look around. You don't connect with an audience by looking straight ahead; you need to make contact with all corners of the room.

Speakers can vastly improve eye contact by following three rules.

Absorb Groups of Words

Glance at the next two sentences for a moment. Then look up and say what you remember.

Tonight, we come together to write a new

chapter in the American story.

Our Forebears enshrined the American

dream—life, liberty, and the pursuit of

happiness.

Can you recite five words? Now read the two sentences aloud, taking in groups of words, like big gulps of Gatorade. Did you beat your previous record? Could you read comfortably looking down just . . . three times?

Those are the first two sentences from the—to speechwriters—famous episode in Bill Clinton's administration, when, about to give his 1993 health care address, he realized the wrong speech was in the teleprompter. Horrors! He had to read from his hard copy until the operators frantically replaced the disc and scrolled down to catch up.

Now, watch Clinton.

AS DELIVERED

Bill Clinton without the Teleprompter.
http://college.cqpress.com/politicalspeech

He looked down three times. Of course, it helped that Clinton also asked for a moment of silence in recognition of a train wreck in Alabama. While he looked down he was no doubt practicing.

But even in the first two minutes of his speech, Clinton looked down only fourteen times for the 158 words. That's pretty good. Note how brief his glances were. The ability to take in groups expands with practice. With practice every one of you reading this chapter should be able to look up for ten of every eleven seconds, just like Clinton.

Think Three Slices of Pizza

Look again at those first two minutes. Notice Clinton turning his head each time he looks down. Left, right, right, center, left—even without the teleprompter he does what public speaking coaches urge clients: to move not just their eyes but their heads. Sometimes we tell speakers to divide the audience in thirds, as if they were looking at three slices of pizza, looking at the tip of each slice, moving at pauses from one slice to the next.

"There is a great deal of research to show that speakers in the United States who refuse to establish eye contact are perceived as tentative or ill at ease and may be seen as insincere or dishonest," says Stephen E. Lucas in his classic text, *The Art of Public Speaking.*[8]

If, during the seven minutes before his teleprompter was working, Clinton still looked up 90 percent of the time, so can you. If you give a floor speech to a deserted chamber, you should still look up. The people watching at home and other offices will see you speaking to them.

This point took on new importance in 2008. That year, television audiences felt Barack Obama was speaking to them. He was looking up and out at them, after all. No one could see his eyes moving.

How does he do that? students would ask. They were amazed to learn that his speech was scrolling down teleprompter screens just out of camera range. They recovered fast, though. *Well, of course,* students told me. If I had a teleprompter, I'd communicate better, too.

Clinton's example is useful to the overwhelming majority of readers, most of whom will never use a teleprompter. With practice, you won't need one to connect.

Work on Your Gestures

It's the most common question people ask when they're trying to improve their delivery: "What do I do with my hands?" American audiences view speakers who use their hands and arms as more open and more believable. But even senators keep their arms pinned to their sides, or in their pockets, or button then unbutton their jackets.

For that reason, some coaches believe speakers should consciously learn and practice gestures that express common emotions. In Box D.1, you'll find a group of basic gestures once popular among public speaking teachers but now the subject of debate because they can seem artificial. As both speaker and teacher, I've seen that many people *can* learn to use them appropriately. But I've also seen speakers use them robotically and seem almost comic, like the wildly gesturing TV financial advisor Jim Cramer.

BOX D.1 Gestures

- *Pointing:* Finger or hand toward listeners when speaker is addressing them.
  (*You have been courageous. . . .*)
- *Giving:* Both hands outstretched when speaker is indicating support.
  (*I have fought for your issues. . . .*)
- *Receiving:* One or both hands at chest level, palm turned toward speaker.
  (*I have seen the pain when. . . .*)
- *Rejecting:* Hand up as if taking an oath, palm toward audience, waggling back and forth.
  (*I will not accept. . . .*)
- *Counting:* Finger of one hand tapping fingers of the other, as speaker enumerates.
  (*First, it's wrong. Second, . . .*)
- *Cautioning:* Index finger up.
  (*But we cannot. . . .*)
- *Dividing:* One hand chopping down, then the other, to indicate different sides. (*On the one hand X . . . on the other hand Y.*)

You can try these by marking where in the text you'd want to use them. Rehearse your speech and check what you look like in the mirror or on video, which even most $100 digital cameras can now record nicely. Give these experiments some time; just like any physical act, gestures will seem awkward at first.

But these seven movements are not the only ways to use your hands and arms. To see someone using gestures in a minimalist but effective way, look at two passages from a celebrated speech from the 2008 presidential election: Obama's July

AS DELIVERED

Barack Obama's Berlin Speech, July 2008.
http://college.cqpress.com/politicalspeech

address in Berlin, Germany. Watch the quiet opening minute in which his hands appear above the lectern just a few times, then compare it to this more animated section in his conclusion—the twenty-second minute.

GESTURE	SPEECH
extends right hand, rhythmically accenting emphasized word	Will we extend our hand
raises right hand again, palm toward chest	to the people in the forgotten corners of this world who yearn
as looks left, raises left hand briefly	for lives marked by dignity and opportunity
left hand in sweeping gesture as if to emphasize scope of the effort	by security and justice? Will we lift the child in Bangladesh from poverty, shelter
right hand lifted, rhythmically accenting emphasized words	the refugee in Chad, and
right hand with finger extended, again rhythmically accenting important words	banish the scourge of AIDS in our time?
lifts left hand to emphasize "or"	Will we stand for the human rights of the dissident in Burma, the blogger in Iran,
right hand up, more pronounced emphasis as if accenting each key word ("never again," "Darfur")	or the voter in Zimbabwe? Will we give meaning
right hand up, then, as pauses, pulls hand down again, before raising it as repeats	to the words "never again" in Darfur? Will we acknowledge
now hand up, palm toward audience in classic rejecting gesture	. . . will we acknowledge that there is no more powerful example than the one each of our nations projects to the world? Will we reject torture
hands toward body in gathering-in gesture	and stand for the rule of law? Will we welcome immigrants from different lands, and
left hand out as if pushing away an idea	shun discrimination against those who don't
right hand out, finger extended in warning gesture	look like us or worship like we do, and
hand up in giving and chopping gesture reminiscent of JFK	keep the promise of equality and opportunity for all of our people?

Notice how many times Obama simply uses his hand, fist loosely closed, to accent his point. He accomplishes a lot with that simple, easy-to-learn way of adding gesture for expression. But notice, too, that it's not his only gesture. He lifts a finger in warning, extends his palm outward, sweeps it from his left to right, and sometimes chops during his most forceful moments. These aren't always the classic gestures of rhetoric. But don't they seem the natural outgrowth of his thought? And wouldn't he seem stilted without them?

There are a few truisms about gestures. First, *use body movements to express your thoughts.* The gestures that accompany a cascade of insults directed at the other side during a debate are not the ones you'd use when delivering a eulogy at a funeral. Second, *different events call for different styles.* Your arms should get more of a workout at a rally in a labor hall than a coffee for fifteen people in an Iowa living room. Finally, *gestures should suit your personality.* What makes one speaker self-conscious might strike another as appropriately expressive. Experiment with gestures as you do with sound. You won't know until you try.

A little later we will look at one clip in which the speaker's gestures don't make that contribution. But remember: If you speak forcefully while your hands and arms are motionless, you are sending two different messages. Whatever you feel fits your style, don't rest until you see your bodily movement helping what you say instead of contradicting it.

VOICE

The student was smart, hardworking, eager to improve, and full of ideas—which he uttered so fast that he swallowed half his words and spoke the rest in short, machinegun-like bursts that all of us in the class had to work hard to decipher.

For the first weeks of the semester, I wrote long descriptions of what he sounded like and talked to him about it after class. "Yeahyeahyeah," he would say.

Then we switched to a new approach American University had made possible: digital tapes we could use, then play back instantly. The student watched and was horrified. "I see what you mean," he said, speaking slowly for the first time. He bought a tape recorder. And for the next week's speech, he articulated every word.

It's like the old joke: "How many psychiatrists does it take to change a light bulb? Just one—if the light bulb wants to change." It's easy to learn the essentials of voice, but you need motivation. That may mean getting someone to give you a frank assessment of how bad you are. More often, you need to see for yourself.

When I coach speakers about voice, I emphasize variety. That means varying three qualities that affect the sounds you make: pitch, rate, and volume; and two techniques for indicating importance or shifts in subject matter: pauses and emphasis. Finally, I cover pronunciation and articulation, two skills linked to both delivery and understanding. Let's look at each.

Pitch

"Singing is just sustained talking," intones the bass member of *The Music Man*'s barbershop quartet. Like a song, a conversation has high and low notes. But the range of highs and lows that's fine in conversation can sound dull in a twenty-minute speech. Announcers consciously learn to extend their pitch range—to see how different they talk from the rest of us, watch any news program listening only for pitch. You don't have to sound like them. But expanding your range beyond the highs and lows you use at the dinner table will make listeners pay attention.

Rate

Normally, people speak at about 150 words per minute. In his Berlin speech, Obama took twenty-five minutes to say about three thousand words; after you subtract several minutes of applause, that was pretty close to average. But these aren't constant rates. For important points, good speakers slow down. At peak moments, they may speed up. Variety is enormously important in maintaining credibility and interest.

Volume

How loud should you be? It depends. Speech coach Michael Sheehan, who preps speakers for the Democratic conventions, reminds them there's no need to shout. The speakers are using a good sound system, and they have a large TV audience. For the folks at home, shouting is as invasive as someone shouting in their living room—which is where the speaker will be. Varying volume also helps you shift your tone and convey different emotions. Watch Obama's quiet opening in the Berlin speech and contrast it with the way he finishes. Should he have done it any other way?

Pauses

The space between words can be an incredibly useful rhetorical tool. A pause can signal listeners that you're switching gears, or have something important coming up, or that you're searching for the right word because you care about being precise. For example, watch Ronald Reagan telling the "sailor" story in his 1989 farewell about two minutes into his speech:

> I've been thinking a bit at that window. I've been reflecting on what the past eight years have meant [PAUSE] and mean. And the image that comes to mind like a refrain is [PAUSE] a nautical one—a small story [PAUSE] about a big ship, and a refugee, and a sailor. It was back in the early eighties, at the height of the boat people. And the sailor was hard at work on the carrier *Midway*, which was patrolling the South China Sea. The sailor, like most American servicemen, was

young, smart, and [PAUSE] fiercely observant. The crew spied on the horizon a leaky little boat. And crammed inside were refugees from Indochina hoping to get to America. The *Midway* sent a small launch to bring them to the ship and safety. As the refugees made their way through the choppy seas, one spied the sailor on deck, and stood up, and called out to him. He yelled, [PAUSE] "Hello, American sailor. Hello, [PAUSE] freedom man."

A small moment with a big meaning, a moment the sailor, who wrote it in a letter, couldn't get out of his mind. And, when I saw it, [PAUSE] neither could I.

I haven't highlighted all the pauses. But note how the ones I included add irony, highlight a compliment, make sure you remember a key word, or just imply emotion.

Emphasis

Read these sentences aloud: *Emphasis* makes a big difference. Emphasis makes a *big* difference. Emphasis makes a big *difference*. Emphasis makes a [PAUSE] *big* difference. Look at Reagan's story again. Can you see how pauses and emphasis work in tandem, making a big [PAUSE] *difference?*

Pronunciation

You might think people running for office would know how to pronounce words. Most do. But even small mistakes hurt—like pronouncing *nuclear* as *new-cue-lar,* or mispronouncing a name, as I learned once when I quoted a singer my boss called Bob *Die*-lan. As a speaker, you shouldn't hesitate to seek pronunciation tips, and speechwriters shouldn't recoil at including them. Checking pronunciation is not a sign of ignorance; it's a sign that you want to get things right.

Articulated Pause

You've heard them: *Uh. Ummm. Er.* Other ingredients in this list suggest things to perfect; this is one to eliminate. Why do speakers lard their speeches with noises that make them seem unsure of themselves? Because silence makes them nervous, or they're afraid that a moment of silence will make audiences doubt them. But silence is infinitely preferable to random noises.

The Elements in Action

The basics of delivery may sound simple, but even frequent speakers often neglect to master them. In this example, Republican senator James Inhofe of Oklahoma begins a floor speech on energy. I include it not to pick on Inhofe— he's no worse than lots of senators in both parties—but to examine the way many politicians handle routine speeches. Watch for ways that his movements distract you, other than the ones noted below. There are plenty.

GESTURE	SPEECH
first AP, or articulated pause	Uh,
Inhofe looks down, puts hand in pocket	Thank you, Mr. President. I think, I wanted a chance and I haven't had a chance to do it, to come down
fixes glasses on nose	and talk about the Democrat bill the,
second AP	th . . . called the Consumer First Energy Act
scratches nose	and I—I—you know we go through this same thing over and over again
looks up	and we have an energy bill which has no energy in it. I said this on the floor last,
third AP	uh, last December. We keep talking about energy and every time we try to expand energy,
fourth AP	uh, try to expand the supply,
looks down; fifth AP	it, it divides right down along party lines. The Consumer First Energy Act does nothing to increase access to America's extensive oil and natural gas reserves, does nothing to promote
sixth AP	uh, nuclear energy, does nothing for, to increase refining capacity, something I've been trying to do for a long period of time, nothing for electricity generation or transmission, and nothing for clean coal technology.
looks up	Instead, this act increases taxes by seventeen billion dollars
left hand out of pocket to gesture	on America's oil and gas producers, which means,
looks down	you're going to pay more at the pump,
hand back in pocket	that's going to be passed on, we know that,
hand out of pocket, but only to place on podium	and it increases government bureaucracy.

Nobody expects a politician delivering a dull floor speech to an empty room to compare with a celebrity using a teleprompter to deliver a convention address before ten thousand screaming fans. But as we've already seen with Bill Clinton, Inhofe didn't need to look down almost two-thirds of the time, or use articulated pauses when he tried to ad-lib. With work he seems perfectly capable of eliminating his many distracting gestures; his rapid, unvarying pace (two hundred words a minute); and his almost completely unvaried pitch or volume.

So here's one suggestion you might hear from a coach in any sport: When the match is routine, work on your game. Why shouldn't people in political life view a routine speech not as something to cruise through on autopilot but as a low-stakes occasion for practicing delivery skills? Which leads us to our final question: What are the best ways to do that?

PRACTICE: THE KEY TO IMPROVING DELIVERY

Once, in high school, my track coach tried to tell me the secret to winning races. "Get out in front and stay there," he said.

Great advice. Just not possible for someone whose dreams outstripped his abilities. My track coach should have told me to up my mileage. That is, to practice on my own.

The same thing is true about speech. You need to get good coaching, and practice often, away from the podium. Practice doesn't make you perfect, but it can make you powerful.

Naturally, not all speeches need the same kind of practice. In the world of public speaking there are four methods of delivery. In politics, two of them, impromptu speeches and memorized speeches, don't count—or shouldn't. Memorized speeches take a prodigious amount of time and aren't worth the effort. Impromptu speeches are too risky.

Instead, the kind of debate prep that presidential candidates go through should be adapted to the daily routine of political life. Even people serving on a city council can work up a briefing book filled with thought-out, crisp answers to the questions most likely to come up at a town hall meeting or on a talk show. You can think, write, then rehearse regularly—while walking the dog, driving home, or taking a shower.

What about the question you didn't expect? If you don't know the answer, admit it, and then study for next time. Or learn what consultants call the "pivot": the kind of answer that begins something like this: *Great question. Yes, I'd like to do X. But the real question is. . . .* Sure, it's an evasion, and (in my view) overdone, but it's one sometimes made necessary by the nearly impossible demands of public life.

Two kinds of delivery dominate political speaking. The first, *manuscript* or *text,* means reading a speech that's been entirely written out. The second is the carefully prepared and practiced but not memorized speech, usually from talking points or some other form of notes, called *extemporaneous*. That's more common with stump speeches.

Practice away from the podium means two things: rehearsing before an actual speech, and improving techniques when there's no event coming up. Let's first review ways to rehearse.

REHEARSING A TEXT SPEECH

During one presidential campaign, I walked into a friend's office to see pages of a speech pasted around his walls, looking a little like miniature sheets on a clothes line. He had printed each sheet in two different colors of ink. Black was the text he had written. Blue were the ad-libs his boss had delivered. The pages were about 80 percent blue—and almost 100 percent incoherent. "He hates being scripted," my friend said, mournfully.

Who could blame him? Nobody likes to think his or her own thoughts are largely irrelevant. But for politicians, there's no way around being scripted. They need to speak fluently about dozens of subjects, and a lot rides on their avoiding errors. Speeches read word for word can sound stiff in front of small groups. For bigger crowds, though, a formal text allows politicians to speak effectively about issues with details only staffers should know—not to mention giving staffers a text to hand reporters.

A speaker with a text can drone through it, or use that same text to sound stirring. Rehearsal helps. Simply sitting at a desk mumbling through the script, occasionally stopping to change a word, does not. In this chapter, aimed at speakers more than writers, here are some steps that do.

Read Speeches Through, and Mark Them Up

On the cover of *Reagan: In His Own Hand* is a photo of the future president sitting at a desk, writing on a manuscript. No speechwriter, no matter how good or how familiar with your style, can make a speech yours. You need to read it aloud, and mark where you want a pause or emphasis. Those preliminary tasks are not part of rehearsal. They make rehearsal useful.

Rehearse Like You Mean It

That means standing at the podium and practicing exactly the voice and tone and gestures you will use. Only in that way will you be able to time the speech accurately and judge what works in your nonverbal language.

Rehearse Not Just to Practice What's There but to Include What Isn't

Use one rehearsal to figure out what you want and don't want. Revise. Then mark up the manuscript and start again.

Cut

Every draft ever written can be cut. Use one rehearsal to cut 10 percent—including words for ideas that could just as easily be conveyed by a gesture alone.

Extend Eye Contact

Even a rehearsal or two will allow you to remember larger groups of words each time, so you can preserve the eye contact so vital to persuasion. Make that an integral part of rehearsal.

LEARNING TO DELIVER AN EXTEMPORANEOUS SPEECH

Speaking extemporaneously is both the most difficult and most valuable delivery method in politics. To give an extended speech without notes, or with only a few talking points, takes careful preparation and many, many hours of rehearsal. If you can learn to deliver an extemporaneous speech well, you'll create the same impact you would with a teleprompter. You'll seem like you know a lot. You'll sound relaxed and conversational. And you'll be looking at your listeners the entire time.

At the local level, state legislators or small-town mayors should rarely rely on prepared texts; the audiences are too small, and the things they need to say are not that different from one event to the next. But even at the national level, politicians should speak extemporaneously much more often than they do. Yes, text speeches make an event easy. You can eat, schmooze with the guests, and not give a thought to the speech until you pull it out of your inside jacket pocket.

But if you want to be really effective, follow this advice, the most important in this chapter: *Use a stump speech, not just during the campaign but as often as possible.*

Other chapters examine the reasons it makes sense to use a stump speech, but let's review them quickly here. First, even if staffers and reporters have heard the stump speech a hundred times, most audiences at different events are different enough that they'll hear it only once. Second, though it may seem that a stock speech can't possibly accommodate everything you want to talk about, most people want to hear about relatively few of the issues that are in the news at any given time.

For instance, in spring 2009 most audiences would have wanted to hear about the fiscal collapse, Iraq and Afghanistan, health care, and perhaps the one big issue in their district. Your ideas about those issues weren't likely to have changed much from speech to speech.

So for most politicians, and except for floor speeches, the stump and a page of talking points should accommodate much of your speaking schedule. Some officeholders scoff at the stump speech. Don't. If you want to exhibit all the skills that make listeners say, *Let's march!*—making constant eye contact, telling jokes well, using gestures expressively, pausing and emphasizing appropriately—you can do it only with carefully prepared and rehearsed material that stays the same from month to month and year to year.

But remember: It won't be an effective stump unless you've planned it carefully. Resist the impulse to jot down a few notes and then amplify them weekly with good ideas you think of and tack on with sticky notes. A speech constructed that way will turn out just as shaky as a house built without plans.

Box D.2 outlines one way to systematically go about creating the kind of stump speech that you can deliver fluently, expressively, and compellingly.

BOX D.2   Stump Speeches

Here are ten steps for preparing a stump or any kind of extemporaneous speech. None of them deal with the content of what you're saying; that's what the rest of *The Political Speechwriter's Companion* is for. In this chapter we look only at how to say things well.

- Write out the speech, with careful attention to themes that work everywhere.
- Limit it to ten to twelve minutes, or about 1,500 to 1,800 words.
- Practice—first with text, then with a speaking outline, then with no notes at all.
- Practice in front of groups of staffers, videotaping each effort.
- Watch videos alone and with staff. Pay special attention to elements of delivery contained in this chapter: pitch, rate, volume, emphasis, pauses, and articulation.
- Revise. Isolate weak sections and practice intensely.
- Try it out with less important groups. Deliver the speech you've prepared; do not vary or digress.
- Make sure stories and jokes remain intact.
- Begin using the speech before groups for whom you might previously have used a text.
- Monitor constantly for creeping length.

Like some drugs, stumps take time to work. You need that time to become fluent, to become confident, to experiment with new material, and to learn from failure. But as you do, remember that this kind of practice can only get you so far. To really become good, remember the mantra that began this chapter: *Great delivery comes not from what you do at the podium, but from what you do away from it.*

EXPANDING YOUR HORIZONS

We've been reviewing one means to becoming a better speaker: rehearsal. But in addition to getting better at things you already do, improvement means experimenting with things you may never have done before.

Great speakers don't think about their speeches only on the day of an event any more than great tennis players contemplate strategy only before a big match. Becoming an excellent political speaker means thinking about it all the time. It also means tackling these five basic things that you could call tasks if they weren't also enjoyable.

LEARN HOW SPEECHES ARE MADE

Delivery cannot be totally divorced from content. If you don't know how repetition or parallel construction can increase power, how can you insist they be in your text? If you are running for office and reading this book, you're learning just the kinds of things that will help you. But check the Web links and watch every example. Look at some of the books listed in this book's bibliography—*The Political Speechwriter's Companion* doesn't have a corner on ideas. The more you read, the more you listen, the more ideas you'll have for your own speeches.

WATCH OTHER SPEAKERS

Not everyone should deliver a speech the same way. But whether you are a state rep in Iowa or a ten-term member of Congress, you've noticed which of your colleagues speak well. Imitating the things they do is a permissible form of plagiarism. In my classes I see that happen every semester. (*Oh!* That's *how litany sounds. Let me try!*) If twenty-year-olds can learn by imitating, so can their parents. We learn how to speak French by listening to people who know how. We learn how to play tennis from a coach. We learn how to dance from— well, okay, some people never do learn. And we can learn to speak by copying others.

If you need evidence, look at the role model admired by so many politicians: Martin Luther King. Taylor Branch's biography describes King at Morehouse College, having decided to become a minister, sneaking into the balcony of Wheat Street Baptist Church with some friends to study the speaking style of William Borders, a minister whose style they admired.

Later, at Crozier Divinity School, King studied oratory: the "proven" sermon structures (the Ladder, the Jewel, the Twin, and others) and how to apply the "three Ps"—proving, painting, and persuasion—"to win over successively the mind, imagination, and heart." Soon, his fellow students were crowding into the chapel to hear King deliver the Thursday morning student sermon.

You can make a case that King was a better speaker than writer. But he wasn't born that way.

STUDY YOUR OWN PERFORMANCE

Constantly. Video has made observation much easier for you than it was for King. Any friend or staffer with a camcorder can unobtrusively provide a tape of every appearance. But don't just watch. Watch critically, watch with friends or staff, and watch with the checklist you will find at the end of this chapter.

BEHIND THE SCENES

Carol Whitney

Carol Whitney first won attention by doing what people thought impossible. Asked in 1978 by an Oregon state senator to run his long-shot campaign for governor, she said, "Sounds like fun."

"He has no chance of winning the primary," one consultant told her about Republican Victor Atiyeh, and promptly quit the campaign. On primary night, a few months later, Whitney had the great pleasure of calling the consultant to say, "Guess what? We won in a landslide!"

After Atiyeh beat a Democratic incumbent to become the first American governor of Arab descent of any party, the Stanford-educated Whitney held a number of Republican Party posts, including executive director of the Republican Governors Association. But then she moved from putting people in office to what always interested her: teaching them how to speak.

Or, as she would put it, "make a connection."

"So many candidates focus on how they sound, rather than whether the audience is getting the message," says Whitney, who is co-program director of American University's Campaign Management Institute, teaches political communications, and works as a communications consultant.

To talk to Whitney is to hear an outpouring of crisply phrased advice about how to speak, honed by that work. "Body language," she says. "A big part of the message." She points to people who lean away from the podium, signaling their discomfort with a question. "Your body has to agree with your speech. And facial expressions! People say [candidates] don't smile enough. No! That's not natural." She mentions the "wolfish grin" of one prominent politician she finds particularly false.

Once, coaching a candidate, Whitney saw his problem. "He was a lawyer. If he had an emotional issue he'd explain it logically."

She asked him, "Don't you care?"

"Of course!"

"Show them!"

As a coach, Whitney makes a practice of building on success. She'll watch videos with the candidates, pointing out what they do well. She believes in listening to candidates' voices. When she writes speeches she tries to hear her clients say them as she writes.

But she also tries to improve them. After a little hesitation and the promise of confidentiality, she lets me see the preliminary assessment she made of one client. Her suggestions, typed in red, involve the things speakers need to hear—and can rarely get from staff:

PRACTICE NEW THINGS SYSTEMATICALLY

One of the frustrating things about coaching people in public life about delivery is that they think talking to a consultant brings change. It doesn't—no more than sitting and talking with a tennis coach improves your forehand.

When you spot a flaw, work on it. And keep working on it. Not overnight, but over time you will not just improve but revolutionize your delivery. And you will make that task easier with one final step.

Remember, you are holding a conversation with your audience . . . talk in conversational language . . . be cognizant of who and where your real audience is . . . they may not be in front of you. . . . It isn't enough to tell the audience where you stand . . . if you want them to really believe they need to know why.

Whitney isn't content to make recommendations. She believes candidates have to practice, and holds practice sessions with them. She talks about spending a three-day weekend with one Midwestern politician, watching tapes together. "We'd [work] on when to raise your voice, lower your voice," she says. "Speeches aren't all at the same level. You can change inflections. Use pauses."

She emphasizes techniques of connection: leaning forward to answer a question, making eye contact, using emotional language, and repeating the same phrase to reinforce a message.

At the end of the assessment I'm reading, Whitney reminds her client about the key question to keep in mind. It is one that involves *what* to say: "What does this audience want and what common values will both help you connect with and persuade them?"

But then this consultant, who over decades has helped dozens of Republicans from county commissioner to governor, ends with a final piece of advice that influences *how* to say it, based on her belief that politicians are too busy telling audiences what they think instead of caring about what the audience thinks.

"Now talk *with* them," she writes.

Carol Whitney's Five Tips for Speakers

1. Always tell the audience you are delighted to be here . . . even if you are not.

2. Remember, this is a conversation with the audience.

3. Use repetition for emphasis and humor to help them remember.

4. "Off the cuff" sounds easy, but it is dangerous; you never know what will come out of your mouth.

5. Focus on the audience, not your own voice.

Source: Carol Whitney spoke with Robert A. Lehrman in April 2009.

RELY ON THE ADVICE OF OTHERS

I leave this tip for last because it is ignored so often. When I was still a young speechwriter, I spent one year working for an excellent governor. It was a miserable year.

The problem wasn't as simple as poor speaking skills. When my boss was in a small group, he would lean over the lectern and tell stories. They were crisply told, witty, and always effective. But as soon as he looked down at his script, he would begin to drone—and never look up.

Afterward, when we would crowd into the elevator going down to the limo, the governor would look around at us staffers. "Gents?" (In those days we were all gents.) "How'd I do?"

I wanted to bring up every applause line he'd muffled, all the places he'd swallowed his words, all the moments when he should have looked up and connected with the audience. I wanted to . . . but I didn't. I was just as cowardly as everyone else.

"Great, governor," I would say, hating myself.

With maturity, I now see that he was right to ask us but wrong to expect candor. As a politician or candidate, you're surrounded by deferential aides. For a young, midlevel staffer, telling you about your bad posture is uncomfortable for both the staffer and you. Neither can you count on an honest critique from the people who invited you to speak. As congressional management consultant Rick Shapiro, more of whose insights you'll see in chapter 17, points out, these people need you. They'll always say, "Great speech."

Still, you cannot rely only on your own evaluation of your abilities. You may be reluctant to face the truth—or too harsh on yourself. You must subject yourself to the honest evaluation of others. Because your voice comes to you altered by the thickness of your own skull, you do not sound to yourself the way they do to others. You don't know when you're slumping, swaying, or droning. Only humiliating, exasperating practice can help, aided by video and the frank assessment of people who care about your goals and know what they're talking about. For politicians used to fawning praise, honest criticism can be tough to take.

My advice: Get over it. You have hired bright people. While you can't simply ask them how you did and expect a frank answer, you can create an atmosphere that fosters good feedback. Tell your chief of staff, "Look, I need your judgment. I need honest reactions from the new speechwriter, too. I know it takes nerve to tell the boss the truth. But I want to sit down after the big speeches, maybe review a tape, and I want you to tell me what you think. No holds barred."

If you encourage honest assessment, deal with it maturely when it comes, and then act on it in ways everyone can see, eventually you'll get plenty of useful advice—even from someone who looks younger than your kids. After all, if you feel comfortable delegating to a twenty-three-year-old the job of deciding how to vote on a $100 million appropriation, you should feel equally comfortable about that person's judgments on the way you make eye contact. Creating an office culture where staffers feel confident sharing opinions will be good for them—and better for you.

It is well worth doing. Except for the clergy, no field other than politics puts such a premium on speaking well. In the 2008 campaign, Mike Huckabee, Sarah Palin, and Barack Obama all moved audiences in different ways, winning voters in the process. This chapter should give you confidence about the elements of delivery, the way to practice, and the way to lift your game to their level. With work and time, you can become a great speaker—in your own, unique way.

Audiences may not remember much of what you say. But if you speak well, they will remember you.

The Speaker's Checklist: Delivery

APPEARANCE

- ☐ Am I standing straight?
- ☐ Did I take time to get a haircut and check my wardrobe?
- ☐ Do I try to stay reasonably physically fit?

MOVEMENT

- ☐ Have I refrained from swaying or other distracting movements?
- ☐ Do my facial expressions resemble those I'd use in conversation?
- ☐ Am I using my hands appropriately and expressively?

EYE CONTACT

- ☐ Have I rehearsed enough so I can look at the audience at least two-thirds of the time?
- ☐ Am I following the "three slices of pizza" rule?

VOICE

- ☐ Am I using a good range of high and low notes?
- ☐ Have I varied my inflections and speaking rate to suit the material?
- ☐ Do I articulate clearly and pronounce everything perfectly?

PREPARATION

- ☐ Do I routinely mark up speeches?
- ☐ Rehearse to cut and reshape?
- ☐ Practice extending eye contact?
- ☐ Systematically prepare my stump?
- ☐ Listen to other speakers?
- ☐ Investigate ways speeches are made?
- ☐ Watch other speakers?
- ☐ Study my own performance?
- ☐ Rely on the advice of others?

PART IV

PUTTING IT TOGETHER

"I don't actually write his speeches—I just nuance them."

Lee Lorenz. Published in *The New Yorker*, June 17, 2002.

chapter 15

A Speech Revisited

Remarks Prepared for Vice President Al Gore at Women's Legal Defense Fund Luncheon

Yes, half of everything you do in politics is useless. You just never know which half. In 1994, not knowing how I might use it, I did a detailed journal entry including every thought I had as I went about writing the speech you'll see here. You saw how I went about researching it in chapter 4, not because my thoughts were brilliant, but because they were typical. Now, having looked at the elements and structure of political speech, it's time to examine the rest.

Is this a little embarrassing? Definitely. Will you see things I should have done differently? Yes. But enough readers have told me to get over it—to let readers see speechwriting in real life. That I'll try. We return to that speech now, with annotations and comments to give you context. If you think it's useless— well, remember the opening line.

Washington, D.C., June 22, 1995

There's an old saying in politics: half of what you do is useless— but you can never tell which half. — Opening joke

Did I have to start with a joke? No. I began this way because I thought it would get a wry nod of the head from the organizing types that fill this kind of luncheon, show Gore as willing to acknowledge how frustrating politics can be—and set the scene for the anecdote that follows. How to get attention? I went with this story because it was an inspiring success story for this group— but also gave credit to someone unknown. Staffers never get enough credit. I was a staffer, too. I thought mentioning Donna Lenhoff was something the group would appreciate.

Eleven years ago, Donna Lenhoff couldn't possibly know if — Attention-getting what she was doing would pay off or not. She came back to the   anecdote old WLDF [Women's Legal Defense Fund] office at 2000 P Street from a meeting on the Hill about maternity leave. She sat down at her typewriter. And over the next few hours, she worked out legislative language for a bill providing a gender-neutral leave policy both for new babies and family emergencies.

> *Notice that this sentence isn't a direct quote; people rarely think in words*

Maybe we can get someone to introduce it in the House, she thought. Maybe we'll get some hearings out of it.

She got a lot more.

Her idea went through lots of changes over the next decade. So did WLDF—for one thing, you got rid of the typewriters and moved into the Information Age.

> *Something Gore, the hi-tech wonk, could get a laugh by pointing out*

But on February 5, 1993—two weeks after inauguration day—when President Bill Clinton signed the Family and Medical Leave Act, it's fair to say he was signing the literal descendant of what came out of Donna Lenhoff's typewriter, that night a decade before.

> *Note first repetition here: "due" repeated three times*

So Judy, while I appreciate your moving words—and while I am so grateful for the way we worked on that issue together, let me give honor where honor is due.

> *Praise for group; it never hurts to remind people that you worked hard on an issue with them*

That great achievement is also due to the thousands of people who worked and lobbied and wrote and petitioned and voted to transform an idea into law. Certainly it is due to the work of this organization.

Oh, and there are two other people who deserve credit.

And who could they be? The two Clintons were very popular at this point. As vice president, Gore is now into his praise mode; he should praise the president, move into the way he has opened up opportunities for women in many ways. Gore devotes the next five minutes to such praise—a little longer than most speeches, in part because there were really a lot of things to point out. I started with a generalization.

President Bill Clinton and Hillary Rodham Clinton, who have consistently fought to make women equal partners in government and American life.

Now a brief example. I had seen this in the schedule and thought it wouldn't hurt to mention it in case listeners were offended that Clinton himself hadn't come.

Actually, at this moment the president and first lady are out at Arlington, for the groundbreaking of the Women's Memorial there.

That's the first major national memorial celebrating women who have been—or are—part of this country's military.

It's long overdue; and the president and first lady feel strongly about the need to commemorate a role that has gone largely unsung since the Revolution.

Okay. Time to state the main theme. In fact, Gore's theme is empowering women—not simply the administration's achievements. He will also talk about problems and solutions, and try to inspire action. But right now, I need to fully flesh out praise for the administration for any doubters.

Today, I want to talk about something I feel strongly about: the president's achievements in the area of empowering women.

> Statement of main theme

Some of these achievements involve facts and figures.

But no figures sum up the president's achievements more than the way Madeline Kunin—our deputy secretary of education—put it awhile back.

> Cueing the audience that boring stats are ahead; but will he find ways to make this praise interesting?

She talked about having been at meetings in the White House under previous administrations. She would sit in the Roosevelt Room with other governors and presidents and see one other woman, sitting against the wall, a staff person. "We kind of winked at one another, as one does on those occasions, and our secret language, was, 'Hey, I'm glad you're there.' I went back to the Roosevelt Room not too long ago, and I couldn't get over it. Half the group was composed of women . . . and I thought, how can I ever have thought that this was such a masculine space and that I did not belong there?"

> The first attempt: surprising them with an unusually personal quote from a government official, one which should resonate with this audience— and show Gore as sensitive to its implications

There's been a change all right. A big change.

Is it worth pointing out the repetition in those two sentences, and a sentence fragment—the kind of colloquial speech that, said right, might sound more natural? And now the dreaded statistics.

Forty-four percent of the president's appointees have been women—by far the highest in history.

He has appointed women to cabinet-level posts never before occupied by women: Attorney General Reno, Secretary of Energy Hazel O'Leary, former Council of Economic Advisors chair Laura D'Andrea Tyson, OMB Director Alice Rivilin.

I'm trying to have Gore say, "I'm looking for posts always given to men to emphasize the extent of change." But now I have to look for some obscure jobs to show that the change has percolated down below the tokens. Here those lists I got from staffers across the driveway came in handy.

An example where the long title, with its strong scent of bureaucracy, might make the point

I don't want to talk only about the well-known names. One of the developments of the last few years is how many women are at the less-noticed jobs traditionally held by men—chief scientist at NASA, for example, or the director for defense research and engineering at the Department of Defense.

I try out an issue of particular interest to a group that brings cases to court. Pretty dull stuff except to the specialists, but maybe some comparisons can make them more interesting. And what about the federal bench?

The president has nominated fifty women out of 165 judicial nominees—two and a half times as many in two years as in the previous twelve years.

In fact, 53 percent of our appointees have been women and minorities—including one to the Supreme Court of the United States.

And more of those nominees, by the way, received the American Bar Association highest rating than the past three administrations.

Stats are a necessary part of persuading people— especially a sophisticated audience like this. But I worry that this is too dry. Time to move on.

The president has made an unprecedented commitment to empowering women.

Now, brief examples to support his point, with short sentences and repetition to build force. Each of these could be applause lines, incidentally. But that would slow the speech too much. He uses short sentences now, rushing through to build to his applause line—which has in it a sop to the right: a reminder that liberals don't actually like abortion.

He repealed . . . he revoked . . . he reversed

He repealed the gag rule. He revoked the import ban on RU-486. He reversed the ban on abortion services at military hospitals.

He has in every way been true to his principle that abortion ──┬── *Applause line clincher*
be safe, legal—and rare.

He has expanded economic, professional, and education
opportunities for women.

That's why the Small Business Administration has estab- ──┬── *More repetition here.*
lished a women's mentoring program and made more busi-   │ *"That's why . . . that's*
ness loans to women.   │ *part . . . that's why."*

That's part of the reason behind the Earned Income Tax
Credit—the equivalent of a 40 percent pay raise for working
mothers with minimum wage jobs.

That's why women soldiers now have access to 259,000
positions in the military that were previously reserved for
men.

That doesn't say they've been filled with women, but
okay. There are political reasons for mentioning these
things, and they add to the support for Gore's overall
point. But this is getting kind of dry, right?

The president has worked to increase safety and security
for women.

That's the point of the Violence Against Women Act
(VAWA)—part of the president's Crime Bill. It improves the
response of law enforcement officials to such crimes. It does so
many things as well, like improving lighting at bus stops, forcing
sex offenders to pay restitution, or tripling the funding for bat-
tered women's shelters.

It also extends "rape shield" protections to all criminal and
civil cases involving alleged sexual misconduct. We want to stop
those embarrassing and irrelevant inquiries into the sex lives of
victims.

You know, sometimes discrimination occurs where you'd
least expect it. There were many well-meaning scientists who
had no idea how exclusively medical research had concentrated
on the diseases of men. Now NIH is correcting that.

And this president has worked to make sure women are no
longer left out

He signed legislation requiring that women and minorities
be included in all clinical research supported by NIH—and he
dramatically increased funding for breast cancer research—by
65 percent at NIH alone.

Enough brief examples! Let me try to enliven things a
little with an anecdote and something light—that
cartoon comes to mind.

Finally, this president has promoted the empowerment of women throughout the world.

This is a point of special concern to me.

The population strategy adopted by the last administration, in Rio, was a disturbing one.

We've turned things around. And I think of [UN Foundation president] Tim Wirth, coming back from the first United Nations meeting at which he discussed the president's ideas.

He said, "Their response was overwhelming. There was a sense of electricity and excitement on the floor. Dozens of delegates came over and said, 'Welcome back to humanity; welcome back to the world.'"

Not a great anecdote. Just the best I could come up with in the limited time I had. At least it has meaning to the audience who really cares about Rio. Oh, I should remind them that Gore was involved.

I was in Cairo. I will never forget how exciting it was to see us finally forge a partnership with more than 150 countries on a platform encouraging gender equality and reproductive rights. The United States is now a leader in the rights of women and we intend to see that there is no going back!

It's a wonderful record of accomplishment.

Does the president get enough credit for it?

Understatement — You'll excuse me for thinking he doesn't—not the president, the administration, or those surrounding him. They don't get enough credit—and get too much blame.

I imagine Gore pausing here, half-smiling, taking a sip of water.

Of course he knows who drew it! — I think of that Wasserman cartoon showing two sullen men, sitting on barstools. "So we're angry white men?" one asks.

"Yeah," the second man says. "Corporations are cutting our pay, exporting our jobs, and laying us off."

"So we're angry at corporations?"

"No," says the second man, his face contorted with anger. "HILLARY CLINTON."

The fact is, regardless of the distorted impressions of some, by working together, we have done so much.

That's the end of the praise section—the recitation of accomplishments both by the group and by the

administration. Gore has used brief examples, anecdote,
statistics, quotes, and a cartoon for humor. Now I'll use
the standard transition to his problem section.

But there is still so much we need to do. —— Transition

Remember—it is 1995, Republicans have just ended forty
years of Democratic rule in the House and are making progress
with their Contract for America. And so it is distressing to see all —— Problem
the things we have worked for now under assault by a Repub-
lican Congress.

Apparently the Republican leadership believes that when it
comes to the challenges facing America, there is no role for
government.

This has been true, whether it is environment or education
or health. But let me mention two [issues.]

If this were a longer speech I might have gone into a long
litany of complaints about the Republican Congress. It
was a lunch, however, and there were two issues of
special interest to the group: a controversial nomination
(later defeated), and affirmative action. It was
important not to send any signal that we were
weakening in our support of the surgeon general
nominee, Dr. Henry Foster. So here I will lump problem/
solution together—direct juxtaposition, remember?—
mention the issue, and defend the administration's
solution.

The first is the issue we are seeing played out on the
Senate floor: the nomination of Dr. Henry Foster. —— Solution

I am so proud that the president nominated this good man,
this distinguished doctor from my state, to be our next surgeon
general.

Here is a man who has given so much hope to the families
of Tennessee.

Here is a man who has devoted his life to giving life to —— Important because it
others.   had come out that he
                                                                                       had occasionally
If we do not win . . . if, as [Sen. J. James Exon, D-Neb.,] put   performed abortions
it, Henry Foster is "sacrificed on the altar of presidential politics," we will be back. And I can assure you we will have a great
surgeon general, one who will work for the kind of values that
Dr. Foster has championed throughout his life.

Translation: Don't bother defeating him—our next
choice will be just as bad.

Problem

Solution

The second issue is affirmative action.

This administration is against quotas and guaranteed results.

But this country has not yet achieved quality of opportunity or stamped out discrimination. The glass ceiling still exists—white males are 43 percent of the workforce but 95 percent of senior management.

And the fact is, affirmative action programs have made a great deal of difference to the lives of Americans.

Some brief examples, given force by repetition of "look." And then, an extended one.

Applause line

Look at the military. The military works hard to make sure there is a promotion pool that reflects the racial and gender makeup of the people in the rank below. In education, training, leadership, the military looks like America—and it works.

Look at the Small Business Administration. Last year it increased loans to minorities by over two-thirds, to women by over 8 percent. We didn't make a single loan to an unqualified person. But we gave people who never had a chance before to get in business.

I'm worried. There's been too much program summary in this speech. I want Gore to seem warmer, less the policy wonk. So now, the personal example.

And let me mention one—more humble—example from my own life.

When I went to high school back in the '60s sports were a major part of my life. But it was unheard of to take seriously any girl's athletic team. If you were ten years old and there was a girl on your team it was a sign that you weren't serious.

Now I have three daughters. I can tell you they take sports seriously. And sports have enriched their lives.

What is it that gave them this chance?

Title Nine. An affirmative action program.

And when I see those who would try to do away with it, I want to ask: Shouldn't your daughters enjoy the same possibilities available to your sons? Don't you want that for them?

Increasing opportunity for all Americans makes citizens more productive, builds stronger communities and a stronger nation. We must find a way to do that, and under this administration we will do that by finding which programs work and giving them our full support.

*Another applause line. In the next chapter you'll see how
linking "we must," which shows belief, and "we will,"
which shows determination, produces applause. It's time
to close—starting with the inspirational example.*

You know, the other day, Tipper and I were at the Race for
the Cure. It was an amazing event. Some of the most moving
moments came listening to those who wore the pink caps
which meant they were breast cancer survivors. Or seeing those
with signs on their backs saying they were running for their
mother—or daughter—or sister.

— Always a little risky to
write folksy expressions
into the text, but it
does work

Inspirational example

*This isn't a great example, but it has the advantage of
being true—something Al and Tipper Gore have done.
I'm hoping that with concrete detail I might evoke a
shock of recognition in the audience, some of whom had
run in the race, too.*

But it was moving, too, just to see how many people were
there. The roads were so packed some people couldn't break
into a jog for the first mile.
And as I ran I thought about how, year by year, because of
the hard work and dedication of hundreds of people, what had
been just an idea became this amazing story of success.
Just like Race for the Cure our work is not a sprint.
You have to look down the road a bit.
I am confident that if we move down that road together,
we will win.
For this is a group that is used to winning.
You have won for pregnant women who lost their jobs. You
have won for victims of sexual harassment who didn't know
where to turn. You won for those who desperately needed time
to take care of a sick child or parent.
During the 1992 campaign, Bill Clinton said, "It's time not
only to make women full partners in government, but to make
government work for women."
This has been the president's goal. This has been his
achievement.

— The moral drawn

— Analogy

Metaphor

Vision of the
future—compressed

Litany of
accomplishment to set
up call for action

Quote

*Remember how whether can link large and small? Now
Gore uses a referral ending to link Clinton to Donna
Lenhoff, the woman he mentioned in his opening
anecdote.*

Let's work together to finish the job. Let us keep alive this
partnership that has served America so well, whether it starts

— Call to action with a
let's litany

with the vision of a man who works at a desk in the Oval Office—or the vision of a woman working late at night at a Women's Legal Defense Fund typewriter.

The typewriter again. Not as consciously deflating as Hillary Clinton's last line in the Yale speech. I'm trying to be serious yet still preserve a hint of humor in this reminder of his reference to wonky technology earlier in the speech.

Done.

chapter 16

Speechwriting and Ethics

He should have given Deval Patrick credit, Barack Obama said afterward.

It was February 16, 2008. The Democratic primary race had become one between Obama and Hillary Clinton, and Obama was attracting attention both for his speeches and his ability to deliver them.

For someone speaking ten times a day, it must hurt to walk onstage imagining people are comparing every line unfavorably to your rival's. An exasperated Clinton criticized Obama for offering "speeches, not solutions." "When there's work to be done," one of her ads argued, "talk doesn't cut it."[1]

Obama knew he had to hit back. Here's how he did it that night, speaking at a Democratic dinner shortly before the Wisconsin primary:

> Don't tell me words don't matter! "I have a dream." Just words? "We hold these truths to be self-evident, that all men are created equal." Just words? "We have nothing to fear but fear itself." Just words—just speeches!

It was effective, dramatic, and moving. Just one problem: as the Clinton campaign soon discovered, Obama's words were almost identical with those uttered by Massachusetts governor Deval Patrick two years earlier, when he answered a similar charge from his Republican opponent, Kerry Healey:

> But her dismissive point, and I hear it a lot from her staff, is that all I have to offer is words—just words. "We hold these truths to be self-evident, that all men are created equal." Just words—just words! "We have nothing to fear but fear itself." Just words! "Ask not what your country can do for you, ask what you can do for your country." Just words! "I have a dream." Just words!

"Clinton Aide Accuses Obama of Plagiarism," read the next day's *Politico* headline, over an article quoting Howard Wolfson, Clinton's combative aide: "When an author plagiarizes from another author, there is damage done."[2]

At first the Obama campaign responded as if the incident were nothing at all like the charge of plagiarism that had finished Joe Biden's presidential campaign twenty years earlier. Obama and Patrick were "friends who share similar views and talk and trade good lines all the time," said an unnamed spokesperson.[3] But two days after the speech, Obama acknowledged that he'd made a mistake.

Plagiarism or not? Ethical or not? And what should the penalties be?

This book wouldn't contain the tools you need to create and deliver a speech without some discussion of ethics, whether about plagiarism or other issues. No such discussions appear in the almost five-hundred-page *Ethics Manual for the House of Representatives,* which covers speeches only to examine whether paying members of Congress for speaking constitutes an honorarium or gift. Payment isn't the only ethical issue for speechwriters. More often, the ethical dilemmas that speakers and speechwriters confront involve five questions:

1. Is it ever ethical to plagiarize or use material without citing a source?

2. Is it ever ethical to knowingly distort an argument?

3. Is it ever ethical to write something you personally oppose?

4. Is it ever ethical to lie?

5. Isn't it unethical by definition for speakers to deliver speeches without acknowledging that they did not write the words themselves?

Of course, in the end most blame for a lie, distortion, or other ethical violation in speechmaking belongs to the one who ordered it. But even spotting these violations can be complicated; what strikes you as a distortion can seem perfectly fair to the speaker. Sometimes, though, there's no doubt. In those cases, speechwriters can certainly become accomplices.

As a speechwriter, you'll find yourself constantly balancing views of what's ethical—not just by your own standards but those of your boss, the rest of the staff, the media, the sponsors of a speech, and the audience that hears it. Without pretending to examine all of their complicated nuances, this chapter will briefly examine those questions, and at least point the way toward steps to deal with them.

PLAGIARISM

A political speech is not a doctoral dissertation; nobody expects it to have footnotes. Still, there are times when citing sources is appropriate and even strategically necessary. One example: when a politician wants to bolster credibility by quoting an expert. There shouldn't have been anything hard about that for Obama, even in the midst of a rousing litany. All he had to do was mention it at the start. (*As my friend Deval Patrick puts it. . . .*)

But did omitting it constitute plagiarism?

In academia, it does. Dan O'Hair, Rob Stewart, and Hannah Rubenstein's excellent *A Speaker's Guidebook* defines it this way: using "other people's ideas or words without acknowledging the source." To demonstrate its essential sinfulness they point to the resignation of Hamilton College president Eugene Tobin after he used a book reviewer's words without attributing them.[4]

Virtually every college punishes plagiarism with penalties including expulsion. American University, for example, leaves no doubt about what it means by the word. Here is its official definition from the student handbook:

> Plagiarism is the representation of someone else's writing, ideas, or work as one's own without attribution. Plagiarism may involve using someone else's wording without using quotation marks—a distinctive name, a phrase, a sentence or an entire passage or essay. Misrepresenting sources is another form of plagiarism. The issue of plagiarism applies to any type of work. . . .[5]

Even one sentence? A phrase? By that standard, Obama's "just words" section was unquestionably plagiarism. So was the example of Martin Luther King and his friend Archibald Carey's speech, mentioned in chapter 14, and Joe Biden's use of British Labour Party leader Neil Kinnock's words in 1987.

But what should the penalty be? At American University, apologizing for plagiarism doesn't end things for students. We can suspend, and in some cases, expel them. Do we expect more of undergraduates than politicians? Do we want the president of a small college to resign for something that earns someone running for president of the United States a slap on the wrist?

The question has become a little more complicated in the last few years because of a major tool of twenty-first century life: search engines. They allow you to find at least the appearance of plagiarism within seconds. For example, Google allowed one reporter to discover that the first four words of the opening litany in John Edwards's stump speech in 2008—"Somewhere in America tonight"—were identical to the opening of the 1996 Democratic National Convention speech by his campaign chair, and my former boss, David Bonior (not written by me). By American University's standards, Edwards's "distinctive" line looks at first like plagiarism that would require a penalty.

But keep Googling. The search engine finds no less than 380,000 sites where others have used the same phrase, including a song by The Outfield and a 1943 New York Central Railroad ad addressed to mothers with sons in the army ("Somewhere in America tonight . . . a young man sits in a railway car bound for a destination unknown"). It's possible that Edwards did lift the phrase from Bonior. It's also possible that the phrase from a song or some other source had lodged deep in the unconscious of Edwards or whoever wrote the line, popping onto the computer screen as if it were original. Or maybe the writer had *never* heard it and really did make it up.

Okay, that last one seems unlikely. Still, the mere existence of an identical phrase or sentence can't be proof of misrepresentation or plagiarism. Take, for example, another phrase politicians commonly use: "There's more to do." A search engine turns up ninety-eight million references. Clearly the existence of a searchable Internet makes it possible to find repetitions that can seem like plagiarism when none existed. To prove plagiarism you need evidence of intent.

But nobody disputes intent with King, Biden, or Obama. They all knew who had spoken the words they used. Each had spent time on campuses where the importance of citing sources was no doubt a constant refrain. So did the three simply think that politics had different standards?

Slate's Jack Schafer offered this defense for Obama: "Most campaign speeches are composed by speechwriters who assume the candidate's persona. The candidate becomes the public 'author' of these words when he speaks them."[6]

The problem with that argument is that Deval Patrick wasn't a speechwriter but a public official who had uttered these words in a public forum. Let's say one of my students borrowed those Deval Patrick lines, but told me, "Hey, I know the guy. It's okay with him." What teacher in their right mind would say, "Oh. Go right ahead." And while teachers need to make sure of originality in order to grade, candidates are also asking for a grade—from voters, who grade them by voting. For Obama in particular, voters graded him partly on eloquence.

Besides, schools don't present plagiarism rules as simply a tool for teachers. "Plagiarism is unethical," the *Guidebook* says. "Whether it's done intentionally or not, plagiarism . . . is stealing . . . you abuse the trust that an audience places in you."[7]

There are other ways to defend Obama (we'll get to one in a few pages). I'm uncomfortable with them all. I don't want my students to go away thinking that in the real world they should ignore ethical standards they learn in class. We should leave the penalty in the hands of voters. But if the American University standard is right for students, why shouldn't it be right for someone who wants to be president?

Besides, plagiarism, or the appearance of plagiarism, is easy to avoid. Politicians may be reluctant to let an audience know they didn't think up a great line. But it's perfectly possible to cite sources without killing your ability to soar. Two suggestions:

- *If you have consciously borrowed material, find an economical way of acknowledging that you have a source.* If Obama had added the words "As Deval Patrick put it" in his litany, his audience's cheers would have been just as loud. That's not the only method speakers can use. Phrases like "I'm not the first to say" signal to listeners that you're not claiming originality.
- *For each speech, keep an annotated record of your sources.* In fact, keep records of anything you've gotten from somewhere else. Why? Because you're going to forget. You have twenty minutes to finish a draft. You find something on a Web site that looks perfect. You add it in, careful to say, "I'm not the first to say." A month later a reporter calls to ask

who was the first. You've completely forgotten. I know—it's happened to me.

There's another reason to keep good records: the recycling that is so common in political speech. Acknowledging a source means acknowledging it every time. Biden, for example, had used Kinnock's words in earlier speeches, acknowledging where they came from. It was when he skipped the acknowledgment that his troubles began.

I would make one exception to the acknowledgment rule: jokes. Some jokes, that is. If it's a quip someone else invented, yes, cite the source (*Mark Twain put it this way*). But so much political humor consists of old jokes with no known author. Preface it by saying, *There's an old joke,* and nobody can accuse you of plagiarism.

Other than that, politicians should hold themselves to the standards they learned in college. Speechwriters can give credit where credit is due with one artful phrase. It's worth fighting to include it. And in case the ethical argument doesn't work, you can tell your boss that Google has made the precepts he or she learned in school too dangerous to ignore.

DISTORTING ARGUMENTS

Lawyers are like cab drivers, one well-known member of the bar has argued. They take you where you want to go. American society accepts the idea that lawyers are not obligated to point out weaknesses in their own arguments or, within the limits of discovery, facts the other side failed to uncover. Regardless of their own beliefs about whether a client is innocent or guilty, society expects lawyers to make whatever arguments will persuade a jury the client is innocent. What about speechwriters? Are you obligated to include a catchy line even when you're sure it distorts the truth? If you don't like what you're being asked to do, should you speak up?

As with many ethical questions, the answer is: It depends. In the heat of politics, absolute truth is one of the less valued commodities, especially at rallies, with their long tradition of permissible hyperbole. Even when Arnold Schwarzenegger uttered his "girlie-men" line, he knew that Democrats' economic views don't really make them effeminate. On the other hand, most politicians believe that truth matters. Certainly, politicians frown at outright fabrication—and not just because it's so easy to get caught.

But most distortions in politics don't involve outright lying. In 2008, when McCain argued that Obama wanted schools to "answer to entrenched bureaucracies," or Obama said that McCain didn't know what it was like to be middle class, couldn't each have argued in good faith that what he said was largely true? What seems like a distortion to you might seem true to your boss.

As a practical matter, it is impossible for speechwriters to put up a fight each time a boss or other staffer insists on using something you believe unethical. Luckily, you have other options. While speechwriting is a collaborative art, the reality of it is that most first drafts eventually get written by one person sitting at a computer, armed with memos, partial drafts, and e-mails from other staffers. Instead of making yourself into a constant nuisance questioning people's motives, you can try these two approaches:

Don't use information or arguments you don't trust. If in your own research you find a piece of information that seems too good to be true, you know enough to check further; you don't want to be responsible for inaccuracies. When other staffers suggest material that doesn't check out, try leaving it out of the draft. This isn't always easy; don't dismiss the danger of ignoring staffers who outrank you. But it may be the person or people who gave you the material knew it was questionable. In a speech conference they're unlikely to insist that you use it (*Where's that half-truth I gave you?*). If someone does insist, you can explain why you didn't include it. If your research is solid, usually no one ends up angry, and you can go away knowing you've done the right thing.

Insert caveats. Sometimes what's unethical about an argument isn't inaccuracy but lack of nuance. *Caveats*—from the Latin for *beware*—are warnings or cautions, handy devices to use. Examples: *The argument is more complicated than we have time for, but . . . ;* or *That issue is not either/or, but. . . .* Like speechwriters, many speakers dislike distortions, so they appreciate having ways to clue listeners in and acknowledge what's been left out.

On the other hand, sometimes your boss doesn't care about the niceties of truth-telling and orders you to insert something you detest. Then, like people in any other job, you have to weigh how important this particular issue is to you. Do you quit? Or do you accept the imperfections of a job you love? This isn't just a question for politics. It's one for life. And for that, there are no hard and fast rules.

WRITING SOMETHING YOU OPPOSE

Speechwriting is a highly partisan job. Unlike schedulers, speechwriters confront policy issues daily, with all their moral implications and potential to affect millions of people. In corporate life speechwriters often decide to write material that makes them uncomfortable for the chance to raise their families in comfort. In politics that kind of trade-off is rare. The salaries are too low.

But no one agrees with *every* position the boss takes. Among my happiest experiences as a speechwriter were the two years I spent writing for David Bonior, an acutely sensitive man who opposed abortion *and* capital punishment, arguing that both positions were part of a "seamless" respect for life.

In one of my first weeks on the job, my immediate boss described his views and told me she guessed I didn't agree about abortion. I said that was true. She told me not to worry, that Bonior had made it clear that he would never ask me to write on that subject. I was so grateful that I went away vowing that if it did seem appropriate, I would help him make his argument on my own. After all, it was his speech, not mine. Because he didn't impose making the "pro-life" case on me, I was willing to impose articulating it on myself.

But that's an incredibly rare event in politics. No matter how carefully you choose whom to write for, you won't escape the need to sometimes write arguments that clash with your own. Two suggestions:

Discuss with your superior

This might work once. If you explain your dilemma in a mature way, many politicians will accept that and assign the work to someone else. They may even like the idea of being sensitive enough to do what Bonior did with his staff.

Look for work elsewhere

If you're uncomfortable with issue after issue, you're in the wrong office. If you need perfect agreement at all times on all points in order to function, political speechwriting is not for you.

LYING

In 1956, Arkansas Democratic senator J. William Fulbright faced a dilemma. He personally disagreed with fighting the Supreme Court decision *Brown v. Board of Education,* which integrated public schools. But if he admitted it, Arkansas residents would vote him out of office. So he joined one hundred other politicians in signing Strom Thurmond's so-called "Southern Manifesto." Drafted by the South Carolina senator when he was still a Democrat, the manifesto opposed racial integration in public places and declared that the Court had exchanged "naked power for established law."

"Fulbright felt the manifesto too extreme," writes Fulbright biographer Randall Bennett Woods, "and did not want to sign it, and . . . had done so for primarily political reasons."[8]

Announcing that he supported it was a lie. It preserved Fulbright's career, allowing him later to lead opposition to the Vietnam War, confounding antiwar activists who didn't want a racist on their side. Was it wrong for Fulbright to lie? If so, everyone in political life is guilty. Some issues are so charged, particularly in their districts, that politicians must pretend to share their constituents' views. They and their speechwriters—who often know the truth—essentially agree to lie. Any time a member of Fulbright's staff reminded listeners of that support, they were lying in his name.

Similar situations arise all the time, on issues far less significant than integration. In fact, any time a group of politicians announces support for a bill, it's likely that their speeches will contain glowing expressions of support. Do all of them really feel so enthusiastic? No, but they've agreed to accept the provisions they don't like in order to get approval from others of the ones they do. "It's a nose holder," I remember one representative saying about a bill—before exuberantly expressing support for it on the floor.

Religious belief poses another problem. About 5 percent of Americans are atheists, and the percentage seems higher among people with graduate degrees.

That means there should be at least twenty-two atheists in the U.S. House. Only one member has acknowledged it.

Let's say speechwriters know that the office expects them to profess faith for their atheist boss. They create lines like the almost reflexive last line we often hear these days: *God bless you, and God Bless America!* This isn't a lie, exactly. But it's a pretty whopping deception. Is such behavior ethical? And what if the boss goes to a prayer breakfast, as some districts require, and asks for eloquent language about the virtues of faith?

With such deception there is, again, no simple answer. People who would wax indignant at politicians' posturing should ask themselves what they would do if telling the truth would deprive them of a job they love. Certainly, lying about illegal acts should make you want to blow the whistle. But for politicians to say openly that they are nonbelievers, or are gay, or believe in the right to own guns when they don't, really does cost them their jobs. It's easy to urge courage on others; it's harder when you're the one taking the risk.

On the other hand, let's say you write for a closeted gay politician who opposes gay marriage to stay in office—not a hypothetical scenario. Or one who calls for a philandering politician to resign while having an affair. Aren't you becoming an accomplice in a lie with social implications? The goal of staying in office can't justify all forms of deception. Clearly, speechwriters might encounter situations—and not just being asked to conceal a crime—in which knowing where to draw the line is easy. But sometimes the answers can be maddeningly imprecise.

In those cases, one way to minimize your complicity: be creative about language. Let's say, for example, your boss wants to state, "I oppose gay marriage; I always have." You know that privately your boss supports gay marriage but fears if voters know, they'll be turned off. Can you change the draft to, "This country *cannot* legalize gay marriage; I've *always* thought that way"? You've removed the implication that this is your boss's belief but an analysis of what the country can accept.

That only works for the first draft, though. If you're overruled, you risk your own job to keep the original line. If there are guidelines about what to do next, I can't think of one. As a political speechwriter, you're likely to find that views on lying depend on some amorphous interplay among the event in question, what you think of your boss, and what you think of the truth you're being asked not to reveal. There's a reason politics is called the "art of compromise." Maybe the only useful piece of advice is that it's realistic to assume that even working for politicians on their way to sainthood will involve some less than saintly compromises on your part.

THE ULTIMATE QUESTION

Finally, the question most people are too diplomatic to bring up to your face—but which they write about often.

Speechwriters are rarely acknowledged by the people for whom they write. Ethically, shouldn't speakers make it clear when the eloquence, information—even the wit—in speeches is not their own?

When Sen. Ed Muskie went through his two-step with Gov. Ann Richards in 1988, pretending he was reading from his own notes instead of mine, he was following a tradition that dates back much further than the night Franklin Roosevelt recopied Raymond Moley's draft of his first inaugural so historians could examine the draft written, as one historian sardonically put it, in "his own hand."[9]

The trend, even since I wrote the first draft of this book, has changed. The publicity Michael Gerson got writing for George W. Bush, and Jon Favreau now gets writing for Barack Obama, came with the permission of both administrations. But deception still exists. Out of one hundred senators, only seventeen list their speechwriter in the *Senate Staff Directory*. Once, weeks after I had written a speech for a college president, I ran across a profile of her and her inability to delegate the really important things. The headline: "She writes her own speeches!"

Why conduct this elaborate charade? Because when politicians tell a joke or a moving story, or analyze a complicated point about global warming, they would be embarrassed if the audience knew that they were reading something composed by a twenty-six-year-old slaving away in a cubicle, or—as at the National Conventions—by a bullpen of speechwriters closeted somewhere backstage.

Compounding such deception is the reality that while some political speechwriters used to be able to sit with the boss, listen to him or her talk, then incorporate some of those ideas into the draft, today such a process is rare. Whether in Washington or at big corporations, trade associations, or nonprofits, speechwriters now often get little face time. At the higher levels of politics, speakers will often head for the floor or up to the podium holding a draft almost 100 percent produced by staffers who haven't talked to them at all.

No wonder academics see a problem. Didn't Aristotle say that demonstrating character (*ethos*) was one of the three ways to persuade? When speechwriters funnel eloquence, wit, or just well-researched paragraphs to politicians, aren't they fooling an audience into seeing in these speakers virtues that they really do not possess?

Having read this far, you know that where you describe a problem, MMS tells you to provide a solution. Thomas H. Bivens, author of the textbook *Public Relations Writing*, cites an ethicist who argues that one test of "ethicality" is whether "the communicator uses ghostwriters to make himself or herself appear to possess personal qualities that he or she really does not have." Bivens's solution: It is wrong to "impart eloquence, wit, coherence, and incisive ideas to a communicator who might not possess these qualities otherwise."[10]

He's not the only one who feels that way. Others argue that writers should give their bosses only the sort of writing their bosses would do if they had the time.

The idea of giving politicians only what they themselves could produce would make speechwriters the only people in the entire workforce hired on the condition that they *not* try their best. The roofers I hire should give me the best roof they can build, not the mess I'd make if I climbed up there myself. The dry cleaner should provide the cleanest shirts, the auto dealer the best thirty-thousand-mile checkup, the doctor the best physical. Hasn't Bivens described exactly what speechwriters *should* do: supply "eloquence, wit, coherence, and incisive ideas" to people who may or may not have those qualities?

After all, plenty of principled, smart, and thoughtful politicians can't write a sentence to save their lives. Would giving them the incoherent speech they might have produced help? I admit that as a highly partisan Democrat, I did my share of grumbling about how the speeches written for George W. Bush masked what I thought were his enormous problems. But bad speeches would not have helped. In fact, it's usually in the public interest for any president to speak well. The country needs politicians who can move, inspire, and offer hope. After 9/11, would the country have been better off if it were Bush—rather than the talented Michael Gerson and Matt Scully—sitting in front of a blank computer screen for a week, trying to find the right words?

There's something self-serving about this argument, though. No one votes for a president because the roof leaks, though clean shirts may be a different issue. Probably because speechwriting can affect history, those who examine this issue sometimes offer a number of other arguments to shore up the idea that speechwriting is an ethical act. After the plagiarism issue arose with Obama, for example, James Fallows, once a White House speechwriter himself (for Jimmy Carter), defended Obama's use of speechwriters on the ground that in his books Obama had shown that he was skilled enough to have written his own speeches.

But he didn't believe this defense applied to every president. "If a public figure's basic quality of mind or ability to express himself is in question," Fallows said, "as frankly is the case with President George W. Bush, then it might be worth investigating whether the words he is uttering actually reflect his underlying outlook and comprehension."[11]

That seems reasonable. But how? Public figures find ways to carefully mask their real abilities. I can't figure out a way reporters or the public could figure out whether "words" and "comprehension" match until long after the fact.

What about a second view—that of Ted Sorensen, who insisted that John F. Kennedy was the true author of *Profiles in Courage* because he "decided the substance, structure, and theme of the book; read and revised each draft; inspired, constructed, and improved the work"?[12] In other words, the speechwriter really isn't the writer at all. This reasoning doesn't hold up, either. If that were true, producers wouldn't need to include screenwriters in the list of movie credits. Kennedy produced and directed; Sorensen wrote the script.

There's a third possibility. Maybe we should define gradations of deception—like a little white lie and a whopper. Surely a speechwriter drafting a senator's floor speech is committing a lesser sin than an academic signing his or her name to an op-ed drafted by a trade association. But "it could be worse" isn't much of a defense. You can't justify running a red light by saying, "At least I didn't hit a pedestrian."

I have heard one argument so often—from friends or from other writers—that it is worth mentioning, if only to rebut: that even if you fully acknowledge a speechwriter's role, *any* speechwriting at all, good or bad, is wrong. "Presidents should write their own speeches," a *Washington Post* reporter told me once, barely concealing his distaste for my chosen career.

Really. In *The Rhetorical Presidency*, Jeffrey K. Tulis estimates that for the first half of this country's history, presidents spoke about ten times a year. When Don Baer became Bill Clinton's chief speechwriter in 1995, he was dumbfounded to find Clinton on track to speak 496 times that year alone.[13]

The public speech—on the floor, on the stump, or on TV—has become a major tool of governing, and not just because it can inspire a nation. For every speech from the Oval Office there are thousands of political speeches each day at Rotary Club lunches and Sierra Club dinners, on statehouse floors, or over coffee in living rooms. The speeches stimulate discussion, promote ideas, and add to knowledge.

Nobody in their right mind should want politicians to write them all. Yes, Abraham Lincoln wrote his speech on the train heading up to Gettysburg, but he had only a page to write—and without a Blackberry, no distractions. If Lincoln had had to deliver three hundred speeches a year, he would have had a few speechwriters, too.

Politicians should spend their days deciding whether to make war or peace. Someone else should write the announcement when they do. But let me make one modest proposal, implied in this book's first pages.

I've already made the point that uncredited lines for others is common in American life: clerks write rulings for Supreme Court justices, assistants write columns for pundits, and public affairs people write the letters that college presidents send to alums. And while the White House acknowledges presidential speechwriters, the thousands of speechwriters at companies, nonprofits, trade associations, or other groups often still work without credit. Last year, when I was speechwriter for Pfizer's CEO, Jeff Kindler, that title was on my business card. Once I gave it to another CEO I'd met. He stared at it. "I'm floored Kindler would let you put that on the card," he said.

Kindler was secure enough to give credit where credit was due. Similarly, in 2009, when Ted Kennedy died, his long-time speechwriter, Bob Shrum, made a point of mentioning how willing Kennedy was to acknowledge him and others. Whether in business or politics, what's the point of doing anything else? Jokewriters who create the monologue for Conan O'Brien do get credit, even if only for a half-second, when nobody's watching. Why should comedians be more honest than politicians, whom voters judge partly on honesty? Rather than trying to conceal the role of speechwriters, why not acknowledge them to the same degree that Hollywood does screenwriters? Why not list them openly in staff directories, quit pretending they "provide research," and stop discouraging reporters from interviewing them? Where is the evidence that acknowledging a speechwriter has ever cost anyone a single vote?

A few years ago, Eric Schnure wrote a roast for Bill Richardson, then governor of New Mexico. The speech went well. As he left the room, someone asked him the secret of his success. According to the *Washington Post*, Richardson answered, "I hired a couple of jokesters and prepared extensively. You can't bomb in a big speech like this."[14]

It didn't seem to hurt him any, and Schnure didn't seem to mind being called a jokester. He kind of enjoyed it. If others followed suit, such honesty might even help.

The Speechwriter's Checklist: Speechwriting and Ethics

☐ Do I cite or imply a source for all words, terms, or phrases I have appropriated from someone else's work?

☐ Have I kept a record of what those sources were?

☐ Have I investigated information or arguments I don't trust?

☐ Have I avoided them if I believe they are false or misleading?

☐ Have I used caveats to fairly indicate to listeners complications the speaker cannot explore?

☐ If I'm uncomfortable writing about issues of personal concern, have I discussed my concerns with my boss?

☐ If asked to lie or conceal illegal actions, have I refused?

☐ If convinced that my boss is lying about issues that are not illegal—personal beliefs or behavior, for example—have I tried to avoid them in my draft?

☐ If ordered to lie about such issues, have I explored every other alternative?

☐ If asked to conceal my role in writing speeches—such as accepting a misleading title—have I suggested other options?

☐ Have I accepted the idea that in writing speeches I must write the very best drafts I can, regardless of my boss's abilities?

☐ Am I comfortable with the compromises I'm asked to accept concerning the ethical issues of political speechwriting?

chapter 17

The Uneasy Partnership

Advice for Speakers and Writers

He sits in the car, the chief of staff beside him, on his way to the Hilton to deliver a keynote. The speech draft rests on his lap. Set in twenty-point type, crisp pages stacked neatly inside a leather speech box, it looks great. The politician hates it.

"These aren't my ideas," he says, aware that the driver will hear and report back to the speechwriter, but too angry to care. "I hate the joke. I've already used it five times—when do I get something new? And these facts? The health stuff? I'm not sure they're right—what if someone asks me about them? He wants me to sound passionate here and I don't give a good goddamn! He mentions my family, Jimmy's broken arm! Jeez! He doesn't *know* my kid! Who gave him the right to—where's a pen? How long do I have?"

"Seven minutes."

"Seven—who's my health guy?"

"Alex. New guy."

"Get him on the phone. Why wasn't *he* involved?"

Now imagine the writer. It's a few hours later. He's having a beer with the driver, who has just delivered a version of what he overheard—sanitized, but not too sanitized to leave any doubt about what happened.

"Well, how can I know what he wants?" the writer says, aware of the futility—what can the driver do?—but too angry to keep quiet. "He canceled the speech meeting! Canceled it! And those facts? They *came* from Alex. He said I *had* to use them. And Jimmy? The arm? He tells me to make the speeches sound personal, but he won't give me any stories. Jimmy's broken arm was in the papers!"

This isn't a story of some poor, victimized speechwriter blamed for everything by an insensitive boss, but one of a speaker and speechwriter who have very different perspectives on the same events. That's not unusual. In fact, one of the interesting insights you can draw from Robert Schlesinger's *White House*

Ghosts is how often presidents and their speechwriters have been unhappy with each other for a similar reason.

As someone who has worked as a staffer for two governors, a senator, two members of the House leadership, and a vice president, I've seen enough offices to know that the basic tenor of any political staff comes from the boss. With apologies to chiefs of staff, if the politician is a miserable son of a bitch it is unusual—though not unheard of—for the rest of the staff to behave in any other way.

Once, when someone I knew was up for a speechwriting job with a senator I didn't know, I asked a friend on the Hill what the senator was like to work for.

Terrible, my friend said.

A week later, I saw my friend again. "She took the job," I told her.

My friend understood. She'd seen this before. "When she leaves, nobody will ask why."

By contrast, someone else I knew took a job as chief of staff for another senator. Because he had told me he was finished with work on the Hill, I said I was surprised.

He said, "Well, he's just a great guy."

The point is, personality at the top can make or break a political office. Corporate CEOs have thousands of people on the payroll who never lay eyes on the boss. Even senators have about fifty. When they are in a bad mood, nobody escapes.

And exacerbating their moods are the emotional highs and lows of an office where every day seems to bring a new crisis. Every job has its pressures, but most don't involve deciding whether to make war on Iraq or approve a $700 billion bailout. Not every member of Congress gets to decide these issues, but they feel as if they might—and so does the staff. Such stakes make people work seventy hours a week for little money and still feel disappointed if they're not asked to come in for a weekend meeting or midnight strategy session. Complicating such tensions are the kinds of people politics attracts: those ambitious and willing to fight others for promotions and face time—or to argue about every word in a sentence.

Meanwhile, though politicians often complain about the sacrifices of their jobs, most of them love what they do. But *because* they love their work, each day brings more worries. Will they get reelected? Should they think about leaving the House and running for that open Senate seat? And what will this bill—or this speech—do to make that possible?

Rick Shapiro, the congressional management consultant whose insights appear on page 282, points out that the same factors creating tension in the rest of a political office can make life tough for the speechwriter, who is often—assuming the office even has a designated speechwriter—the sole staffer who understands how hard a job writing is. It's stressful to have a constant stream of people ducking their heads into your office and shouting, "Got it? Got it? He needs it in *five minutes! Five!*"

Tight deadlines. High stakes. The inevitable clashes of personalities and egos. And one other thing: political speechwriting is tense because it has changed. In the public imagination—to the limited extent that most people imagine speechwriters at all—the stereotype has been the Ted Sorensen model: the trusted aide meeting every day with the boss, or sitting together on a plane batting ideas back and forth, as Sorenson did with Kennedy.

These days, though, even full-time speechwriters are midlevel staffers who get material filtered to them through a communications director. They have to fight for time to ask the questions policy people won't ask (*When Jimmy broke his arm, did you go to the hospital?*). When they do, they may meet resistance. Even politicians can be intensely private people who shrink from the idea of using their personal lives to affect an audience. They sometimes resent feeling scripted by someone often half their age, whom they barely know. Meanwhile at any given moment, every politician has a hundred claims on his or her attention that seem at least as important as meeting with a writer for a speech conference.

The result: they cancel speech conferences, maybe without even articulating the reasons to themselves, leaving speechwriters unable to get the direction they need, having to obey higher-ranking staffers whose only interest is policy, producing something for an event that makes the boss more nervous than any other part of the day. It's a wonder these awkward but necessary relationships work at all.

But they can. Just as speechwriters and their bosses both need to think about the needs of an audience, they need to consider each other's needs as well.

FOR SPEAKERS: WHAT SPEECHWRITERS NEED FROM YOU

The more you clarify what you want and expect from the people who work for you, the more likely you are to get it, and the less time you'll have to spend cleaning up messes. Here's what that advice means when it comes to speechwriters.

CLEARLY DEFINE THE SPEECHWRITER'S ROLE

Do you want to review drafts of all speeches, or just the big ones? How much time do you need? How much turnaround time do you think is fair for incorporating your suggestions? Do you want the speechwriter to handle just the text, or will he or she also be responsible for the list of acknowledgments and thank-yous? How long should your speeches be? How comfortable are you taking Q&A?

Nobody can answer these questions, and dozens more, except you. What Shapiro says later is worth mentioning here: make sure your chief of staff, communications director, and speechwriter know what makes you comfortable. Spell everything out in writing.

Include in the job description these elements: the need to make changes quickly, understand that criticism is inevitable but not personal, provide sources for data, work with staff, and learn about not just the issues but the politics surrounding them.

When I worked as a staffer, no speaker ever talked to me about these matters. But confusion about each was a constant source of tension on both sides. It took years for me to understand that the problem was not—always—an insensitive boss, but the catch-as-catch-can culture of political life. Clarity is an asset in speeches *and* in producing them.

PROVIDE TRAINING

Even if speechwriters come to your office with a portfolio of professional work, the odds are great that they learned on the fly in someone else's office rather than through any kind of formal training. They believe speechwriting is . . . whatever it was in the last place they worked. As Shapiro points out, if you want speechwriters who share your standards, perspectives, and ideas, you not only have to train them but allow them the training you can't provide. Public speaking courses, books, and conferences can all help. It's not unusual for people in government to attend management workshops or seminars in legislative process; speechwriters could benefit from them, too.

LEARN MORE ABOUT WHAT MAKES SPEECHES GOOD

Some aspects of giving a good speech are up to you, not your writers. Anyone who's walked into a bookstore to pick up a book on playing tennis shouldn't look askance at reading a book about persuasive speech. There are a lot of good ones besides the one you now hold. If you read systematically about the role that concrete detail or story can play in moving audiences, if you know why research matters or why Monroe's Motivated Sequence is so effective, you will become a better speaker. You'll also be able to articulate more clearly to your writers exactly what you want them to provide. Since in most political offices the speechwriters are also learning on the job, you can educate each other.

FOR DELIVERY, HIRE A CONSULTANT

Virtually everyone in politics can dramatically improve delivery. First, gird yourself to watch and listen to yourself on tape. Then get candid advice. No matter how honest your staffers try to be, no one you have the power to fire feels comfortable mentioning that you slumped over the podium, swallowed your words, and ad-libbed a tasteless joke. Consultants can. Hiring them doesn't have to mean spending a fortune. You can find, say, public speaking teachers at a community college who would be happy to volunteer their time or work for a modest fee.

But during those sessions, involve anyone on the staff who writes speeches for you. No one else in the office knows more about what you need or can spot problems faster. If you make clear that you really want candor about the things consultants point out—even the genuinely embarrassing ones—over time, and if they see you're really listening and changing, staffers will relax and start telling you the truth.

INVOLVE YOURSELF IN FINDING CONTENT

For most officeholders, speech conferences—if they happen at all—can feel like a waste of time. You're busy right up until the minute your staff files in to talk. Your mind's a blank. You barely remember what event they're talking about. You're grateful that someone seems to have ideas, because right now you don't.

But five minutes' advance work on your part could hugely increase the value of a speech conference. Spend that time jotting down points that reflect your thinking, including material from your personal life. Really think about what you want to convey. Usually, you'll surprise yourself by how much you know. And because you see your own language in the draft you get, you'll feel more comfortable delivering it.

Better still, don't wait for a speech conference to think about material. Issues are relatively easy for your staff to research, but you're the only who can tell them what's been happening in your life. Have you heard a joke you liked recently? Did a staffer show you a moving letter from a constituent? Yes, writers can provide you with jokes, and most speeches should have them—but only you know what you find compelling.

In the old days, sharing ideas with staff was cumbersome; you had to clip and copy articles and send them around. Now things are simpler. Bombard your speechwriters with e-mails. (*Check this health article in the* Post . . . *Good stuff . . . Heard a joke I like the other day. . . .*) They would have to be idiots not to include them in the next draft. And if you ask why they didn't (*Didn't I send you . . .*), even idiots should know enough to change.

ENCOURAGE RECYCLING

If you have read this entire book, skip these paragraphs. If you haven't, allow me to encourage you to reread Chapter 4's story about Wyatt Tee Walker, and recycle my advice on recycling. In speeches, originality is no virtue. And in politics, the reluctance to recycle can be disastrous.

First, powerful material doesn't grow on trees. Second, audiences haven't heard what you've used a thousand times, as you and your staff have. To find something good and then discard it is like closing down a hit show after opening night.

Recycled material lets you look out at the crowd and build fluently toward a climax with the confidence that comes only from familiarity. Everyone in politics has seen candidates stammer over a stump speech at the start of a campaign—and deliver the same speech powerfully just before election day. Practice makes perfect.

Especially with humor. As mentioned in chapter 9, the comedian David Brenner used to say he would never use a joke on the *Tonight Show* until it had been in his act for six months. If a professional comedian is wary of new material, shouldn't amateurs be?

AS DELIVERED

Bono at the 2007 NAACP Awards.
http://college.cqpress.com/politicalspeech

For more evidence, watch Bono's 2007 speech to the NAACP, available on YouTube. You'll see him wrestle with the text he's been handed—until the closing litany, which he's done for years. Suddenly he doesn't need his notes. After thirty seconds he has the whole audience on its feet.

It's an object lesson for speakers. Recycled material allows speakers to use their greatest hits, and like any actor, get good at doing them. Recycling also makes things easier for speechwriters by giving them more time to spend on drafts of new speeches.

GIVE SPEECHWRITERS FACE TIME

Resist the trend that encourages you to deal with speechwriters through other staffers, often the communications director.

Yes, speechwriters can get statistics, ideas, and acknowledgments from other staffers. But they need personal contact with you even more than some staffers who outrank them do. Only speechwriters will ask, *Did the caseworkers send you anything moving this week? Do you have a favorite story about this? Did your kids say anything funny this week? Did you read anything in the papers that made you mad?* Answering their questions will help make your speeches personal in a way that audiences love.

It's sometimes useful to include speechwriters in meetings for which they have no official role. You may say something as an aside that staffers concerned with policy will ignore. Good speechwriters will hear that aside as something important to you and take it down verbatim, then find a way to include it in the draft, phrased in a way that makes you comfortable. That's good for you, good for the speechwriter, and good for the speech.

DON'T EXPECT PERFECT FIRST DRAFTS

Even if you hire the best speechwriters and follow every tip in this chapter, a perfect draft exactly reflecting your own vision can't possibly appear on your desk every time. First drafts are never perfect in any kind of writing; speechwriting in particular calls for give-and-take. Working with speechwriters means learning to read analytically and give concrete feedback on a draft's virtues and problems. *I hate it; do it over* doesn't help anyone. Even a compliment works better if it's specific. (*Love this part about the [fill in the blank]; can you do more like that?*) And scolding writers for guessing wrong is a sure way to make them give you only the safest—and blandest—material.

FOR SPEECHWRITERS: WHAT SPEAKERS NEED FROM YOU

The boss owes you feedback. You owe the boss and everyone else in the office not just your best efforts but your respect. Writing may be a solitary occupation, but a speechwriter is part of what's at best a cohesive political team. Here are some ways to help that team work together, and help your own contributions.

BE REALISTIC

Even in the beginning, Ted Sorensen wasn't Ted Sorensen. Relationships with your boss develop over time, not overnight. From your boss's perspective, you are one midlevel staffer who will probably leave in two or three years. It might not seem at first that you're worth investing the time and thought you crave.

Meanwhile, just as relationships take time, so do skills. Being a good writer isn't all you need. You will have to listen carefully and work hard to become great at writing speeches for politicians. How long do they like to speak? What kinds of stories will they tell? Do they want to rehearse? There are dozens of questions that you'll answer only through trial and error or bad mistakes—like the old man renowned for his good judgment who said, "I learned good judgment . . . through bad judgment." That takes time.

LEARN MORE ABOUT WHAT MAKES A GOOD SPEECH

Yes, you.

Earlier in this book I mentioned being part of a presentation to about 125 speechwriters, all working full time, only a handful of whom had ever heard of Monroe, the classic and most appropriate structure for writing policy speeches. In retrospect, that's not surprising. Speechwriting is often an accidental career; people come to it from journalism, law, or other areas. Very few have systematically explored the variety of techniques taught in any college public speaking course.

They should. Books like the one you're holding aren't the only way. Journalists learn by reading journalism. Screenwriters learn by watching movies. You should read and listen to speeches. Because of YouTube, you can do this slouched in your chair, switching from speech to speech literally by moving one finger. Find the ones you admire most. What made them great? How can you apply those ideas to your own drafts? You should not only write better than your boss—you should know more.

Rick Shapiro

From the air above Washington, you see them flank the Capitol: three office buildings to the north and east, and three just south along Independence Avenue. Named for people who were once household names, like Rayburn, or Dirksen, they hold the offices of 435 members of the House of Representatives and a hundred senators, all worried about how to make those offices run better.

For the last two decades, many of them have turned to Rick Shapiro. For eighteen years Shapiro directed the Congressional Management Foundation, which helps congressional offices run more effectively. Now he has his own business.

Shapiro agrees that writing—not just speechwriting—is a problem in political offices. He knows at least one reason why.

"It's tied mostly to the way politicians manage," he says. "Politicians pick chiefs of staff not because they know how to manage or coach staff but because they were productive line employees. The member trusts their political judgments."

Managing an office also takes time and management training skills, Shapiro says—two commodities chiefs of staff tend to have in short supply. "Instead of trying to manage the office and staff effectively, most COS hope they can avoid actually managing by hiring smart people and letting them do their job."

And when the boss needs a speech?

Usually, Shapiro points out, congressional offices don't have a delegated speechwriter. "The culture gives issue specialists ownership of their issue areas—including the writing of speeches. Speeches tend to be produced by a number of different issue specialists who all adopt different approaches."

Sometimes, though, the member turns out to like his or her communications director or legislative director's writing better than the others. The member might say about the leg director, "I like the way Bob does it. Run this speech through him.' This gives Bob a responsibility he may not like—consulting about style."

"Members or their managers compound that problem," Shapiro says. "They rarely find the time to provide the speechwriters feedback on their speeches. That undermines the learning process."

RESEARCH BEFORE (AND MORE THAN) YOU WRITE

Ask skillful print feature writers how many hours they research—that is, read, interview, or spend time following a subject around. They will invariably say that the time researching far outstrips the time writing. With good reason. Only research can give them the anecdote, concrete detail, and insight that make stories come to life.

If I ever needed help remembering this, the daily work on this book would remind me. Take the Delivery chapter's sections on Barack Obama's Berlin speech and James Inhofe's speech on the Senate floor. Drafting the general points took me, in the first draft, a few minutes. But to find and delineate the

Shapiro suggests five ways offices could improve their speechwriting.

1. *Train.* The chief of staff or legislative director should spend time outlining the steps, from how to research to the deadlines for drafts to revisions. In the beginning they may have to do this with each speech, since the process may not always be the same.

2. *Create templates.* Create clear expectations of what a good speech looks like in this office, with examples of what approaches don't work well. Of course, this means building a shared speech filing system, so you can find that speech that went well a few years back.

3. *Coach.* Don't let the new writer go off for several days and create a lengthy draft that is way off the mark. Review the speech in stages as it is being developed and offer concrete, candid feedback at each stage.

4. *Debrief.* Writers need to know what worked, what didn't, and why—even if they don't want to hear it. Without this feedback and chance to debrief the process, they will improve slowly, if at all.

"Don't just tell them it went fine," Shapiro says. "If the speech is in the district, have a conference call afterwards with the district director, the writer, the communications director. And yes, the member. Sometimes a member's delivery or failure to stick closely to the text of the speech is the principal problem. The member doesn't want to hear it. But the challenge of a good chief of staff is to make sure the bad news gets delivered and discussed and everyone learns and improves—even the member."

Shapiro has one other suggestion: "Be patient."

He points out that there are offices where the member and the managers can set priorities, develop plans, and manage the work of the office. There are actually offices where the staff views each other as part of a family.

"That takes time," he says. "And work. Great offices just don't happen."

Source: Rick Shapiro spoke with Robert A. Lehrman in March 2009.

precise examples to illustrate those points? Sifting through different possibilities, locating them, and deciding which details were vital took a full day. And it wasn't until several drafts later, and the persistent questions of a brilliant editor, that I did even more research to produce the detail that satisfied us both. The section involved about a morning of writing time but two days of research to produce material even the thorough reader will cover in a half hour.

It was worth it. And speechwriting is no different. One sure way to write a bad speech is to think you need only what is in your head. Your job as a speechwriter is to find the stories, wit, pithy quotes, concrete detail, and instantly persuasive examples that will keep people listening. It may take hours looking at horrible jokes to uncover the one that's perfect, or the concrete detail that puts a dry statistic into startling context. But remember: They can be more memorable for an audience than all of the draft's policy ideas put together.

WORK FOR MORE FACE TIME

Like children, staffers compete for the attention of their boss. Even your friends may try to cut you out of speech conferences. You'll know this is happening when you hear tell-tale sentences like, *Oh, you don't have to come;* or, *I'll get you everything you need;* or the classic, *We'll just be talking about logistics.*

Smile and tell them you need to know about logistics, too. Then go to the meeting. If you can't get permission, try again next time. Otherwise the big boss won't identify you with the draft. He or she won't call you with ideas. And you won't get the chance to ask the questions that no one else will ask.

LEARN HOW TO HANDLE SPEECH CONFERENCES

It's not just a speech. It's *the* speech. So on this day, the boss has called everybody in to talk about it.

Don't waste the chance. First, prepare. Go to the other staffers and find out what they're going to say, so you'll know how to head them off if they're wrong, or support them if they make sense. Read some old speeches to see what's been done for similar groups. Write out the questions you need to ask—not just to sound smart, but because in the heat of discussion and the distraction of note-taking you're unlikely to remember the questions that occurred to you during the quiet moments at your desk.

Second, take voluminous notes—and certainly every word your boss says. You need the information for yourself, and if questions come up later you want to be the smart one who knows exactly what was said.

Third, whatever you do, make sure every idea the boss comes up with appears in some form in your draft. Bosses mention ideas because they want to see them in the speech. They'll notice if their thoughts don't appear.

Speech conferences will never give you all you need. But they will tell you what you need to find.

CULTIVATE RELATIONSHIPS

No speechwriter is an island. You need other staffers not just to work as partners with you but to enjoy doing it. If you go to them for advice and take it, you will find they support you in meetings, go out of their way to find material you can use—and undercut you less.

Never say, *Oh, I fight with Joe, but the boss likes me.* You can't always tell who likes you, and you won't always hear about complaints. Speechwriters like to make fun of policy wonks. But even if the wonks don't write well, they think well, and they know more about their area than you could ever learn. Work to make them like you, too.

Do this for staffers at every level. Recently, one freelance speechwriter I know did a draft for a senator on contract. He didn't know that the senator had asked a personal friend—I'll call him Fred—to do a competing draft, then picked Fred's draft without reading my friend's.

My friend lucked out. As the senator was leaving for the day, his receptionist said, "You took Fred's? The other one is much better."

The senator was so startled, he sat down and read both—and changed his mind. The lesson: In a political office, everyone is smart and everyone might be part of the process.

WORK HARD ON THE COVER MEMO

Yes, you can send a quick e-mail or write a sticky note reading, *Here's the draft. Tell me what you think.* But that would be a colossal mistake and a missed opportunity. Speakers and other staffers are busy. They can't pore over your draft to appreciate each fine point you want them to notice. So write a cover memo that directs their attention by including three sections:

- *I've done what you've asked.* Make sure your memo says something like, *You will see your ideas incorporated throughout the draft. For example . . .* and list each example.
- *Here's what I didn't change, and why.* Some suggestions made in brainstorming sessions just don't work when you get to the computer. Highlight them. (*One change I didn't make was X, only because. . . .*) Usually the boss will agree. Even if he or she does not, at least it won't seem like you were trying to hide something. Warning: If you haven't incorporated far more of the boss's ideas than you've ignored, think again.
- *Here's how you can check everything I did.* Provide a draft with tracked changes and one that's clean. Bosses may never even download the tracked version, but they will appreciate your openness. They'll know you value their views, and that will make them value you.

GO TO EVERY SPEECH

That means *every* speech. Two reasons.

First, hearing your speeches delivered is in your boss's interest. You will see—and cringe at—each mistake you've made: a clumsy sentence, a joke that gets no reaction, a story that goes on too long. Seeing your boss come to the punch line, look up, and hear only silence will make you more careful about what you hand in next time. In addition, you will see what your boss can and can't do. Is he or she too inhibited to be forceful? Too animated telling a story? Unable to expand from sketchy talking points? Taking the boss's strengths and limitations into account is your job, too.

Equally important is what happens afterwards. That's the best time to get feedback on how the speaker felt about the speech. Even a few minutes in the elevator or car can give you insights you'll get no other way.

Second, being there is in your interest. It brings you closer to your boss. They will identify you with these drafts that appear on their desks, and some-times—especially when they are in the expansive mood that comes after a speech is done—they'll include you in the relaxed conversations that lift you at least temporarily above the rank of midlevel staffer. And—not a small point—if things go well, you can bask in the high-fives.

TAKE RESPONSIBILITY FOR MORE THAN THE DRAFTS

Keep an anecdote file. Include every story, joke, and quote your boss ever uses. It will prove invaluable. I still use the one my office created for Al Gore almost fifteen years ago.

Arrange video for the big speeches. These days a $100 digital camcorder can give you a useful version. There's no better way for your boss to see what's not working than to watch his or her own performance with no one else in the room. When you've shown yourself as someone to trust, you might get invited to sit in. Then you can advise on delivery—with the evidence right there, you can be more candid—and find one more way of making yourself indispensable.

RECYCLE

This is good advice for writers for the same reasons it's good for speakers—and one more. Most political speechwriters are incredibly rushed. Anyone produc-ing a short speech for House members ten minutes before they speak, or finish-ing a speech conference and beginning revisions a half hour before *Air Force Two* touches down, or producing sixty speeches in a single month will under-stand how useful it is to pull up an old draft, insert a few small changes to make it current, and hit Send before your deadline.

DO MORE THAN CAPTURE YOUR BOSS'S VOICE

This classic piece of speechwriter's advice contains a germ of truth. Not all speakers use exactly the same diction or tone, or tell a joke or story the same way, or feel the same about how partisan to be. As a speechwriter, you need to listen and learn how your boss thinks and speaks.

But don't count on listening to give you everything you need. You may never hear some elements of a good speech—simple, concrete, uncluttered language; storytelling and wit—in your boss's conversations or see them in the drafts of the writers who preceded you. That doesn't matter. All the best tech-niques should be represented in your drafts whether you've heard the speaker use them or not.

"The job of a speechwriter," says Eric Schnure, "isn't just finding the speaker's voice. It's helping them find their own—then making it better."[1]

DON'T EXPECT TO HEAR YOUR MATERIAL WORD FOR WORD

It's common for a speechwriter to start out thinking that the fun of speechwriting will be hearing a famous and powerful person mouth the words you have created. Think again.

Any speaker with a brain will want to change some things you've written. Sometimes they'll have a thought up on the podium and want to digress. Sometimes they'll deliver your lines well. Sometimes they'll butcher them. And sometimes, hearing your lines, you'll wish you had done one more rewrite. If your only idea of a reward is hearing someone say exactly what you wrote, you're destined to have a miserable time.

Instead, look for the things you've done that make a contribution: the joke you found, the line that got applause, the story that moved an audience, the dry stat you put into context, and the sound bite everybody's talking about when it makes the evening news.

A speechwriter is part of a team. You don't always score the only run.

The Speechwriter's Checklist: The Uneasy Partnership—Advice for Speakers and Writers

FOR THE SPEAKER

- ☐ Have I clearly defined in writing the speechwriter's role, making clear important issues that include:
  - ☐ workload?
  - ☐ deadlines?
  - ☐ process?
  - ☐ sources for data?
  - ☐ appropriate staff to consult?
  - ☐ issues to know?
  - ☐ political context?

- ☐ Have I offered the speechwriter opportunities for training, including conferences, coursework, and mentoring?
- ☐ For delivery issues do I understand the difficulties of achieving candor from staff?
- ☐ Have I explored hiring outside consultants for help with delivery?
- ☐ Do I understand the need for recycled material both for me and those writing drafts?

☐ Do I give speechwriters the face time they need?

☐ Do I include the speechwriter in discussions of the political needs of an appearance?

☐ Do I provide candid feedback not just about drafts but about all aspects of a speech, including scheduling, advance, and briefing?

FOR THE SPEECHWRITER

☐ Am I realistic about the relationship I can expect with my boss?

☐ Have I explored ways to educate myself about speech including:
    ☐ reading?
    ☐ courses?
    ☐ conferences?
    ☐ consulting with others?
    ☐ regular exploration of speeches by others and old speeches by my boss?

☐ To the extent possible, do I research more than I write?

☐ Do I make an effort to work well with staff?

☐ Do I attend every speech possible?

☐ Do I prepare well for speech conferences?

☐ Does my cover memo fairly explain how I tried to achieve my boss's goals?

☐ Do I take responsibility for more than drafts, including files of jokes, quotes, and other material that worked well?

☐ Do I urge recycling?

☐ Do I take satisfaction in contributing rather than hearing my work delivered word for word?

☐ Do I solicit candid feedback and try to apply what I have heard?

18

Final Words

During the frenetic last month of working on this book, when I was sure I was done finding new things to write about, one incident took me by surprise. I was talking to David Kusnet, who had been Bill Clinton's chief speechwriter and whose interview about Clinton's inauguration speech appears in chapter 7. There were some memorable lines in that speech, and I wanted to find out the story behind them.

"Well, you have a line in it," he said.

"I do?"

"Sure."

Silence while David apparently flipped through the draft—or maybe scrolled through it—then read it to me.

"I wrote that?"

David reminded me that after the election I, like other Democratic speechwriters, had written a draft of the inaugural for him; he had liked one line and stuck it in his first draft. "Didn't you hear the speech?"

I remembered inauguration day, 1993. It was freezing; my kids were cold and bored. I wasn't paying much attention to Clinton.

Really, the line wasn't that good—you'll notice I haven't mentioned which one it was. The surprising thing was how absurdly pleased I felt that he'd included it. One not very distinguished line in a fourteen-minute speech! What's the big deal?

But I knew. The big deal was that most of us who write political speeches believe passionately that politics matters. We don't do it for money or fame—certainly not fame—but to further the ideas of someone we're convinced can make life better. I had been elated that Clinton was president; from inside the White House I saw him do things I valued every day. Having even a tiny role in one of his big speeches was something to cherish.

This doesn't mean Clinton or everybody who worked for him in those days actually did make life better. To read the interviews in this book of, say,

Lissa Muscatine and David Frum is to see equally informed, decent people, each holding views the other sees as dangerous. History has proven wrong all kinds of brilliant people who were certain they knew what's true. On the preposterous chance that I'm wrong about mine, I've written a book I hope can help people of every ideological stripe.

But will it help? Do you really have to understand parallel construction or know the five steps of Monroe to write great speeches? Didn't I point out that Abraham Lincoln used those steps before Monroe was born?

Those questions go to the very reason this book exists. If you've read it from beginning to end—not a requirement—you know it focuses not on introducing new techniques but on examining those common to successful speeches. Certainly some speechwriters have used those approaches well without ever having studied them in a classroom.

But those of you who read the Preface and remember Bernard Grebanier's belief in the systematic study of playwriting know why I think the same approach applies to other forms.[1] I've tried to do the same thing here. This isn't the place for discussion about the sometimes overwrought debate over whether you can teach writing. But systematic teaching seems to help most people become at least competent, whether at tennis, piano, or screenwriting. Why not speechwriting?

In fact, speechwriters might find this approach especially valuable. Someone who wants to be a novelist—as I did—grows up reading thousands of stories and novels, all models for the unconscious imitation that writers use as they write. It's different with speechwriters. Most learn on the job. Except for the Gettysburg Address, King's "Dream" speech, and a few other staples of high school literature courses, most speechwriters start paying attention to speeches only when they have to write one.

In my experience, even the best work speechwriters have done in the past is new to just about everyone, which is why examples lace each chapter in this book. I want speechwriters to see what's worked. In our course at American University, Eric Schnure and I see the difference this makes, semester after semester.

Formal study might also be useful because there are things about writing speeches you won't learn in any other writing course—like the approach to ideas. It's a staple of literary criticism that novelists and playwrights are better served by parking their political agenda. English majors hear teachers laud Shakespeare for hiding his feelings about the views of his characters, and heap contempt on the proletarian novels of the 1930s, where the ideologies of the characters determined how likable they were.

Political speeches, though, *exist* to further ideas: story, wit, and imaginative language are tools to persuade audiences to believe. For partisan audiences this fusion of idea and, say, story gives speeches incredible power. It's the combination that makes Republican delegates leap to their feet as Arnold

Schwarzenegger describes himself as a small boy, or Democrats weep as Barack Obama describes 106-year-old Ann Nixon Cooper as a symbol of her country.

For that reason, speeches, unlike novels, rarely have universal appeal. It's hard for Democrats to be moved by a Sarah Palin speech, or Republicans by one from Bill Clinton's lips, no matter how imaginative. They're just too infuriated by the ideas.

But while it's hard to move listeners on the other side, it's not impossible. In reexamining old speeches with the intensity of someone thinking about what belongs between the covers of a book, I've been struck by how often I, as partisan a Democrat as there is, could respond to the emotion in Ronald Reagan's voice as he describes a Vietnamese boat person, or the mixture of humor and sadness in Reagan's son's story of the "thumbs-up" sign in the eulogy of his father.

So one thing studying political speeches can do is make you see that even the most partisan ones can be about more than ideology. They can tell stories, display genuine wit, or offer insight that transcends the ideas they illustrate. In this book I hope you've found truly moving and original passages in speeches uttered by people you can't stand, created by writers mostly unknown to the people who've heard their work. And then I hope you saw that being able to handle language doesn't guarantee that you can create those effects any more than being a great athlete helped Michael Jordan in his brief attempt to play professional baseball. You need skills.

Naturally, even if you have those skills, the job can be frustrating. Other writers have described those frustrations in detail: having to give voice to unpalatable views; seeing bad editors wreck good drafts; hearing other writers hold you in contempt for writing under someone else's name; working for speakers who say they're grateful for your work but try hard to disguise your role; and trying to produce intellectually coherent arguments about policies produced by compromise. Budding speechwriters, entranced by the highly overrated experience of hearing famous people utter words they've invented, should be under no illusions about the romance of the job.

On the other hand, why not see some romance about writing the actual words for people you believe in, accomplishing things you believe worth doing, whether a U.S. president or a city councilman pushing for a stop sign? Some writers resent the fact that speeches are ephemeral. *You work three days, your boss reads it in ten minutes, and—on to the next.* So what? If being remembered is the test of a worthwhile life, then most people are doomed to disappointment. Should it matter that the words with which William Jennings Bryan electrified millions in 1896 dealt with an issue nobody cares about now? Issues don't have to be eternal to matter. It should be satisfaction enough that, even for an hour or a day, you have helped move an audience toward accepting views you believe.

And there are other satisfactions besides writing about the important issues of the day. In 2000 I wrote speeches for the Million Mom March, the well-publicized and entirely ineffective rally about gun deaths. I wrote a lot of speeches for celebrities. But the most satisfying were those for two mothers whose children had been killed with illegal handguns.

By coincidence, their children had been in my son's high school class. I remembered the shooting well. Two boys had a fight at a basketball game. Later, one of them got a gun, waited by the house until the other boy came home from shopping for his mother, and shot him and his girlfriend while they were unloading groceries.

How do you help people who have had an unspeakable loss, are terrified of speaking with millions watching, but are determined to tell their story so it might not happen to others?

I met them, having scribbled down some lines I thought could make their speeches memorable. But as I sat listening, I realized that the thing to do was not to give them my lines but find a framework for theirs.

In the end, much of what the two mothers said that day in front of the Capitol came from them. But even today, knowing that these two women trusted me to listen to their stories, ask questions, and distill their thoughts and emotions into words that made them comfortable remains as thrilling as anything I've ever done.

And over the last five years, the satisfaction of teaching speechwriting has fully equaled the best moments of writing them. It's incredibly gratifying to work out ways to put into words what speechwriters do intuitively and see how quickly twenty-two-year-olds in a college classroom learn to do what sophisticated White House speechwriters have done.

Each year, near the end of our speechwriting class, we run what we call the "charity contest." Students come in, put $5 in a pot matched by their teachers—then give speeches designed to persuade the group to donate that pot to their favorite charity.

The assignment has a profound effect. Some students have links between a charity and their own lives: a grandfather with Lou Gehrig's disease; a mother with breast cancer; or in one case, a student who had been told he was dying, granted a last wish by the Make-A-Wish Foundation. Others just admire the work others do, whether treating children in Sudan or rescuing animals from a slaughterhouse.

They use techniques they've learned as homework. But because they care, they harness them to speeches so compelling we sometimes call a recess to recover. They have learned how to take something that matters to them, and make it matter to us.

And if there is one thing I hope readers carry away from this book, it is that. Politics, in the end, is not about whether a senator had an affair or took a bribe. It is about whether people can find work, see a doctor, go to a good school, or get sent to fight a war. It is about things that matter. And despite demagoguery and dullness, despite Google and YouTube, despite the need for news anchors to limit what they show to eight seconds, despite the limitations of writing by committee, an entire speech given live by a politician still has the capacity to make listeners see why politics must matter to them.

The story, imagery, vivid detail, and rhythms called rhetoric make it possible for an action hero governor to move an audience through a story of his childhood that rings true; for an unknown state senator from Illinois to electrify an audience of Democrats with his "Blue State–Red State" litany; or for a president to remind his listeners of the pain and heroism of those who saw or felt planes plowing into a building. But they apply to smaller events, too: a commencement address that sums up the reasons college seniors and their parents should celebrate; an angry speech expressing the fury of people who feel ignored; a eulogy that shows the feelings of someone grateful because he had a good dad.

William Safire, the former speechwriter who has enlightened us for decades with his interest in language, once called oratory "human persuasion in action."[2] Artfully composed, persuasive speeches remain an enduring custom of American political life. I hope that when you finish this book you'll feel you've learned not just how to write good ones but why they are worth the trouble.

And then I hope what you've read allows you to take a little more satisfaction in contributing to them. They are worth the not-inconsiderable trouble. Because the reverse of what our students learn is also true; since speeches matter so much to others, doing them well should matter to you, whether you do it for a year or a lifetime, for yourself or for others, to further ideas or stir emotion; whether you've written every word of a senator's floor statement, part of a rally speech for a grief-stricken mother—or just a single, somewhat turgid line for the speech of a new president on inauguration day.

Speeches for *Almost* Every Occasion

Almost? Why not all of them? Have a heart. No book can cover every single event at which a politician is asked to talk.

But while the ways we've examined to use language, story, humor, or evidence are almost always appropriate in politics, each type of event has some needs that make it unique. So here we examine six of the most common: stump, floor, keynote, commencement, eulogy, and roast. Naturally, there are others. Politicians speak at hearings, fund-raisers, rallies, and prayer breakfasts. They deliver tributes and toasts. They declare victory and concede defeat. Most of what this book suggests can apply to those events as well.

For the ones I include here, you will find a general discussion of each kind, along with some tips; a sample outline; and a full-length example complete with Flesch-Kincaid stats, word count, the approximate grade level at which it reads, average sentence length, and percentage of passive voice. You'll see that those who wrote these speeches sometimes ignored things this book recommends. They are worth studying anyway. Aside from the two speeches I wrote—and thus leave judgment to others—you'll find in this section imaginative language, moving story, graceful wit, and pointed use of evidence. Remember: elsewhere in the book are three full speeches also worth study, as well as many for which other chapters provide links available on this book's Web site: college.cqpress. com/politicalspeech. Read them with an eye for what you can imitate—and how you can do them one better.

THE STUMP SPEECH

It's impossible to deliver the same speech four hundred times without getting bored. Speakers sometimes feel that since the audience must have heard this one before, they're bored too. They aren't. Politicians and staffers must separate their own reactions from those of the crowd. They need stumps. Like rehearsing a play, endless repetition is precisely what allows speakers to deliver lines without thinking—and thus to concentrate on being expressive.

Sometimes people think stump speeches exist only for campaigns. Not true. Elected officials need them *in* office too. Plenty of appearances call for the same material. They also call for the modified version of Monroe's Motivated Sequence (MMS) detailed in chapter 5. Winning *attention* through opening jokes, *acknowledging* local politicians, detailing *problem* and *solution,* using the inspirational example to *visualize* success, and *calling to action*—each meets needs that remain whether you're in a race or in office. Some tips:

- **Prepare with care.** Often, politicians allow stumps to develop haphazardly, improvising from event to event. That's a mistake. It's too hard to be effective without planning. Finding the most compelling way to start, the most inspirational way to close, and the best examples for every point takes sitting down at a computer, thinking, talking, writing, and rehearsing. Stumps evolve, just as do all our plans. But let them evolve from a plan.

- **Work for audience response.** There is nothing worse than a political rally where the audience sits on its hands. Stumps are for events where you want the crowd to interrupt. Whether in a campaign or at a keynote, speakers are energized by applause. Use the ways to make applause lines effective, yes. But even the most unimaginative applause line (*Isn't Joe great?*) works better than nothing.

- **Take advantage of audience anger.** If schedulers have done their job, politicians will almost always talk to friendly crowds. Political audiences are animated not just by love of their side but hostility to the other. Applause lines come not just from what you're for, but from sarcasm and other ways to excoriate what you're against.

- **Leave one section—preferably at the end of the solution section—for the special issues of this crowd.** Your basic issues should stay the same from group to group. But every group and every town has its own pet issue. Make sure you cover it, and in a way that leads to an applause line. It may be the loudest and longest of the night.

- **Customize.** Even if 90 percent of the speech stays the same, tailor it a little for every event. Howdahells are crucial; mentioning examples and real people important to the group carry weight. Don't make the audience think you're dialing the speech in.

STUMP SPEECH OUTLINE

Introduction

Opening joke (Often something barbed about the other side.)
Acknowledgments (The perfect place for crowd response.)
Howdahells
Serious attention-getter
Praise for the group (Remember to work for audience response.)
Statement of purpose (Reason you're there.)

Body

Record of accomplishment by party (The reminder of principles shared, accomplishments won. Common litany: *We're the party that . . .*)
Problems (Both failures by the other side and social problems. Common litany: *How can we be satisfied, when . . . ?*)
Transition to solutions (*We have a different idea.*)
Solutions (Bills and policies you support, laced with startling statistics, anecdote, humor—and applause lines. Remember the special needs of the group. Common litanies: *We can . . . we must . . . we will.*)

Conclusion

Reflective section
Inspirational example/vision of success
Lesson drawn (A litany of things we can do if everyone works together. Common litany: *I believe we can . . .*)
Call to action (Another chance for audience response.)
Clincher (Remember referral endings and antithesis.)

SEN. BARACK OBAMA, STUMP SPEECH, DECEMBER 2007

This stump speech comes from early in Barack Obama's presidential campaign. You won't see story or some other ingredients common to stumps. You will see the hallmarks of what characterized his speeches over two years: alliteration, antithesis, concrete detail, and constant litany ("We were promised . . . I am running . . . That is why . . .").

Words: 2,625
Grade level: 8.8
Sentence length: 19.8
Passive: 6 percent

Longer than most stumps, Obama's includes many of the ingredients you see in the outline below, often as litany, including:

- **Opening joke** ("Here's the good news . . .")
- **Statement of purpose** ("I'm running for president because . . .")
- **Problem** ("We were promised . . .")
- **Solution** ("One year from now . . .")

Note the way he appeals both to fear ("I don't want . . .") and hope ("One year from now, we can . . .") in his conclusion. Note too how he balances the need to criticize without alienating a rival who may become an ally and member of his administration. Later, Obama's stump would evolve, and he'd be able to use these elements in five minutes or twenty. But his structure and many of his examples would stay the same till election day.

One year from now, you will have the chance to walk into a voting booth, pull back the curtain, and choose the next President of the United States.

Here's the good news—for the first time in a long time, the name George Bush will not appear on the ballot. The name Dick Cheney will not appear on the ballot. The era of Scooter Libby justice, and Brownie incompetence, and the Karl Rove politics of fear and cynicism will be over.

But the question you will have to ask yourselves when you pick up your ballot a year from today is, "What next?" How do we repair the enormous damage of these dismal years and recapture that sense of common purpose that has seen America through our toughest times?

I'm running for president because I believe we find ourselves in a moment of great challenge and great promise—a moment that comes along once in a generation.

It's a moment of challenge because America is less safe and less respected than at any time in recent history. We are more dependent on oil from dictators and closer to the day when climate change becomes a climate catastrophe.

In the midst of great prosperity, families all across this country feel further from the American Dream. You know this from your own lives. Most Americans are working harder for less and paying more for health care and college than ever before. It's harder to save. Harder to retire. And the policies of the last seven years have added to that unfairness.

George Bush said whatever the politics of the moment required in order to get elected in 2000. And those seven years of broken promises have left the American people with less trust in their leaders and less faith in their government than they have in years.

We were promised compassion and conservatism, but we got Katrina and wiretaps.

We were promised a uniter, but we got a divider who couldn't even lead the half of the country who voted for him.

We were promised a kinder, gentler Washington but got a town that's more bitter, secretive, and corrupt than ever before. And the only mission ever accomplished was using fear and falsehoods to take us to a war that should've never been authorized and never been waged.

This catastrophic failure of leadership has led us to a moment where it's not just Democrats who are listening to what we have to say, but Independents and Republicans who have never been more disillusioned with what the state of our leadership in Washington has done to this country.

That's why this is also a moment of great promise. It's a chance to turn the page by offering the American people a fundamentally different choice in 2008—not just in the policies we offer, but in the kind of leadership we offer. It's a chance to come together and finally solve the challenges that were made worse by George Bush, but existed long before he took office—challenges like health care and energy and education that we haven't met for decades because of a political system in Washington that has failed the American people.

And that's what this debate in our party right now is all about.

Much has been said about the exchanges between Senator Clinton and myself this week. Now, understand that Hillary Clinton is a colleague and a friend. She's also a skilled politician, and she's run what Washington would call a "textbook" campaign. But the problem is the textbook itself.

It's a textbook that's all about winning elections, but says nothing about how to bring the country together to solve problems. As we saw in the debate last week, it encourages vague, calculated answers to suit the politics of the moment, instead of clear, consistent principles about how you would lead America. It teaches you that you can promise progress for everyday people while striking a bargain with the very special interests who crowd them out.

Now, Senator Clinton is certainly not the only one in Washington to play this game. It's gone on for years, and I understand the reasoning behind it. It's a game that usually gets politicians where they need to go. But I don't believe it gets America where we need to go. When it comes to issues like war and diplomacy, energy and health care, I don't believe we can bring about real change if all we do is change our positions based on what's popular or politically convenient. If we are going to seize this moment of challenge and promise, the American people deserve more when they head to the voting booth in 2008.

I believe that our party has made the most difference in people's lives and the life of this country when we have led not by polls but by principle; not by calculation but by conviction; when we've been able to summon the entire nation to a common purpose—a higher purpose. That's how Roosevelt led us through war and lifted us from depression. It's how Kennedy called on a new generation to ask what they could do for America. And I am running for the Democratic nomination for President of the United States because that's the kind of leadership America needs right now.

I don't pretend to be a perfect man, and I will not be a perfect president. But I am in this race because I believe that if we want to break from the failures of the past and finally make progress as a country, we can't keep telling different people what we think they want to hear—we have to tell every American what they need to know. We have to be honest about the challenges we face.

When I called for higher fuel standards so we could reduce our dependence on foreign oil, I didn't say it to some environmental group in California—I said it in front of automakers in Detroit. When I called for corporate responsibility so that middle-class Americans could get a tax cut, I said it in front of CEOs on Wall Street. And when I was invited to speak out against George Bush's plan to invade Iraq as a Senate candidate five years ago, I didn't listen to those who warned me that it was a politically risky position to take, I listened to my gut, and I said loud and clear that this was the wrong war at the wrong time and Congress should stand up and say so.

That's the kind of leadership we need right now. That's why I'm in this race. Because I don't think you should settle for a president who's only there for you when it's easy or convenient or popular—I think you deserve a president who's willing to fight for you every hour of every day for the next four years.

That's the change we can offer in 2008—not change as a slogan, but change we can believe in.

One year from now, we have the chance to tell all those corporate lobbyists that the days of them setting the agenda in Washington are over. I have done more to take on lobbyists than any other candidate in this race—and I've won. I don't take a dime of their money, and when I am president, they won't find a job in my White House. Because real change isn't another four years of defending lobbyists who don't represent real Americans—it's standing with working Americans who have seen their jobs disappear and their wages decline and their hope for the future slip further and further away. That's the change we can offer in 2008.

When I am president, I will end the tax giveaways to companies that ship our jobs overseas, and I will put the money in the pockets of working Americans, and seniors, and homeowners who deserve a break. I won't wait ten years to raise the minimum wage—I'll raise it to keep pace every single year. And if American workers are being denied their right to organize when I'm in the White House, I will put on a comfortable pair of shoes and I will walk on that picket line with you as President of the United States.

One year from now, we can stop campaigning on the outrage of 47 million uninsured Americans and finally start doing something about it. I reformed health care in Illinois, and I didn't do it alone—I did it by reaching out to Democrats and Republicans. We took on the insurance industry, and we won. That's how I'll pass a universal health care bill that allows every American to get the same kind of health care that members of Congress get for themselves and cuts every family's premiums by up to $2,500. And mark my words—I will sign this bill by the end of my first term as president. That's the change we can offer in 2008.

One year from now, we can stop sending our children down corridors of shame and start putting them on a pathway to success. When I am president, we will stop passing bills called No Child Left Behind that leave the money behind and start making real investments in education from cradle to adulthood. That means early childhood education. That means recruiting an army of new teachers, and paying them better, and supporting them more so they're not just teaching to test, but teaching to teach. And it means finally putting a college education within reach of every American. That's the change we can offer in 2008.

One year from now, we can stop sending hundreds of millions of dollars to dictators for their oil while we melt the polar ice caps in the bargain. I will raise our fuel standards, and put a cap on carbon emissions to reduce them 80 percent by 2050. We'll tell polluters that they have to pay for their pollution, because they don't own the skies, the American people own the skies. And we'll use the money to invest in the clean, renewable fuels that are our future. That's the change we can offer in 2008.

In this election, we have the chance to turn the page on the last six years of being told that the only way for Democrats to look tough on national security is to talk, and act, and vote like George Bush Republicans.

When I'm your nominee, my opponent won't be able to say that I was for the war in Iraq before I was against it; or that I supported an extension of the Iraq war into Iran; or that I support the Bush-Cheney diplomacy of not talking to leaders we don't like. And he won't be able to say that I flip-flopped on something as fundamental as whether our nation should use torture. Because we are not a nation that makes excuses for torture, we are a nation that rejects it. That's the change we can offer in 2008.

When I am president, I will end this war in Iraq. I will bring our troops home within sixteen months. I'll finish the fight against al Qaeda in Afghanistan. And I will lead the world against the common threats of the twenty-first century—nuclear weapons and terrorism; climate change and poverty; genocide and disease. That's what Democrats must stand for, and that's what America must stand for. And I'll be a president who finally sends a message to the black, white, and brown faces beyond our shores; from the halls of power to the huts of Africa that says, "You matter to America. Your future is our future. And our moment is now."

America, our moment is now. Now is our chance to turn the page. Now is our chance to write a new chapter.

I am in this race because I don't want to see us spend the next year re-fighting the Washington battles of the 1990s. I don't want to pit Blue America against Red America, I want to lead a United States of America. I don't want this election to be about the past, because if it's about the future, we all win. If this election is about whether or not to end this war, or pass universal health care, or make more college affordable, it won't just be a Democratic victory; it will be an American victory.

That's the victory this country needs right now. This election and this moment are too important to settle for what we already know. The time has come to reach for what we know is possible.

I am not running for this office to fulfill any long-held plans or because I believe it is somehow owed to me. I never expected to be here, and I always knew the journey would be improbable. I've never been on one that wasn't.

I am running because of what Dr. King called "the fierce urgency of now." I am running because I do believe there's such a thing as being too late. And that hour is almost here.

I'm running because I don't want to wake up one morning four years from now, and turn on one of those cable talk shows, and see that Washington is still stuck in the same food fight it's been in for over a decade. I don't want to see that more Americans lost their health care and fell into bankruptcy because we let the insurance industry spend millions to stop us for yet another year. I don't want to see that.

I don't want to see that the oceans rose another few inches and the planet has reached the point of no return because we couldn't find a way to stop ourselves from buying oil from dictators. I don't want to see that.

I don't want to see that we risked more American lives in another misguided war because no one had the judgment to ask the tough questions before we sent our troops to fight. I don't want to see that.

I don't want to see homeless veterans on the street. I don't want to send another generation of children through corridors of shame. I don't want this future for my daughters and I do not accept this future for America. It is time to turn the page.

I run for the presidency for the same reason I drove halfway across the country over two decades ago to bring jobs to the jobless and hope to the hopeless on the streets of Chicago; for the same reason I stood up for justice and equality as a civil rights lawyer; for the same reason I've fought for Illinois families for over a decade. Because I will never forget that the only reason I am standing here today is because someone, somewhere stood up when it wasn't popular, when it was risky, when it was hard. And because that someone stood up, a few more did. And then a few thousand. And then a few million. And together, they changed the world.

That's why I run in this election. I run to give my children and their children the same chances that someone, somewhere gave me. I run so that a year from today, there is a chance that the world will look at America differently, and that America will look at itself differently. And I run to keep the promise of the United States of America alive for all those who still hunger for opportunity and thirst for equality and long to believe again.

That is the change that's possible in this election. That is the moment I want to seize as president. And I ask you all to join me in this journey. Thank you.

THE FLOOR SPEECH

Written in haste, often by staff aides whose strength is not language, floor speeches—especially those during debate—are the orphan children of the political speech world. It's clear why. First, floor speeches often, though not always, deal with a specific solution—a bill, often a long one with many provisions, written in the arcane language of legislation. It seems logical that the staff aides who know the bill should write the speech. Besides, it might seem like the only audience is legislators presumably familiar with the bill and able to handle technical discussion. Actually, legislators can be the least important listeners. Floor speeches rarely change votes. By the time a bill is up for a vote, both parties know almost to a person what the total will be and how everyone will vote.

But floor speeches carry weight with *secondary* audiences: staffers who might pay attention to an interesting approach, reporters, trade association lobbyists wanting to see who's really with them, and people back home who might see a line or two in the local paper or on TV. And, for members of Congress, those watching on C-Span.

Floor speeches have another use. They provide a record of what a politician has done or said. Members of Congress can put excerpts in their newsletters, which eagle-eyed opponents scour to pick up stupid things and reporters file for possible in-depth stories. Each can help speakers or hurt them.

Floor speeches aren't all the same. There's a big difference between writing the short, often angry speeches that pass for debate in the House of Representatives and the longer, more measured addresses in a body whose members have to win support throughout an entire state. They differ too because they reflect the different personalities of the speaker and the importance of the issue.

That said, well-written and well-rehearsed floor speeches of every variety can attract attention and win influence far beyond their minimal effect on switching votes. Tips:

- **Make them brief.** Well, of course. Aren't we limited by debate? When that happens, everything gets compressed. A two-minute floor speech means you don't have room for story jokes or detailed anecdote—though you can look for quips, quotes, and headlines to win attention. Not every speech has time limits, though. But even in the longer ones—permitted by special orders, for example—resist rambling on the floor for a long time; you can still get all the benefits you need in a short speech.

- **Fit them to an overall strategy.** Work with the leadership to create an approach not duplicated by everyone else on your side.

- **Make them quotable**. Too often, speakers think they've discharged their duty by appearing in the well and handing in the text for the *Congressional Record*. Resist! Reporters are listening.

- **Deliver them well!** Because politicians often speak to an empty chamber, they think they can read their speech without ever looking up. But people watch members of Congress on C-Span. Reporters are in the gallery. Even one or two rehearsals will make speakers able to look up so the TV audience thinks they're speaking to them.

- **Get mileage from them.** Put them in newsletters; quote the best lines in other speeches; and mail them to the reporters, supporters, and lobbyists who will like them.

FLOOR SPEECH OUTLINE

Introduction

Attention step (*Brief* story illustrating the problem, solved by the bill up for a vote.)

Statement of purpose (What the general problem is and how the bill helps or hurts.)

Body

Problems (Both failures by the other side and social problems. Common litany: *How can we be satisfied, when . . . ?*)

Solution (Bills and policies you support, laced with startling statistics, anecdote, humor—and applause lines. Remember the special needs of the group. Common litanies: *We can . . . we must . . . we will.*)

Conclusion (forty-five seconds)

Inspirational example

Draw the lesson (A litany of things we can do if everyone works together. Common litany: *I believe we can . . .*)

Call to action (Address to members.)

Clincher (Remember referral endings and antithesis.)

Because floor speeches can differ so radically, we look at two—the full-length versions of Senator Obama's as a model for what you can do with about five minutes, and Majority Whip Bonior's—to show what is possible when debate time is limited to a minute.

SEN. BARACK OBAMA, FLOOR STATEMENT ON AMENDMENT TO PROVIDE MEALS AND PHONE SERVICE TO WOUNDED VETERANS, APRIL 14, 2005

Sometimes in floor speeches it's necessary to include boilerplate paragraphs of appreciation to other members. Obama's statement on the Amendment to

Provide Meals and Phone Service to Wounded Veterans really begins in the second paragraph and ends in the next-to-last one. But, as in his stump, note how closely he hews to MMS:

Words: 804
Grade level: 9.9
Sentence length: 19.1
Passive: 6 percent

- **Opening story** ("The other day, I . . .")
- **Problem** ("Because the Department of Defense . . .")
- **Solution** ("The first amendment I'm offering . . .")
- **Call to action** ("I ask . . .")
- **Clincher** (A referral ending bringing us back to his opening story— "These are our kids out there . . .")

In addition to structure, note the personal touch with which Obama opens: his colloquial litany about "our kids" puts a human face on a budget amendment. And don't overlook the concrete detail in his summary of the problem, the economy of his solution, and the antithesis with which he ends. For a second example, examine Obama's floor speech used to illustrate MMS in chapter 5.

Mr. President, today I am offering an amendment to the fiscal year 2005 Emergency Supplemental, which I am pleased to announce is being cosponsored by Senators Corzine, Bingaman, and Graham. This amendment would meet certain needs of our injured service members in recognition of the tremendous sacrifices they have made in defense of our country.

The other day I had the opportunity to visit some of our wounded heroes at Walter Reed Army Medical Center.

I know that many of my colleagues have made the same trip and I'd heard about their visits, but there is nothing that can fully prepare you for what you see when you take that first step into the Physical Therapy room.

These are kids in there. Our kids. The ones we watched grow up. The ones we hoped would live lives that were happy, healthy, and safe. These kids left their homes and families for a dangerous place halfway around the world. After years of being protected by their parents, these kids risked their lives to protect us.

And now, some of them have come home from that war with scars that may change their lives forever—scars that may never heal. And yet they sit there in that hospital, so full of hope and still so proud of their country.

These kids are the best of America. They deserve our highest respect, and they deserve our help.

Recently, I learned that some of our most severely wounded soldiers are being forced to pay for their own meals and their own phone calls while being treated in medical hospitals.

Up until last year, there was a law on the books that prohibited soldiers from receiving both their basic subsistence allowance and free meals from the military. Basically, this law allowed the government to charge our wounded heroes for food while they were recovering from their war injuries.

Thankfully, this body acted to change this law in 2003 so that wounded soldiers wouldn't have to pay for their meals.

But, we're dealing with a bureaucracy here, and as we all know, nothing is ever simple in a bureaucracy. So now, because the Department of Defense doesn't consider getting physical therapy or rehabilitation services in a medical hospital as "being hospitalized," there are wounded veterans who still do not qualify for the free meals other veterans receive. And after ninety days, even those classified as hospitalized on an outpatient status lose their free meals as well.

Also, while our soldiers in the field qualify for free phone service, injured service men and women who may be hospitalized hundreds or thousands of miles from home do not receive this benefit.

For soldiers whose family members aren't able to take off work and travel to a military hospital, hearing the familiar voice of a mom or dad or husband or wife on the other side of the phone can make all the difference in the world.

And yet, our government will not help pay for these calls. And it will not help pay for those meals.

Think about that. Think about the sacrifice these kids have made for their country, many of them literally risking life and sacrificing limb.

And now, at $8.10 a meal, they could end up with a $250 bill from the government that sent them to war every single month. This is wrong, and we have a moral obligation to fix it.

The first amendment that I'm offering today will do this. It will expand the group of "hospitalized" soldiers who cannot be charged for their meals to include those service members undergoing medical recuperation, therapy, or otherwise on "medical hold." The number of people affected by this amendment will be small. Only about four thousand service members are estimated to fall under the category of "non-hospitalized."

The amendment is retroactive to January 1, 2005, in an effort to provide those injured service members who may have received bills for their meals with some relief from those costs. The amendment will also extend free phone service to those injured service members who are hospitalized or otherwise undergoing medical recuperation or therapy. I am proud that this amendment is supported by the American Legion, and I hope my colleagues will join them in that support.

I ask my colleagues to join me in supporting this amendment. These are our kids out there, and they're risking their lives for us. When they come home with injuries, the government that asked these kids to serve should provide them with the best possible care and support. This is a small price to pay for those who have sacrificed so much for their country.

I thank the Senior Senator from Alaska and my colleague from Mississippi for working with me on this issue. I am hopeful we can reach an agreement on this.

MAJORITY WHIP DAVID BONIOR, FLOOR STATEMENT: "NOTHING CAN BE DONE?" OCTOBER 29, 1991

Bonior's one-minute, delivered during a recession as an unpopular president boarded *Air Force One* for a conference in Switzerland, received wide publicity.

It's an example of how floor speeches can win attention out of proportion to the time they take. Bonior gets attention with a damning quote from the other side before presenting problem and solution, and he finishes with a clincher that uses metaphor and antithesis to win wide publicity—all with only 149 words.

Words: 149
Grade level: 5.6
Sentence length: 8.2
Passive: 16 percent

Mr. Speaker, a top White House aide says George Bush doesn't need to pay attention to the home front because there isn't anything that can be done right now.

Nothing that can be done? He could read a few headlines!

"Economic ills . . . Economy weaker!"

"Economy absolutely stalled."

Nothing that can be done?

Sign our unemployment bill! 437,000 people in my home state of Michigan are out of work. His bill helps none of them. Zippo!

Nothing that can be done?

Forget the capital gains cut for the wealthy. Support a middle-class tax cut to put money back in the hands of working Americans.

There's plenty to do.

Bush's aide said yesterday that the president's not ignoring us. "It's just that he likes foreign policy better."

Maybe it's more fun to jet off all around the world.

We need a pilot who can get this dismal economy off the ground.

THE KEYNOTE

In music, the key note is the tonic—or ruling—note in a chord. In tonal music it determines what key the piece is in.

In politics, a keynote speech strikes the ruling theme of the event. In its discussion of litany, this book talks about political and issue-driven keynotes. But for politicians, both kinds are essentially political. Whether speaking at a meeting of county Democrats or talking to the Sierra Club, politicians offer or imply the same message: vote for me.

That is not to say the differences are tiny. Here are the basic elements of each, with some attention to where they differ.

POLITICAL

Basically, a political keynote follows the format of an expanded stump. In addition to the Monroe steps, someone keynoting the big political dinners—Jefferson-Jackson Day dinners for Democrats or Lincoln-Reagan Day dinners for Republicans—will make sure to include these elements:

- **Acknowledgments.** Sometimes called shout-outs, because you shout out each name, hoping to generate applause. (*And isn't it great to see Janet Jones, who has fought so hard for etc.*)

- **Praise.** For the party and for the achievements of people in the audience.

- **A problem section.** Consisting of an extensive list of failures of the other party over a wide range of subjects.

- **Solutions.** Ending memorably enough to generate applause.

- **A call to action that ends in specific action.** Writing checks, taking yard signs, or working on election day.

- **Audience interaction**. Questions designed to elicit reaction. (*Has there ever been an administration more unwilling to face X? Audience: NO!*)

ISSUE

To talk of "issue" keynotes is not to imply they are the only keynotes dealing with issues. Political keynotes are filled with issues. Still, there are differences. When politicians speak to groups like the Sierra Club, or Business Roundtable, they mute their personal attacks on the opposition, add nuance to their assessment of the issues, and devote more time to the issues that concern the group. While the six elements we list are the same as they are for political keynoter, here's what often looks different in the draft for an issue-driven one:

- **Acknowledgments.** Generally fewer, since politicians are less worried about insulting anyone. Since the atmosphere is a little less circuslike at conferences, they often aren't done as shout-outs.

- **Praise.** Here it is for the group, and sometimes the larger movement of which it's a part—as well as those in the audience.

- **A problem section.** Might involve a discussion of the issue itself, more background, and only a hint at the other party's failures in this one area.

- **Solutions.** Should still end memorably enough to generate applause—but about a much narrower range of issues. They often include a discussion of legislative prospects and announce support for a particular bill.

- **A call to action.** Much more likely to stress the theme of partnership—since the group may not agree with everything the speaker has done.

- **Audience interaction.** Less likely, but not unheard of, particularly for the crowd at nonprofit events who basically fall in one political camp—the Federalist Society for Republicans, for example, and Alliance for Justice for Democrats.

Aside from those differences, here are three points to keep in mind for both:

1. **Length.** There is almost never a need to go more than twenty minutes for either. Audiences get bored, it's tiring, and a longer Q&A will be more interesting for almost everybody, including the speaker.

2. **Tone.** Party dinners are red-meat affairs. The tone is highly partisan. Speakers can be more reflective in issues keynotes. Groups don't expect to agree with you on every issue. Decide where you can agree with the group without going on record with support you'll later regret. They'll understand.

3. **Evidence.** Because the audience knows the issue, your discussion at issue keynoters can include more technical evidence—and will need fact-checking, because listeners love to find errors.

KEYNOTE SPEECH OUTLINE

Introduction

Opening joke (Often something barbed about the other side.)
Acknowledgments (Less likely to get crowd reaction in an issues keynote response.)
Howdahells
Praise for the group
Serious attention-getter
Statement of purpose

Body

Record of accomplishment by party or group (The reminder of principles shared, accomplishments won. Common litany: *We're the party that . . .* for political; *you're the ones who . . .* for nonpolitical.)

Problems (Both failures by the other side and social problems. Common litany: *How can we be satisfied, when . . . ?*)

Solutions (Bills and policies you support, laced with startling statistics, anecdote, and humor-and-applause lines. Remember the special needs of the group. Common litanies: *We can . . . we must . . . we will.*)

Conclusion

Reflective section

Inspirational example

The lesson drawn (Litany of things we can do if everyone works together. Common litany: *I believe we can . . .*)

Call to action (Another chance for audience response.)

Clincher

PRESIDENT RONALD REAGAN, REMARKS ON THE FORTIETH ANNIVERSARY OF D DAY, POINTE DU HOC, NORMANDY, FRANCE, JUNE 6, 1984

Words: 1,850
Grade level: 7.4
Sentence length: 17.2
Passive: 10 percent

I've selected this most well-known speech by Ronald Reagan to illustrate keynote speeches partly because much of it remains excellent today. We examine it, though, mostly because while at first glance it seems different than most keynotes and more like a tribute, a close look shows how useful the Monroe structure is in this speech. Like Obama's floor speech, it too starts with paragraph two: "I had decided on a plan."

Then comes the gripping, concrete, cinematic, and richly detailed story of what happened; some stories of individual heroism; and a ruminative passage speculating on what made the "Boys of Pointe du Hoc" risk so much.

But about two-thirds of the way through the speech, speechwriter Peggy Noonan turns to the problem of 1984, a solution, and a standard, four-part close. The basic steps:

- **Attention** ("We stand on a lonely . . .")
- **Praise for group** ("These are the boys of Pointe du Hoc.")
- **Problem** ("The Soviet troops . . . did not leave . . .")
- **Solution** (The Soviets "must give up the ways of conquest.")
- **Inspiration and lesson learned** ("We're bound today by what bound us forty years ago . . .")

- **Call to action** ("Let us make a vow to our dead.")
- **Clincher** ("Strengthened by their courage . . .")

One might wish the speech had an ending as concrete as its opening, but remember: on TV, the visions of cemetery crosses and the old men seated before Reagan make words less important. In fact, Noonan's account in *What I Saw at the Revolution* is a particularly instructive story of how speeches are not entirely in the hands of the writer.

What speechwriters should note, among many other things, is the concrete detail of the opening and the reflective middle section; and similar to others, from Lincoln ("With malice towards none . . .") to Palin ("If character is the measure . . ."), is her use of suspense ("Strengthened by their courage . . .") in the clincher.

We're here to mark that day in history when the Allied armies joined in battle to reclaim this continent to liberty. For four long years, much of Europe had been under a terrible shadow. Free nations had fallen, Jews cried out in the camps, millions cried out for liberation. Europe was enslaved and the world prayed for its rescue. Here, in Normandy, the rescue began. Here, the Allies stood and fought against tyranny, in a giant undertaking unparalleled in human history.

We stand on a lonely, windswept point on the northern shore of France. The air is soft, but forty years ago at this moment, the air was dense with smoke and the cries of men, and the air was filled with the crack of rifle fire and the roar of cannon. At dawn, on the morning of the 6th of June, 1944, 225 Rangers jumped off the British landing craft and ran to the bottom of these cliffs.

Their mission was one of the most difficult and daring of the invasion: to climb these sheer and desolate cliffs and take out the enemy guns. The Allies had been told that some of the mightiest of these guns were here, and they would be trained on the beaches to stop the Allied advance.

The Rangers looked up and saw the enemy soldiers at the edge of the cliffs, shooting down at them with machine guns and throwing grenades. And the American Rangers began to climb. They shot rope ladders over the face of these cliffs and began to pull themselves up. When one Ranger fell, another would take his place. When one rope was cut, a Ranger would grab another and begin his climb again. They climbed, shot back, and held their footing. Soon, one by one, the Rangers pulled themselves over the top, and in seizing the firm land at the top of these cliffs, they began to seize back the continent of Europe. Two hundred and twenty-five came here. After two days of fighting, only ninety could still bear arms.

And behind me is a memorial that symbolizes the Ranger daggers that were thrust into the top of these cliffs. And before me are the men who put them there. These are the boys of Pointe du Hoc. These are the men who took the cliffs. These are the champions who helped free a continent. And these are the heroes who helped end a war. Gentlemen, I look at you and I think of the words of Stephen Spender's poem. You are men who in your "lives fought for life and left the vivid air signed with your honor."

I think I know what you may be thinking right now—thinking "we were just part of a bigger effort; everyone was brave that day." Well everyone was. Do you remember the story of Bill Millin of the 51st Highlanders? Forty years ago today, British troops were pinned down near a bridge, waiting desperately for help. Suddenly, they heard the sound of bagpipes, and some thought they were dreaming. Well, they weren't. They looked up and saw Bill Millin with his bagpipes, leading the reinforcements and ignoring the smack of the bullets into the ground around him.

Lord Lovat was with him—Lord Lovat of Scotland, who calmly announced when he got to the bridge, "Sorry, I'm a few minutes late," as if he'd been delayed by a traffic jam, when in truth he'd just come from the bloody fighting on Sword Beach, which he and his men had just taken.

There was the impossible valor of the Poles, who threw themselves between the enemy and the rest of Europe as the invasion took hold; and the unsurpassed courage of the Canadians, who had already seen the horrors of war on this coast. They knew what awaited them there, but they would not be deterred. And once they hit Juno Beach, they never looked back.

All of these men were part of a roll call of honor with names that spoke of a pride as bright as the colors they bore: the Royal Winnipeg Rifles, Poland's 24th Lancers, the Royal Scots' Fusiliers, the Screaming Eagles, the Yeomen of England's armored divisions, the forces of Free France, the Coast Guard's "Matchbox Fleet," and you, the American Rangers.

Forty summers have passed since the battle that you fought here. You were young the day you took these cliffs; some of you were hardly more than boys, with the deepest joys of life before you. Yet you risked everything here. Why? Why did you do it? What impelled you to put aside the instinct for self-preservation and risk your lives to take these cliffs? What inspired all the men of the armies that met here? We look at you, and somehow we know the answer. It was faith and belief. It was loyalty and love.

The men of Normandy had faith that what they were doing was right, faith that they fought for all humanity, faith that a just God would grant them mercy on this beachhead, or on the next. It was the deep knowledge—and pray God we have not lost it—that there is a profound moral difference between the use of force for liberation and the use of force for conquest. You were here to liberate, not to conquer, and so you and those others did not doubt your cause. And you were right not to doubt.

You all knew that some things are worth dying for. One's country is worth dying for, and democracy is worth dying for, because it's the most deeply honorable form of government ever devised by man. All of you loved liberty. All of you were willing to fight tyranny, and you knew the people of your countries were behind you.

The Americans who fought here that morning knew word of the invasion was spreading through the darkness back home. They fought—or felt in their hearts, though they couldn't know in fact, that in Georgia they were filling the churches at 4:00 A.M. In Kansas they were kneeling on their porches and praying. And in Philadelphia they were ringing the Liberty Bell.

Something else helped the men of D day; their rock-hard belief that Providence would have a great hand in the events that would unfold here; that God was an ally in this great cause. And so, the night before the invasion, when Colonel Wolverton asked his parachute troops to kneel with him in prayer, he told them: "Do not bow your heads, but look up so you can see God and ask His blessing in what we're about to do." Also, that night, General Matthew Ridgway on his cot, listening in the darkness for the promise God made to Joshua: "I will not fail thee nor forsake thee."

These are the things that impelled them; these are the things that shaped the unity of the Allies.

When the war was over, there were lives to be rebuilt and governments to be returned to the people. There were nations to be reborn. Above all, there was a new peace to be assured. These were huge and daunting tasks. But the Allies summoned strength from the faith, belief, loyalty, and love of those who fell here. They rebuilt a new Europe together. There was first a great reconciliation among those who had been enemies, all of whom had suffered so greatly. The United States did its part, creating the Marshall Plan to help rebuild our allies and our former enemies. The Marshall Plan led to the Atlantic alliance—a great alliance that serves to this day as our shield for freedom, for prosperity, and for peace.

In spite of our great efforts and successes, not all that followed the end of the war was happy or planned. Some liberated countries were lost. The great sadness of this loss echoes down to our own time in the streets of Warsaw, Prague, and East Berlin. The Soviet troops that came to the center of this continent did not leave when peace came. They're still there, uninvited, unwanted, unyielding, almost forty years after the war. Because of this, allied forces still stand on this continent. Today, as forty years ago, our armies are here for only one purpose: to protect and defend democracy. The only territories we hold are memorials like this one and graveyards where our heroes rest.

We in America have learned bitter lessons from two world wars. It is better to be here ready to protect the peace, than to take blind shelter across the sea, rushing to respond only after freedom is lost. We've learned that isolationism never was and never will be an acceptable response to tyrannical governments with an expansionist intent. But we try always to be prepared for peace, prepared to deter aggression, prepared to negotiate the reduction of arms, and yes, prepared to reach out again in the spirit of reconciliation. In truth, there is no reconciliation we would welcome more than a reconciliation with the Soviet Union, so, together, we can lessen the risks of war, now and forever.

It's fitting to remember here the great losses also suffered by the Russian people during World War II. Twenty million perished, a terrible price that testifies to all the world the necessity of ending war. I tell you from my heart that we in the United States do not want war. We want to wipe from the face of the earth the terrible weapons that man now has in his hands. And I tell you, we are ready to seize that beachhead. We look for some sign from the Soviet Union that they are willing to move forward, that they share our desire and love for peace, and that they will give up the ways of conquest. There must be a changing there that will allow us to turn our hope into action.

We will pray forever that someday that changing will come. But for now, particularly today, it is good and fitting to renew our commitment to each other, to our freedom, and to the alliance that protects it.

We're bound today by what bound us forty years ago, the same loyalties, traditions, and beliefs. We're bound by reality. The strength of America's allies is vital to the United States, and the American security guarantee is essential to the continued freedom of Europe's democracies. We were with you then; we're with you now. Your hopes are our hopes, and your destiny is our destiny.

Here, in this place where the West held together, let us make a vow to our dead. Let us show them by our actions that we understand what they died for. Let our actions say to them the words for which Matthew Ridgway listened: "I will not fail thee nor forsake thee."

Strengthened by their courage and heartened by their value [valor] and borne by their memory, let us continue to stand for the ideals for which they lived and died.

Thank you very much, and God bless you all.

THE COMMENCEMENT

Political life is contentious. One person's president is another's war criminal. We expect argument in political speeches. Commencements, though, are celebrations, where people who may disagree about politics celebrate together. They don't want to hear views that set their teeth on edge.

Does that mean speakers have to be bland? Not at all.

First of all, not all campuses are alike. Some schools may overwhelmingly share a speaker's views. Sometimes that's why the school invites them. What might be controversial elsewhere becomes the right approach there.

Most campuses, though, are mixed. When politicians speak at commencements, they should at least think about soft-pedaling views offensive to people who want to feel comfortable. Once in a while, it's possible to be celebratory and insightful without controversy.

And whether speakers are controversial or not, they usually conform to the traditional things commencement speakers are expected to do:

- Express thanks for the invitation and honorary degree (if there is one).
- Talk about some personal connection to the school, no matter how tenuous.
- Applaud the students, school—and parents.
- Make a few serious points about something for which the school is known.
- Challenge the students to make the world better.
- Acknowledge the sadness of leaving the campus, but inspire them with a vision of what lies ahead.

Is there one reason commencement speeches are so unmemorable? Not really. These are the elements graduates need. What makes them unmemorable is that so many are abstract—the kinds of statements that could work on any campus. Five suggestions:

1. **Personalize.** Don't just mouth general words of praise. Look on the school's Web site to find some genuine accomplishments and people who illustrate them—especially in the graduating class. This will make it clear that the speaker cares about the event.

2. **Talk to people on campus.** Find out what's really going on. It will help make the draft relevant.

3. **Include stories involving classmates.** That is, if you talk about intellectual growth, relate it to a class others have taken, or to an event others have experienced.

4. **Provide a shock of recognition.** Find the concrete details graduates will recognize from their own experiences to make them feel your speech represents them too.

5. **Do all that in about ten minutes.** Students are listening. They—and certainly their parents—can be moved. But they're also eager to have the ceremony end.

COMMENCEMENT SPEECH OUTLINE

Introduction

Brief opening joke

Express thanks for invitation

Praise the students and parents

Attention step (Story or description of some personal connection with campus.)

Praise the school, using concrete examples

Statement of purpose (Often, that the speaker will demonstrate conviction that these graduates can help solve what the speaker sees as the challenge of our time.)

Body

Problem (Graphic litany of some problems the world faces, including stories to illustrate.)

Solution (Specific support for the idea that these graduates can make a difference. As in any persuasive speech, lace this section with story, startling statistics, anecdote, humor—and applause lines—but with examples from the school and student body.)

Conclusion

Inspirational example. (Again, often one that involves a connection to this campus.)

Draw the lesson. (A litany of things we can do if everyone works together.)

Call to action (Paint your vision of what these students can do.)

Clincher (Again, revolve your final sentence around something relevant to this campus.)

SEN. JOHN KERRY, COMMENCEMENT SPEECH, KENYON COLLEGE, MAY 20, 2006

Words: 2,435
Grade level: 6.5
Sentence length: 14.1
Passive: 4 percent

A little longer than most commencements, this speech had its origin in a coincidence, and though written by me and thus a little embarrassing, I include it because it illustrates what speakers can do to make events meaningful.

The coincidence was that on election night 2004 the last state that would decide whether John Kerry won or lost was Ohio. And the last place where polls stayed open was tiny Kenyon College, where students lined up to vote at its two voting machines until well after midnight.

The overwhelmingly pro-Kerry campus really wanted Kerry to come, and he was similarly emotional about that night. Kerry did what speakers rarely do: he assembled a group of Kenyon alums and spent an hour asking them questions and taking notes. Those notes provided material that allowed me to infuse the speech with a wealth of detail about the school. (Truth in advertising: my son had gone to Kenyon, giving me a head start on the kind of material I would need.) "He took notes!" raved the student speaker, Hayes Wong, introducing Kerry.

The lesson we all learned: effective commencement speeches are not about what the speaker thinks; they're about what's special about this campus and this commencement.

Thank you, President Nugent.

President! Some people would do a lot for that title.

Class of 2006—fellow survivors of November 2, 2004.

I'm happy to be here at this beautiful school . . . which had my admiration long before that night when the country wondered whether I would win—and whether you would vote.

Your Web site has a profile of a very smart math major in the class of 2006: Joe Neilson. He said that once, after a statistics course here, he realized "the probability of any event in our lives is about zero."

"I probably spent a week," Joe said, "annoying my friends by saying: 'What are the odds?'"

Joe, what were the odds that we'd be linked by those long hours—not that I keep track—560 days ago?

Like everyone that night, I admired the tenacity of Kenyon students.

But what you did went far beyond tenacity.

My wife, Teresa, is honored by the degree you grant her today. But she's also here because when you grow up in a dictatorship as she did . . . when you don't get a chance to vote until you're thirty-one . . . when you see your father voting for the first time in his seventies . . . you know what a privilege it is to cast a ballot.

Through that long night, we in Massachusetts watched you in Gambier. We were honored. We were inspired. We were determined not to concede until our team had checked every possibility.

If you could stay up all night to vote, we could certainly stay up that next day to make sure your vote would count.

We couldn't close the gap. I say to my supporters: I would have given anything to have fulfilled your hopes. Thank you for your faith in our campaign.

And I thank those who cast a ballot for my opponent.

I say to them: I wish all Republicans had been just like you at Kenyon—informed, willing to stand up for your views . . . and only 10 percent of the vote.

Actually, all of you, through your patience and good humor, showed Americans that politics matters to young people. I really do thank every student here.

And I want to thank someone who *isn't* a student.

Because at the meeting Hayes was kind enough to mention—and I did take notes—the alums made it clear how much they'd been influenced by great friends, great teachers.

Or a great coach.

I happen to know what it's like to be on a team before an important game. I know how crucial that last practice can be.

For the field hockey team, that November 2 was the last day before the Oberlin game. Winning meant getting into the league championship—and from there to the NCAAs.

So I can understand why players were upset after hours waiting in line at the polling place that afternoon. When Maggie Hill called her coach to ask if she should come back to practice—you'd expect the coach to say yes.

This coach had a different reaction. "I'll cancel practice," she said, "and I'm sending the whole team to vote."

In that one moment she became a hero to me. It takes a big coach to know there are more important things than a big game.

So I'd like a *huge* round of applause for Robin Cash.

[APPLAUSE]

Her values are the values of Kenyon.

By the way, for parents who may not remember—Kenyon played brilliantly—and won that Oberlin game 3–zip.

Now—it's not as if seeing brilliance here is a surprise. Like everybody, I know that when you look at a resume and see a Kenyon degree, you think, "Smart. Committed. Good writer."

And maybe, "Likes to see a lot of stars at night."

But there's more. The Kenyon alums were so eloquent about what it meant to be here, where all your friends live, study, and play along a one-mile path in a town surrounded by cornfields.

"I came here on a cold, rainy October," one of them said, "but after my interview I saw professors having coffee at the deli, and heard everybody so excited about the Tom Stoppard play they were putting on—and fell in love with the place."

"Intelligent conversation permeates the whole campus," someone else said.

Another one said—I don't think he was kidding—"Nobody gets drunk at Commencement."

We talked till I got dragged into an intelligence briefing from the White House.

Believe me, I learned more at the Kenyon meeting.

What they said sounded very familiar. And wonderful. Because there are other places where you can find a small community—where the bonds you forge will never dissolve. You can find it on a tiny boat in Vietnam's Cam Ranh Bay.

You can even find it in the Senate.

Someone described to me what it's like walking into Gund for dinner after your girlfriend breaks up with you. You see every single person staring to make sure you're all right.

I thought, "Sounds like walking into the Democratic Caucus after that first New Hampshire poll."

The Kenyon grads in Washington didn't agree on everything. But they agreed that Kenyon is a place where you have the luxury of examining an issue not for whether it sounds good but for whether it is good

Actually, one Kenyon parent told me something that bothered him. His son took *Quest for Justice* his first semester at Kenyon. That's not what bothered him. But, the class met early in the morning—and his son made every class.

After years of pushing this kid to get out of bed, the father wanted to know, "What changed?"

His son said, "Dad, I could disappoint you. But not Professor Baumann."

And that brings up one of the things I want to talk about.

For the election day event that united us was a disappointment. There's no way around it. Even as we flew in over Columbus this morning, I was looking down at the Ohio landscape, thinking: we came so close.

So what.

You cannot go through life without disappointment. No team, no politician, no writer, no scientist—*no* one avoids defeat.

The question is: What do you do next?

Here's what I think.

You pick yourself up and keep on fighting. Losing a battle doesn't mean you've lost the war. Whether it's a term paper, an experiment . . . or a race for president . . . you will learn from experience, and experience success.

That's important, because there are so many things to fight for.

By that, I don't just mean the things we fight over in the halls of Congress. Kenyon produces graduates that produce our literature and drama—like E. L. Doctorow did with *The March,* fifty-four years after leaving Gambier. Or Allison Janney did on *West Wing*—the first show ever to portray politics with something approaching the complexity it deserves. Your challenge is to produce and perform the rich imaginative works that move and illuminate your time.

Kenyon has vastly expanded its science programs. And your challenge is to fight in laboratories against enemies like the tiny HIV virus that has created the most devastating epidemic in human history—killing more people every two hours than there are in this graduating class.

At a time when we read about the high-tech jobs of a globalized world, your challenge is to find a way to educate the millions of Americans who can't get those jobs—because they can't read well enough to understand how to get online.

And now, we are engaged in a misguided war.

Like the war of my generation, it began with an official deception.

It's a war that in addition to the human cost—the tragedy of tens of thousands of Iraqis and Americans dead and wounded—will cost a trillion dollars.

Enough to endow ten thousand Kenyons.

Money that could fight poverty, disease, and hunger.

To me, we cannot stand by and watch our troops sacrificed for a policy that isn't working.

We cannot tolerate those who brand unpatriotic dissenters who ask tough questions.

As it was with Vietnam, it is again right to make clear that the best way to support the troops is to oppose a course that squanders their lives.

And so, your challenge is also to find a way to reclaim America's conscience.

I have no doubt you will.

For one thing, you have great role models. Like your parents, sitting out there under the trees.

You may laugh looking at the old photos of your dad in a ponytail, and your mom in bellbottoms and that crazy, tie-dyed shirt.

But their generation too faced the task of ending a war. And they did.

And went on to invent Earth Day, march against racism, bring women into the workplace, and become the first generation to usher in an acceptance for people regardless of sexual preference.

They honored democracy by making government face issues of conscience—and I ask you to applaud them for making the world better *before* they made it better by making you what you are!

[REACTION]

And of course, in addition to those sitting behind you . . . you have great role models sitting *among* you. Students from this class who had a dream, took a chance, and have already achieved great things.

I know, because sitting here is a student who dreamed of being published, and felt ambitious enough to send a poem he'd written for class to the *Chautauqua Literary Journal*. And so Sam Anderson became a published poet at the age of twenty-one.

I know, because sitting here is a student who, watching a cousin struggle with Duchenne Muscular Dystrophy, dreamed of finding a way to help—and designed a project that involved her with the leading DMD researcher in the world. Now Amy Aloe's been invited to work in his groundbreaking lab.

I know, because sitting here is a student who dreamed of returning to the country of her birth, the country that shaped much of my life. And in Vietnam, Nhu Truong could examine not just issues, but the more difficult job of examining herself.

They all took a chance. If you ever despair of making a difference you'll have Kenyon people to remind you of what's possible if *you* take a chance.

And not just from the class of '06.

One of the alums mentioned that every week, a group of them meet to talk about issues. They don't think alike about every idea, he said. But they share a *passion* for ideas they learned here.

Another asked me to tell those of you suspicious of government, that "it's made up of people like us, trying to make things better."

The group included one alum who's well known here—and getting well known in Washington.

But a while back he was just a nervous twenty-four-year old, sitting silently in a meeting with a new secretary of state. Until he got up the nerve to raise his hand and make a point.

"Who's that young, red-haired kid?" Condoleezza Rice said afterward, to an aide. "Keep your eye on him."

No, she didn't mean he was a security risk. He'd said something that, as a *Washington Post* reporter put it, "crystallized her thoughts about foreign policy."

And now Chris Brose, Kenyon 2002, travels everywhere with Secretary Rice, not just crafting her speeches but talking about policy.

I wish the policies were a little different . . .

But he's making a mark. He's making a difference.

"I whimsically tripped into political science," Chris said, "and it changed my life." He has no doubt that every day he uses in Washington what he learned in Gambier.

You know, during World War II, my father was flying planes in the Army Air Corps. While he was away on duty, my mother was volunteering at home. She sent him a letter about it.

"You have no idea of the ways in which one can be useful right now," she wrote. "There's something for everyone to do."

She was right about her time. What she wrote is right about yours.

In a few minutes you will walk across this stage for your diploma. You'll line up on the steps of Rosse Hall to sing for the last time. You'll turn in your hoods, go back and finish packing. Maybe sell that ratty sofa to somebody from the class of 2007. And then you'll watch the cars pull away.

I know you've heard the old saying that commencement is not an end but a beginning.

The truth is, it's both.

It is a day to feel sad about leaving Gambier. It's a day to feel eager about what lies ahead.

Because you have a special mission.

Those who worked to end a war long ago, now ask you to help end new wars.

Those who worked to end poverty ask you to finish what we have left undone.

We ask you to take a chance.

We ask you work for change.

Promise yourselves, promise your parents, promise your teachers that you will use what you have learned.

Don't doubt that you can.

Only doubt those pessimists who say you can't.

For all along the way, I promise, that while you leave the campus, Kenyon will never leave you.

You will be linked by the experiences vividly brought to life today by Hayes Wong, who experienced them with you.

As you fight for justice in this world, you will be linked by the insights you all had in courses like *Quest for Justice.*

You will be linked to classmates whose success you predict will take the world by storm—and to some whose success takes you by surprise.

You will be linked by the times you sat on a bench in Middle Path and argued about politics with people whose views you opposed—and learned you could be friends, anyway.

At some point you'll see that this small campus that changed you has produced enormous change in the world.

And you will see that it came from what you learned here: from a class so compelling you were awake at the crack of dawn . . . from that night Teresa and I will never forget when you waited patiently till 4:15 at a polling place in Gambier . . . or from a coach who knew that her mission was to teach you how to win on and off the field.

THE EULOGY

One of the peculiarities of political life is that people you don't know well ask you to speak at funerals. Once, I wrote a eulogy for one of my bosses to deliver for the mother of someone he knew. I put in the requisite compliments to the dead woman. In a spasm of *hubris* I wrote that she had "inculcated" high moral values to her children.

My boss looked across the desk at me and said, "Clearly you don't know the family." Then he went out and delivered it anyway.

To steal a line from Wilford Brimley, it was the right thing to do. You don't speak ill of the dead—at least not at the funeral. Eulogies are not events at which you note the complexities of the dead person's life or character, or the tensions, rivalries, and disappointments of family life. People at a funeral service are usually saddened, some bereft, and even those present merely out of obligation will weep, even if only because they have confronted the idea of their own mortality.

For people in public life, eulogies should do more than express grief. Often, speakers are talking about colleagues. By celebrating their achievements, they remind listeners about the importance of the causes they cared about. Since audiences usually have worked for the same causes, this drives home another useful point: that the speaker admires not just the dead person, but them.

"We don't just mourn a loss," eulogizers often say, "but celebrate a life." *Eulogy* actually comes from the Greek word meaning "praise." *Euphemism* comes from the same root. Even in the most tragic circumstances, listeners need to feel the dead person's life had lasting value. Some tips:

• **Use anecdote.** Abstractions cannot hold an audience's attention and—more important—won't move it.

• **Be funny.** Mourners need the relief. Stories that make gentle fun of the dead person can work well as long as they are gentle. One way to tell: ask yourself if the dead person would be upset if they could hear.

• **Try poetry.** This is a time when lines that might seem too literary for politics can sum up feeling. Peggy Noonan's reputation comes mostly from a poem she found, which President Reagan used at the end of his eulogy for the *Challenger* astronauts.

• **Use phrases that bond the group.** (*All of us who cared for . . .*) It makes those not speaking feel their views have been heard.

• **Give the loss a larger significance.** In mentioning that the dead person will be mourned by his or her family *and* those sharing his or her concerns, you further those causes and please the audience, who will usually share them.

• **Talk little about yourself.** Unless it's to express gratitude for the dead person's influence. Audiences want to hear about the person they mourn, not the speaker.

• **Don't feel you have to mask grief.** It's natural to choke up. Nobody will be offended.

EULOGY OUTLINE

Introduction

Attention step (Story or description of the dead person relating to your theme.)

Statement of purpose (Often, that we're not here just to mourn a loss but celebrate a life; religious mourners may take comfort by asserting that the dead have joined their Maker, or are free of earthly cares.)

Body

Praise general qualities of person (Use concrete examples.)

Describe the larger context (The causes they fought for, the successes they achieved.)

Return to individual (More stories illustrating different qualities.)

Conclusion

Inspirational example (Here is a chance to be moving with poetry or other literary allusions—or something the dead person once said.)

Draw the lesson (Sum up why what you've quoted sums up the dead person.)

Call to action (Ask the audience to remember them in this way they would want.)

Clincher (Yes, even here. Remember referral endings and antithesis—but again, revolve around the dead person.)

RON REAGAN, EULOGY FOR HIS FATHER, RONALD REAGAN, JUNE 14, 2004

Sometimes those writing eulogies feel awkward examining their techniques. Does everything have to be analyzed? Can't you just mourn? And don't gimmicks in political speech—a clincher, for God's sake!—cheapen the event? But just as the organist at a funeral doesn't forget technique, neither should a speaker.

> Words: 760
> Grade level: 6.1
> Sentence length: 12.8
> Passive: 3 percent

So, with apologies to the dead, and those who had the ineffably sad job of writing and speaking, let's look at one: Ron Reagan's of his father.

While Ronald Reagan's funeral was certainly a public event, his son's eulogy was intensely personal. All the traditional elements were there: praise for his father, comfort because he is "home" and "free," and celebration of his life. But while Reagan tries to unify the speech by returning in the end to the "home" and "free" themes, he disposes of all that quickly to get to the strengths of this eulogy: concrete detail and revealing anecdote.

The detail comes in the way Ron Reagan imagines his father in a heaven specially designed for him. Of the anecdotes, the best is the "thumbs-up" story.

Rather than a eulogy that pokes fun at the dead person, this story, stylishly told, shows Reagan (the father) making fun of himself in a self-deprecating and likable way.

He is home now. He is free. In his final letter to the American people, Dad wrote, "I now begin the journey that will lead me into the sunset of my life." This evening, he has arrived.

History will record his worth as a leader. We here have long since measured his worth as a man: honest, compassionate, graceful, brave. He was the most plainly decent man you could ever hope to meet.

He used to say, "A gentleman always does the kind thing." And, he was a gentleman in the truest sense of the word: a gentle man.

Big as he was, he never tried to make anyone feel small. Powerful as he became, he never took advantage of those who were weaker. Strength, he believed, was never more admirable than when it was applied with restraint. Shopkeeper, doorman, king or queen, it made no difference. Dad treated everyone with the same unfailing courtesy— acknowledging the innate dignity in us all.

The idea that all people are created equal was more than mere words on a page; it was how he lived his life. And he lived a good, long life—the kind of life good men lead.

But I guess I'm just telling you things you already know.

Here's something you may not know, a little Ronald Reagan trivia for you. His entire life, Dad had an inordinate fondness for earlobes. Even as a boy, back in Dixon, Illinois, hanging out on a street corner with his friends, they knew that if they were standing next to Dutch, sooner or later, he was going to reach over and grab a hold of their lobe, give it a workout there.

Sitting on his lap watching TV as a kid, same story. He'd have hold of my earlobe. I'm surprised I have any lobes left after all of that.

And you didn't have to be a kid to enjoy that sort of treatment. Serving in the Screen Actors Guild with his great friend William Holden, the actor, best man at his wedding, well, Bill got used to it. They'd be there at the meetings, and Dad would have hold of his earlobe. There they'd be, some tense labor negotiation, two big Hollywood movie stars, hand in earlobe.

He was, as you know, a famously optimistic man. Sometimes such optimism leads you to see the world as you wish it were as opposed to how it really is. At a certain point in his presidency, Dad decided he was going to revive the thumbs-up gesture. So he went all over the country, of course, giving everybody the thumbs-up. Dory [Ron's wife, Doria] and I found ourselves in the presidential limousine one day returning from some big event. My mother was there and Dad was, of course, thumbs-upping the crowd along the way.

And suddenly, looming in the window on his side of the car, was this snarling face. This fellow was reviving an entirely different hand gesture and hoisted an entirely different digit in our direction. Dad saw this and without missing a beat turned to us and said, "You see? I think it's catching on."

Dad was also a deeply, unabashedly religious man. But he never made the fatal mistake of so many politicians—wearing his faith on his sleeve to gain political advantage. True, after he was shot and nearly killed early in his presidency, he came to believe that God had spared him in order that he might do good. But he accepted that as a responsibility, not a mandate. And there is a profound difference.

Humble as he was, he never would have assumed a free pass to heaven. But in his heart of hearts, I suspect he felt he would be welcome there.

And so he is home. He is free.

Those of us who knew him well will have no trouble imagining his paradise. Golden fields will spread beneath the blue dome of a western sky. Live oaks will shadow the rolling hillsides. And someplace, flowing from years long past, a river will wind towards the sea. Across those fields, he will ride a gray mare he calls Nancy D. They will sail over jumps he has built with his own hands. He will, at the river, carry him over the shining stones. He will rest in the shade of the trees.

Our cares are no longer his. We meet him now only in memory.

But we will join him soon enough—all of us.

When we are home.

When we are free.

THE ROAST

Each year, in the American University speechwriting class I teach with Eric Schnure, we divide the students into groups and give them fifteen minutes to write four jokes Jay Leno might use in his *Tonight Show* monologue—in the days when he was still hosting the *Tonight Show.*

We try to get them to cluster to make lists of who is in the news, and why, then connect the items on that list in unexpected ways. When they're done, the groups read their jokes aloud. We compliment everyone for trying, but let the class decide who wrote the best one.

Last fall's winner was an undergrad: Miguel Vieira. Leno had been telling jokes about how bad the economy was. It was also the week Yankee star Alex Rodriguez—A-Rod—had confessed to using steroids.

Miguel had never written humor before. His joke: "The economy's so bad that A-Rod switched from steroids to Flintstone vitamins."

The class ended. We got home just in time to turn on Leno as he said: "The economy's so bad, A-Rod switched . . ." Practically word for word.

Miguel was as amazed as anyone. We were pleased, but not amazed; both of us remembered when he and his Humor Cabinet partner Jeff Nussbaum began writing jokes. Nobody was more surprised than they at how good they turned out to be.

Why that is so I'll leave for another book. But for those of you who want to try this expanding political tradition, it's worth examining the Tom Daschle roast reprinted here, the full story of which appears in chapter 8.

Roasts are popular for two reasons. They are fun for the audience, and they are great for political careers. Like any other political speech, roasts characterize the speaker. They need to be likable. Does that mean they can't poke fun at others? Of course not. But they should make sure that at the end they've reassured the audience the jokes were all in good fun, and even served a larger purpose: bringing people together.

While we don't provide a detailed outline for a string of what are sometimes loosely connected jokes, what follows is a brief outline of one popular structure:

- Make fun of the emcee.
- Make fun of other guests.
- Make fun of yourself.
- Reassure the audience that it's all in good fun.
- Close with a final zinger.

Political roasts resemble only in format the Friars Club and Comedy Central roasts, which actually do burn, while the targets pretend to enjoy it. The Gridiron's motto, "Singe, don't burn," is still the mantra for political roast scriptwriters. Self-deprecating humor is still the rule. In the Daschle example you'll see the elements we suggest.

And while political humor is supposed to be topical—and obsolete in days—a surprising number remain funny.

As you read, note a few things that made people praise this script so highly:

- **The skit.** The Daschle roast isn't a series of unconnected jokes. The first few minutes involve a unified skit: the parody of an Alcoholics Anonymous confession, with the hangdog Daschle playing a character. This gives his jokes continuity, and as each joke tops the last, allows the laughter to build.

- **The pun.** As someone targeted by Republicans for preventing legislation from passing, Daschle takes the audience by surprise by using the word *pass* in an unexpected way with his "pass the salt" joke.

- **The story joke.** *Where's he going?* the audience asks as Daschle begins his tale of selling lemonade. Yes, the punch line ("I would let nothing pass") is another surprise. But look more closely. The *aside* ("plus tax") gets a laugh as a self-deprecating joke from a tax-and-spend Democrat. The *inflated language* ("I vowed . . . then and there . . ."), a parody of rags to riches stories, uses suspense to set up the punch line.

- **Untraditional self-mockery.** In Washington, the cosmetic work politicians use—whether Botox, hair plugs, or face lifts—is usually too sensitive to mention even in jokes. When Daschle admits to his own ("When my hair started to turn gray . . . I put a stop to that . . .") he gets credit for going the extra step of candor.

- **Misdirection.** Using a staple of political humor, Daschle lets us think he's referring to himself when he tells how right-wing attacks "hurt." We're fooled—and surprised into laughter when it turns out to be John McCain.

There isn't enough space in this book to detail the ways to write humor, or even to analyze the many other ways this script uses humor that works in politics. But you should try it. Whether you become the next generation's "go-to guy" for political humor or an undergrad writing your first joke, you might surprise yourself.

SEN. TOM DASCHLE, REMARKS AT THE 117TH ANNUAL GRIDIRON DINNER, WASHINGTON, D.C., MARCH 9, 2002

Hi. My name is Tom. And I'm an obstructionist.

This is my first meeting. I haven't obstructed anything in the last twenty-four hours.

Well, actually . . . just a couple of minutes ago, the president asked me to pass . . . the salt. I wanted to. I *tried* to. I just can't bring myself to pass anything.

I guess I started obstructing when I was growing up in rural South Dakota . . . or as the rest of the country thinks of it: a secret undisclosed location.

Words: 1,856

Grade level: 6.1

Sentence length: 12.8

Passive: 3 percent

Actually, South Dakota's a lot like Crawford, Texas . . . without the sophisticated nightlife.

We were poor. Not Bob Byrd poor or Paul O'Neill poor. But, we were poor.

As a young boy, I wanted to help out . . . so I'd sit in front of the farm trying to sell lemonade to passing cars.

It was just five cents a cup—plus tax.

But no one would stop.

As car after car sped by . . . I vowed . . . then and there . . . if ever I was fortunate enough to attain a position of power . . .

I would let nothing pass.

But it turned out that I liked stopping things. I really liked it. . . . And I was good at it. In fact, I just kept getting better.

In my time, I've stopped budget cuts. I've stopped tax breaks.

When my hair started to turn gray . . . I put a stop to that, too. So I admit, I have a problem. And I'm not surprised that people have tried to demonize me for it.

People . . . and also Tom DeLay.

This demon label might be starting to stick. In a recent ad, I was compared to Saddam Hussein . . . and *he* was offended.

In fact, the other day, I was talking with one of my closest friends in the Senate about how much it hurts—*really* hurts—to be vilified by the right-wing hate machine.

All I could say was . . . "McCain . . . don't be such a wuss."

But hey, I really can't complain . . . at least the press coverage of this Republican strategy hasn't been all bad. Although, *USA Today* did skewer me with a *vicious* pie chart.

But on the whole, the reporting has been balanced. So, I don't think of you as adversaries. Tonight, I prefer to think of you as . . . fellow detainees.

I will say this, however: If sitting through a Broder skit isn't considered inhumane treatment under the Geneva Convention—I don't know what is.

Hey, I was told you guys could sing. Apparently, the Office of Strategic Influence is still up and running.

But I deeply appreciate the invitation to come here. Frankly, it's a welcome change to be in a place where people would rather drink a fifth than plead it. As many of you know, this is my first time at the Gridiron Club. That means until tonight, I've never seen Bob Novak in a dress . . . it's usually a pleated skirt and conservative pumps.

But I've done my homework. I know that the Gridiron is as respected as it is inclusive. I also know that you singe but never burn—like the Chlorine Dioxide in my office. I know that this is part of what the powerbrokers call the "invisible primary." Which would explain Dick Cheney being here.

And I know that this is the one hundred and seventeenth annual Gridiron Dinner.

Of course, so much has changed since 1885 . . . but one thing has remained constant. The obligatory bad Strom Thurmond joke. So here goes: Since when did Walter Reed go condo?

I do want to acknowledge and thank the one person who is responsible for me being invited here tonight: Jim Jeffords.

I also want to say hello to my counterpart this evening, Christie Todd Whitman.

As you know, she's in charge of EPA, which, in this administration, stands for Essentially Powerless Agency.

And in the spirit of bipartisanship and unity that marks this dinner, I want to join the top White House officials here . . . and disavow everything Governor Whitman will say. Has ever said. Or is even thinking of saying.

In these trying times, I should also acknowledge Secretary Rumsfeld. If you want to know how out of touch we are inside the Beltway . . . I'll give you four words: Don Rumsfeld, Sex Symbol.

That's enough to make Jack Germond wish he did more TV.

Actually, better to be print press than working for ABC. What a mess. Ted Koppel may be replaced. Cokie's leaving. And, to add insult to injury, Sam Donaldson just announced he's staying.

Yep, the times are changing.

Things are so unpredictable . . . that the only person guaranteed in 2002 to serve a six-year term is Jim Traficant.

And once campaign finance reform becomes law, things will only get crazier.

Lobbyists are going to have to go back to gaining influence the old-fashioned way—asking Bob Strauss for it.

My good friend Mitch McConnell opposes campaign reform. He says it tampers with the Bill of Rights. He says that's not Congress's job. He's right. It's John Ashcroft's job.

Speaking of the attorney general . . . what do you make of that "Statue of Justice" thing?

After all of his time in Washington, you would think that John Ashcroft would have learned: It's not the woman that gets you. It's the cover-up.

Of course, we're all working to change the tone. I've hugged President Bush. It was the first time in a while that a president could hug somebody and not get impeached.

I hear Jerry Falwell was outraged. I don't know what upset Reverend Falwell more—two men embracing in public . . . or that a Republican hugged me. I would like to congratulate the new Gridiron president—and South Dakotan—Marianne Means.

Marianne, it was a stroke of genius to have the "Speech in the Dark" sponsored by Enron. I really enjoyed it . . . but then again, I'm used to being kept in the dark.

Actually, I've known Marianne for a long time. And I can't think of a South Dakotan more deserving of being elected "president."

Hmmmm. . . .

But, you know, the governor of South Dakota just signed a bill that prohibits a senator from simultaneously seeking reelection and running for president.

Boy, is Tim Johnson going to be pissed.

Well, maybe I should give running for president some more thought. South Dakota *is* a very diverse state—it's a rainbow of all shades of German and Norwegian immigrants . . . the kind of place that makes Carl Leubsdorf feel at home.

Don't laugh . . . if we joined forces with North Dakota, we'd have as many electoral votes as Kansas.

But you know, running for president is actually too intimidating to really think about. Nobody has had an approval rating as high as President Bush since . . . well, his father.

I guess that's why only twenty or maybe twenty-five Democrats have expressed interest. These days, if I want to get a quorum, I've got to go to Des Moines.

It's a tough field.

We've got some fresh new faces—like Dick Gephardt.

Al Gore won last time, so he'll be tough to beat. And Al sure looks like a President . . . Rutherford B. Hayes.

John Kerry's formidable. But I don't know about his new slogan. Have you seen it? "John Kerry . . . the tall Dukakis."

Being president sure would be tempting. Mostly because majority leader isn't very glamorous. I mean, it's not all Rose Garden ceremonies, afternoon workouts, and naps.

My schedule is packed. For me, every day is a Brokaw day.

- Let's take a look at Monday: Go to the Dodd's and change diapers. Go into the nursery and change the baby's diaper too.
- Draw Jim Jeffords his bath, just the way he likes it.
- Arrive at office and do "Good Morning South Dakota." Mr. President, it's not a show. I actually call everyone in the state.
- Apologize to John Kerry for the Mike Dukakis joke.
- Apologize to Mike Dukakis for the John Kerry joke.
- Apologize to Zell Miller . . . just in case.
- Meet with Senator Lott and listen to him carry on—yet again—that America needs a Strategic Hairspray Reserve.
- Agree with Robert Byrd that it belongs in West Virginia.
- Watch *Access Hollywood* to see who Bob Torricelli is dating this week.

Trust me, my days are much like this evening. . . . Long and tortured.

In fact, some days the only thing that keeps me going are the letters of support I receive from so many Americans.

Just today, I got this one.

It says it's from a second-grade class at a school outside of Trenton, New Jersey. The Greenville School.

Maybe, I'll just wait and open it back in my office.

Actually, the day we got the real anthrax letter, I was having breakfast at the White House. Remember that, Mr. President? It was quite a morning. My staff called, and told me what had happened. I told the president immediately.

I have to tell you all . . . it was at that moment, I saw in this man—the steely resolve and calm confidence seen only before by Karen Hughes and Bob Woodward.

I joke. But even in tough times, it's my job and my constitutional responsibility to ask the tough questions.

For example: If Washington DC has a shadow senator in the *real* government, do they get a *real* senator in the shadow government?

And, more philosophically, if the shadow government falls, but nobody knew about it, did it ever really exist to begin with?

* * *

It has been such a relief to hear you all laugh.

It wasn't so long ago that we wondered when we would laugh again.

Once, at the height of the Civil War, President Lincoln was presiding over a particularly somber meeting of his cabinet. He made a small joke.

When no one responded, President Lincoln asked them: "Gentlemen, why don't you laugh? With the fearful strain that is upon me night and day, if I did not laugh, I should die. You need this medicine as much as I do."

These continue to be challenging times—for my profession . . . for yours . . . and for our nation.

Just when our hearts had begun to heal from September 11, they broke again for Daniel Pearl—a brave journalist and good man.

His murder—and the loss of eight more of our soldiers in Afghanistan—underscores a terrible truth: there are those today for whom democracy itself is a target.

It's a privilege to be here tonight with a president who has been so strong and steadfast in leading our nation in this war against terrorism.

And it's an honor to be among so many people for whom defending our democracy is, literally, a life's work.

Not everyone in this room always agrees with each other. But when we are able to laugh together, it makes it easier to work together.

And, as we have shown in the days since September 11: united, there is nothing Americans cannot do.

I'm going to stop before this Gridiron Dinner turns into a Sperling Breakfast.

But I want to thank you all for this "healing medicine."

Thank you. God bless you.

Notes

NOTES TO CHAPTER 1

1. Ann Devroy, "Clinton: 'There Is Room' to Pray in Public School; White House Conciliatory Toward GOP," *Washington Post,* November 16, 1994.
2. Chris Sittenfeld, "What Michelle Obama Would Bring to the White House," *Time Magazine*, September 27, 2008.
3. Stephen Lucas, *The Art of Public Speaking,* 9th ed. (Columbus, Ohio: McGraw-Hill, 2007), 372.
4. Ibid., 400.
5. Patrick Anderson, *Electing Jimmy Carter: The Campaign of 1976* (Baton Rouge: Louisiana State University Press, 1976), 167.
6. Ibid.
7. Elvin T. Lim, *The Anti-Intellectual Presidency: The Decline of Presidential Rhetoric from George Washington to George W. Bush* (Oxford: Oxford University Press, 2008).

NOTES TO CHAPTER 2

1. W. Rhys Roberts, trans., Aristotle's *Rhetoric,* compiled by Lee Honeycutt (hypertext of Aristotle's *Rhetoric,* June 2004), www.public.iastate.edu/~honeyl/Rhetoric/index.html.
2. ABC News Online, September 9, 2005, www.abc.net.au/News/newsitems/200509/s1456650.htm.
3. Roberts, Aristotle's *Rhetoric.*
4. Sharon Begley, "Heard Any Good Stories Lately?" *Newsweek*, September 22, 2008.
5. Roberts, Aristotle's *Rhetoric.*
6. Stephanie Rosenbloom, "Names That Match Forge a Bond on the Internet," *New York Times,* April 10, 2008.
7. Fox News Sunday transcript (September 7, 2008), www.foxnews.com/story/02933.418342.00.htm.
8. "The Choice: Comment," *The New Yorker,* October 13, 2008.
9. To watch the ad, see www.youtube.com/watch?v=OKs-bTL-pRg.
10. Edmund Fuller, ed., *Thesaurus of Anecdotes* (New York: Crown Publishers, 1942).

NOTES TO CHAPTER 3

1. David Mills, "Sister Souljah's Call to Arms," *Washington Post,* May 13, 1992.
2. Michael A. Cohen, "The Souljah Legacy," http://campaignstops.blogs.nytimes.com/2008/06/15/the-souljah-legacy/#more-258.

3. Robert Gordon and James Kvaal, "McContradiction," *The New Republic,* July 9, 2008.

4. Stephen E. Lucas, *The Art of Public Speaking* (New York: McGraw-Hill, 2004).

NOTES TO CHAPTER 4

1. Drew D. Hansen, *The Dream: Martin Luther King, Jr. and the Speech That Inspired a Nation* (New York: HarperCollins, 2003), 67.

2. Glenn Kessler, "The Young Speechwriter Who Captured Rice's Voice," *Washington Post,* March 14, 2006.

3. Peggy Noonan, *What I Saw at the Revolution* (New York: Random House, 1990), 229.

4. Chuck Baldwin, "You Know Things Are in Bad Shape When Jay Leno Makes More Sense than Either G. W. Bush or John Kerry," *Covenant News,* article posted April 6, 2004, www.covenantnews.com/baldwin040406.htm (accessed July 13, 2009).

5. Personal conversation with Nan Aron; www.newswithviews.com/baldwin/baldwin174.htm.

NOTES TO CHAPTER 5

1. Carnegie, Dale, *The Quick and Easy Way to Effective Speaking,* rev. Dorothy Carnegie (New York: Pocket Books, 1962).

2. Tanya Gregory, "Writing for Publication: 10 Steps to Success," www.emorypa.org/Gregory/Writing10Steps.pdf.

NOTES TO CHAPTER 6

1. James C. Humes, *Confessions of a White House Ghostwriter* (Jackson, Tenn.: Perseus Distribution Services, 1997).

2. David Zarefsky, *Strategies for Success,* 3rd ed. (New York: Allyn and Bacon, 2002), 261.

3. Robert Schlesinger, *White House Ghosts* (New York: Simon and Schuster, 2008), 1.

4. Alan Cheuse, "Endings—Few of Them Happy—Under a Big Western Sky," *San Francisco Chronicle,* July 2, 2006.

5. Dan O'Hair, Rob Stewart, and Hannah Rubenstein, *A Speaker's Guidebook: Text and Reference,* 4th ed. (Boston: Bedford/St. Martin's, 2008), 198.

NOTES TO CHAPTER 7

1. Aaron J. Palmer, *Dictionary of American History* (Farmington Hills, Mich.: Gale Cengage Learning, 2003).

2. Edward P. J. Corbett, *Classical Rhetoric for the Modern Student,* 2nd ed. (Oxford: Oxford University Press, 1971), 459.

3. Ralph Keyes, *The Quote Verifier* (New York: St. Martin's Griffin, 2006), 88.

4. George Orwell, "Politics and the English Language," *Horizon,* April 1946.
5. "Mike Huckabee: Republican National Convention Speech," *American Rhetoric,* www.americanrhetoric.com/speeches/convention2008/mikehuckabee2008rnc.htm (accessed July 13, 2009).

NOTES TO CHAPTER 8

1. Chris Matthews, *Hardball: How Politics Is Played, Told By One Who Knows the Game* (New York: Simon and Schuster, 1988).
2. Bas A. Andeweg, Jaap C. deJong, and Hans Hoeken, "'May I Have Your Attention': Exordial Techniques in Informative Oral Presentations," *Technical Communication Quarterly* 7, no. 3 (1998): 271–284.
3. Sharon Begley, "Heard Any Good Stories Lately?" *Newsweek,* Sept. 22, 2008.
4. George Schultz, foreword from *Reagan in His Own Hand: The Writings of Ronald Reagan That Reveal His Revolutionary Vision for America,* edited by Kiron K. Skinner, Annelise Anderson, and Martin Anderson (New York: The Free Press, 2001), 1–2.

NOTES TO CHAPTER 9

1. Joel Achenbach, "Land of the Giants," *Washington Post Magazine*, May 20, 2007.
2. Ibid.
3. John F. Kennedy Presidential Library and Museum, "Remarks of Senator John F. Kennedy at Syracuse University in Syracuse, New York, June 3, 1957," www.jfklibrary.org/Historical+Resources/Archives/Reference+Desk/Speeches/JFK/JFK+Pre-Pres/1957/002PREPRES12SPEECHES_57JUN03.htm (accessed July 13, 2009).
4. Washingtonpost.com Special Report: Clinton Accused, "Jesse Jackson's 'Hymietown' Remark—1984," www.washingtonpost.com/wp-srv/politics/special/clinton/frenzy/jackson.htm (accessed July 13, 2009); BBC News, "Bush: No Apology for Gaffe," September 5, 2000, http://news.bbc.co.uk/1/hi/world/americas/910614.stm (accessed July 13, 2009).
5. Morris K. Udall, with Bob Neuman and Randy Udall, *Too Funny to Be President* (New York: Henry Holt, 1987).

NOTES TO CHAPTER 10

1. Lisa Olen, Daily News Central: Health News, "Dr. Graham's Testimony to Senate Committee on Vioxx, FDA Failures," November 20, 2004, http://health.dailynewscentral.com/content/view/000160/40 (accessed July 13, 2009).
2. Ibid.
3. Stifled Mind, "Logical Fallacies in Politics," July 30, 2008, http://stifledmind.blogspot.com/search?q=This+is+a+pretty+good+example+of+the+fallacy+of+ad+hominem (accessed July 13, 2009).
4. CanDoGo, www.candogo.com/search/insight?i=716.

NOTES TO CHAPTER 11

1. "Shackleton's Expedition," NOVA Online, February 2002, www.pbs.org/wgbh/nova/shackleton (accessed July 24, 2009).
2. Morris K. Udall, with Bob Neuman and Randy Udall, *Too Funny to Be President* (New York: Henry Holt, 1987).
3. James C. Humes, *Roles Speakers Play* (New York: Harper and Row, 1976).
4. Author interview with Schnure.
5. Laura Miller, "Far From Narnia," *New Yorker*, December 26, 2005.
6. Peggy Noonan, *What I Saw at the Revolution* (New York: Random House, 1990), 86.

NOTES TO CHAPTER 12

1. Eyewitness to History.com, "Writing the Declaration of Independence, 1776," www.eyewitnesstohistory.com/jefferson.htm (accessed July 13, 2009).
2. Ibid.
3. Ibid.
4. Meredith Wilson, screenplay, *The Music Man*, www.allmusicals.com.
5. Cited in William Safire, ed., *Lend Me Your Ears: Great Speeches in History* (New York: W.W. Norton, and Co., 1992), 568–569.
6. CommonDreams.org, "'A Chill Wind Is Blowing in This Nation … ': Transcript of the speech given by actor Tim Robbins to the National Press Club in Washington, D.C., on April 15, 2003," www.commondreams.org/views03/0416-01.htm (accessed July 13, 2009).
7. American Rhetoric, "Elie Wiesel: The Perils of Indifference," www.americanrhetoric.com/speeches/ewieselperilsofindifference.html (accessed July 13, 2009).
8. Philip Rucker, "Orszag Is Washington Centrist Who Knows How to Deal," *Washington Post*, February 26, 2009.
9. Anne Kornblut, "For Obama's Political Knots, He's the Fixer," *Washington Post*, February 21, 2009.

NOTES TO CHAPTER 13

1. Peggy Noonan, *What I Saw at the Revolution* (New York: Random House, 1990), 229.
2. Robert Rossen, screenplay, *All the King's Men*, in *Three Screenplays*, ed. Steven Rossen (Garden City, N.Y.: Anchor Books, 1972).
3. Arron Sorkin, screenplay, *The American President* (1995); www.dailyscript.com/movie.html.
4. Daniel J. O'Keefe, *Persuasion: Theory and Research* (Thousand Oaks, Calif.: Sage Publications, 2002), 187.

NOTES TO CHAPTER 14

1. Taylor Branch, *Parting the Waters: America in the King Years, 1954–63* (New York: Simon and Schuster, 1988).

2. Paul Begala, "Commentary: Obama Summons Ghost of American History," www.cnn.com/2009/POLITICS/01/21/begala.obama/index.html.
3. Taylor Branch, *Parting the Waters.*
4. Ernest J. Simmons, *Chekhov: A Biography* (Chicago: Chicago University Press, 1962).

NOTES TO DELIVERY CHAPTER

1. Robert Schlesinger, *White House Ghosts* (New York: Simon and Schuster, 2008), 364.
2. Shelly Chaiken, "Physical Appearance and Social Influence." In C. Peter Herman, Mark P. Zanna, and E. Tory Higgins, eds., *Physical Appearance, Stigma, and Social Behavior: The Ontario Symposium,* Vol. 3 (Hillsdale, N.J.: Lawrence Erlbaum, 1986), 143–177.
3. Jo Sprague, Douglas Stuart, and David Bodary, *The Speaker's Handbook* (Belmont, Calif.: Thomson/Wadsworth Publishing, 2008).
4. Dale Carnegie, *Public Speaking and Influencing Men in Business* (Whitefish, Mont.: Kessinger Publishing, 2003).
5. Francine Parnes, "In Business, From Dressing Down to Suiting Up," www.nytimes.com/2001/07/15/nyregion/in-business-from-dressing-down-to-suiting-up.html?pagewanted=all (downloaded July 23, 2009).
6. Steven Brydon and Michael Scott, *Between One and Many: The Art and Science of Public Speaking* (Mountain View, Calif.: Mayfield, 2007).
7. Schlesinger, *White House Ghosts,* 271.
8. Stephen E. Lucas, *The Art of Public Speaking* (New York: McGraw-Hill, 2004), 372.
9. Schlesinger, *White House Ghosts,* 395.

NOTES TO CHAPTER 16

1. "Clinton Ads in Ohio, Texas," Associated Press, Feb. 23, 2008.
2. Mike Allen, "Clinton Aide Accuses Obama of Plagiarism," *Politico,* February 18, 2008.
3. Ibid.
4. Dan O'Hair, Rob Stewart, and Hannah Rubenstein, *A Speaker's Guidebook: Text and Reference* (Boston: Bedford St. Martins, 2006).
5. American University student handbook.
6. Jack Schafer, "Don't Call It Plagiarism: Obama's Sound Bite, Considered," *Slate,* February 19, 2008.
7. O'Hair, et al., *A Speaker's Guidebook.*
8. Randall Bennett Woods, *Fulbright: A Biography* (New York: Cambridge University Press, 1998).
9. Elvin T. Lim, *The Anti-Intellectual Presidency: The Decline of Presidential Rhetoric from George Washington to George W. Bush* (New York: Oxford University Press, 2008), 166.
10. Thomas H. Bivens, *Public Relations Writing: The Essentials of Style and Format,* 6th ed. (New York: McGraw-Hill 2007).

11. James Fallows, "More on Speechwriting and Obama," *The Atlantic*, jamesfallows .theatlancic.com/archives/2008 (accessed July 14, 2009).

12. Richard J. Tofel, "In His Own Words," *Wall Street Journal*, May 9, 2008, W3.

13. Jeffrey K. Tulis, *The Rhetorical Presidency* (Princeton: Princeton University Press, 1988).

14. Neely Tucker, "Careful, That Dish Is Hot: At the Gridiron Dinner, Hames Glazed with Condi," March 13, 2005, D01.

NOTE TO CHAPTER 17

1. Eric Schnure, personal conversation.

NOTES TO CHAPTER 18

1. Bernard Grebanier, *Playwriting: How to Write for the Theater*, Apollo ed. (New York: Thomas Y. Crowell Co., 1965), v.

2. William Safire, *Lend Me Your Ears: Great Speeches in History* (New York: W.W. Norton and Company, 1997).

Bibliography

Yes, *The Political Speechwriter's Companion* is the only book specifically about how to write and deliver political speeches. But there exist many books about speech, including political speech: scholarly books on rhetoric or persuasion, public speaking textbooks, anthologies, quote books, joke and anecdote compendiums, histories, memoirs, biographies, and how-to books on humor or argument, among others. In addition, during the 2008 campaign, when rhetoric was an important issue, reporters produced hundreds of useful articles about the candidates' speeches.

Meanwhile, each year sees an explosion of new, unwacky Web sites useful for speechwriters in politics. Some don't meet the standards for scholarship that would allow me to cite them here—www.wikipedia.org, for example. But there's no questioning how helpful Wikipedia and others are for the practical work of getting a speech done.

In this bibliography you'll find many of the books, articles, and Web sites cited in this book—as well as others I've found useful. I've prefaced each section with a brief guide to what you might find useful about them.

In no way is this a complete list; it's a sampling of the kinds of books that harried speechwriters in politics can use. Spending some time with these can lead you to many others.

Final note: Some of the items on this list are out of print. Even ten years ago it would have been pointless to list them. Now, however, Google and Amazon make it easy to track them down, place an order, and for a few dollars find a useful book on your doorstep within two or three days.

BOOKS ON RHETORIC OR PERSUASION

Each is interesting for different reasons: Aristotle to amaze you with how many ideas are still useful after 2,300 years; Corbitt because it still provides a complete overview of rhetorical techniques only touched on in this book; O'Keefe because it gives you confidence that meticulous research lies beyond the tips on persuasion covered here; and Toulmin et al. for its surprisingly readable way of making us see that techniques of persuasion in politics aren't much different than what we do in the rest of our lives.

Aristotle. *Ars Rhetorica*. New York: Oxford University Press, 1959.
Corbitt, Edward P. J., and Robert Connors. *Classical Rhetoric for the Modern Student.*
    4th ed. New York: Oxford University Press, 1998.

O'Keefe, Daniel J. *Persuasion, Theory, and Research.* 2nd ed. Thousand Oaks, Calif.: Sage Publications, 2002.

Toulmin, Stephen, Richard Rieke, and Allen Janik. *An Introduction to Reasoning.* New York: Macmillan, 1979.

PUBLIC SPEAKING TEXTBOOKS

While Lucas is the best-selling public speaking book now in print, for many good reasons O'Hair et al. is useful for its handy yet not simplistic way of approaching every part of speechmaking, and Wolvin for its insight into the often overlooked idea that speaking involves interaction between speaker and listeners. While there are more current editions of Monroe, I include it out of sentiment, and because there should be some readers interested in what the author whose ideas so influenced this book wrote on his own, fifty years ago.

Lucas, Stephen E. *The Art of Public Speaking.* 10th ed. New York: McGraw-Hill, 2009.

Monroe, Alan H., and Douglas Ehninger. *Principles of Speech.* 5th brief ed. Glenview, Ill.: Scott, Foresman, 1964.

O'Hair, Daniel, Rob Stewart, and Hannah Rubenstein. *Speaker's Guidebook: Text and Reference.* 3rd ed. Boston, New York: Bedford/St. Martins, 2007.

Wolvin, Andrew D., Roy M. Berko, and Darlyn R. Wolvin. *The Public Speaker/The Public Listener.* 2nd ed. Los Angeles: Roxbury Publishing Company, 1999.

BOOKS ON POLITICAL SPEECH

It shouldn't surprise you that not everyone agrees with every idea in *The Political Speechwriter's Companion.* You don't have to completely share Jamieson and Lim's alarm about the trends in political speech to profit from the substance, nuance, and insight with which the authors make their case. Schlesinger will give you an anecdotal look at presidential speechwriting that both could and should influence the way you work. And Tulis offers you historical context, covering two centuries that can explain the way political speeches get written in this one.

Jamieson, Kathleen Hall. *Eloquence in an Electronic Age: The Transformation of Political Speechmaking.* New York: Oxford University Press, 1988.

Jamieson, Kathleen Hall, and Karlyn Kohrs Campbell. *The Interplay of Influence: News Advertising, Politics, and the Mass Media.* 4th ed. Belmont, Calif.: Wadsworth Publishing Company, 1997.

Lim, Elvin. *The Anti-Intellectual Presidency: The Decline of Presidential Rhetoric from George Washington to George W. Bush.* New York: Oxford University Press, 2008.

Schlesinger, Robert. *White House Ghosts: Presidents and Their Speechwriters.* New York: Simon and Schuster, 2008.

Tulis, Jeffrey K. *The Rhetorical Presidency.* Princeton: Princeton University Press, 1988.

ANTHOLOGIES

No one would try writing a novel or screenplay without first reading hundreds of them. Why should speechwriting be any different? There are hundreds of speech anthologies. Here are three, useful for different reasons. The Penguin anthology teaches us that there are many famous speeches effective for a single line while not particularly effective elsewhere; Olive gives us a look at the president whose speeches were central to his election; and Safire, justifiably a classic, should interest readers not just because of the selections or how Safire groups them, but for his interesting introductions to each one.

MacArthur, Brian, ed. *The Penguin Book of Historic Speeches.* London: Penguin, 1996.

Olive, David. *An American Story: The Speeches of Barack Obama.* Toronto: ECW Press, 2008.

Safire, William, ed. *Lend Me Your Ears: Great Speeches in History.* New York: W. W. Norton, 1992.

QUOTATIONS, JOKES, AND ANECDOTES

Such books come in for stinging criticism, and not without reason. Listeners who hear a speaker quote Mark Twain don't automatically assume they are reading a line picked out by some staffer from a book. On the other hand, there is no simple way to find the variety of pithy ways people have expressed the ideas you'd like to include. The quote books here all emphasize subjects suited to politics: Grothe is full of interesting examples about a figure of speech only touched on in this book; The Quote Verifier not only helps you avoid making embarrassing mistakes, it provides material you can actually include because its nuggets of information are so interesting; Dole and Udall offers the advantage of jokes that the authors actually used in politics; and the anecdote books, especially Fadiman, provide stories you can use at any stage in your speech.

QUOTATIONS

Eigen, Lewis D., and Jonathan P. Siegel, eds. *The MacMillan Dictionary of Political Quotations.* New York: MacMillan Publishing Company, 1993.

Goldstein, Sharon, ed. *Langenscheidt's Pocket Merriam-Webster Guide to Quotations.* New York, Berlin: Langescheidt Publishing Group, 2002.

Grothe, Mardy. *Never Let a Fool Kiss You or a Kiss Fool You.* New York: Penguin Group, 2002.

Humes, James C. *The Wit and Wisdom of Winston Churchill.* New York: Harper Perennial, 1995.

Jay, Antony. *The Oxford Dictionary of Political Quotations.* New York: Oxford University Press, 2001.

Keyes, Ralph. *The Quote Verifier: Who Said What, Where, and When.* New York: St. Martin's Griffin, 2006.

Petros, Ross, and Kathryn Petros. *The Stupidest Things Ever Said by Politicians.* New York, London: Pocket Books, 1999.

Platt, Suzy. *Respectfully Quoted: A Dictionary of Quotations from the Library of Congress.* Washington, D.C.: Congressional Quarterly, 1992.

Shapiro, Fred, ed. *The Yale Book of Quotations.* New Haven, London: Yale University Press, 2006.

Torricelli, Robert G., ed. *Quotations for Public Speakers: A Historical, Literary, and Political Anthology.* New Brunswick: Rutgers University Press, 2000.

HUMOR

Dole, Bob. *Great Political Wit.* New York, Toronto: Nan Talese/Doubleday, 1998.

Udall, Morris. *Too Funny to Be President.* New York: Henry Holt and Company, 1987.

ANECDOTES

Fadiman, Clifton, ed. *The Little, Brown Book of Anecdotes.* Boston: Little, Brown, 1985.

Fuller, Edmund, ed. *2500 Anecdotes for All Occasions.* New York: Avenel Books, 1942, 1970.

REFERENCE

It goes without saying that speechwriters need a dictionary. Actually, you need several; *American Heritage* is good because it reflects common usage—and it's little enough to carry around with you.

Why *Chase's Calendar*? Because I have never failed to be amazed by how often it helps make speeches interesting ("Today happens to be Walter Raleigh's birthday. He once said . . ."). But here's a tip—you don't need this year's version, or the CD-ROM. Get an old one online for a few dollars. Most events throughout history remain useful, and my 1996 version still serves me just fine. And while there are Internet books, I include this one because its creators update it, which is absolutely essential with researching online.

The American Heritage Dictionary. 4th ed. Paper. Boston: Houghton Mifflin, 1996.

Chase's Calendar of Events. New York: McGraw-Hill Professional. Annual.

Searching the Internet: Search Engines and Subject Indexes. www.sldirectory.com/search.html.

BOOKS ABOUT POLITICS

Rhetorical techniques don't vary much by ideology, but language does. Here is a variety of books that show you how to be effective with language in the different ways Republicans and Democrats need. Luntz and Lakoff have become famous for the way politicians use their insights. Kusnet was written for a specific campaign but remains relevant. Greenfield, long out of print, is easy to find online: look for the parody of the political stump speech. Matthews's insight into politics, on display each day by the former Carter speechwriter, includes a lot that's relevant for speechwriters today. Finally, Heinrich manages to take Aristotle and show you how what he said is as contemporary as yesterday's argument with your kids.

Greenfield, Jeff. *Playing to Win: An Insider's Guide to Politics.* New York: Simon and Schuster, 1980.
Heinrichs, Jay. *Thank You for Arguing: What Aristotle, Lincoln, and Homer Simpson Can Teach Us about the Art of Persuasion.* New York: Three River Press, 2007.
Kusnet, David. *Speaking American: How the Democrats Can Win in the Nineties.* New York: Thunder's Mouth Press, 1992.
Lakoff, George. *Don't Think of an Elephant.* White River Jct., Vt.: Chelsea Green Publishing, 2004.
Luntz, Frank. *Words That Work: It's Not What You Say, It's What People Hear.* New York: Hyperion, 2007.
Matthews, Christopher. *Hardball: How Politics Is Played, Told by One Who Knows the Game.* Rev. ed. New York: Touchstone, 1999.

MEMOIRS

Each of these, candid and detailed, presents portraits of the different ways speakers and writers interact. The liveliest is Noonan—it reads as if the former Reagan speechwriter were keeping a daily journal. But Shrum covers far more than speech issues: the former McGovern speechwriter provides a candid look at over three decades of presidential campaigns.

Anderson, Patrick. *Electing Jimmy Carter.* Baton Rouge: Louisiana State University Press, 1994.
Noonan, Peggy. *What I Saw at the Revolution: A Political life in the Reagan Era.* New York: Random House, 1990.
Shrum, Robert. *No Excuses: Concessions of a Serial Campaigner.* New York: Simon and Schuster, 2007.
Sorensen, Ted. *Counselor.* New York: HarperCollins, 2008.
Waldman, Michael. *POTUS Speaks: Finding the Words That Defined the Clinton Presidency.* New York: Simon and Schuster, 2000.

HOW-TO BOOKS

While not just about politics, Noonan and Cook are useful and succinct. The E. B. White revision of Strunk may have first appeared fifty years ago, but various editors have revised it, and it still has useful suggestions for writers—though not more than Clark's less well-known but graceful and sensible book. And Grebanier? Cited in this book, it reminds us that speechwriting isn't the only kind of writing for which systematic study helps.

Clark, Roy Peter. *Writing Tools: Fifty Essential Strategies for Every Writer.* Washington, D.C.: CQ Press, 2008.
Cook, Jeff Scott. *The Elements of Speechwriting and Public Speaking.* New York: MacMillan Publishing Company, 1988.

Grebanier, Bernard. *Playwriting: How to Write for the Theater.* Apollo ed. New York: Thomas Y. Crowell Company, 1965.

Noonan, Peggy. *On Speaking Well: How to Give a Speech with Style, Substance, and Clarity.* New York: Harper Perennial, 1999.

Strunk, William, Jr., and E. B. White. *The Elements of Style.* 4th ed. London: Longman, 1995.

ARTICLES

Frobish and Lucas are useful for readers interested in the scholarly differences about rhetoric that are relevant to political speeches. Scully provides the kind of candid discussion almost unheard of in the field. And the articles about 2008 are a selection of the hundreds that dealt with a campaign in which rhetoric didn't just shape debate but spawned it.

SCHOLARLY

Frobish, T. "Jamieson Meets Lucas: Eloquence and Pedagogical Model(s) in the Art of Public Speaking." *Communication Education* 49 (July 2000): 239–252.

Lucas, Stephen E. "Speechwriting, Pedagogy, and Civic Responsibility." *American Communication Journal* 5, no. 2 (Winter 2002); www.acjournal.org/holdings/vol5/iss2/special/lucas.htm.

ON SPEECHWRITING

McGrath, David. "In the Words of my Speechwriter . . ." *Washington Post,* September 4, 2008; www.washingtonpost.com/wp-dyn/content/article/2008/09/03/AR2008090303133.html.

Scully, Matthew. "Present at the Creation." *Atlantic* (September 2007); www.theatlantic.com/doc/200709/michael-gerson.

ON THE 2008 CAMPAIGN

Alter, Jonathan. "A Reality Check on 'Change.'" *Newsweek,* September 22, 2008, 41; www.newsweek.com/id/158767.

Bailey, Jonathan. "The Obama Plagiarism Scandal." *Plagiarism Today,* February 20, 2008; www.plagiarismtoday.com/2008/02/20/the-obama-plagiarism-scandal.

Begley, Sharon. "Heard Any Good Stories Lately?" *Newsweek,* September 22, 2008, 42; www.newsweek.com/id/158749.

Bernstein, David. "The Speech." Chicagomag.com, June 2007; www.chicagomag.com/Chicago-Magazine/June-2007/The-Speech/.

Braun, Stephen, and Maria L. Laganga. "Candidates Buoyed by Their Own Words." *Los Angeles Times,* January 6, 2008; http://articles.latimes.com/2008/jan/06/nation/na-speeches6.

Gallo, Carmine. "In Praise of the Sound Bite." Business week.com, February 8, 2008; www.businessweek.com/smallbiz/content/feb2008/sb2008028_436537.htm.

Klein, Joe. "Obama's Speech 'Very Tough.'" Time.com, August 29, 2008; www.time.com/time/politics/article/0,8599,1837433,00.html.

Liasson, Mara. "The Anatomy of McCain's Stump Speech." NPR.org, October 27, 2008; www.npr.org/templates/story/story.php?storyId=96187955.

Liasson, Mara. "How Obama's Stump Speech Has Evolved." NPR.org, October 28, 2008; www.npr.org/templates/story/story.php?storyId=96231055.

Newton-Small, Jay. "How Obama Writes His Speeches." Time.com, August 28, 2008; www.time.com/time/politics/article/0,8599,1837368,00.html.

Saslow, Eli. "Helping to Write History." *Washington Post,* December 18, 2008, A01; www.washingtonpost.com/wp-dyn/content/article/2008/12/17/AR2008121703903.html.

Stelter, Brian. "Finding the Humor in the Election, Each Other, and Themselves." *New York Times,* October 17, 2008; www.nytimes.com/2008/10/18/arts/television/18joke.html.

WEB SITES

The Internet has revolutionized the way speechwriters approach speech-writing—they can access transcripts instantly and watch speeches on YouTube minutes or years after a speech has been given. Some of the sites below will help you diversify your speechwriting resources.

These are not just sites for people in Washington, D.C. Politics is still local—but even at the state legislative level, not entirely. Don't neglect books, but keep this list and be alert for others that will appear long after this book is out.

American Rhetoric (www.americanrhetoric.com). Of all the sites whose URLs should be at your fingertips, Stephen Lucas's is, hands down, the most useful. Its enormous bank of political speeches, usually providing both video and transcript, is indispensable for anyone seriously interested in seeing what has been done. The speech bank generally organizes speeches alphabetically by speaker's *first* name.

Bartleby (www.bartleby.com). A great source for quotes and inspiration ("the poetry").

Congressional Record (www.gpoaccess.gov/crecord/). This has a transcript of every speech delivered on the House and Senate floors in Washington.

Democratic National Committee (www.dnc.org) and Republican National Committee (www.rnc.org). The Web sites of the DNC and RNC are good for a quick look at what your party urges on every issue.

Factcheck (www.Factcheck.org) and others (www.politfact.com/truth-o-meter). These should be consulted for their rigorous analysis of whether politicians are telling the truth.

Harris Interactive Poll (www.harrisinteractive.com/harris_poll/). This has an incredible archive of American attitudes on specific issues.

New York Speechwriter's Roundtable (www.nyspeechwriters.com).

Ragan Communications (www.Ragan.com). This publisher puts on the mammoth biannual national conference of speechwriters and covers speech issues, with some newsletters available by subscription.

U.S. House of Representatives (www.house.gov/).

U.S. Senate (www.senate.gov/).

Washington Speechwriters Roundtable (www.washingtonspeechwriters.com/). Visit this site not only for insights into speech but also job listings.

Index

Index of Speakers

About the Author

Robert A. Lehrman served as Chief Speechwriter to Vice President Al Gore and, in 2004, as Chief Speechwriter for the Democratic National Committee during his more than three decades of experience writing speeches. He has written for political figures, celebrities, heads of nonprofits, and corporate CEOs, most recently as speechwriter to the Chairman and CEO of Pfizer. He created and co-teaches the political speechwriting course at American University and speaks often at other campuses, conferences, and associations, on the topic of political speechwriting. Author of a number of award-winning novels and coauthor of a highly acclaimed non-fiction book for young adults, Lehrman has a B.A. from Tufts University and an M.F.A. from the University of Iowa's Writer's Workshop, where he studied with Kurt Vonnegut and Richard Yates.